"Generation after generation man is born anew. Each generation gives rise to new aspirations in life and brings a new quest for fulfillment. Each man needs sound physical and mental health, greater ability in action, a greater capacity to think clearly, increased efficiency in work, and more loving and rewarding relationships with others. He needs enough vitality and intelligence to satisfy the desires of his mind and bring contentment to his life. We have seen that all this can be gained through the regular practice of Transcendental Meditation." — *Maharishi*

MAHARISHI MAHESH YOGI, founder of the Transcendental Meditation program, inspired teaching of this simple, natural, and effective practice worldwide. *Science of Being and Art of Living: Transcendental Meditation* demonstrates why Maharishi is acknowledged as the greatest teacher of enlightenment in our time.

SCIENCE OF BEING AND ART OF LIVING

TRANSCENDENTAL MEDITATION®

Maharishi Mahesh Yogi

Maharishi International University Press

First published in 1963 by Allied Publishers, New Delhi

Copyright © 1963 Maharishi Mahesh Yogi
Copyright © 2020 Maharishi Vedic University Limited and Maharishi Foundation Limited
All rights reserved worldwide

For further information, contact: MVULtd@Maharishi.net

Without limiting the rights under copyright reserved above, no part of this publication may be reproduced, stored in or introduced into a retrieval system, or transmitted, in any form, or by any means (electronic, mechanical, photocopying, recording, or otherwise), without the prior written permission of the copyright owner of this book.

Maharishi Mahesh Yogi inaugurated the Spiritual Regeneration Movement as the first organization teaching Transcendental Meditation on January 1, 1958. Since that time, the Spiritual Regeneration Movement has evolved into a global structure of Transcendental Meditation centers in countries around the world, which have been established in the name of educational organizations authorized in each country to teach the Transcendental Meditation program. For information on learning the Transcendental Meditation technique, please refer to *Contact Information*, page 435.

In *Science of Being and Art of Living: Transcendental Meditation*, terms such as "mankind" and "man" refer to humankind regardless of gender; the pronouns "he" and "his" refer to all individuals. These terms have been retained from the original edition.

Transcendental Meditation, TM, Maharishi, Maharishi Sthapatya Veda, Maharishi AyurVeda, Maharishi Yagya, Maharishi Jyotish, Raam Raj, and other terms used in this publication are subject to trademark protection in many countries around the world, including the United States and Canada. See page 438 for more detail.

First Maharishi International University Press edition, 2020

Maharishi International University Press
Fairfield, Iowa 52557 USA
Website: miupress.shop

ISBN 978-0-923569-81-5

TO

THE LOTUS FEET OF SHRI GURU DEV,

HIS DIVINITY

BRAHMANANDA SARASWATI,

JAGADGURU BHAGAVAN SHANKARACHARYA

OF JYOTIR MATH, HIMALAYAS,

AND

AS BLESSINGS FROM HIM

THIS BOOK IS PRESENTED

TO ALL LOVERS OF LIFE

DESIROUS OF ENJOYING ALL GLORIES,

WORLDLY AND DIVINE

Contents

INTRODUCTION xi

Section I: SCIENCE OF BEING 1

WHAT IS BEING? 3
BEING, THE ESSENTIAL CONSTITUENT OF CREATION 4
OMNIPRESENCE OF BEING 6
BEING, THE FIELD OF ETERNAL LIFE 8
BEING, THE BASIS OF ALL LIVING 9
    (The basis of all activity and Karma*)*
BEING, THE PLANE OF COSMIC LAW 10
BEING, THE ABSOLUTE AND THE RELATIVE 13
BEING, THE ETERNAL AND ULTIMATE REALITY 15
PRĀṆA AND BEING 17
    (Attunement with the cosmic life force)
MIND AND BEING 19
    (Unfoldment of mental faculties)
KARMA AND BEING 23
    (Creation of senses, nervous system, and the body)
HOW TO CONTACT BEING 27
HOW TO LIVE BEING 36
    (Self-consciousness and Cosmic Consciousness)
ADVANTAGES OF THE EXPERIENCE OF BEING 40

Section II: LIFE 43

WHAT IS LIFE? 45
(Purpose of life, status, and significance)

NORMAL LIFE 51
(Cosmic Consciousness, human values, and realization)

INDIVIDUAL AND COSMIC LIFE 53
(The universe reacts to individual action)

Section III: ART OF LIVING 59

MAN'S FULL POTENTIAL 63

HOW TO USE ONE'S FULL POTENTIAL 65
(For maximum benefit to one's self and the universe)

HOW TO MAKE FULL USE OF THE SURROUNDINGS 69

HOW TO MAKE FULL USE OF THE ALMIGHTY POWER OF NATURE 77

ART OF BEING 87
(Harmony of material and spiritual values; how to live life in eternal freedom while accomplishing the maximum in the world)

ART OF THINKING 127
(Key to clear, powerful, and fruitful thinking)

ART OF SPEAKING 134

ART OF ACTION 141
(Key to self-confidence, increased efficiency, and success in undertakings)

ART OF BEHAVIOR 174
(Key to fruitful relationships)

KEY TO GOOD HEALTH 180
(Key to all health: mental, physical, and environmental)

EDUCATION 205
(Education from within; unfoldment of full mental potential)

HIGHWAY TO REHABILITATION 217
(Eradication of delinquency and crime; a natural remedy to neutralize evil)

RECREATION AND RAPID REJUVENATION 218

RIGHT AND WRONG 219
(Criterion and discrimination)

LIFE IN FREEDOM 229
  (Peace in life; elimination of fear, tension, and suffering; The Problem of World Peace)

Section IV: FULFILLMENT 243

FULFILLMENT OF LIFE 245
FULFILLMENT OF RELIGION 250
FULFILLMENT OF PSYCHOLOGY 256
FULFILLMENT OF PHILOSOPHY 264
PATHS TO GOD-REALIZATION 267
GENERATION AFTER GENERATION 300
  (A move to safeguard human values and divine existence)

APPENDICES and AFTERWORD 309

APPENDIX I: A Proposal to the World Parliament Association, Paris, October 1962 311

APPENDIX II: Timely Call to the Leaders of Today and Tomorrow 329

AFTERWORD: Sequential Unfoldment of Maharishi's Teaching, by Dr. Bevan Morris 333

APPENDIX A: Overview of the Scientific Research on the *Transcendental Meditation* and *Transcendental Meditation Sidhi* Programs Including *Yogic Flying* 363

APPENDIX B: Human Physiology — Expression of Veda and the Vedic Literature: *Modern Science and Ancient Vedic Science Discover the Fabrics of Immortality in the Human Physiology*, by Dr. Tony Nader, MD, PhD, MARR .. 376

APPENDIX C: Introduction to the Bhagavad-Gītā 380

APPENDIX D: Maharishi's Master Plan to Create Heaven on Earth: *Reconstruction of the Whole World* 382

APPENDIX E: A Glimpse of Maharishi's Achievements: *1957–2008 Continuing* 384

APPENDIX F: Maharishi's Books — *Enlightenment for Everyone and Every Nation* 388

INDEX 393

CONTACT INFORMATION for Maharishi's Global Programs 435

Introduction

THE Science of Being and Art of Living is the summation of both the practical wisdom of integrated life advanced by the Vedic *Ṛishis* of ancient India and the growth of scientific thinking in the present-day Western world.

It presents a philosophy of life in fulfillment and brings forth a practice suitable for all men everywhere in the world to glorify all aspects of their day-to-day life. It deals with the fundamentals of all problems of life and suggests one sure cure to eradicate all sufferings.

This book presents a practical thesis of integrated life which has long been the abstract goal of the various sciences, religions, and metaphysical thought groups. This thesis will enable all men to harmonize their inner spiritual content with the glories of the outer material life and find their God within themselves.

Science explores into the actuality of forms and phenomena. All the branches of science are the various ways to realize the truth of existence. The approach of each of them starts from the obvious known and aims at investigating the hidden unknown. The ultimate truth of life is being approached from all directions. All the sciences are exploring the various strata of creation, from the gross to the subtler fields of existence.

The Science of Being, as does every other science, starts its investigation into the truth of existence from the gross, obvious level of life and later enters into the subtle regions of experience. The Science of Being, however, eventually transcends these subtle regions and arrives at the direct experience of the transcendental field of eternal Being.

The Science of Being is a deep and practical philosophy of life. It is a systematic investigation into the true nature of the ultimate reality. Although, like any other science, it is theoretical in its nature, its applied aspects reach much farther horizons of the supreme reality of life than those of abstract metaphysical speculations.

This book is divided into four sections: "Science of Being," "Life," "Art of Living," and "Fulfillment." The last three sections of the book present the most practical wisdom of day-to-day life, and this greatest wisdom of practical life is based on the deep philosophical significance contained in the section on the Science of Being.

The Science of Being serves to provide a deep and significant basis for the art of living. As a matter of fact, the art of living is the applied Science of Being.

To those who have never had an interest in metaphysical study, the section on "Science of Being" may at first appear to be highly abstract, but once they have stepped into "Life" and "Art of Living" and have completed the section on "Fulfillment," they will find that without dwelling on the abstract features of the Science of Being, the whole wisdom of the book would have no practical basis.

A gardener has to have a knowledge of the unseen root of the tree before he can be expected to give his concentrated effort to watering its root so that the whole tree remains fresh and green.

Likewise, a man in the practical field of life must first be given a good understanding about the fundamental reality of life that lies in the field of abstract Being, in order to glorify the whole of the rest of life. That is why the Science of Being is the first section of this book, and the sections of practical value follow.

The word "science" comes from the Latin root word *scire*, to know. It means knowledge; systematized knowledge is science.

The Science of Being means systematized knowledge of Being — systematized knowledge of existence or the actuality of life.

The field of Being or absolute existence was for many centuries considered in terms of mysticism. The present scientific age hesitates to assign value to anything shrouded in the garb of mysticism, and that is why the study of Being, the absolute field of creation, has not been a part of any branch of science until now.

The growth of scientific thinking in the present generation has brought Being to the level of scientific study and scrutiny.

A systematic method has been developed that enables an individual to experience directly the pure state of Being. It is done by consciously entering into the experience of the subtle strata of a thought, eventually arriving at the direct experience of the subtlest state of the thought, and then arriving at the very source of thought. Then the conscious mind attains the pure state of Being.

The Science of Being, which gives rise to the practical art of living, is a science which is much more valuable for human life than all the sciences known so far to the human mind. For, up to now, the basis of all the sciences has been the human mind functioning from a limited field of consciousness or limited potential. The Science of Being, through the practice of Transcendental Meditation, enlarges the conscious capacity of the mind to infinite values and therefore functions not only as the basis for the great expansion of knowledge in every field of science, but also brings to man a direct way to fulfillment.

For all this knowledge my indebtedness is to the Holy Tradition of Jagadguru Bhagavan Shankaracharya, the main source of all my inspirations and activity.

My first thanks are due to Henry Nyburg, the head of the Spiritual Regeneration Movement in Europe, who first felt the need and conceived the idea of such a book as this one about three years ago.

My thanks are also due to blessed *Ma* from London, who, like a mother, sat with a stick over the child to get the task completed. Leona Simpson from Canada, Guri Mehellis from Norway, and Dick Bock from Los Angeles have also been of great assistance in maintaining the breath of the writing and the writer. Jerry Jarvis and his dear wife, Debby, who worked hard transcribing and editing the tapes[1] and preparing the final manuscript, also deserve to share my feelings of appreciation and thanks for them. Certainly the warmth of the atmosphere created by love of Mother Olson and Roland

---

1 This book is a record of Maharishi's spoken words. In late 1962 Maharishi took time in seclusion to speak his thoughts onto audio tapes, which were transcribed and put into the form of this book, a treasury of pure knowledge to guide mankind in its evolution to perfection.

Olson, Helen Lutes, and the dear Verrills and Granvilles had its own share in bringing out this book.

This is a book of revival for the age. If the golden era is ever to dawn on human society, if the Age of Enlightenment is ever to be on Earth, this book will provide a freeway for it to come. A new humanity will be born, fuller in conception and richer in experience and accomplishments in all fields. Joy of life will belong to every man, love will dominate human society, truth and virtue will reign in the world, peace on Earth will be permanent, and all will live in fulfillment in fullness of life in God Consciousness.

Jai Guru Dev

MAHARISHI MAHESH YOGI

Lake Arrowhead
California
January 12, 1963

Section I

SCIENCE OF BEING

WHAT IS BEING? 3
BEING, THE ESSENTIAL CONSTITUENT OF CREATION 4
OMNIPRESENCE OF BEING 6
BEING, THE FIELD OF ETERNAL LIFE 8
BEING, THE BASIS OF ALL LIVING 9
BEING, THE PLANE OF COSMIC LAW 10
BEING, THE ABSOLUTE AND THE RELATIVE 13
BEING, THE ETERNAL AND ULTIMATE REALITY 15
PRĀṆA AND BEING 17
MIND AND BEING 19
KARMA AND BEING 23
HOW TO CONTACT BEING 27
    Transcendental Meditation 29
    The Main Principle of Transcendental Meditation 30
    The Technique 32
    Increasing Charm on the Path of Transcending 32
    Increased Conscious Capacity of the Mind 33
    Importance of a Proper Thought 34
    Necessity of Personal Guidance 36
HOW TO LIVE BEING 36
ADVANTAGES OF THE EXPERIENCE OF BEING 40

What Is Being?

Being is Life. It is existence. To be is to live, to exist. Being or existence finds expression in the different aspects of living: thinking, speaking, doing, experiencing, feeling. All aspects of life have their basis in Being.

The question arises, then, of how to understand Being in terms of all the different aspects of life with which we are familiar. How can we know Being in terms of the world, and what is Its relationship with the world of forms and phenomena in which we live?

How can we distinguish existence from that which exists?

Existence is abstract; that which exists is concrete.

We may say that existence is life itself, while that which exists is the ever-changing phenomenal phase of the never-changing reality of existence. Existence is the abstract aspect of life on which are built what we call the concrete phases of life which encompass all aspects of the individual — body, mind, thinking, speaking, acting, behaving, experiencing, and influencing the surroundings, including all aspects of Cosmic Existence.

Life expresses itself in different modes of living. That which is lived is the expression of life; that which exists is the expression of existence.

Existence, life, or Being is the unmanifested reality of all that exists, lives, or is. Being is the ultimate reality of all that was, is, or will be. It is eternal and unbounded, the basis of all the phenomenal existence of the Cosmic Life. It is the source of all time, space, and causation. It is the be-all and end-all of existence, the all-pervading eternal field of the almighty creative intelligence. *I am That eternal Being, Thou art That, and all this is That eternal Being in Its essential nature.*

Experience shows that Being is Bliss Consciousness, the source of all thinking, of all existing creation. It lies out of relative existence where the experiencer or mind is left awake by itself in full awareness of itself without any experience of an object. The conscious mind reaches the state of pure consciousness which is the source of all thinking. The almighty creative intelligence of the Absolute is the source of all intelligence. Being is the source of all power. It is the source of all Nature and of the Natural Laws which maintain the different forms and phenomena in creation.

The essential nature of Being is absolute Bliss Consciousness.[1] Without the knowledge of the fundamental of life, absolute Bliss Consciousness, life is like a building without a foundation. All relative life without the conscious basis of Being is like a ship without a rudder, ever at the mercy of the tossing sea. It is like a dry leaf on the ground left to the mercy of the wind, drifting aimlessly in any direction the wind takes it, for it has no roots to anchor it. The life of the individual without the realization of Being is baseless, meaningless, and fruitless.

Thus, Being is that which is the basis of life, gives it meaning, and makes it fruitful. Being is the living presence of God, the reality of life. It is eternal Truth. It is the Absolute in eternal freedom.

Being, the Essential Constituent of Creation

Physical science informs us that the whole of creation is built up of layers of energy, one inside the other. The subtlest is at the innermost stratum of creation and builds up around itself different qualities, becoming bigger and bigger.

Recent discoveries of physics indicate the existence of various types of elementary particles lying at the basis of all creation. The family of elementary particles is found increasing all the time to show that the creation exists in innumerable strata of energy. Fine particles give rise to neutrons and pro-

---

[1] *Sat-Chid-Ānanda* — It is *Sat* which never changes; it is *Chid* which is consciousness; it is *Ānanda* which is bliss.

tons which build up into the nucleus of an atom, which in turn builds up into an atom. The atoms comprise molecules, and the molecules make up the different forms of phenomena and constitute the entire visible universe. This is how physics is discovering finer layers of creation.

There was a time when physics declared the indestructibility of matter because the atom, which was thought to be the subtlest part of matter, was thought to be indestructible. Later on, experiments in the field of physics split the atom and found another world. Investigations into the nucleus of the atom gave rise to nuclear physics. Investigations into the field of electrons gave rise to electronics. The growing knowledge in these fields has advanced man's ability far beyond what could have been imagined a few decades ago.

As our knowledge of the finer fields of creation is increasing, it is enabling us to be more powerful in life.

Underneath the subtlest layer of all that exists in the relative field is the abstract, absolute field of pure Being, which is unmanifested and transcendental. It is neither matter nor energy. It is pure Being, the state of existence.

This state of pure existence underlies all that exists. Everything is the expression of this pure existence or absolute Being which is the essential constituent of all relative life.

The one eternal unmanifested absolute Being manifests Itself in many forms of lives and existences in creation. As our knowledge of the finer strata of existence increases, we gain advantage of that knowledge and grow in understanding about life. Our life becomes more comprehensive, more powerful, more useful, more creative; our aspirations, also, are found increasing.

Similarly, the knowledge of Being as the ultimate and essential constituent of creation raises the standards of all aspects of life to the unbounded status of the absolute existence. Relative life gains the absolute standard, and, based on this, stability and permanence are given to the relative field.

Energy, intelligence, and creativity rise to their limitless value and the limitations of individual life gain the status of unlimited Cosmic Existence. This is the glory of the discovery that Being is the essential constituent of creation.

Omnipresence of Being

It has been seen that Being is the essential constituent of creation and that It is present in every stratum of creation. It is present in all forms, words, smells, tastes, and objects of touch. In all the objects of experience, in all the senses of perception and organs of action, in every phenomenon, in the doer and the work done, in all directions — north, south, east, and west — in all times — past, present, and future — It is uniformly present. It is present in front of man, behind him, to the left and right of him, above him, below him, in him — everywhere and under all circumstances the essential constituent of creation, Being, is permeating everything. It is the omnipresent God for those who know and understand It, feel It, and live It in their lives.

The whole of creation is the field of consciousness in different forms and phenomena. Consciousness is the radiation from the center of pure Being. For example, the electrical current from a battery reaches the lightbulb and radiates out as a beam of light. As the beam proceeds further from its source, its intensity diminishes until it reaches a limit when the light may be said to be nil. Likewise, from the inexhaustible battery of Being, Bliss Consciousness radiates, and as it proceeds further from its source the degree of bliss diminishes. We could speak of consciousness appearing in all subtle and gross forms of life.

Those whose hearts and minds are not cultured, whose vision concentrates on the gross, only see the surface value of life. They only find qualities of matter and energy; they do not find innocent, ever-present, omnipresent Being. The softness of Its presence is beyond any relative degree of softness. They do not enjoy almighty Being in Its innocent, never-changing status of fullness and abundance of everything that lies beyond the obvious phase of forms and phenomena of matter and energy, and of mind and individual.

Pure Being is of transcendental nature because of Its status as the essential constituent of the universe. It is finer than the finest in creation; because of Its nature, It is not exposed to the senses which primarily are formed to give only the experience of the manifested reality of life. It is not obviously exposed to the perception of the mind, because the mind is connected for the most part with the senses. The constitution of the mind is such that for any experience it has to associate itself with the senses and come in contact with the outside world of forms and phenomena.

Experience shows that Being is the essential, basic nature of the mind; but, since it commonly remains in tune with the senses projecting outwards toward the manifested realms of creation, the mind misses or fails to appreciate its own essential nature, just as the eyes are unable to see themselves. Everything but the eyes themselves can be seen through the eyes. Similarly, everything is based on the essential nature of the mind, omnipresent Being, and yet, while the mind is engaged in the projected field of manifested diversity, Being is not appreciated by the mind, although It is its very basis and essential constituent. Because It is at the root of everything, It is, as it were, supporting the existence of life and the creation and not exposing Itself. The great dignity, the great splendor and grandeur of Its innocent, almighty, omnipresent Nature is present in man as the basis of ego, intellect, mind, senses, body, and surroundings. But It is not obvious; It underlies all creation.

It is like a powerful business owner who is rarely found in the actual place of business, who remains obscure and yet effectively controls his business operations. In order to see him it is necessary to meet him in seclusion, far from the main activity of the business scene. Likewise, the all-controller of the universe, being present everywhere, influencing everything, remaining at the basis of the conduct of all universal activity and phenomenal life, dwells in the silent chamber of the heart of everyone and everything.

It is the omnipresence of Being that is responsible for hiding Its nature somewhere in seclusion, out of the marketplace of the world. It is the omnipresence of Being that is responsible for hiding Being behind the scenes and giving It the status of the omniscient, omnipotent supreme lord of the universe.

The lord of the universe so kindly dwells in the heart of everyone to see that no one suffers. To maintain the unlimited love, happiness, and evolution of everyone, the omnipresent lord of the universe is so kind that he is naturally abiding in everything. No one can possibly remove himself from It. It is the omnipresence of Being that is life eternal, the essence of eternal life.

Being, the Field of Eternal Life

As the omnipresent, essential constituent of creation, Being lies at the basis of everything, beyond all relative existence, beyond all forms and phenomena. Because It has Its pure and full status in the Transcendent, It lies out of the realm of time, space, and causation, and out of the boundaries of the ever-changing phenomenal field of creation. It is, It was, It will be, in the status of Its absolute purity. It always has the status which knows no change, the status of eternal life.

Absolute Being and Its relationship with the relative universe can be understood by an example. Being is like a limitless ocean of life, silent and ever-existing in the same status. The different aspects of creation can be taken to be as ripples and waves of the vast ocean of eternal Being. All the forms and phenomena and ever-changing states of life in the world have their basis in that eternal life of omnipresent Being.

The eternal ocean of Being can be conceived of as an ocean of water. The only difference is that the pure status of the ocean of Being lies beyond all relative existence. It is the unlimited vastness of pure existence or pure consciousness, the essential constituent and content of life. It is the field of unlimited, unbounded, eternal life, pure intelligence, pure existence, the Absolute.

Having thus found that Being is the field of eternal life, what is encouraging on the practical level is the fact that the ever-changing phenomenal phases of daily life in the world can be supplemented with the unlimited power of eternal life of Being. How this is achieved in different phases of individual life is dealt with in "How to Contact Being,"[2] and "Art of Being."[3]

BEING, THE BASIS OF ALL LIVING

Living constitutes the practical life of day-to-day activity. Being, which is the essential constituent of creation, is at the basis of all activity, lying at the field of the Absolute. Being forms the basic source of all activity of the individual, and, naturally, in It and by It is sustained the activity in all the complex and diversified fields of day-to-day life.

Naturally we know our life starts with breathing and thinking. In "*Prāṇa*[4] and Being"[5] and "Mind and Being"[6] we shall see how unmanifested, transcendental Being manifests Itself in the form of *Prāṇa* and mind, which is the level of thinking and breathing. Thus we will see how all activity in our life is based on the absolute, eternal field of Being. The start of activity is from the level of thinking and the start of thinking is at the level of transcendental Being. Therefore, we find Being at the basis of all activity, behavior, and the variety of ways and forms of living.

All tendencies and the various states of likes and dislikes are modes of mind. Once we have fathomed the basis of mind and *Prāṇa* it will be easy to establish Being as the basis of all living. Because Being lies at the root of all creation, at the root of all tendencies of man, at the root of all the complexities of behavior and society, it is easy to conclude that Being is the basis of all living.

It is possible to glorify all fields of life and living by consciously infusing the nature of Being into all the different fields of activity and behavior.[7]

---

2 See page 27.
3 See page 87.
4 The Sanskrit *Prāṇa* is used because there is no corresponding word in English.
5 See page 17.
6 See page 19.
7 This is dealt with in detail under Section III on "Art of Living."

We know that activity depends upon thinking. One has first to think in order to do anything. However, people rarely consider what their thinking depends upon. Thinking is the basis of doing; what, then, is the basis of thinking? In order to think, one has at least to be. Being is the basis of thinking and thinking is the basis of doing. Being is the basis of all living, just as without the sap and root there would be no tree. If we can take care of the sap the whole tree will be taken care of. Similarly, if we can take care of Being, the whole field of thinking and doing will be taken care of. The whole field of life can be glorified by consciously taking care of Being. Being is the most glorified, most precious, and most laudable basis of all living. Being is the plane of Cosmic Law, the basis of all the Laws of Nature, which lies at the root of all creation and evolution.

Being, the Plane of Cosmic Law

Law means a rule of procedure. Cosmic Law means the rule of procedure of Cosmic Life, the rule that governs the purpose of Cosmic Existence and evolution. Cosmic Law means the rule of procedure of cosmic creative intelligence which creates, maintains, and dissolves the universe.

Cosmic means all-inclusive; it means "of the entire universe." All that there is in Nature in its static state of existence or in its dynamic state of life is included when we say cosmic.

What we find in the universe is progression of life; life seems to be in a progressive mode. Something is created, it grows, develops to its fullest extent, and at last begins to decay. It decays and becomes transformed again. We find a status of things changing. It is the change of life pattern, a change of the state that sustains evolution. It is the aspect of change that gives status to the universe.

We find that things are changing in the universe. But, besides change, there is maintenance. Life maintains itself and evolves at the same time. The aspect of maintenance is one of stability; the aspect of evolution is one of change.

The maintenance of something created is stable, but when it changes into another thing, evolves to a higher state or degrades itself to a lower state, this is called the changeable phase. When we think of Cosmic Law, therefore, we have to consider these two factors: the factor of stability and the factor of change in the universe. And we see that they are found simultaneously.

This is the law of creation, the law of maintenance, the law of evolution. Something is created, it is maintained, and, while it is maintained, it evolves, reaches the height of evolution, then dissolves. This cycle of creation, maintenance, evolution, and dissolution continues, and, in its continuity, the life of the universe goes on.

When we consider universal law we have to consider all the different features of the universe, creation of things and creation of life, maintenance of the status of the created things of life, evolution of the maintained life, and, eventually, dissolution.

In order to have a clear picture of the nature of Cosmic Law, let us take an example: Hydrogen is gas, oxygen is gas; they combine to make water, H_2O. The qualities of gas have changed to qualities of water, but "H" and "O," hydrogen and oxygen, remain "H" and "O." Again, the water freezes and is transformed into ice. The qualities of water have changed into the qualities of ice, but hydrogen and oxygen, the essential constituents, remain the same. Hydrogen and oxygen remaining the same means there is some force, there is some law or system, which maintains the integrity of hydrogen and oxygen. Yet there are certain laws which keep on changing the qualities of gas to water and water into ice.

There is one law which does not allow the status of oxygen and hydrogen to change, and that law itself does not change. The law that does not allow hydrogen and oxygen to change into anything else is itself unchanging, uniform, and eternal. Allowing hydrogen and oxygen to go through all the different levels of creation, it maintains the integrity of hydrogen and oxygen.

That law is the same one law that maintains the status quo of the essential constituent; but, at different levels of creation, this stream of law gives rise to other laws which transform the quality of this plane to that plane, transform the quality of gas into water and water into ice.

Different levels of creation in different forms keep on evolving. The appearance of new qualities is necessarily due to new laws coming into play. Thus we find all these new laws coming into play even when that eternal law goes on in its unchanging state. All the changes take place on the unchanging platform of the essential constituent. This gives a clear picture of the Cosmic Law.

There is one law of the universe which never changes, and there are innumerable laws which are responsible for all the changes in creation. The law that never changes ever maintains the integrity of the ultimate, essential constituent of creation. So this Cosmic Law is such that it never changes; yet, even while it never changes, it keeps on bringing forth newer and newer laws at different strata of Nature. This results in the different states of creation, the different forms and phenomena.

The essential and ultimate constituent of creation is the absolute state of Being or the state of pure consciousness. This absolute state of pure consciousness is of unmanifested nature which is ever maintained as that by virtue of the never-changing Cosmic Law. Pure consciousness, pure Being, is maintained as pure consciousness and pure Being all the time, and yet it is transformed into all the different forms and phenomena. Here is the Cosmic Law, one law which never changes and which never allows absolute Being to change. Absolute Being remains absolute Being throughout, although It is found in changed qualities here and there in all the different strata.

The Cosmic Law is that absolute state of pure consciousness which knows no change. It is the basis of all the Laws of Nature and it maintains the status quo of the different strata of creation, and at the same time evolves them into higher ones in conformity with the cosmic purpose of creation and evolution, and thus maintains the stream of evolution. Thus, although the maintenance and evolution of creation is directly carried on by different laws of creation, the basis of all these laws is the eternal Cosmic Law at the plane of Being, which is the basis of all creation.

Cosmic Law functions from the level in between the absolute and the relative planes of life. It harmonizes unmanifested eternal Being and the manifested field of diverse relative existence. It is the power of the Cosmic Law that maintains the eternal Being in the absolute state and at the same time maintains the ever-changing phenomenal creation of diversity in the relative states of life. It is the power of the Cosmic Law that maintains never-changing eternal Being along with the ever-changing phenomenal diversity of creation. Oneness of unity of life of absolute Being and diversity of the multiple creation are both maintained in their proper status of never-changing and ever-changing states. This is the mysterious and all-powerful nature of the Cosmic Law that has its eternal status in the plane of Being.

Being, the Absolute and the Relative

The unbounded field of Being ranges from the unmanifested, absolute, eternal state to the gross, relative, ever-changing states of phenomenal life, as the ocean ranges from the eternal silence at its bottom to the great activity of ever-changing nature on the surface of the waves. One extremity is eternally silent, never-changing in its nature, and the other is active and ever-changing.

The active, ever-changing phase of the ocean represents the relative phase of Being, and the ever-silent aspect of the bottom of the ocean represents the never-changing, eternal, absolute state. This is the relationship of Being with the world of forms and phenomena in which we live. Both these states, the relative and the Absolute, are the states of Being. Being is eternally never-changing in Its absolute state, and It is eternally ever-changing in Its relative states.

We have seen that Being is the ultimate reality of existence and the essential constituent of creation; It is omnipresent. This reveals that Being has two sides to Its essential nature: one is absolute, the other, relative. Being, ever remaining in Its omnipresent absolute status, is found to be in the ever-changing phases of phenomenal existence and relative creation. The entire field of life from the individual to the cosmos is nothing but the expression of eternal, absolute, never-changing, omnipresent Being in the relative, ever-changing phases of existence.

An example will illustrate the nature of Being in a more comprehensive manner. As we have seen, the oxygen and the hydrogen atoms in one state present the qualities of gas, in another they combine and exhibit the qualities of water, and in yet another state they exhibit the qualities of solid ice. The essential content of gas, water, and ice is the same, but it changes in its properties. Even when the properties of gas, water, and ice are quite contradictory to each other, the essential constituents, H and O, are always the same.

As the oxygen and hydrogen remaining in their never-changing state are found exhibiting different qualities, so also Being, remaining in Its never-changing, eternal, absolute character, is found expressing Itself in the different forms and phenomena of the diverse creation.

Here is a statement which, to some of the scientifically minded people of modern times, might seem contradictory to the established theories of physical science. Dr. Albert Einstein propounded the theory of relativity and said that everything in the universe is relative and the existence of different worlds and forms and phenomena can only be accounted for in terms of relativity. But here we have made a statement which says that the Absolute, remaining Absolute, expresses Itself in the relative states of creation. Being, remaining in Its never-changing, eternal absolute character, is found expressing Itself in the different forms and phenomena of the diverse creation.

Is there any consistency in these two expressions? Yes. When Einstein says all that exists in the universe can only be understood in terms of relativity, he is not wrong, because his theory of relativity concerns itself only with the manifested field of creation, which is the realm of physical science.

Certainly, in his attempts to scientifically establish the unified field theory, Einstein seems to have been clearly aware of the possibility of one ultimate basis of all diversity, one common denominator of all creation. At least he was trying to establish one element at the basis of all relative existence. If and when physical science arrives at what Einstein was trying to pinpoint by his unified field theory, one element will be established as the basis of all relative creation. With the rapid pace of development of nuclear physics, the day does not seem to be far off when some theoretical physicist will succeed in establishing a unified field theory. It may be given a different name but the content will establish the principle of unity in the midst of diversity, the basic unity of material existence.

The discovery of the field of this one basis of material existence will mark the ultimate achievement in the history of development of physical science. This will serve to turn the world of physical science to the science of mental phenomena. Theories of mind, intellect, and ego will supersede the findings of physical science. At the ultimate or the extreme limit of investigation into the nature of reality in the field of the mind will eventually be located the state of pure consciousness, the field of the transcendental nature lying beyond all relative existence of material and mental values of life. The ultimate field of Being lies beyond the field of mental phenomena and is the truth of life in all its phases, relative and absolute. The Science of Being is the transcendental science of mind. The Science of Being transcends the science of mind which in its turn transcends the science of matter which, again, in turn, transcends the diversity of material existence.

Being is the ultimate reality of all that exists; It is absolute in nature. Everything in the universe is of a relative order, but the truth is that eternal Being, the ultimate life principle of unmanifested Nature, is expressing Itself in different forms and maintaining the status quo of all that exists. The absolute and relative existence are the two aspects of eternal Being; It is both absolute and relative.

BEING, THE ETERNAL AND ULTIMATE REALITY

The glory of Being as the ultimate reality can be fathomed and known by direct experience. By experiencing the subtle states of a sound or a thought the mind could be systematically led on to the subtlest limit of experience, and, transcending this subtlest experience of the relative order, can reach a field of what may be called the ultimate.

The Upanishads bring out Being as the ultimate reality which is imperishable and eternal. The hymns of the Vedas and Bhagavad-Gītā sing the glory of the imperishable Self, Being, the ultimate reality, the Brahman which is the supreme ultimate Absolute. They say: "Water cannot wet It nor can fire burn It. Wind cannot dry It and weapons cannot slay It. It is in front, It is behind, It is above and below, It is to the right and left. It is all-pervading, omnipresent, divine Being."

The Upanishads explain Being in terms of *Ānanda*, or bliss, and locate It at the source of creation permeating everything — all time, past, present, and future; all space of all times and all aspects of causation — and explore It in the transcendental region of life.

The Upanishads explore Being as Brahman in the regions where cosmic *Prāṇa* takes its birth and explore it for man within himself. The great words of enlightenment found in the Vedas express Being as the ultimate reality and find It within man as his own inseparable Self. They reveal the truth in the expressions: "I am That," "Thou art That," "All this is That," "That alone is," and "There is nothing else but That." In these expressions and many like them, which have been the source of inspiration and enlightenment to millions of people from time immemorial, the Indian philosophy expounds the oneness of life as the ultimate reality, absolute Being.

The idea of Being as the ultimate reality is contained in the oldest records of Indian thought. The eternal texts of the Vedas, crowned with the philosophy of the Upanishads, bring out the relative and the Absolute as two aspects of the one reality of Brahman, absolute Being, which, although unmanifest in Its essential nature, manifests Itself as the relative creation.

Life is nothing but Being in all Its phases of absolute and relative existence: oneness of Being is the diversity of life, imperishable Being is the ever-changing perishable universe.

The thesis of Being as the eternal ultimate reality of life is certainly founded on the strength of a direct and practical way for every man to directly experience It. The Bhagavad-Gītā gives a very clear exposition of the path of enlightenment, Transcendental Meditation, and claims that there is no obstacle to it, there is no hurdle on the way. A slight practice relieves man of great fears.

This practical message of the direct experience of Being as the ultimate reality is one of glorification of all aspects of life. It is unique in establishing

Being as the Absolute and as the ultimate reality of all the relative phases of life.

Being as the ultimate is of transcendental nature. That is why the field of Being is not concrete. It can only be said to be abstract, although the words abstract and concrete are both relative, and neither of them truthfully expresses the nature of Being. But, for the sake of understanding, if we have to use a word to convey the nature of Being, we can only say that It is abstract and not concrete, even though Its experience is much more concrete than any concreteness of relative life.

Because of Its abstract nature, the study of Being has until recently been considered to be mystical in nature, and such a tendency is responsible for depriving the common man for hundreds of generations past of the great advantages of experiencing Being.

Now, with the availability of a systematic way to directly experience transcendental ultimate Being, Being not only steps out of the mystical field into the daylight of modern science, but It also provides a rescue and refuge against the fear of annihilation that is promoted by man's increasing knowledge in the various sciences.

The finding of Being as the eternal and ultimate reality has provided a possibility of supplementing and reinforcing the individual life with the profound basis of eternal life of the Absolute. The ever-changing phases of individual life have to be based[8] on the never-changing phase of Being, the eternal and ultimate reality. A delicate link of *Prāṇa* connects the never-changing field of eternal Being with the ever-changing phases of relative life.

PRĀṆA AND BEING

Prāṇa is the expression of manifesting Being. It is the tendency of the unmanifested to manifest. It can be said to be the impulse of abstract absolute Being. Being is the absolute existence of unmanifested nature. Its tendency to vibrate and manifest is referred to as *Prāṇa*. Being vibrates by virtue of *Prāṇa* and manifests. Assuming a subjective nature, Being becomes mind;

---

8 See Section III on "Art of Living."

assuming an objective nature, It becomes matter. Remaining innocent, It serves as a link between the subject and the object, creating the subject–object relationship and making possible the start of the multiple creation for the eternal one divine Being to have Its play in the field of the great variety of life.

Thus we find that *Prāṇa* is the power of Being which is latent in its unmanifested state and comes into play in the process of manifestation when Being assumes the role of the subjective and objective creation.

The question may then arise: What makes *Prāṇa* assume subjective and objective qualities?

That Cosmic Intelligence or creative power which is the very nature of Being generates *Prāṇa* out of Itself, absolute Being. *Prāṇa* shoots forth from the fountainhead of unmanifested Being; absolute Being assumes the role of *Prāṇa*. This is how the very nature of Being starts the process of creation and evolution begins.

What is responsible for this?

The very nature of Being is responsible. It is as if the Absolute wants to be creative and relative.

And the question, Why? may be asked.

Because of Its own nature; perhaps for the sake of variety!

Expansion of happiness is the purpose of creation.

The unity of Beingness, without undergoing any change in Itself, assumes the role of the multiplicity of creation, the diversity of Being. The Absolute assuming the role of relativity, or unity appearing as multiplicity, is nothing else but the very nature of absolute Being appearing in different manifestations. That is why, while the Absolute is eternal in Its never-changing status, the relative diversity of creation is eternal in its ever-changing nature.

This resolves the enigma of creation.

The unity of unmanifested absolute Being is the diversity and variety of manifested creation in all its relative phases of existence. The Absolute and the relative both together present the whole truth of life. One hundred percent of absolute and one hundred percent of relative existence combine to form the one hundred percent of life in creation.

It should be borne in mind that manifested creation and unmanifested Being, although appearing to be different, in reality are one and the same.

The reality of duality is unity. Even though different in their characteristics, absolute Being and relative creation together form the one reality. The whole process of what we understand as creation and evolution is just the state of Being in *Prāṇa*, and the change belongs to the very nature of Beingness. Creativity lies in the nature of absolute Being, creation is Its play, and evolution is Its expansion in Its Beingness. Being remains Being and the creation comes to be.

Prāṇa can thus be said to be the nature of Being, the motivating force of creation; it is the basic force of the mind.

MIND AND BEING

Mind is a wave of the ocean of Being. Unmanifested absolute Being, stimulated by Its own nature, *Prāṇa*, appears as mind, as an ocean stimulated by the wind appears as a wave.

Karma[9] acts as the force of wind to produce a wave of the mind in the ocean of unmanifested Being. To sum up, it may be said that *Prāṇa*, supplemented by the influence of *Karma*, is the mind.

This statement introduces the idea that if there were no influence of *Karma*, mind would not be. A question may arise as to whether *Karma* has to exist first so that the mind may be.

When we look at *Karma*, we find that without the mind (the doer), *Karma* or action cannot be produced. This shows the interdependence of mind and *Karma* and thus it seems difficult to decide whether *Karma* is produced by mind or mind is produced by *Karma*.

The riddle is resolved in the expression that the mind is born of *Karma* and creates *Karma* and *Karma* is born of mind and creates mind. The seed produces the tree and the tree produces the seed. It cannot be determined which gave rise to which in the beginning. The starting point of the cycle of

9 *Prāṇa* and *Karma*: see Section III, "Breathing and the Art of Being," p. 92 and "*Karma* and the Art of Being," p. 117.

the seed and the tree cannot be specifically determined. It can only be said that the seed is the cause of the tree and that the tree is the cause of the seed. But which started the cycle cannot be ascertained.

Metaphysics is mute on this point and finds solace in recognizing that the cycle of the seed and the tree has existed and continues to exist. Similarly, there is no evidence to prove whether *Prāṇa* gives rise to mind or mind gives rise to *Prāṇa*.

For all practical purposes the interdependence of mind and *Prāṇa* is the only established principle left at hand.

This can be understood in terms of *Karma*. *Karma* of the past life is responsible for the mind's identity in the present life; the level of evolution gained by the mind in the past life gives it its status in the present life, and, based on the *Karma* of the past life, the mind starts in the present life.

Karma is inert. This inert *Karma* supplemented by the life force, *Prāṇa*, gives rise to the mind. This mind is a composite of *Prāṇa* and *Karma*, and through *Prāṇa* it is connected with unmanifested Being. Thus we find that mind is the second stage in the process of manifestation or creation, and the first, *Prāṇa*.

This clarifies the position of the mind in the field of creation and its relationship with Being, which is the ultimate.

Prāṇa is the first expression of Cosmic Intelligence. Reflected upon by *Karma*, the *Prāṇa* gains individuality and appears as individual mind. Thus the individual mind is found to be the reflection of cosmic mind or Cosmic Intelligence. Just as *Prāṇa* is the manifesting expression of the eternal ocean of unmanifested Being, mind is the reflection of Cosmic Intelligence on *Karma*.

This shows that before the creation of the mind, there existed in principle the agency of *Karma*. This leads us to conclude that there was creation before creation. There existed a day before this day and a night before this night. The cycle of creation and dissolution is the eternal cycle in the eternity of Being.

In the process of creation, mind comes to be because there has been a mind before, which created some *Karma* that continues to exist to form the basis of the present mind.

Thus we can conceive of two realities at the basis of creation. One is the eternal reality of absolute Being and the other is the reality of *Karma* which, although it lies in the ever-changing field of relative existence, finds its eternal status in the ever-continuing cycle of action, experience, and impression. The impression of an experience is the finest remains of the *Karma* or action which maintains its existence at the finest level of the mind, almost at the meeting point of the mind and the *Prāṇa*. It is just at that plane that the creation begins — where Being becomes mind — and by virtue of this finest impression of *Karma*, *Prāṇa* simultaneously assumes the role of mind. It could be said that the next step in creation is almost simultaneously produced in principle — the mechanics of the senses of perception to enable the mind to function and to materialize the reality of mind and senses. The matter comes into being to form the physical machinery through which the five senses of perception find their expression in order to justify the validity of their creation and be and act as the agents of the mind in the process of evolution and creation. This is the process of formation of the senses, nervous system, and body.

This clarifies the subtle mechanics of creation and illustrates the principles underlying the creation of mind, senses, nervous system, and body, and their relationship with Being.

Being is the unbounded eternal ocean of absolute life. It is of a transcendental nature and, as such, It is without any attribute. It is experienced, certainly, but Its experience is always in Its own field of transcendental existence of pure consciousness where the mind transcends all fields of relative experience and becomes one with Being, gains the status of Being, and is no longer conscious mind. This state of attributeless absolute existence lies completely beyond imagination or any intellectual conception or understanding.

The human mind naturally tries to understand the ultimate reality and to stand at the shore of the limitless ocean of wisdom of the Absolute. In its attempt to fathom the unfathomable and understand the Transcendent it takes the course of understanding the finer fields of creation in the hope that if and when the finest stratum of creation is understood, it will then be possible to understand the real nature of the ultimate supreme.

To help such intellectual inquiries into the nature of Being and Its relationship with the finer fields of subjective and objective creation, we will discuss precisely and briefly the status of Being and the successive creation of the *Prāṇa*, the mind, the senses, the nervous system, and the body.

It has been made clear that it is not Being that manifests[10] (because of Its completely transcendental and attributeless nature It is not in a position to manifest or to resist manifesting), but that it is the instrumentality of *Karma* that reflects upon Being or accepts the reflection of Being and becomes the tendency to create, thereby gaining the attribute of *Prāṇa*. From that point, based on that reflection, the whole creation starts, leaving Being to remain unchanged in Its eternal status of the Absolute. Thus, nothing happens to absolute Being, and creation begins in its multifarious forms and phenomena, based on the instrumentality of *Karma*, propelled by *Prāṇa*, and carried out by the mind, leaving Being untouched.

Because Being is omnipresent, all the multiplicity of creation is pervaded by It. Nothing is without It. Everything is It. Thus, the status of creation is irrespective of Being, and, at the same time, Being is the whole creation. Mind is irrespective of Being and at the same time its essential nature is Being.

The wheel of *Karma* keeps on creating, evolving, and dissolving the phenomenal creation in cycles of existence and nonexistence of the cosmos as a whole, and the individual finds his share in it as a part of it.

We find that, in essence, life is eternal and absolute. In reality nothing but That alone is. All the ever-changing relative forms and phenomena and the entire Cosmic Existence have their life in eternal Being, and at the same time their phenomenal phase of existence is based on the plane of *Karma*, which has no absolute status in itself. The relative phase finds an everlasting status in the cycles of creation and dissolution.[11] This gives us the idea that there are two foundations of life — absolute Being and *Karma*. The question arises: Can there be two ultimate realities?

Obviously, this leaves the quest of ultimate reality in despair and the seeker of truth in uncertainty.

Certainly there cannot be two ultimate realities of life — Being and *Karma*. Obviously there can be only one ultimate reality. It remains to be discovered what the ultimate is, whether Being or *Karma*.

It has been seen that Being in Its essential nature is the absolute existence and that alone can certainly be accepted as the ultimate reality of life and

10 See "Being, the Plane of Cosmic Law," page 10.
11 See "Being, the Absolute and the Relative," page 13.

existence. But we have also seen that this ultimate reality, Being, is absolute, and, being so, is attributeless and cannot create. It has been said that the creation comes out of the reflection of Being on *Karma* or the reflection of *Karma* on Being which holds together the instrumentality of *Prāṇa*, *Karma*, and mind. It has also been said that the creation comes out of what we call *Karma*, which, by virtue of itself, assumes the role of *Prāṇa*, the vital force of life and creation.

This feature of *Karma* assuming the role of *Prāṇa* to start creation in the omnipresence of eternal Being brings hope to the seeker of one ultimate supreme reality. The understanding of *Karma* emerging from Being brings justification to the quest of the one ultimate reality.

The omnipresent nature of Being does not allow *Karma* to be given an independent status as the ultimate. *Karma* finds itself imbibed in the very nature of Being and creation finds its source in it. Thus stands Being as one supreme reality which has the instrumentality of *Karma* as Its own nature for the purpose of creation.

The realization of eternal Being as the one ultimate supreme reality of existence finds that this cause of creation or the almighty creativity is latent in the very nature of Being and expresses Itself in the form of creation. Thus, it is found that absolute attributeless eternal Being is the ultimate reality of existence and by virtue of Its own nature, the process of creation, evolution, and dissolution continues eternally without affecting the absolute status of eternal Being.

This gives the whole picture of absolute eternal Being in relation to Its own almighty cosmic creative intelligence, or universal mind, and the individual mind.

KARMA AND BEING

Karma means action or activity.

We have seen in the previous part the relationship of Being and *Karma* and have found that *Karma* is opposed to the essential nature of Being. Being is just to be. Being is absolute existence while *Karma* is the instrument through which the cycle of creation, evolution, and dissolution is kept going continuously. Thus we see that the essential nature of *Karma* is certainly not in conformity with the essential nature of Being, which is just to be.

No *Karma* can ever reach the state of Being. By the process of *Karma*, one has to keep on moving in activity: the eternal cycle of birth and death, creation, evolution, and dissolution. When *Karma* is thus opposed to the state of Being, then any process of bringing *Karma* to an end would certainly result in the state of Being.

We have seen that although the state of Being is forever the same omnipresent, transcendental, absolute existence — It is forever there — but moving in the wheel of *Karma*, the life of the individual always remains in the field of relative existence and obviously misses the glory of Being. As we have already seen, the life of the individual and that of the cosmos is being created, maintained, and dissolved by the force of *Karma*. That is why every individual and all the beings in the world are subject to the force of *Karma*. And the force of *Karma* keeps maintaining the life in the relative field, and the individual is constantly kept out of the realm of pure Being.

If there were a way available to avoid the grip of *Karma*, that would be the way to attain the state of eternal Being. In the part on "How to Contact Being,"[12] we will see that through a technique of minimizing the activity of experiencing and eventually transcending the subtlest field of activity, one arrives at the state of Being, the field of eternal life.

This truth that the nature of Being and *Karma* are incompatible with one another has been greatly misinterpreted by those who did not know the technique of minimizing the force of *Karma* and coming out of its influence. When such people of incomplete vision read in metaphysical books that absolute Bliss Consciousness is opposed to the nature of *Karma*, they evolve their own theories. They theorize that the life of activity in the world opposes the state of absolute Bliss Consciousness. This misunderstanding has created a gulf between spiritual and material values of life that has existed for many centuries past.

---

12 See page 27.

Certainly the nature of the Absolute and the relative, the nature of Being and *Karma*, are incompatible with each other. But by the technique which will be described[13] it is certainly possible to glorify the field of *Karma* by the light of Being. This is the point that hundreds of generations within the past many centuries have missed. The knowledge that it only needs skill in action to accomplish this glorification of *Karma* has been missed. That has been the main reason for the growing suffering, misery, and tension and the increasing negativity in all fields of activity in life.

It is high time that the mistake be corrected and that it be realized by all that through the system of Transcendental Meditation it is possible for every mind to come out of the relative state of experience and attain the state of Being. Having been in that state, the mind is infused with the full value of Being because, in the field of the Transcendent, it is out of the field of *Karma* and it ceases to be individual mind and becomes one with absolute eternal Being. When it has gained this state of eternal Being, the force of *Karma* draws the mind out again, and when it comes back into the relative field of activity, it realizes that the state of transcendental Being was certainly better in its unlimited status of absolute bliss than the relative state of transitory happiness in the field of activity.

The state of Bliss Consciousness of the Transcendent makes a real impact upon the nature of the mind, and we find the mind thus becomes more powerful, having tasted the unbounded state of limitless expanded consciousness. Coming out into the relative field where time, space, and causation keep everything bound within very small boundaries, the mind begins to retain some of that unbounded status in its nature. And with repeated practice, the mind becomes familiar with that transcendental state of consciousness, and when it comes out into the field of relative experience, its nature is transformed to a much higher state of consciousness.

The practice of Transcendental Meditation results in such a great impact of the nature of Being on the nature of the mind that the mind begins to live the nature of eternal Being and yet continues to behave and experience in the field of relative existence. This is the tremendous value to the mind

13 See page 36, "How to Live Being" and page 27, "How to Contact Being."

achieved through the association of transcendental Being in the day-to-day practical life in the world.

What has been lacking is the skill in action to harmonize the value of Being with the value of the field of activity or *Karma*. And it is not difficult to understand. The skill in action lies in bringing the action of the mind to recede to its source and to start conscious activity from the source of thought. This is the skill in action that succeeds in infusing the power of Being into the field of *Karma* through the instrumentality of the mind, glorifies it at all levels, and, at the same time, leaves the mind free from the bondage of *Karma*; for the mind is then established in eternal Bliss Consciousness. Just as, in the bright sunlight, candlelight loses its relative significance, so also, in the eternal light of the absolute bliss, the relative joys of life lose their attraction. This is said to be the loss of the binding influence of *Karma* under the influence of the experience of the absolute bliss of eternal Being.

The skill in action is to first bring the activity to nil, and from there start to act. It is like drawing the arrow back on the bow before we wish to shoot ahead. The skill lies in pulling the arrow back on the bow as far as possible until it reaches the state of no activity. From that point, the arrow can be shot by just releasing the catch, without effort. So this skill in action is only a matter of pulling the arrow back and then releasing it. It will, with the least amount of effort, naturally shoot ahead with the maximum force.

Likewise, by utilizing the skill of bringing the activity of the mind to a state of stillness and from that point starting the activity, the energy necessary to perform the action will be least. The action will be performed for the greatest results, and the doer will cultivate a state of eternal freedom. The doer will act established in eternal Being, and therefore will not be under the binding influence of action. This is true skill in action.

We may thus conclude that although the nature of *Karma* and the nature of Being are incompatible, it is possible to glorify *Karma* by the bliss of Being. It is possible for a man to live in the field of action and yet simultaneously live a life of eternal freedom in the Bliss Consciousness of absolute Being. It is possible for a man to act with full interest in the world and yet simultaneously live God Consciousness, thereby bringing together the values of the absolute and the relative existence. To reveal this to man is the purpose of the Science of Being.

It must be borne in mind that, while this Science of Being is perfect in its theory, it is also a practical science in which results are found only when the experiment is made. It is open to every individual to experience this state of Being and create in his life a state of eternal freedom while bringing greater success in all fields of activity.

How to Contact Being

The Science of Being not only postulates a theory of one absolute element at the basis of the entire creation, but also provides a systematic way whereby any man may have direct experience of the essential nature of transcendental absolute Being.

First we shall look into the possibility of the direct experience of the Absolute from a theoretical point of view and then consider the practical results of such an experience in day-to-day life.

We have seen that Being lies beyond the subtlest stratum of creation in the transcendental field of absolute existence. In order to experience this transcendental reality, it is necessary that our attention be led in a concrete manner through all the subtle strata of creation. Then, arriving at the subtlest level, it must transcend that experience to know transcendental Being.

What do we have in the gross level of creation? We have gross things to see through the eyes, gross words or sounds to hear through the ears, gross smells to smell through the nose, varieties of sensations to feel through the sense of touch, and varieties of tastes to taste with the tongue. We think, and the process of thinking normally seems to have no connection with these senses of perception. But the process of thinking does include one or many of these senses of perception.

Our experience in the field of perception shows that we experience gross things and we experience subtle things. We use our eyes to see, ears to hear, and so on, but we know there is a limit to which the eyes can see, the ears can hear, and the tongue can taste. This limit marks the experience of gross creation.

Eyes can see forms as long as they do not become refined beyond a certain point. The ears can hear sound within a certain range of frequency. The nose can smell different smells as long as the smells are gross enough. This is the case with all the senses of experience. They are only able to experience the gross objects.

Thus we understand that our field of experience ordinarily is limited to the gross field of creation only. The subtle fields are out of our common range of experience. We know that there are forms much finer than the eyes can see and that these may be experienced through the microscope. We know that there are waves which the ears cannot sense but which we hear with the help of radio. This shows that there are subtle strata of creation in existence with which we are not familiar because our common capacity of experience is limited to the experience of the gross only. Therefore, in order to experience transcendental Being, it is necessary to improve the faculty of experience.

If we could improve our faculty of experience through any of the senses, or improve our ability to experience the thought before it comes to the conscious level of the mind, and if this ability to perceive the thought could be so improved that it reached the source of thought, then, having transcended the source, it would be possible to reach the transcendental state of pure Being. This establishes a way to experience transcendental Being — to experience finer and finer states of creation through any sense of experience, to experience the finest stratum of creation, and to transcend that to get to the state of Being.

Since Being is of transcendental nature, It does not belong to the range of any of the senses of perception. Only when sensory perception has come to an end can the transcendental field of Being be reached. As long as we are experiencing through the senses, we are in the relative field. Therefore, Being certainly cannot be experienced by means of any of the senses. This shows that through whatever sense of experience we proceed, we must come to the ultimate limit of experience through that sense. Transcending that, we will reach a state of consciousness where the experiencer no longer experiences.

The word "experiencer" implies a relative state; it is a relative word. For the experiencer to be, there has to be an object of experience. The experiencer and the object of experience are both relative. When we have transcended the field of the experience of the subtlest object, the experiencer is left by himself without an experience, without an object of experience, and without the process of experiencing. When the subject is left without an object of experience, having transcended the subtlest state of the object, the experiencer steps out of the process of experiencing and arrives at the state of Being. The mind is then found in the state of Being which is out of the relative.

The state of Being is neither a state of objective nor subjective existence, because both of these states belong to the relative field of life. When the subtlest state of objective experience has been transcended, the subtlest state of consciousness is then said to be pure consciousness, the state of absolute Being.

This is how, by bringing the attention to the field of the Transcendent, it is possible to contact and experience Being. It cannot be experienced on the level of thinking because, as far as thinking goes, it is still a field of relative existence; the whole field of hearing, touching, seeing, tasting, and smelling lies in the relative existence.

The transcendental state of Being lies beyond all seeing, hearing, touching, smelling, and tasting — beyond all thinking and beyond all feeling. This state of unmanifested, absolute pure consciousness of Being is the ultimate of life. It is easily experienced through the system of Transcendental Meditation.

Transcendental Meditation

The process of bringing the attention to the level of transcendental Being is known as the system of Transcendental Meditation.

In the practice of Transcendental Meditation, a proper thought is selected and the technique of experiencing that thought in its infant states of development enables the conscious mind to arrive systematically at the source of thought, the field of Being.

Thus, the way to experience transcendental Being lies in selecting a proper thought and experiencing its subtle states until its subtlest state is experienced and transcended.

We shall now deal with the main principle of the system of Transcendental Meditation.

The Main Principle of Transcendental Meditation

We have seen that Being is the state of eternal and absolute existence and that the way to experience Being is to experience from the gross to the subtle states of creation until the mind arrives at the Transcendent.

We have seen that we could proceed through any sense of experience. For example, through the sense of sight we could experience gradually subtler and subtler forms and eventually our eyes would reach a point where they were unable to perceive a form beyond a certain degree of subtlety. If we could close our eyes and train the inner eye — the eye of the mind — to perceive the object at the point at which we failed to perceive it through our open eyes, we would have a mental image of the object. If there were a way to experience the finer and finer fields of that mental image, experience its finest state and transcend it, we would then reach the state of Being. Likewise, through any sense of experience we could start experiencing the object and eventually arrive at the transcendental state of Being.

Through the experience of a thought we could experience the subtle states of thinking and, transcending the subtlest state of thinking, we would be sure to arrive at the transcendental state of Being.

Thinking, in itself, is the subtle state of speech. When we speak, our words are audible to the ears, but if we do not speak, the words do not become perceptible to the organ of hearing. Thus we find that thought is a subtle form of sound.

Experience shows that the process of thinking starts from the deepest, most refined level of consciousness and becomes grosser as it develops. Eventually it becomes gross enough to be perceived on the surface level of the ocean of consciousness, on the common level of thinking. An analogy will clarify the principle.

A thought starts from the deepest level of consciousness, from the deepest level of the ocean of mind, as a bubble starts at the bottom of the sea. As the bubble rises, it gradually becomes bigger. When it comes to the surface of the water it is perceived as a bubble.

Mind is like an ocean, and, as in an ocean, the surface layers are active in waves and the deeper levels are silent. The surface layers of the mind are actively functioning while the deeper levels are silent. The surface functioning level of the ocean of mind is said to be the conscious mind. Any thought on the surface level is conscious mind. Any thought on the surface level is consciously cognized. The level of the ocean of mind at which the thoughts are appreciated as thoughts is the conscious level of the mind.

A thought starts from the deepest level of consciousness, travels through the whole depth of the ocean of mind, and finally appears as a conscious thought on the surface. Thus we find that every thought stirs the whole range of the depth of consciousness, but it is consciously appreciated only when it has come to the conscious level; the rest of its many stages of development are not appreciated. That is why, for all practical purposes, we say that the deeper levels of the ocean of consciousness are as though silent. If there were a way to consciously appreciate all the states of the bubble of thought prior to its reaching the surface level, that would be the way to transcend thought and experience transcendental Being.

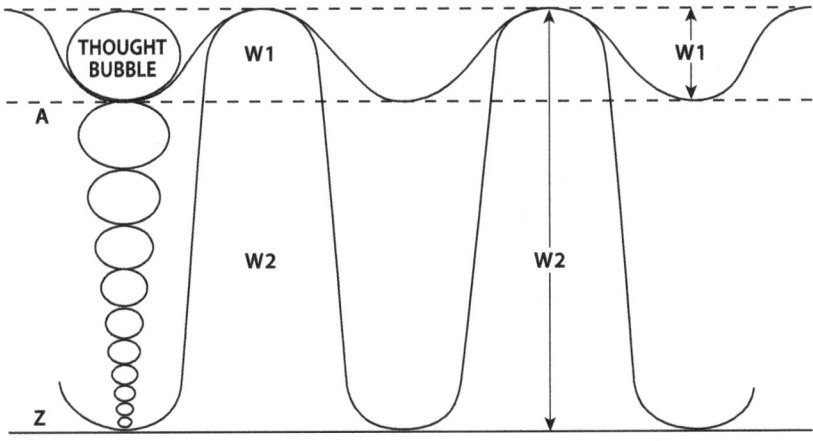

The Main Principle of Transcendental Meditation

The bubble of thought rising from the level Z becomes bigger (*see illustration*). By the time it reaches the surface level A, it has developed enough to be appreciated as a thought. This is the level of the conscious mind.

The subtle states of the bubble of thought below the level of the conscious state are not consciously appreciated. If there were a way to appreciate consciously the bubble of thought at all levels of its development, and at the source Z, and if it were possible to transcend this experience, then the mind would gain the state of Transcendental Consciousness.

If the bubble of thought could be consciously appreciated at the level below A and at all levels of subtlety from A to Z, it would then be possible to bring the level Z within the range of the conscious mind. In this way the depth of the conscious mind (represented by W1) would become greater (as represented by W2), and the power of the conscious mind would be increased manyfold. This expansion of the conscious capacity of the mind will again be, on the mental level, on the way to experiencing Being.

The Technique

Bubbles of thought are produced in a stream, one after the other, and the mind is trained to experience the oncoming bubble at an earlier and earlier stage of its development (*see illustration*). When the attention has reached level Z, it has traversed the whole depth of the mind, and has reached the source of creative intelligence in man.

This source of thought thus comes within the scope of the conscious mind. When it transcends the subtlest state of thought, the conscious mind transcends the subtlest state of relative experience and arrives at the state of transcendental Being, the state of pure consciousness or Self-awareness.

This is how, in a systematic manner, the conscious mind is led on, step by step, to the direct experience of transcendental absolute Being.

Increasing Charm on the Path of Transcending

To go to a field of greater happiness is the natural tendency of the mind. Because in this practice of Transcendental Meditation the conscious mind is set on its way to transcending and experiencing transcendental absolute Being, whose nature is Bliss Consciousness, the mind finds that the way is increasingly attractive as it advances in the direction of bliss. A light becomes faint and dim as we go away from its source, and the intensity increases as we proceed toward the source. Similarly, when the mind goes in the direction of the absolute bliss of transcendental Being, it finds increasing charm at every step of its march. The mind is charmed and is led to experience transcendental Being.

Thus we find the practice of Transcendental Meditation is a pleasant practice for every mind. Whatever the state of evolution of the aspirant, whether or not he is emotionally developed or intellectually advanced, his mind, by its very tendency to go to a field of greater happiness, finds its way to transcend the subtlest state of thinking and arrive at the bliss of absolute Being. That is why the practice of Transcendental Meditation is not only simple, but also automatic.

Increased Conscious Capacity of the Mind

We will analyze in detail what has happened to the conscious mind during Transcendental Meditation when it fathoms the subtle states of thought. This, of course, is not a part of our consideration of how to experience Being, but it is interesting to note what happens to the mind on its way to directly experiencing the transcendental. In the diagram, the area of the conscious mind represented by W1 has become the much larger area represented by W2. It is as if the waves on the surface of the ocean have communicated themselves with the deeper levels of water, with the result that each wave is mightier than the wave before.

On the path to experiencing Being, the conscious capacity of the mind is enlarged and the whole ocean of mind becomes capable of being conscious. The full mental potential is thus unfolded, and the conscious capacity of the mind is increased to the maximum limit. How it is technically achieved is a matter of personal instruction from those who have been trained to impart this technique of experiencing Being.

Importance of a Proper Thought

A proper thought means a thought whose nature is harmonious and useful to the thinker and the surroundings. Every thought, as every spoken word, has some influence on the thinker and on his surroundings. Just as a stone thrown into a pond produces waves that reach all the extremities of the pond, any thought, word, or action produces waves in the atmosphere, and these waves travel in all directions and strike against everything in the atmosphere. They produce some influence in every level of creation. The whole universe is influenced by every thought, word, and action of every individual.

When such is the wide range of the influence of a thought, one has to be very particular about the quality of thought one creates in his mind. There may be a thought whose influence is detrimental to the thinker and to the rest of the universe. Likewise, there may be a thought whose influence is favorable and useful to the thinker and to the world at large. Because each personality has its own quality, it is extremely necessary that each man should have selected for him a special quality of thought whose physical influence will be conducive and useful to himself and the world at large.

The influence of a spoken word that is carried by the waves of vibrations in the atmosphere does not depend upon the meaning of the word. It lies in the quality of the vibrations that are set forth. Therefore, where it is necessary to produce vibrations of good quality that produce an influence of harmony and happiness, it also is necessary that the quality of vibration should correspond to that of the individual.

Individuals differ in the quality of their vibrations which constitute their individual personalities.

That is why the selection of a proper thought for a particular individual is a vital factor in the practice of Transcendental Meditation.

Since the quality of each man is different from that of every other man, it is all the more difficult to be able to select the right type of vibration or the proper quality of thought for the practice of Transcendental Meditation. This problem of selecting a proper thought whose physical quality corresponds to the physical quality of the thinker becomes increasingly important when we consider that the power of thought increases when the thought is appreciated in its infant states of development.

We know that power is greater in the subtle strata of creation than in the gross. If we throw a stone at someone it will hurt him, but if we could enter into its subtle strata and excite an atom of the stone, tremendous energy would be released and the effect would be far greater. Similarly, when we enter into the subtler states of a thought, we appreciate its finer levels and the power is much greater than it would be on the common conscious level of the mind. With this in view, it is essential that, before starting the practice of Transcendental Meditation, a proper quality of sound should be selected.

The question of selecting a proper thought for a particular individual presents an enormous problem when we consider the far-reaching influence of an action in the entire universe.

An action performed by a particular individual in a particular place at a particular time may produce favorable results for the doer and the surroundings. The same action, however, may produce a different influence under different circumstances.

The consideration of action and its influence is highly complicated. It virtually goes beyond the capacity of the human mind to fathom the influence of an action at any level of creation. Therefore, the problem of selecting a proper thought for the daily practice of Transcendental Meditation is something which cannot be successfully decided by any and every individual.

For the sake of facilitating the finding of a proper word for every individual, certain individuals have been trained in the art of selecting a proper sound or word to correspond to the special quality of the individual. These trained teachers of Transcendental Meditation are found in almost every country of the world in the centers of the Spiritual Regeneration Movement.[14]

---

14 Maharishi was inspired to inaugurate the Spiritual Regeneration Movement on December 31, 1957, in Madras (Chennai), India, to spiritually regenerate mankind. The formal inauguration took place the following day, January 1, 1958. Under Maharishi's guidance, the Spiritual Regeneration Movement evolved into a global structure of Transcendental Meditation centers in countries around the world, which have been established in the name of educational organizations authorized in each country to teach the Transcendental Meditation program (see Contact Information for Maharishi's Global Programs, page 435).

Necessity of Personal Guidance

By necessity, the teaching of Transcendental Meditation is verbal; it is imparted by personal instruction. It cannot be imparted through a book because it not only involves telling an aspirant how to experience the subtle states of thinking, but an even greater responsibility lies in finding out what the aspirant experiences when he proceeds on that path.

A thought itself is a very abstract experience to a common man, and if he is asked to experience the subtle states of thought, he is being asked to experience the finer states of that abstract experience. To be able to do this seems to be an impossibility to the ordinary mind, which has always been used to the experience of gross, concrete objects.

The experiences on the path of Transcendental Meditation are very subtle, and the experiencer himself often is not certain that he is experiencing anything, because the moment he begins to experience the subtle state of thought, he finds himself drifting away to nothingness. It takes a while for the beginner to be able to pinpoint his experiences of the subtle state of thought. That is why it is not possible to put into writing how the mind passes through the experiences of the subtle states of thought. The practice of Transcendental Meditation must *always* be given by the expert teachers of Transcendental Meditation who have been properly trained to give it and who have been trained to check the experiences.

The checking of experiences is a vital point in the practice of Transcendental Meditation. Again, it cannot be done through books. The practice must result in all good in life, but by its nature it is delicate and therefore highly technical. Under personal instruction and guidance the way is smooth and easy.

How to Live Being

Being is not something that exists and can be brought from somewhere and lived. It is existence, the very life of everything. It is the all-pervading, omnipresent state of absolute consciousness. In order to live It, the conscious mind first has to become acquainted with It by the means described under the heading, "How to Contact Being."[15]

In Transcendental Meditation, when the mind transcends the subtlest state of thinking, it arrives at the state of Being. It is the state of no experience because the whole field of relativity has been transcended. It is just the state of transcendence, the state of existence, pure consciousness, *is*-ness, *am*-ness.

From this state of pure Being the mind comes back again to experience thought in the relative world. Through constantly going into the realm of the Transcendent and back out into the field of relativity, familiarity with the essential nature of Being deepens, and the mind becomes gradually more aware of its own essential nature. With more and more practice, the ability of the mind to maintain its essential nature while experiencing objects through the senses increases. When this happens the mind and its essential nature, the state of transcendental Being, become one, and the mind is then capable of retaining its essential nature — Being — while engaged in thought, speech, or action.

In order to achieve such a state of mind, two things are necessary. One, as we have already seen, is the practice of Transcendental Meditation, and the other, equally important for the rapid attainment of the desired goal, is that the mind should not be strained when it comes out after meditation to engage in the field of activity. The whole field of activity should be properly attended to, everything experienced, and all necessary action performed, but the mind should not be overtaxed. Everything should be done in a very easy manner. Taking life naturally and easily is very important for the quick infusion of Being into the nature of the active mind.

When the conscious mind transcends and attains the state of Being, it becomes one hundred percent of the state of Being. The mind loses its individuality and becomes cosmic mind; it becomes omnipresent and gains pure, eternal existence. In the Transcendent it has no capacity for experience. Here the mind does not exist, it becomes existence.

When the mind comes back into the field of relative life, it gains individuality again, but it also seems to retain some of the great unbounded, universal status which it had just attained. With practice it is able to retain more and more of that experience in the activity of daily life.

15 See page 27.

Any engagement of the mind in the field of activity is naturally a strain for the essential nature of the mind, which is pure Being. But if the mind engages itself in the activity in an easy, unstrained, simple, and natural manner, the infusion of the faculty of Being into the nature of the mind becomes greater. If, on the other hand, the mind is strained during activity, the infusion of Being into the nature of the mind becomes less effective. For example, when a white cloth is dipped into yellow dye it becomes yellow. When it is brought out, the depth of color is not as great as it appeared while the cloth was still in the dye. If the cloth is put in the shade for some time, the color fades still more and, if the cloth is placed in the direct Sun, it is found that the color fades even more rapidly.

Likewise, when the mind gets to the transcendental state of Being, it becomes pure Being. If it is put to activity in a very normal and natural manner when it comes out of the Transcendent, the infusion of the faculty of Being is retained for some time. But, if the mind is strained in activity, then the intensity of infusion is much less. Therefore, it is very important when one engages oneself in the field of activity that it is done in a very natural manner so that the activity serves as a means to culture the mind to be in the state of Being.

Thus we find that the regular practice of Transcendental Meditation and regulated activity in life is a direct way of living Being, or, a shortcut for creating a state of consciousness where absolute Being and the relative field of life both will be simultaneously lived, and one will not be a barrier for the other.

In the "Art of Living,"[16] it is made clear that, by the system of Transcendental Meditation, it is not only possible but easy for everyone to cultivate the state of Cosmic Consciousness in which Being is lived along with all values of relative life.

Those who start the practice of Transcendental Meditation feel more energy, greater clarity of mind, and better health. They become more efficient and energetic in all fields of activity. They should bear in mind, however, that, as their mental and physical efficiency increases, they should not blow themselves up into activity to such an extent that they become exhausted

16 See "Art of Action" and "Art of Behavior" in Section III.

and find no time for meditation. When the root is watered, the tree becomes green and more vital for the purpose of growing more. If the activity of growing is cherished by the tree to such an extent that it has no time to draw in the water from the root, then the very basis of the growth will be lost.

It is important to note that, while the infusion of the faculty of Being into the nature of the mind apparently results in rejuvenation of personality, clear thinking, and greater energy, it is a very delicate process. It is on the level of Being, the very existence of the individual, and it is never on the level of the conscious mind.[17] Therefore, we caution all aspirants not to expect to feel Being on the level of the conscious mind.

Whatever influence of Transcendental Meditation there is takes place in the field of Being. It is like a tree which receives water at its root and consequently all the parts of the tree automatically receive nourishment and flourish. No other part of the tree, however, knows or experiences the process of the root receiving the water. Its influence is seen in the increasing freshness of all parts of the tree. Perhaps a leaf puts up the argument that it feels better but does not feel that it is receiving any nourishment. Its constitution from the beginning has been such that it naturally received life energy from the roots. The same process is just continuing on a greater scale. This is why the leaf does not recognize that anything is happening to it. What is happening to it is appreciated, however, by all those who have seen the leaf drying up and who now see that it is becoming fresh and is flourishing.

Likewise, when one meditates, one experiences increased energy and clarity of mind, but does not experience the actual process of the infusion of Being into the nature of the mind. The whole process is silent on the level of pure Being. Whatever the mind's experiences during meditation, they are just relative states of the medium of meditation. These states become finer and finer until eventually nothing is left of the medium and the mind is left all by itself in the state of pure consciousness.

With regular practice, one does succeed in living Being. The infusion of the nature of Being into the nature of the mind is on the level of Being, the very nature of the mind.

17 Surface level of the mind.

Therefore, living Being is a state which cannot be described; it can only be lived, because description cannot give a complete exposition of that state.

It is as in the case of someone who has been eating something and is asked to describe the taste. It is very difficult to put the exact taste into words even though he was able to taste the food perfectly well. Similarly, Being is very well lived in life and is a state of experience, but It cannot be expressed precisely. In the beginning of the practice, Being is very delicately impressed on the nature of the mind. But, as the practice is continued, It becomes more and more deeply infused in the mind and eventually becomes so deep, significant, and unshakable that It is lived all the time through all the experiences of the wakeful, dreaming, and deep-sleep states. Then one lives eternal freedom in the life of relative experience.

Advantages of the Experience of Being

There are innumerable advantages to the experience of absolute Being through the practice of Transcendental Meditation. It influences the life of the individual on all levels to such a great degree that the whole life is transformed to a value beyond the human mind's imagination.

How can it be possible for a mortal man to gauge the advantages of his individual life coming in conscious contact with the Cosmic Life of absolute Being of eternal status? How can ordinary human intelligence fathom the greatness of Cosmic Intelligence found in the field of transcendental Being? How can it be possible for an individual functioning with a limited degree of his mental potential to gauge the great possibilities of creative energy when he would be able to function with the whole of his potential and remain in tune with the center of creative intelligence of absolute Being?

The mind, the body, and the surroundings are the three main spheres of life. The advantages of the direct experience of Being in these aspects of life in all their variety of expressions will be dealt with in the parts that follow.

We shall see in the section on "Life" how the experience of Being permits one to live life in its full status and significance, how it leads one to live the normal life of man — Cosmic Consciousness. The advantages of experiencing Being with regard to the body and mind are dealt with in "Key to Good Health,"[18] and the unfoldment of mental faculties is discussed in "Education."[19]

The effect of the experience of Being on relationships with others is dealt with in the parts on "Art of Being" and "Art of Behavior";[20] rejuvenation of the individual is discussed in the part on "Recreation and Rapid Rejuvenation."[21]

We shall see how there can be peace in life through elimination of fear, tension, and suffering on both the individual and international planes, through the direct experience of Being. This is dealt with in "Life in Freedom."[22]

In the section on the "Art of Living," it is shown that the direct experience of Being enables man to use his full potential and to make full use of his surroundings and of the almighty power of Nature. This brings into harmony the material and spiritual values of life and makes it possible to live life in eternal freedom, while still accomplishing the maximum in the material field. It is shown how Being may be lived in all phases of life: the body, mind, nervous system, action, speech, thought, breath, behavior, and surroundings.

Being brought to the level of the individual mind provides the key to clear, purposeful, and fruitful thinking; put into action, it provides the key to self-confidence and increased efficiency in all undertakings.

In the section on "Fulfillment," we shall discover that Transcendental Meditation fulfills a man's religious life, provides true fulfillment of psychology and philosophy, and is the key to God-Realization.

---

18 See "Key to Good Health" in Section III on "Art of Living."
19 See "Education" in Section III on "Art of Living."
20 See "Art of Being" and "Art of Behavior" in Section III on "Art of Living."
21 See "Recreation and Rapid Rejuvenation" in Section III on "Art of Living."
22 See "Life in Freedom" in Section III on "Art of Living."

Section II

LIFE

WHAT IS LIFE? 45
    Purpose of Life 48
NORMAL LIFE 51
INDIVIDUAL AND COSMIC LIFE 53
    The Universe Reacts to Individual Action 54

What Is Life?

Life is the Light of God, the expression of Divinity. It is Divine. It is the stream of eternal Being, a flow of existence, intelligence, creativity, purity, and bliss.

Life is unity on the basis of the absolute and eternal unity of life. On the surface of eternity, we are mortal beings in an ever-changing phenomenal existence.

Life is unity in God Consciousness. It is multiplicity in the Light of God. Life is absolute in Bliss Consciousness and relative in the variety of phenomenal joy.

Essentially life is Being. Life, in its essential nature, is the unbounded, eternal ocean of Being.

When we state that life is the ocean of Being, we do not mean life is only that. It is also the stream, the flow of Being. The "flow of Being" means Being in Its manifested, relative aspects.

Let us consider the ocean, since we have said life is the ocean of Being. At the bottom of the ocean the water is cool. As we rise toward the surface we find that the water becomes warmer at each level and that at the surface of the ocean the temperature is highest. The various degrees of temperature at different levels constitute the temperature of the ocean. The water is essentially the same at all levels, but, according to the temperature of each different level, it varies in its density.

Likewise, Being is the same and yet different at each level of creation. It is composed of different levels of understanding, different levels of intelligence and creativity, and different levels of peace and happiness.

All these levels of peace and happiness, creativity, intelligence, and power are nothing but the different levels of Being. One extreme of Being is absolute, and the other is the grossest state of relative existence. The different states of Being between these two extremes constitute the different states of manifested Being. This is how we find that life is the ocean of Being. Eternally remaining absolute Being, It is found in the different qualities, forms, and phenomena of the diverse creation.

Another example will serve to illustrate the nature of life. We know that hydrogen and oxygen are gases and when they combine as H_2O they become water. Although gas becomes water, the essential constituents, H and O, remain the same hydrogen and oxygen.

When water freezes to become ice, the qualities change again, but the essential constituents remain the same. The fluidity of water has changed into the solidity of ice. The transparency of water has changed into the opacity of ice, but with all these changes, the essential constituents of hydrogen and oxygen have not changed. The same element is found in all the different states, appearing in different qualities, giving rise to different phenomena.

It is as if one and the same man is found as an actor on the stage, a player on the playing field, a student in the class, and a customer in the market.

When a judge sits in the courtroom, he wears robes befitting a judge, but when he goes to his club he appears in the clothes that are worn at a club. When he is at home he wears clothes that differ from those he wears on the street. And, before retiring at night, he changes his clothes once again. The garments keep on changing, but the man remains the same. He is addressed in different ways by different people, yet the man is forever the same man.

Likewise, all different forms and phenomena in creation differ in their qualities. No two forms in the world appear to be the same, for nothing in creation seems to be stable. All is changing from one to the other, yet, at the basis of all these ever-changing phases of forms and phenomena of creation, the underlying reality is the same never-changing eternal absolute Being.

What life is could be illustrated by the example of a tree. All the various attributes of the outer aspect of the tree — trunk, branches, leaves, flowers, and fruit — together with the various attributes of the inner root, go to make up the whole life of the tree. But when we look more closely into the life of the tree we find that, although the root is the basis of the outer tree, it has no absolute, independent status. The root depends upon the nourishment, or sap, that comes from the area outside the root itself. This sap is the essence of the entire tree. It makes the root and, passing through the root, gives rise to the various aspects of the tree.

We thus find the tree is nothing but the nourishment that comes from outside the boundary of the individual tree. The tree is obviously limited within the bounds of the root and outer tree, but its basis is outside these bounds.

This basis of life is of transcendental nature; it transcends the boundaries of the inner and outer tree. It is the field of the essential constituent of life.

Similarly, the life of man, or any individual life in creation, has three aspects: the outer, the inner, and the transcendental. The outer aspect of life is the body; the inner is the subjective aspect of the personality which is concerned with the process of experience and action; and the transcendental aspect of life is Being.

The various aspects of life may be compared with a coconut. The outer part of a coconut consists of a hard shell and husk of many fibers. The husk and its particular shape may be compared with the outer or gross physical aspect of life, the body. Underneath the shell is a more precious aspect of the coconut which is the solidified layer of milk, the kernel. Beyond the kernel is the essence of the coconut, the milk in its pure form. The milk in its pure form has solidified into a firm inner layer and surrounds itself with the harder and more solidified layer of the shell in order to protect the precious inner aspect of the coconut.

Similarly, in the life of the individual we find that inner Being is unmanifested absolute Being which manifests as the ego, intellect, mind, senses, and *Prāṇa*. All these subtle states of life make up the inner man or the subject within, the subjective aspect of life. The subjective aspect of life differs from the objective aspect of life, which is the body in all its various attributes.

When we consider life we have to consider it in all its phases, and, if we succeed in having a clear picture of all aspects of an individual existence, then we know the full scope of life.

Thus, life in its full scope has three aspects: the objective aspect, the subjective aspect, and the transcendental aspect. This is life in its totality.

Purpose of Life

Expansion of happiness is the purpose of life, and evolution is the process through which it is fulfilled. Life begins in a natural way,[1] it evolves, and happiness expands. The expansion of happiness carries with it the expansion of intelligence, power, creativity, and everything that may be said to be of significance in life.

The purpose of individual life is also the purpose of the life of the entire cosmos. The purpose of creation is expansion of happiness which is fulfilled through the process of cosmic evolution. The significance and purpose of individual life is the same as that of the life of the cosmos. The difference lies in the scale.

The individual life is the basic unit of the life of the cosmos. Evolution of the cosmos is basically served by the evolution of the individual life. Thus, if the purpose of individual life is served, the purpose of Cosmic Life is also served spontaneously and simultaneously to that degree and on that scale.

If one has fulfilled the purpose of his own life, he has done his best to serve the cosmic purpose.

If one is not happy, one has lost the very purpose of life. If one is not constantly developing his intelligence, power, creativity, peace, and happiness, then he has lost the very purpose of life. Life is not meant to be lived in dullness, idleness, and suffering; these do not belong to the essential nature of life.

Life is dynamic, not static. It is energetic, progressing, evolving, developing through activity, and multiplying itself. The nature and purpose of life is progress, evolution, activity, and improvement.

Activity maintains the stream of evolution, and the physical vehicle that is responsible for activity is the nervous system of the individual. In the species lower than man the nervous system is not as fully evolved and so the activity leading to evolution is on a much smaller scale. The activity of the lower species, while carrying out the process of evolution, does not produce a high degree of evolution. As the nervous system evolves, the rate of evolution increases.

1 See page 19, "Mind and Being."

Man's nervous system is the most highly evolved. Therefore, the scope of evolution of man is unlimited in this life. We note how, when a child is born, his intelligence, power, and creativity are low, but as he grows he indulges in the field of activity where his power is great, his intelligence is great, his creativity is great, and the degree of happiness which he experiences in himself and projects outside himself is great. The nervous system is developed to the extent that through proper activity (the revelation of which is the purpose of this book) the man can contact absolute bliss, creativity, intelligence, power, and energy.

Man's nervous system is said to be a complete nervous system. So the purpose of man's life is to live a state of unlimited energy, intelligence, power, creativity, and bliss of absolute Being.

To live a life of freedom is the purpose of life in the human species. If one is not able to live such a life, the very purpose of life is blurred. Man is born to live a perfect life holding within its range all values of the transcendental absolute Divine of unlimited energy, intelligence, power, peace, and bliss, along with the unlimited values of the world of multiplicity in relative existence. He is born to project the abundance of the absolute state of life into the world of relative existence.

Man's life is meant to be a bridge of abundance between Divine Intelligence and the whole creation. Man's life is to cultivate and give — cultivate the divine power, the Divine Intelligence, happiness and abundance, and give it out to all of creation. This is the high purpose of the life of man, and it is fortunate to find that every man is capable of reaching this by improving the conscious capacity of his mind and consciously contacting the field of the absolute energy, peace, happiness, and abundance of the eternal, divine consciousness.

Every man is capable of spreading the divine splendor in the whole creation. He is able to project all values of the Absolute into the world of relative existence for all creatures to enjoy and to glorify the whole creation of God. Every man is capable of living a life of full values. If one fails to live it, it is a disgrace to oneself, and it abuses the glory of almighty God within and above us.

Here is an invitation for every man on Earth to start picking up the divine consciousness of the Absolute, and, by bringing it out through all his activity into the world of variety, enjoy it for himself and project it for all others to enjoy as well.

A man projecting himself out in the world through a limited mind is not able to appreciate the real purpose of life. With a small capacity of mind, he engages himself in doing little things of which he thinks in very limited terms. He can engage himself in very limited activity. He can create only a limited number of small things of limited value. The conscious mind of an ordinary man is so limited that he is not even able to enjoy life. He is found to be suffering for the most part on many levels of his life. This state of suffering is merely due to his not using his full potential.[2]

By not using his full potential, man is not able to fulfill the purpose of his life. He is found suffering in many ways because he is not using the full conscious capacity of his mind; he is not using the great energy he carries within himself. He is not experiencing and expressing in his life the abundance of absolute bliss that he naturally possesses, the great absolute field of creativity and power that he has within himself. He is like a millionaire who has forgotten all his wealth and status and who goes begging in the street and at every moment feels the lack of money.

All suffering is due to not knowing a way to unfold the divine glory present within oneself. Lack of knowledge to "dive" within oneself is the root of all ills and sufferings of human life. Not having the capacity of divine unfoldment, the ignorance of a technique for diving within oneself is responsible for misery in life. Without divine consciousness, man is found lacking in energy, intelligence, and clear thinking. He is tired, worried, tense, and anxious.

This state of human existence and human intelligence has come to such a deplorable condition that from the field of psychology — the great science of the mind — it is found suggested that tension is necessary for creative intelligence. What a shame it is to believe that tension is necessary to improve life!

It is said that poets and artists have created their inspiring literature and art under tension. All such statements come from ignorance and from an inability to release tensions.

---

2 See page 63, "Man's Full Potential."

Our modern scientific age unfortunately is increasing in tension. The individual life seems to be growing in tension instead of growing in ease and comfort, even though material comforts certainly are increasing. This is only because the individuals have no way of improving their ability and efficiency through contact with the fields of greater energy and intelligence that every man has within himself. It is only necessary to consciously contact that field of inner life and profit by it.

The man of today is blind to the purpose of life, not able to see that he is born to enjoy, create, and live a life useful to himself and to others. He plunges into whatever activity lies ahead and works hard to put forth his best effort in that field. It is commendable to work hard for things; to be creative in any aspect of life is what man is here for. But when the activity increases, a man often finds himself unable to cope with the increased pressure. His efficiency declines, or he does not find energy enough to cope with the increased activity. This is why tensions and strain develop.

As a man engages in greater activity he should be able to produce more energy and greater intelligence within himself to cope with the increased activity. This he does not know how to do, and, therefore, he loses the entire purpose of life.

NORMAL LIFE

While dealing with the question "What is Life?" it has been made clear that life has two aspects, relative and absolute. Therefore, normal life should mean that the values of both these aspects are lived and enjoyed in a natural way — to fulfill the overall purpose of life.

A normal life means the use of full values of full life — all values of relative fields of life and all values of the absolute field of life. Taken together they make up the normal life.

We have also seen that in the relative aspect of life we have both the subjective and objective aspects. The subject is the inner aspect of the individual, and the object is the outer body. The values of the outer life of the individual (the body) and the inner life of the individual (which includes the ego, intellect, mind, senses, *Prāṇa*, and absolute Being), taken together, represent the normal state of life.

The body and mind should be functioning normally, Being should supplement all fields of relative existence, and the surroundings should be harmonious and useful. Such a life is said to be a normal life. When one naturally uses all the resources of mind, body, and Being for the natural process of evolution, then life can be said to be normal. When one enjoys all values of human existence, which includes the eternal value of Bliss Consciousness of divine Being along with the maximum use of all the potential glories of material life, then is life said to be in its normal state. When all values of relative life pertaining to the body, mind, and surroundings are supplemented with the divine values, the blissful nature of absolute Being, then the worldly life in fullness of eternal freedom is the normal life of a human being. The normal standard of human life is a life of all glory in the material field of the world, supplemented by the eternal freedom in God Consciousness. Cosmic Consciousness is meant to be the normal consciousness of human beings.

The standard of human life is not, as is often thought, restricted to our different ways of living, dressing, sleeping, walking, playing, talking, or behaving in society; these are the gross levels of human values. The real, substantial value of human life is the Bliss Consciousness that places a man on the high pedestal of eternal freedom while he is engaged in the day-to-day world of transitory values.

Cosmic Consciousness is the state of normal human life, and to attain that is to begin to live a normal life. One who has not achieved Cosmic Consciousness has not yet reached the platform of normal human life. His standard of living is not the standard of normal human life; it is below the standards of human life; it is nearer the level of animal life.

What makes the difference between the life of man and that of the animal? The process of maintaining life is the same in both cases. Animals and man eat, drink, sleep, and are active. All the joys of the senses that man has in his contact with the object of senses are also naturally found in the life of animals. Animals shrink from death just as man does. There does not seem to be any superiority in the life of man over the animals insofar as the maintenance of life is concerned.

Man is superior to the animal species because of his ability of greater understanding, his ability to perceive a greater range of life, his ability to live full values of life, and his ability to act independently. Man has freedom of action, whereas the activities of the animals are governed by the Laws of Nature. Mother Nature takes care of all the activities of the animals and they are all in a set pattern. Their lord of evolution maintains their life in a particular pattern. No animal has a developed mind to deviate from its channels of activity brought to it by the natural laws. Man, however, has a developed nervous system through which he can either maintain his activity in accordance with the laws of evolution or he can deviate from these laws. He has the choice either to make great headway in the process of evolution or go in the opposite direction toward devolution.

Man has a developed brain, and he is thus in a position to distinguish between right and wrong; this is why the great responsibility of proper behavior lies within the power of man. Man has the ability to directly experience the abstract field of Bliss Consciousness. Man has the ability to experience subtle fields of creation. Man's highly developed nervous system provides him with the ability to experience subtler states of thought, to transcend the subtlest thought and to arrive at the transcendental state of pure consciousness, the state of absolute Being. This is a great special value of human life over that of the animals.

The ability of living the transcendental state of Being along with the experiences of transitory nature of relative existence is the normal capacity of human life.

When one does not live a normal life or a life using his full potential, he feels miserable and tense and suffers in many ways.

Individual and Cosmic Life

We have seen that life has two aspects, absolute and relative. We have also seen that the relative aspect is only the expression of the absolute phase of life, which is the omnipresent, unlimited, unbounded ocean of pure consciousness or eternal existence. This unbounded ocean of eternal existence is said to be Cosmic Life, and its expression in the relative field is called individual life.

Thus it is found that the absolute state of life corresponds to Cosmic Life, and the relative states of life correspond to the individual life. Individual life is the expression of Cosmic Life, just as a wave is the expression of the ocean. The ocean, while remaining the same, is affected by every wave and its activity.

The Universe Reacts to Individual Action

If a stone is thrown into a pond, waves are produced that travel throughout the pond. Every wave produces effects in every part of the pond, resulting in some influence or other. Similarly, the wave of individual life through its activity produces an influence in all fields of the cosmos.

Life is one continuous and homogeneous whole from which rise the waves of individual life without breaking the continuity and all-pervading status of eternal absolute Being. The entire creation is the expression of that Cosmic Life and all the innumerable Laws of Nature carrying out the process of creation, evolution, and dissolution, in different parts of the universe, are all the diverse expressions of the one eternal Cosmic Law.[3]

When individuality is gained at different points in the creation, the continuity and homogeneity of Cosmic Life is not disturbed. Life exists in the body, and all the different limbs are at the command of the life force of that one individual. But the hand itself, for example, is a composite of millions of cells, each of which has its own life and function to perform. Although the life of the cell is a life in itself and has its own sphere of activity and individuality, it is a part of the whole life of the individual. The life of every cell influences the whole life of man. If something happens to one cell in one tissue of the body, the entire body is altered. The smooth running of every tissue in the body produces a harmonious and powerful influence in the individual life. But some defect, misery, inactivity, or dullness in one cell of a tissue can bring about a corresponding effect in the whole life of the individual. Similarly, the whole universe reacts to individual action.

Through every thought, word, and action we are producing an influence

3 See page 45, "What Is Life?"

to affect all our surroundings. Physics has revealed that through everything we do we are producing vibrations in the atmosphere. Waves of activity are set up inside our individual system and are emitted from the body to reach all strata of the atmosphere. Recently we have seen that devices installed in the satellites traveling at hundreds of miles per minute receive commands from Earth at great distances. These machines carry out the commands and send back information. This has shown the continuity of life and its reaction to our action in the unlimited space field that is much beyond our immediate surroundings. Our every thought, word, or action produces an influence in the atmosphere, and the quality of that influence depends upon the quality of the vibrations emitted from us. Everything in the universe is constantly influencing every other thing.

This shows how dependent and how powerful is the life of the individual. One may not be aware of the influence that he produces in the surroundings, but the influence is produced nonetheless. A good, sweet, loving expression to a child produces a loving and life-supporting influence in the whole of the cosmos. One harsh, cruel word to an individual in a quiet corner will produce that influence of harshness and cruelty throughout the creation.

Experiments with plants have been reported indicating that a plant which is properly attended to with feelings of love and kindness grows stronger and more quickly than a plant which has received abuses and condemnation.

One kind look to an innocent child draws the child to you. One hard look at the child makes him cry and run away. This is how, quite silently, one influence pervades throughout the whole of Nature. Innocently, one becomes the victim of the vibrations of all other people; one is subjected to and influenced by the thoughts of other individuals.

Life in the animal species does not know that it is producing wide influence through every little action, but man with his highly developed nervous system should know that such wide influence is produced.

If a man has a kind and compassionate nature, then naturally he will produce a good influence in the vicinity. When one enters the home of a friend, one often feels either elated or depressed. If the friend is virtuous and a man of good intention, good thought, and good action, then certainly he creates a very good atmosphere around him. Wherever he lives or goes he carries with him that influence of happiness and harmony. Someone passes by you in the street and you feel attracted to him and begin to feel love toward him. Another man passes by and you are repulsed by him. This is because of the qualities of the men and their reaction upon your own vibrations.

It has been seen that many houses attract passersby; just a look at them brings impulses of harmony, peace, and happiness. Some houses produce an influence of sadness, dryness, coldness — a sense of repulsion. All this is due to the quality of the people living in the house, to the quality of the person who built the house, or to the quality of the wealth with which it was built.

When we speak of the quality of wealth, what do we mean?

A good quality of wealth is that which is earned through means which have helped to elevate the society and improve the life of the people. A poor quality of wealth is that which is gained through illegal or sinful means or through a type of business which provides means to degenerate the spiritual standards of society, lower its consciousness, or directly or indirectly create a situation whereby the moral, spiritual, and religious sentiments of the people are lowered.

The quality of the wealth is determined by the method of earning — virtuous or impious — as well as by the effects it produces for others. For example, the wealth earned by a business which helps the people in society to grow, to maintain life, and to elevate themselves, certainly produces a very good influence. Any house built with that wealth and any act done with this wealth will produce a good influence in the atmosphere.

The wealth of a business which has either been gained from illegal activities or has helped the society to degenerate into lower consciousness, however, has a very bad influence, and any work done with that wealth, or any house erected with it, has that overall depressing influence.

It can be seen that big properties earned through an activity which lowers the consciousness of the people or by damaging the life of the people do not produce a healthy influence for the heirs who inherit them. Sickness, a low state of consciousness, degenerate ways of life, and a mind clouded with petty and low thoughts are the result; moreover, the individual upon whom such wealth has been bestowed does not know that he is suffering from the demoralizing influence of the inherited wealth.

These innocent and basically harmless people become the victims of the great harm their parents or forefathers have perpetrated on society. Such wealth does not initiate in them any feeling to help others, nor does it permit them to have good health or good, useful surroundings. Its overall influence is to suppress the consciousness. The way out of such a situation is charity for such works that are directly dedicated to the raising of the consciousness of the people. This counteracts the adverse effects produced at the time of earning the wealth. A good proportion between the wealth and the charity certainly brings forth results to a significant and appreciable measure.

The relative fields of life are so concentrated, and the influence of each aspect of life on every other aspect of life in the cosmos is so complex and diverse, that it is highly important that a situation should somehow be created in the world that every man is a righteous man. Each man should be a compassionate, loving, and helpful man whose every thought should be kind, loving, and virtuous, so that it produces a good influence on the thinker, both in his immediate surroundings and in the whole of creation.

In view of this understanding of the individual and his influence on the cosmos, it can be seen that it is highly important that every individual should develop his consciousness in such a manner that he is always right and good. Through his every thought, word, and action, he must always create life-supporting and life-sustaining influences for himself and for the whole creation. This may only be created by each individual for himself by transforming the nature of his mind in such a way, and to such an extent, that, by nature, the mind can pick up only right thoughts and engage itself in right speech and action.[4]

Each man has to rise to this state by himself. Nobody else can possibly raise the standard of another's consciousness. Certainly some help by way of information and guidance could be offered to others by those who know the way, but the responsibility of raising one's consciousness lies in oneself. Everyone has to work out his own destiny, even though each man's destiny

---
4 This is dealt with in "Art of Being" in Section III.

influences the destiny of others and that of the entire universe. There lies an intimate and inseparable connection between the individual and the universe. Others would help themselves by bringing out this great wisdom of life; but it is up to each individual within himself to choose his own path.

If all those to whom such information comes through this book would inform their neighbors, associates, and circles of friends that there is a way to improve the consciousness of the individual and transform one's nature in a way which will make the individual spontaneously good for his own benefit, and for that of all creation, it would be of great help to humanity. There is a very great responsibility on every individual.

Everyone should know that he is part of the whole life of the universe and that his relationship to universal life is what one cell is to the whole body. If every cell is not alert, energetic, and healthy, the body as a whole begins to suffer. Therefore, for the sake of the life of the individual, and equally so for the life of everything in the entire universe, it is necessary that the individual be healthy, virtuous, good, and right in his every thought, word, and deed. It is a scientific fact that the whole universe reacts to every individual action.[5]

The boundaries of individual life are not restricted to the boundaries of the body, and not even to those of one's family or one's home; they extend far beyond that sphere to the limitless horizons of Cosmic Life.

Every action of an individual influences every other thing in the universe.

The universe influences the individual and the individual influences the universe.

None of them is independent. One is intimately connected with the other.

---

5 Refer to "The Problem of World Peace" in Section III on "Art of Living," page 237.

Section III

ART OF LIVING

MAN'S FULL POTENTIAL 63
HOW TO USE ONE'S FULL POTENTIAL 65
HOW TO MAKE FULL USE OF THE SURROUNDINGS 69
HOW TO MAKE FULL USE OF THE ALMIGHTY POWER OF NATURE 77
ART OF BEING 87
   Thinking and the Art of Being 88
   Speaking and the Art of Being 90
   Breathing and the Art of Being 92
   Experiencing and the Art of Being 96
   Behavior and the Art of Being 98
   Health and the Art of Being 100
   Mind and the Art of Being 101
      The Influence of Food; The Influence of Activity
   The Senses and the Art of Being 108
   The Body and the Art of Being 112
   The Nervous System and the Art of Being 113
   The Surroundings and the Art of Being 116
   Karma and the Art of Being 117
ART OF THINKING 127
   Right Thought 130
   Useful and Creative Thought 131
   Powerful Thinking 132
   Thoughts to Liberate the Thinker 133
ART OF SPEAKING 134
   Speaking with a Minimum Consumption of Energy 134
   Speaking Rightly 137
   Speaking Harmoniously 138
   Speaking Pleasingly 139
   Speaking Powerfully 140

Speaking Usefully 140
Speaking in Such a Manner That the Speaker Remains Free from
   the Binding Influence of Speech 141
ART OF ACTION 141
   The Art of Performing an Action with the Least Amount of Energy 144
   The Art of Performing an Action in the Least Amount of Time 145
   The Art of Performing Only Useful Action 147
   The Art of Performing Action to Produce the Most Effective and
      Desirable Results 148
      *Strong Thought Force; Great Energy; Favorable Surroundings and
      Circumstances; Ability to Perform Right Action; Self-Confidence*
   Fixity of Purpose in Performance of Action for the Most Effective
      and Desirable Results 162
   The Art of Performing Action Without Harming Anyone 164
   The Art of Performing Action to Yield Maximum Results 165
   The Art of Performing an Action So That the Performance Remains
      a Joy and Does Not Become Tiring, Tedious, or a Boring Task 169
   The Art of Proper Planning of Action 171
   The Art of Effective Execution of the Plan 173
ART OF BEHAVIOR 174
   Behavior and the Surroundings 177
KEY TO GOOD HEALTH 180
   Mental Health 186
   Physical Health 188
   Physiological Effects of Transcendental Meditation 189
   Health of the Atmosphere 196
EDUCATION 205
   Economics 210
   Humanities 211
   Political Science 212
   Sociology 213
   Psychology 214
   Natural Sciences 215
HIGHWAY TO REHABILITATION 217
RECREATION AND RAPID REJUVENATION 218
RIGHT AND WRONG 219
LIFE IN FREEDOM 229
   The Problem of World Peace 237

"Art" implies a graceful and skillful method of accomplishment. The art of living any phase of life is to master that phase. The only way one can master any or all phases of life is by using latent potentialities and applied techniques.

The art of living enables a man to live full values of life, accomplish the maximum in the world, and at the same time, live a life of eternal freedom in God Consciousness. The art of living is the art of letting the life stream flow in such a manner that every aspect of living is supplemented with intelligence, power, creativity, and the magnificence of the whole life. As the art of making a flower arrangement is to glorify every flower by the beauty and glory of every other flower, in a similar way the art of living is such that every aspect of life is supplemented by the glories of every other aspect. It is in this way that the transcendental aspect of life supplements the subjective and objective aspects of existence so that the entire range of subjectivity and objectivity enjoys the absolute strength, intelligence, bliss, and creativity of eternal Being.

When the power of the Absolute supplements all aspects of subjectivity, the ego is full, the intellect is profound, sharp, and one-pointed, the mind is concentrated and powerful, thought force is great, and the senses are fully alert. When the ego, intellect, mind, and senses are fully supplemented by absolute Being, experience is more profound, activity is powerful, and, at the same time, the intellect, ego, mind, and senses are useful in all spheres of life, in all spheres of action and experience in the individual life in society and in the entire cosmos.[1]

We have seen earlier that it is the sap which is the basis of the root and the entire tree. In this example, we find the root lying between the transcendental area of the tree and the outer tree. Likewise, the subjective aspect of life, the

---

[1] This aspect of the individual influencing Cosmic Life has been dealt with in detail in "Individual and Cosmic Life," page 53.

inner man (ego, mind, and senses) lies between transcendental Being (the basis of our life) and the outer gross field of objective existence. The art of living demands proper and effective existence. The art of living demands the proper and effective intake of Being in the subjective aspect of life, and Its infusion in all the fields of objective existence; the art of living requires that the mind draw the power of Being and pass it on to the body and surroundings.

For a tree to grow to maturity, efficiency is demanded on the part of the root so that the nourishment from the surrounding area is properly absorbed by the root and given out to all the different aspects of the outer tree. This provides the key to the art of living.

The inner man should be such that it absorbs the value of the transcendental absolute state of life and passes it on to the outer gross relative state of life, enriching each aspect and supplementing it with the power of absolute Being. This technique amounts to thinking in such a way that each individual thought enjoys the strength of Cosmic Intelligence of absolute Being. Every action enjoys the power of absolute unlimited Being, as the experience is supplemented by the bliss of transcendental Being. The individual creative energy is supplemented by the unlimited, unbounded creative energy of cosmic Being.

Thus we conclude that the art of living demands that the mind be in constant communion with the absolute state of life, so that whatever the mind is thinking, in whatever action of experience it is engaged, it is never away from the influence of eternal absolute Being.

The art of life demands that the mind cultivate within itself the eternal state of absolute Being. For without constant and continuous infusion of the Absolute into the very nature of the mind, the mind can never be all-comprehensive and all-powerful.

If a businessman does not invest all his wealth in his business, he does not gain the most profit possible. If the individual mind does not bring out the bliss of absolute Being and experience things in the outside relative field of life while remaining saturated with that bliss, then nothing that is experienced will bring contentment. The mind will always be searching for greater happiness. But if the mind is saturated with the bliss of absolute Being, it derives joy from the variety of multiple creation and remains well established in contentment. Only then does the mind fully enjoy variety.

If it is left without the basis of the bliss of unity within, the mind is as though it were being tossed about like a football, from one point to the other, having no stable status of its own. That is why, in order that the experiences in life give the maximum charm and the world of variety prove itself to be of real value, it is necessary that the bliss of absolute Being remain infused into the very nature of the mind.

The variety of the world can be enjoyed only when the mind has gained an unshakable status in the bliss of absolute Being. Otherwise, the very purpose of the multiplicity of joyful, glorious variety of creation is undermined. If experience is only one-sided, if the mind experiences only the variety of relative, gross fields of life, then it is clear that the values of the relative life are not being supplemented by the absolute state of life. Such a one-sided life is due only to the lack of knowledge of the art of living.

Thus, the art of living demands that, for life to be lived in all its values, the subjective aspect of life be infused with the power of Being. Then only will it be possible to make use of one's full potential for glorification of all aspects of life.

In order to make this clear, we shall first analyze what man's full potential is and then see how the power of Being can be infused on the various different levels of life so that one may take advantage of all aspects of the art of living.

MAN'S FULL POTENTIAL

We have seen that the nervous system of man is the most highly developed nervous system in creation. With such a highly developed nervous system the full potential of man indicates that man should be able to live the supreme state of life — at the least, a life without suffering and, at its best, a life of absolute bliss in God Consciousness.

The full potential of man means that on all levels of life — physical, mental, and spiritual — one should live to one's maximum capacity.

The full potential of man on the physical plane means the ability to have a healthy body in which all the limbs, the senses, and the nervous system are functioning normally and in good coordination with each other. The full potential on the mental plane of life means the ability of man to make use of his full mental capacity. The full potential on the spiritual plane of life means man's ability to live the value of spiritual Being in all fields of daily life.

Man's full potential on the physical, mental, and spiritual levels of existence also implies that there should be a perfect coordination between these planes of life. The physical plane of life should be in perfect coordination with the mental plane; the mental plane should be in perfect coordination with the spiritual plane.

The full potential means a perfect coordination of the Divine with the physical levels of man's life, the full functioning capacity of the mind, perfect health, and the value of divine life being infused in the day-to-day material life of man.

Man generally does not use his full mind. The conscious mind is only an insignificant part of the total mind that a man possesses, and, as long as man functions on only the ordinary level of conscious mind, he is not using his full mental potential. The conscious capacity of man should be the normal functioning capacity of the full mental potential.

Over and above these considerations, the use of full potential should enable a man to think, speak, and act in such a manner that every thought, word, and action not only accomplishes the maximum in material life, but also becomes a means of remaining in tune with almighty God, thereby bringing the blessing of the Almighty on all levels of human life.

We have seen[2] that the human mind has the ability of taking within its consciousness the field of transcendental absolute divine Being. This shows that the whole range of creation and the field of the ultimate creator, almighty universal Being, lies within the scope of human life. The full potential of man in this sequence is the full Cosmic Life open to each individual. The full potential of man is the unlimited potential of universal Being.

2 See page 29, "Transcendental Meditation."

A normal human life means living a life of divine consciousness; a normal human mind is one that should function on human levels but should also have the status of universal cosmic mind.

Cosmic Consciousness should not be considered as something far beyond the reach of normal man. The state of Cosmic Consciousness should be the state of normal human consciousness. Any state below Cosmic Consciousness can only be taken to be subnormal human consciousness. The human mind should be a cosmically conscious mind. The potential of human life should mean the potential of the almighty Divine on Earth. The normal life of man should be a God-realized life in divine consciousness, a fruitful life in universal Being.

The full potential of man is such that it can bring to every man this blessed and graceful state of divine life in a natural and easy manner with no struggle and maintain it in all phases of daily life.

A direct and simple technique for beginning to express one's full potential in a natural way is the practice of Transcendental Meditation, which unfolds all the Divine in man and brings human consciousness to the high pedestal of God Consciousness. It brings life to a state of eternal freedom, supplementing it with unlimited creative energy and harmonizing the abstract absolute values of divine Being with the concrete physical material values of day-to-day human life.

How to Use One's Full Potential

In "Individual and Cosmic Life" we have seen that "the boundaries of individual life are not restricted to the boundaries of the body, and not even to those of one's family or one's home; they extend far beyond that sphere to the limitless horizons of Cosmic Life."[3]

And in "Man's Full Potential," we have seen that man's full potential means that "man should be able to live the supreme state of life — at the

3 See page 58.

least, a life without suffering and, at its best, a life of absolute bliss in God Consciousness."[4]

In view of this, the art of using one's full potential means that the wave of individual life should not be confined only to the surface value of the ocean of eternal absolute Being, but should also extend to the depths of the unbounded ocean of Being, so that all the potentialities are unfolded, and life becomes strong and powerful.

When one's full potential is unfolded, then every phase of life supplements every other phase, strengthens it and makes life more substantial, more glorified, more useful, and more worthwhile on all levels for oneself and for others. A small wave on the surface of the ocean would not be a very powerful wave, but the same wave becomes powerful when it connects with deeper levels of water. So, the art of improving and strengthening a wave is to enable it to contact directly deeper levels of water.

If the wave is to rise high to accomplish more and be more powerful, then the act of rising high should be supplemented by drawing in more water at the base. When the wave is able to supplement the act of rising high by drawing in more water at its base, it is possible for it to rise up in an integrated and powerful manner. Otherwise, if it failed to draw more water at its base while rising higher, it would become weak at the crest and even a slight breeze could disintegrate it.

The art of using one's full potential necessitates that the surface value of relative life be supplemented by the power which lies at the depth of the ocean of absolute Being. It means that the relative life should be supplemented with the absolute state of life. The art of using one's full potential is the art of deepening the stream of individual life to the maximum depth possible by taking the wave of relative experience and existence to the limit of absolute experience and existence. The art of using one's full potential lies basically in supplementing the wave of individual life with the power of the ocean of Being.

The art of living is the ability to supplement and reinforce individual life with the power of absolute cosmic Being. It is within the reach of every individual to fathom the great depth of absolute Being, thereby supplementing and reinforcing the individual life with the life of eternal cosmic Being.

4 See page 63.

Every wave on the sea has the opportunity to embrace within itself as great an amount of water at its base as it likes. The whole ocean could be drawn in a single wave; it is possible that one wave could draw upon the strength of the entire ocean and rise with infinite power.

Similarly, every individual has an opportunity available to gain for himself the strength of unlimited, eternal, absolute Being and thus be powerful to the maximum extent possible.

When there is a possibility for a wave to enjoy the limitless strength of the ocean, does it not amount to a sheer waste to be tossed about by the breeze in a weak and powerless manner? When there is open to every man the opportunity of gaining unlimited power, energy, existence, intelligence, peace, and happiness, then is it not a waste of life to remain in a limited, weak, and powerless state?

The art of using one's full potential demands that life as a whole should have a solid basis for itself. For without a strong basis, life will be just as unstable as a building without a strong foundation. In the first place, the building cannot be properly built, and will not be stable. Thus, a solid foundation for life is the first requisite for an all-comprehensive and powerful life.

Life in its relative stages is ever-changing. The ever-changing phases of life leave no stable status of life. Therefore, in order to be able to use one's full potential, the first step will be to infuse stability into the ever-changing phases of relative life.

Stability belongs to the absolute status. Stability is attributed to that factor of life which never changes, and that which never changes is the truth of life, the ultimate reality, eternal Being. Life, then, in its absolute state alone is stable. And when stability is gained by the mind and retained through all the mind's activity of experience and action, the whole field of activity is supplemented by the power of never-changing absolute Being. This forms the basic platform for using one's full potential; it reinforces and enriches the ever-unstable phases of relative existence.

If the basis of life is weak, if the life is not based on the eternal and stable status of absolute Being, then apart from being ever-changing in its character, it will always remain weak.

The art of using one's full potential is the same as the art of shooting an arrow ahead; one begins by pulling the arrow back on the bow. As the arrow is drawn back, it gains the maximum strength for going forward. A useless shot will result if the arrow is not first pulled back.

The art of using one's full potential demands bringing the mind back to the field of absolute Being before it is brought out to face the gross aspect of the relative fields of life. Fortunately, this art of living has been developed to bring most effective results in life and all its glory has been centered in a technique of bringing the mind to the field of Being in a simple and effective way.

The ever-changing phase of relative existence must remain ever-changing all the time. This ever-changing phase cannot be transformed into a never-changing status. This is relative life. But the subject within, the inner man, could gain a simultaneous status in eternal, absolute Being. For, while it is maintaining its status in the ever-changing phenomenal phases of life, it is not devoid of its status in absolute, never-changing Being.

This is how the never-changing Absolute might supplement the ever-changing phenomenal phases of life, and these two, together, go to make life complete.

This absolute stable factor in life, Being of the Transcendent, is always out of the field of the ever-changing phenomenal creation and experience.

The art of using one's full potential is in harmonizing the Absolute and the relative, which is easily accomplished through the simple system of Transcendental Meditation.

A man has two sides, left and right, and the art of living demands that the left and right sides both be used to full advantage. If only the left side is used and the right remains unused, the latter might become immobile and the left side would be over-strained in action. The right side too, will be over-strained, being in a state of inactivity. Therefore, in order to live all values of life, it is necessary that we should have the left and right working together in good coordination, working together for the same cause.

The Absolute and the relative are the two phases of one's existence. It is the art of living that brings these two together, enabling all values of life to be lived. Otherwise, on the one hand, the Absolute remains transcendental, out of the field of activity, out of sight, and as if of no practical value. On the other hand, it leaves the field of the relative life to be over-strained, due to constant activity, and the relative life remains weak in the unstable, ever-changing field.

That is why the art of living brings together the never-active Absolute of transcendental nature with the ever-changing field of relative existence and links them together. Both are brought together on the level of the mind, just as in the life of the tree the surrounding area of the nourishment and the outer sphere of the tree are brought together by the instrumentality of the root, which draws nourishment from one side and supplies it to the other.

The art of using one's full potential is to live a life supplemented by the power of unlimited eternal absolute Being. It is easy to learn this art because, as we have seen in "Transcendental Meditation,"[5] when the mind proceeds on the experience of subtler states of thought and experiences transcendental Being, the full potentiality of the mind is unfolded, and one naturally begins to make use of one's full mental potential in one's daily activities. By this process one also begins to make full use of one's potential in the fields of one's senses, body, and surroundings. These aspects are dealt with in detail in the following heading.

Thus we find it is easy to learn the art of using one's full potential. It is easy to live a life of full values of power, intelligence, creativity, peace, and bliss of eternal absolute Being through the regular practice of the simple system of Transcendental Meditation.

How to Make Full Use of the Surroundings

In order to understand the technique of making full use of the surroundings, it is first necessary to understand what constitutes one's surroundings. One finds that they are not always the same. At home a man's surroundings are different from those in his office. The surroundings of a man change according to his own desire; they are the creation of the individual.

The creation of the surroundings is of two types: there are those which

---

5 See page 29.

are consciously created and those which are created without the individual's conscious knowledge, as the result of his own thought, speech, or action. If a man, for example, builds a new house, he does so consciously and intentionally. If he invites a friend to the house and his friend interprets the invitation to have an ulterior motive, the friend may become an enemy. The friend's enmity is the creation and responsibility of the man who invited him, even though it was not his intention to make an enemy of him.

Looking into this question more deeply, we find the unintentional creation of the surroundings is in accordance with the theory of *Karma*. The present surroundings are the result of something we have done in the past. Our present intentions and efforts are the materialization of the influence of the past. It is not only that our present surroundings are the result of the past, because the fruits of our past actions have to be accepted and supplemented by our intention of the present. Therefore, our surroundings are not only the result of our past, but the result of a combination of past and present. Such is the life of a man in the present.

Take the example of a man whose relations with others are bad. Many people with whom he is associated speak ill of him and misunderstand his actions although the man knows he has not harmed anyone. This he might take to be the result of past action which, again, is nothing but his own creation that is coming to him in the present.

A gardener who plants trees assumes responsibility for whether they grow or whether they die. If the trees flourish and bloom and bear fruit, the gardener enjoys them as a result of his own action in the past. If a beautiful flower suddenly wilts because of excessive heat, it is not due to the action or *Karma* of the gardener, but *is* due to his failure to protect the flower from the heat wave. But the gardener takes what happens in his garden as it comes.

Likewise, the individual has to take his surroundings as they are, knowing that they are his own creation. If a rose's thorn pricks the hand of someone who is enjoying the rose's beauty, both the beauty of the rose and the thorn prick may be attributed to the labor of the gardener.

Thus, when we enjoy, we are enjoying the result of our own action, and we also suffer as a result of our own *Karma*. So, whether we have joy or misery, the surroundings in themselves are not at fault.

When we build a house, we make full use of the surroundings that we have created in it. If we plant a garden outside, we enjoy it, but if we do not plant a garden, we enjoy the warmth of the living room. Thus, we make full use of the surroundings we have created.

Since our surroundings are our own creation, they naturally are meant to assist us in obtaining what we desire. The technique of receiving help from the surroundings is in our attitude of giving. If we want to receive the maximum at all times, we must have an attitude of giving. "If you want to receive, you must give" is a Law of Nature.

In the life of a tree, the root has the responsibility of taking the sap from the surrounding area and passing it on to the outer tree. Only when it is prepared to pass it on to the outer tree is it able to take it in. If the tree is cut at the root, the root no longer takes in the sap to the extent it did when the tree was intact.

If a sales manager in a factory keeps making sales, the production manager keeps the factory producing. If the product is not sold, the production also comes to a standstill. Production depends upon the consumption.

It is natural that one receives what he is in a position to give. The mother gives to the child and, in return, receives from the child; the father gives to the son all his love, wealth, strength, and mind, and in return receives the confidence, love, and happiness of the son.

If you are open with someone, he will be open with you. If you want love from someone, give your love to him. If you want kind and sympathetic behavior from someone, be kind and sympathetic to him. If you want comfort from him, prove yourself comforting to him. If you want admiration from others, do something to show your admiration for them. If you are sincere in giving, you receive it in return manyfold. The teacher learns by teaching; in obeying, the student commands the respect of the teacher. If your son readily is obedient to you, he captures your heart as a natural return of his obedience. If you are kind to a child he will be kind to you; if you are harsh to him, he will revolt against you. This is action and reaction.

That action and reaction are equal is a scientifically established truth. You react to someone in a certain way and he, in turn, will react to you in a similar way. If he does not react to you, then Nature will bring to you a similar type of reaction. If you hurt someone, even if he himself does not react, other agencies of Nature will bring the reaction of your behavior to you. It is a Law of Nature that as you sow, so you reap. In whatever way one wants the surroundings to react to him, his behavior toward the surroundings must be in accordance with that. This is the fundamental principle of making the best use of one's surroundings.

The Laws of Nature cannot be deceived; the reaction will come. If a man is jealous of you, you will find, when you search your heart, that you have been jealous either of him or of someone else sometime in the past. Be kind to him, and the surroundings will be kind to you; be loving to him, and the surroundings will be loving to you; begin to doubt, and the surroundings begin to doubt you. If you hate, the surroundings begin to hate you. If the surroundings begin to hate you, do not blame the surroundings, blame your own inner conscience.

It is necessary to clear your conscience and to be compassionate and sincere in your behavior. Good outward behavior is certainly of great value in life, but what is a greater value is the state of pure inner conscience. If you are clear in your conscience and loving, kind, and virtuous to your fellow men, you will naturally receive good behavior from everyone and great joy from the surroundings.

If you feel you have all these qualities and are clear in your conscience and yet feel there is something wrong in your surroundings, then take it as it comes; it is the result of some action in the past.

If you retaliate, you are brought to the level of the wrong. Rather, let the wrong be just a drop in the ocean of your virtue. A common saying is, "Do not resist evil." If evil is resisted, first you must stoop to that level of evil, and, second, you are further responsible for the evil influence you are producing in retaliating.

Let the impurities of the atmosphere find a refuge in the ocean of purity in your heart, the unfathomable joy of your inner pure conscience. When you forgive, all Nature enjoys your brilliance and returns joy to you. Forgiveness, tolerance, purity of heart, sincerity, love, and kindness are the basic platforms from which to enjoy and make full use of the surroundings on the fundamental principle of giving.

The surroundings are of two types — animate and inanimate, or, living and nonliving. It may be said that nothing is not living in the universe; physics has told us that nothing is really inert, that everything is vibration and activity, and that nothing is passivity. Nonetheless, in the field of relative existence, we do distinguish a man from a house, a dog from a garden. A house and a garden we take to be inert surroundings, and the dog and the man we take to be lively surroundings. Our purpose is to make the best use of both the lively and the inert types of surroundings.

To make full use of both types of surroundings, the basic principle is the same as that with which we have dealt: the principle of giving. Love the dog, and the dog will love you; hate the dog, and the dog will bite you. Love your mother, and there will be no end to her love for you; create dissension, and, while her love for you is so great that she will not react, any dissension on your part will certainly influence the surroundings. Therefore, in all walks of life, under all circumstances, in all types of surroundings, animate or inanimate, living or nonliving, it is necessary to have a very loving, kind, and sympathetic view in the inner core of our heart. Our outward behavior should be based on that.

This is the fundamental technique of making full use of the surroundings. This means you will derive maximum advantage from the surroundings. You will enjoy the surroundings and will make them do the most for you only if you are grounded in loving kindness and sympathy for them.

Again, we find there are two types of surroundings on a different level: the immediate surroundings and the surroundings that are distant and remote. The surroundings that are near to you are affected by how you behave, speak, and act in relation to them. If a flower is placed in your room, it blooms and remains fresh. If, on the other hand, the flower is left to wither on the ground in the dust, it reflects your neglect. Thus the surroundings that are near to you are directly affected by your behavior. But surroundings that are remote from you are mostly reacting to your feelings and thoughts. For instance, if you are in India and have a friend in America, his feeling of heart and mind will be according to the feeling of your heart and mind.

Thought waves are much more powerful than the waves of speech and action. Through every thought, word, and action we are creating some wave in the atmosphere, but thought waves are especially penetrating. If we are joyful, happy, and full of kindness and love for the whole world, we receive love from every quarter.

In "*Karma* and Being,"[6] we have seen in detail how both thought and action influence the entire field of the universe, and, in the preceding part, we have seen how the universe reacts to the individual action. We are creating the quality of life in the atmosphere according to the quality of our heart. Whether we consider the surroundings that are near to or remote from us, the technique of making full use of all types of surroundings for our best advantage will be manifested when, in the center of our being, heart, and mind, we have kind, loving, forgiving, and sympathetic thoughts for all surroundings. If one is guided throughout his life by this principle — "Give, if you want to receive" — naturally the receiving will be equal to or more than what is given because it rebounds from many parts of the surroundings.

If you want the surroundings to be of best use to you, be of best use to your surroundings. If you want your house to give you joy and comfort, be joyful in it, bring to it beautiful things. If you project love to the plants in your garden, they will reward you with beautiful flowers to give you joy. If you cultivate within yourself a natural state of kindness, compassion, love, and forgiveness, you will receive a thousandfold reward from the surroundings. In order to make full use of the surroundings it is necessary to develop these qualities within yourself to the fullest capacity; these are merely the potentialities that are within you. If one is able to rise to this full value of human life, one may receive the maximum possible and make full use of the surroundings to his own best advantage.

We have seen in the previous part that, to make full use of one's own human potential, it is only necessary to be regular in the practice of Transcendental Meditation, which readily unfolds all the inner mental potential-

6 See page 23.

ities and the inner divine Nature. With the direct experience of Bliss Consciousness, one gains that fullness of life to which all types of surroundings will react in a favorable way and will offer the best use of their values.

In order to really make full use of the surroundings, one has to be a normal man, and, as we have seen in the previous part, a normal man is a man of Cosmic Consciousness — a fully grown man is a perfectly developed personality. It is in this state that one receives full advantage from the surroundings, because in this state one's heart and mind are established on that level from which all the Laws of Nature are working out the evolution of everything. That level of Nature alone knows how to give because the Laws of Nature are based on that level. Only from that level of Cosmic Consciousness can one really give. When one sets himself on this level of maximum giving, then one is in a position to receive the maximum.

Cosmic Consciousness is a state where one has put oneself in the service of the Divine, because, as we have seen in "Cosmic Law,"[7] the thought, speech, and action of one who has reached this state is only guided by the divine will. He is an individual, but he is a living instrument of God, a tool in the hands of the Divine. What comes out of him is naturally of service to the Cosmic Life. He is by nature the most obedient servant of the Divine. By attaining the state of Cosmic Consciousness — the state of normality — through the regular practice of Transcendental Meditation, one naturally puts himself in a state where he will not only be making full use of the surroundings, but also where the surroundings will be of full use to him. It is not necessary for him to do anything to derive the most from the surroundings; they naturally will be of full use to him. By virtue of his status he will be naturally deriving the best advantage from the surroundings and everything in his surroundings will naturally be of great value to others.

One not only derives the advantages of the surroundings for himself by raising his consciousness, but he creates a situation so that everything in the surroundings draws the maximum from every other. This way the surroundings gain and man gains by the constant practice[8] of Transcendental Meditation.

7 See page 10, "Being, the Plane of Cosmic Law."
8 Dedicated, regular practice.

This is the purpose of making full use of the surroundings in a very automatic way. This may appear to be a farfetched principle of life, but it is just the expression of the truth on this level. It is not otherwise possible to turn one's surroundings to all good for oneself. Even those who try to change their surroundings and convert them to their own use by force are recorded in history to have received only partial success in their attempt. The greatest monarchs and dictators of the world have only been recorded to have achieved partial success in life; it was not possible for them to make the full use of the surroundings because they did not develop themselves on all levels of life.

It is necessary to be in tune with Nature and raise the consciousness so that it enters the realm of all harmony, peace, and happiness that lies in the eternal status of the absolute, transcendental pure consciousness. Neither by force nor moral pressure nor suggestion is it possible to change the surroundings or make full use of them for oneself.

The attempt of modern psychology to reconcile the surroundings of a man by the system of improving his relationship through suggestion and psychological training is just ridiculous. The attempt of modern psychology to improve the relationships, surroundings, and outlook on life has nothing to do with the basic fundamentals of life. It is like a child's attempt to build a castle on the beach with the sand that is available. Trying to build up human life purely on the consideration of surface values of psychology can amuse the intellect of some ignorant people, but it cannot serve the real purpose of life.

If a petal of a flower starts to wither, a skilled gardener does not water the petal, he waters the root. If a relationship begins to create tension, very little can be gained by trying to reconcile the parties by suggestions on the surface. Bad relationships should be handled by improving the quality of heart and mind of both parties.

We have seen in "How to Contact Being,"[9] how quickly the conscious capacity of the mind is improved by the practice of Transcendental Meditation. It has been experienced throughout the world that if someone feels sad because of some tragedy, it is hard for him to assemble in his mind all the suggestions and goodwill with which others try to console him. But, if

9 See page 27.

he starts the practice of Transcendental Meditation, within ten minutes he finds that his mind calms down, doubts begin to be dispelled from inside, the tension begins to resolve, and compassion begins to glow.

He is able to view the situation from an enlarged consciousness and vision, and, immediately, he finds himself forgiving and tolerant about the same thing which was a terrible problem a few minutes before. The tragedy is the same, the circumstances are the same. At one moment he fails to derive the advantage and is miserable from the surroundings, but, at the next moment, by virtue of raising his consciousness through the method of Transcendental Meditation, he begins to enjoy the surroundings and to develop maximum advantage for himself and for others.

This is what leads us to conclude that, in order to be able to make full use of the surroundings, it is first necessary to raise one's consciousness through the regular practice of Transcendental Meditation; all the surroundings and circumstances will by nature be helpful and be fully used to the best advantage of oneself and all others.

How to Make Full Use of the Almighty Power of Nature

In determining the full potential of man, it has been found that, whereas the individual personality of man apparently seems to be bound by time, space, and causation, the boundaries of the individual life actually touch the unlimited horizon of eternal life. It has been maintained that a man is not only a part of Divine Intelligence — the individual life is not only a wave on the surface of the ocean of eternal life — but also that the individual has the ability of fathoming the unlimited field of Cosmic Life and of deriving the maximum from the absolute power of Being.

It has also been seen in "How to Contact Being"[10] that it not only lies within the capacity of each individual to contact and live absolute Being in his day-to-day life, but that it is simple and easy for everyone to do so.

10 See page 27.

And it has been seen in "Cosmic Law"[11] that it is easy for every individual to place himself at the control switchboard of all the Laws of Nature and make use of the almighty power of Nature according to his desire, need, or convenience.

When it is possible for a man to have the value of transcendental Being infused into the very nature of his mind, irrespective of its condition in the wakeful, dreaming, or deep-sleep states, then he naturally has gained the level of Being which is the source of inspiration, or the basic foundation for all the Laws of Nature to function. Then he has placed himself in a position where he is naturally able to use the almighty power of Nature.

This may sound strange to those who have little understanding of the value of Being and who have not started the practice of Transcendental Meditation, because for a man who is gripped by the tensions of day-to-day life, and who finds before him so many complicated and unsolved problems of life, the information that he could place himself where he will be using the almighty power of Nature is much beyond the imagination. He might consider it a flight of fancy which has no bearing on practical life. But, with all sincerity it is being recorded, it is being written, it is being brought home to the innocent, ignorant, simple people of the world who are undergoing much suffering in life, yet who are in a position to rise above all the miseries and tensions of life and to make all their circumstances favorable to themselves and agreeable to all the evolution possible for their life.

In order to use the almighty power of Nature, one has to actually put oneself in the hands of the almighty power of Nature. For a son to be able to use the status of his father's millionaireship, it is only necessary for him to show a willingness to obey the father. The love and sympathy of the son for what his father is will bring all the influence and strength of the father to the son. This is similar to the technique of making full use of the almighty power of Nature.

In order to derive the great strength needed for making use of the almighty power of Nature, one has to put oneself completely in the hands of almighty Nature. If one is able to submit oneself to Nature, then Nature will

---

11 See page 10, "Being, the Plane of Cosmic Law."

react to his needs. All-powerful and all-loving is the almighty hand of Nature because all the Laws of Nature are for the creation and evolution of all the beings and creatures of the entire cosmos.

There is no greater kindness than the kindness of Nature, which only moves one way to bring fulfillment of evolution and life to all these things in all their states of evolution, under all circumstances. When a man, because of some misdeeds, seems to be punished by Nature and suffers for it, this also is the manifestation of the kindness and helpfulness of Nature. If a child has smeared mud on himself, his mother will wipe the mud off. Even if the process of wiping off the mud is not liked by the child, it is good for him because the mud could harm his skin. The child, however, does not understand the injury that the mud would cause him and rebels against his mother's efforts.

When a doctor is to operate on a patient, he cuts into the body in all kindness, sympathy, and willingness to help the patient, but he can only start operating when the patient has completely given himself to him. The patient has to put himself at the mercy of the doctor and only then can the doctor operate for the patient's benefit. Similarly, if one submits oneself to Nature, Nature begins to operate on him and all that Nature does is for his own evolution and good. Therefore, in order to make full use of the almighty power of Nature, one has to submit oneself fully to that almighty will.

We have seen in the previous part on "How to Make Full Use of the Surroundings"[12] that the main principle lies in giving in order to gain. So the principle of giving oneself to the almighty hand of Nature enables oneself to make full use of the almighty power of Nature. It is certainly not possible for man to intellectually understand all the Laws of Nature, nor is it possible to feel what the strength of Nature is in a certain place at a certain time for a certain individual.

All this intellectual understanding about the Laws of Nature, in an attempt to put oneself in accordance with the natural flow of evolution governed by Nature, is physically impossible. The constant and eternal process of creation and evolution of the multiple variety of creation is so complex and diversified in its nature that it is only the almighty intelligence that could

12 See page 69.

possibly set the whole thing in the functioning order. It is not possible to fathom all the depths of complexity and variety of circumstances which constitute the unlimited span of the universe. But there is one factor in the entire field of creation on which one could base an attempt to meet the order of the Laws of Nature: This is that all the Laws of Nature are functioning in the direction of evolution.

This one-way flow of Nature to take everything on to a higher evolution is a flow in which the individual can consciously put himself to permit Nature to work on him — a natural flow of evolution of the individual in accordance with the cosmic evolution.

This is possible, fortunately, thanks to the great tradition of the Yogis of India and to the blessings of Shri Guru Dev. A simple system of Transcendental Meditation has brought to the present generation a technique whereby one's consciousness could be easily placed on the level of the natural flow of evolution, the basic plane on which all the Laws of Nature function. Only if the individual places his consciousness on that level is it possible to put one's whole life on the basic level of the functioning of the almighty power of Nature.

When one has submitted oneself in this manner to the almighty power of Mother Nature, then one is the loving, submissive, and obedient child who will certainly enjoy all the power of the Divine.

This is the simple way of making use of the almighty power of Nature. Life finds its fulfillment in submission, surrender, devotion, losing oneself, and gaining the power of the Almighty. From here springs the ideology of devotion and surrender, but the basis of all this is that, as we have seen in the section on "Life," the life of the individual is relative and absolute, both together; the individual is already in contact with absolute Being. It is only conscious contact which has to be established.

We have seen in "Transcendental Meditation"[13] that the practice does not need anything on the part of the individual except innocence and simplicity, and he need not put forth any effort for that. He must be devoid of any intellectual play or emotional twist. Such simplicity and innocence is already deeply rooted in the very nature of each individual. Here is a technique to

13 See page 29.

surrender oneself to the almighty power of Nature and arrive at the absolute, eternal field of Divine Intelligence. Having arrived at that plane, one begins to enjoy the almighty power of Nature quite automatically for great good to himself. When we say one naturally begins to enjoy the almighty power of Nature, we mean that it is on that almighty level of Nature that it is possible, not on the level of human understanding or human life.

Thus we find that it is quite possible to live life on the level of Cosmic Law, naturally enjoying the almighty power of Mother Nature, but that it is not possible to understand that almighty power or the Cosmic Law and its various components, intricacies, and complexities. That is why the technique of how to make full use of the almighty power of Nature is not on the level of thinking, understanding, reasoning, discriminating, or feeling. It is on the level of Being.

The field of surrender is never on the level of thinking; it is on the level of Being only. Many who want to surrender to God or to Mother Nature try to surrender on the level of thinking. They make a mood of surrender to God and mood-making necessarily is on the gross conscious thinking level.

Unless the level of individual being[14] comes to the level of almighty Nature, the individual does not enjoy the power of the Almighty. Just thinking "I have surrendered to God" and making a mood of that surrender only creates dullness and passivity on the part of the individual and deprives him of the opportunity to advance in life. True surrender to God cannot be on the thinking level. This sense of surrender is always on the level of Being, and, unless the level of Being is consciously gained by the mind, any attempt at making a mood of surrender will only result in a fanciful passivity of individual life and not a grand and successful attunement with the almighty power of Nature.

Unless the conscious mind transcends thinking and feeling, it cannot arrive at the plane of Being. Unless the individual consciousness is infused with the state of divine Being, the state of surrender does not arise. As long as the individual is on the thinking level, he maintains his identity, because

---

14 "The art of using one's full potential means that the wave of individual life should not be confined only to the surface value of the ocean of eternal absolute Being, but should also extend to the depths of the unbounded ocean of Being, so that all the potentialities are unfolded, and life becomes strong and powerful" (see page 66).

to maintain a thought, even a thought of surrender, one has to remain an individual thinker. As long as the individuality is maintained, the state of surrender cannot be. This is the weak point in the understanding of the ideology of surrender.

Surrender to the almighty will of God, surrender to the almighty Nature, is the most advanced ideology of life. If one really surrenders, one loses the petty individuality of the time-space-causation-bound mind and gains the unlimited eternal status of absolute Being. This is possible only in the state of Transcendental Consciousness, which is easily arrived at by the simple system of Transcendental Meditation.

The words "surrender to the will of God" are very significant and provide a direct way for the individual to gain the almighty power. But without the technique of easily transcending the limits of relative existence this expression has had no practical meaning for the past centuries. It has come to express an abstract, metaphysical or mystical sense of life. But with the knowledge of Transcendental Meditation, these words have become a significant, practical reality of life. They are no longer shrouded in the garb of mysticism. It is now the truth of daily experience, and through this experience comes the ability of making full use of the almighty power.

To those unaware of the practice of Transcendental Meditation, the idea of making full use of the almighty power of Nature remains only a fascinating and fanciful thought. However, with the knowledge and practice of Transcendental Meditation, the idea of making full use of the almighty power naturally gains a tangible status. For the son of a millionaire, the use of the power of his father's wealth should be natural and normal. Similarly, for man, the son of the almighty God, it should be natural and normal to make use of the almighty power of Nature. It is certainly within the scope of each individual to make full use of this power of Nature.

Only the regular practice of Transcendental Meditation brings a man to that status where he finds himself placed in the situation in which the almighty power of Nature works for him. It is not that he is required to make use of it, but that he is given the full advantage of it. Without rising to a state of Cosmic Consciousness, or at least putting oneself on the path, it is simply not possible to make use of even the partial strength of Mother Nature, not to speak of the almighty power.

Fortunate is he who has established within himself a state of natural attunement with cosmic Being. The whole of Nature moves in accordance with his needs; all his desires are in accordance with the cosmic purpose and his life serves the purpose of cosmic evolution. He is in the hands of God for the purpose of God, and God is for him and for his purpose. He uses the almighty power of Mother Nature, and Mother Nature uses his life for the glorious purpose of creation and evolution. Very fortunate is he.

The height of fortune is now available to all through the practice of Transcendental Meditation. The point will be brought out in the section on "Fulfillment," in the part "Generation After Generation,"[15] that it lies within the easy reach of the present generation to lay a solid foundation for all generations to keep on deriving the unlimited advantages of Transcendental Meditation, so that all the people in every generation will know the technique of how to use the almighty power of Nature.

There are some who try to make use of the supernatural power of creation by contacting the spirit world through a medium or through invoking spirits. That is on a very limited level of strength because no spirit is in possession of the total power of Nature. There may be spirits who may be more powerful than man, but invoking these spirits or behaving as a medium for them is not a practice to be encouraged because of two reasons. First, the power gained through these spirits is an insignificant, infinitesimal fraction of the power of almighty Nature; second, in order to receive that portion of the power of Nature, one has to give oneself completely to the influence of that spirit. To become a medium of a spirit one has to give oneself to it completely or else the spirit will not come. Instead of giving oneself completely to a spirit to gain a small amount of power, why not give oneself completely to divine consciousness through Transcendental Meditation and gain the unlimited almighty power of Mother Nature?

When you have to invest your money in a business, why not invest it in a business which will bring you the maximum profit in the minimum amount of time? Contacting the spirits and trying to gain some information of the

---

15 See page 300, "Generation After Generation."

universe or trying to do some work here and there is a very unfortunate formula for losing oneself in surrender to God. Those who try to achieve these supernatural or psychic powers are merely pitiable. This is only due to lack of proper guidance. Man's aspiration to come into contact with the higher powers and to accomplish great things in life is a very legitimate desire, but the contacting of spirits is an attempt to do this on a very low level of life.

Because of the lack of proper guidance, a large number of the seekers of power and higher spiritual life are misled to follow the path of spiritualistic influence. Those who fall prey to spiritualistic investigations and such practices are not at fault themselves. They are the seekers of something higher than what man's life apparently presents, but what is the basic disgrace is the lack of proper guidance.

There have not been enough teachers of Transcendental Meditation, and that is why spiritualistic and like teachings have become quite popular, especially in the Western countries.

The desire of people to gain higher powers together with lack of proper guidance has led many to try anything that is said to be out of the commonplace. In order that the people may receive the right technique to make full use of the almighty power of Nature, it is necessary that large numbers of teachers of Transcendental Meditation be available everywhere. This would make it possible for the life of all people to be set naturally on a sound foundation where they might enjoy the great benefits of the almighty power of Nature.

There is yet another type of people who, in their enthusiasm to develop higher power within themselves, take to practices of concentration and control of the mind. After much time in these practices they seem to achieve something in line with their aspirations, but the great effort that they have put into it has no bearing upon the small amount of gain. All this amounts to a waste of human aspirations and a waste of the great possibilities of achievements on the way to higher power.

If there is a fort, and the whole territory belongs to it, it is wise to go straight to the fort and capture it. Having captured the fort, all that is in the surrounding territory will naturally be possessed. If there is a gold mine on one side of the road and a diamond mine on the other and some other precious material on this side or that side, and one captures the fort, he is able to possess all the precious things in the territory automatically. Otherwise, if one takes possession of the gold mine, directs others to take the diamond mine, and later directs them to capture the other mines, all the strength and the time lost in capturing one will be so great that there will be little time left for taking the others.

All the psychic powers belong naturally to the field of Being. If there could be a way to directly come in contact and be familiar with the field of Being, then all the psychic powers and all the powers of Nature belonging to almighty eternal Being will be available. That is why, when there is a chance through the practice of Transcendental Meditation for everyone to contact Being in an easy manner, it is unwise to practice concentration or mind control, which takes years to give appreciable results.

Here is an invitation to all the seekers of power in the world to rise and start the practice of Transcendental Meditation and raise the standard of their consciousness to the plane of Cosmic Consciousness. They will gain the advantage of being naturally placed in a position where, without their intention or overtly trying to use the power of Nature, the almighty power of Mother Nature will be at their disposal and will naturally be serving the cause of their life. All that they want or need, the need of their surroundings and all concerned, will naturally be met in the most magnanimous and glorious way.

There is still another type of people who have been told to believe that the power of positive thinking is the greatest power in Nature. They are told to base their life on positive thinking. It is only childish and ridiculous to base one's life on the level of thinking. Thinking can never be a profound basis of living. Being is the natural basis. Instead of wasting one's time in thinking positively and waiting for the positive thought to be materialized, it is necessary to positively *be*. Positive Being through the practice of Transcendental Meditation provides the greatest status to life, which brings the possibility of the power of almighty Nature in the day-to-day practical life. Thinking, on the other hand, is only imaginary. We will see in the "Art of Thinking"[16] that in order to make thinking powerful, it is necessary to *be*. The technique of Being is the technique of making thought powerful.

16 See page 127.

While positive thoughts are better than negative thoughts, if we base our life solely on positive thinking, it will be just an imaginary basis. Positive thinking may have its value against negative thinking, but it has practically no value when compared with the power of Being. Trying to attain the powers of Nature on the basis of thinking is to delude oneself. In using the principle of positive thinking, if one starts thinking and gives all positivity to "I am a king," it may be that he will delude himself with the idea of being a king to such an extent that he begins to feel that he is a king, but that feeling of kingship will be far removed from the reality of being a king.

The philosophy of positive thinking has to be replaced by the philosophy of positive Being. It is not the science of mind that is the topmost and most useful science of life. It is the Science of Being that cherishes the topmost status in all the sciences of life and living. Remaining only in the mere hope of gaining abundance and fulfillment of life amounts only to running after mirages or building castles in the air.

The mind has to be supplemented by the power of Being; it is the power of Being which is the real basis of life, not the mind. All the material sciences — physics, chemistry, biology, etc. — are in the relative field. Likewise, the field of mind is also part of the relative field of existence. The science of mind, like any other science, is merely the science of relative fields of life. It is the Science of Being that is the science of the absolute eternal existence. It is the Science of Being that could bring stability, intelligence, the almighty power of Nature, and the eternal bliss of the Absolute into the relative field of life. It is the power of Being that must be acquired, and it is easy for all people all over the world to acquire it, even in the midst of their hustle and bustle of the modern business of day-to-day life.

Thus, we find that the principle of making full use of the almighty power of Nature lies in the Science of Being, the technique of which is found in the regular practice of Transcendental Meditation.

Art of Being

Each field of life should be lived and handled in such a manner that the maximum is gained for the individual and for the universe. We shall deal with these different fields of life and find out the technique that makes it possible to use all these different fields of life to best advantage for the individual and the universe.

Being, as we have seen in the section on "Science of Being," is the basic element of life. Ordinarily, It is of transcendental nature; It has Its value in a field beyond the obvious features of day-to-day life. The art of Being implies that the value of Being should be more thoroughly utilized for the sake of the good of the individual and the universe.

The art of Being means not only that the value of Being should not be lost in the different spheres of life but also that it should be naturally and fully retained in all spheres of life under all circumstances, in all the states of consciousness, and be utilized to glorify all aspects of life leading to fulfillment.

The different aspects of life are the nervous system, body, mind, senses, surroundings, *Karma*, breathing, thinking, speaking, experiencing, and behaving. The three states of consciousness are waking, dreaming, and sleeping.

Even without the art of living Being, Being is there because by Its very existence, nothing could be without Being. What could there be without Being? Being is the basis of the existence of everything, even though It is hidden behind the obvious.

In the section on "Science of Being" we have seen that the nature of Being is Bliss Consciousness; It is concentrated happiness of absolute nature and permanent status. Therefore the art of Being means that the concentrated state of happiness should be constantly lived under all circumstances. The art of Being demands that at least Being should not be lost and that normally Being should dominate life and be in the forefront of all aspects of life under all circumstances.

This means that life by nature must be blissful, naturally free from suffering, misery, tension, confusion, and disharmony. All spheres of life — thinking, speaking, acting, and behaving — become and remain permeated with the conscious awareness of Being, and life is thus able to live the value of Being.

The art of Being is necessarily the technique of first fathoming Being in the innermost level of one's own life and then bringing It out from the transcendental field of unmanifested nature into the relative existence. Thus the art of Being is comprised of a technique which has two aspects. It first explores the region of Being by taking the conscious mind from the gross relative field of experience to the field of unmanifest Being, and then brings the mind out well-infused with the value of Being. Thus the art of Being, or the technique of gaining that state of Being, lies in contacting Being and living It. Transcendental Meditation is a practical technique for the art of Being.

A technique or an art of something necessarily means that it should be done without strain and be accomplished thoroughly for greater advantage. In considering the scope of the art of Being we shall take the different aspects of life and go into details in view of those aspects.

Thinking and the Art of Being

We have seen in the previous part that, when Being is maintained on the conscious level, all the thoughts naturally find their place at the level of Being. This is the art of Being in thinking, where thinking and Being find their co-existence.

When one thinks with the conscious mind established in the level of Being, then Being is naturally maintained through the process of thinking. So, the art of Being with regard to thinking necessitates the infusion of the value of transcendental Being into the nature of the mind.

The relationship of thought with Being is like the relationship that exists between a child and his mother. Being is the source of thinking. The process of thinking brings the mind out of the essential nature of its Being. Thus we find that the process of thinking is opposed to the state of Being. This is the reason that only when the mind transcends the subtlest stage of thinking during Transcendental Meditation is it able to arrive at the state of Being. When it starts thinking again, it must come out of the transcendental field of Being.

Thus, the conscious mind is either engaged in the process of thinking or in the transcendental state of pure Being. Thus, thinking is, in a way, a challenge to Being. However, this is only because the mind has not been trained to hold Being and the thought simultaneously. By and large, the ingrained habit of the mind to remain mostly in the field of thinking is the reason why the process of thinking becomes a challenge to the state of Being. When with the practice of Transcendental Meditation the conscious mind fathoms the source of thought and becomes familiar with the state of Being, then the state of pure Being is so harmonious, blissful, and so pure in Its nature that the mind, having become familiar with It, will not part with It under any circumstances. It is then that the nature of the mind is transformed into the very nature of Being so that the mind, while yet remaining a thinking mind, is naturally established in the field of Being. This is the art of Being in the field of thought.

If the mind is without Being, the process of thinking is as though lifeless, and, when the mind is not familiar with Being, the process of thinking and the thought force are very weak. If these are weak, so will be the resultant activity, and, as a result of weak activity, the accomplishments are not satisfying and the fulfillment of life is not gained. So it is the art of Being while thinking that is the basis of all accomplishments and fulfillment in life. The regular practice of Transcendental Meditation takes care of it.

When we consider the art of Being while thinking, then we must make it clear that the art of Being lies in creating a condition of Being in the mind, and this is done when the attention is brought to the transcendental field of Being. This cannot be accomplished by any other process.

Any attempt to be aware of Being without bringing the conscious mind to the field of transcendental Being through the practice of Transcendental Meditation could only mean that the conscious mind cherishes the *thought* of Being. And when the conscious mind cherishes the thought of It, it is devoid of the state of Being because the thought of Being is not the state of Being Itself. Any attempt to hold the thought of Being with the hope of maintaining the awareness of Being on the conscious level will only result in division of the mind. The practice of cherishing the thought of Being will neither cultivate Being in the mind nor will it allow the full mind to be engaged in the thinking process. This means neither Being nor the thinking will be profound.

There are some misguided schools of thought which provoke the seekers of truth to maintain Being on the conscious level while they are engaged in thinking, speaking, or acting. Any attempt to maintain Being or try to maintain self-awareness on the conscious thinking level without allowing the mind to transcend is only a vain attempt to live Being in life. It only creates a false idea about the state of realization of Being during thinking or activity. The aspirants of truth and those who want to make thinking powerful by the power of Being should be aware of the mental effects of only *thinking* about Being. It is a state of life which cannot be thought and lived; Being is naturally lived without a thought about It. The reason the state of Being has gone out of conscious awareness is because we have not been acquainted with the field of transcendental pure Being. For that, the only way is that the conscious attention should be brought from the gross state of thinking to the subtlest state of thought where the field of Being is consciously reached.

The art of Being with regard to thinking lies in the system of Transcendental Meditation.

Speaking and the Art of Being

Speaking is the gross form of thinking. Speaking requires more energy than thinking, and, thus, the process of speaking naturally engages the mind more than the process of thinking. So the art of Being on the level of speaking is necessarily a greater art than the art of Being on the level of thinking.

While dealing with the main principle of enlarging the conscious capacity of the mind,[17] we have seen that a thought starts from the subtlest level of

17 See page 30.

consciousness and becomes bigger and bigger until it eventually comes to be appreciated as a full thought on the conscious level. This same process of the thought bubble becoming bigger continues and the thought that was appreciated as a thought on the conscious level is expressed as speech.

The process of speaking is basically in no way different from that of thinking, so the art of Being and speaking will be no other than the art of Being on the various levels of thinking. The only difference will be in scale, because the energy consumed in speaking is greater than in thinking. The art of maintaining Being on the level of speaking is more intensified than the art of maintaining Being on the level of thinking.

Thus it is clear that the practice of Transcendental Meditation, which is, as we have seen, the art of maintaining Being on the level of thinking, is also the practice for maintaining Being on the level of speaking. The difference will be only in scale. Greater practice of Transcendental Meditation will be needed for speaking. Thus we find that the art of Being at the level of speaking finds its fulfillment in the regular and steady practice of the system of Transcendental Meditation.

When, with steady practice, Being begins to be maintained at the level of speaking, speech finds as its basis the state of Being or of Cosmic Law. Speech then produces an influence congenial to all the Laws of Nature. This is how, with the practice of Transcendental Meditation, Being naturally begins to be maintained at the level of speech, and, when speech supplements and reinforces the functioning of the Laws of Nature, it becomes a help in the process of cosmic evolution and maintains harmony and rhythm of life in Nature. A great influence of harmony everywhere is the result of the art of Being on the level of speaking.

Again, it should be borne in mind that any conscious attempt to hold the thought of Being while engaged in the process of speaking results in just holding the *thought* of Being alone. Similarly, when we consider the maintenance of the state of Being at the level of speaking, we should know that any attempt to maintain Being at that level without the practice of Transcendental Meditation will only result in dividing the mind between the thought of Being and the process of speaking. In the practical field this will only result in retardation of speech. Part of the mind is engaged in maintaining the *thought* of Being, while another part is engaged in speaking; this divides the mind and produces retardation in the natural flow of speech.

It is interesting to note that many philosopher-teachers have been instructing their followers to think before speaking as a way to maintain awareness while speaking. Thinking before speaking and simultaneously trying to maintain the inner awareness of Being only results in a retardation of speech because the process of thinking and speaking are in the same flow. There are many such people following the teachings of these masters, particularly in London. These personalities were found to be retarded in their actions as well as in their speech. This is not the art of Being at the level of speaking. The art of Being at the level of speaking lies in the regular and steady practice of Transcendental Meditation, which brings Being to fullness on the level of the mind at all times.

Breathing and the Art of Being

It is breathing that lies between the individual being and cosmic Being, between the individual stream of life and the eternal cosmic ocean of life; it is as if breathing sets forth an individual stream out of the cosmic ocean of Being.

Breathing in its subtlest aspect is referred to as *Prāṇa*. *Prāṇa* is the vibratory nature of Being which transforms the unmanifested ocean of Being into the manifested life stream of individual beings. When transcendental omnipresent absolute cosmic Being, by virtue of the *Prāṇa* which is Its own nature, vibrates into manifested streams of life, the *Prāṇa* assumes the role of breathing and maintains the individual life stream and keeps it connected at its basis with the Cosmic Life of the Absolute.

At every rise of the breath, the cosmic *Prāṇa* receives the identity of individual life force, and, at every fall of the breath, the stream of individual life contacts cosmic Being so that between the fall and the rise of breath the state of the individual life is in communion with cosmic Being. This is how breathing on the one hand produces the individual life from the Cosmic Life, and, on the other hand, maintains the harmony of attunement of the individual with cosmic Being. The art of Being with regard to breathing means that, even while the breath is in action, the contact of the individual life stream is not broken with the eternal life of cosmic Being.

How can this be accomplished?

In order to discover a formula for Being to be maintained along with the process of breathing, it is first necessary to see how the breathing starts and what it is that makes the breath or the *Prāṇa* emerge from Being. We have said that *Prāṇa* is the vibratory nature of Being. But how and why does the vibratory nature of Being adopt a particular pattern to give rise to a specific stream of individual life by virtue of breathing? Because breathing, as we have seen, sets forth the stream of the individual life.

There should be something more than mere *Prāṇa*, however, to bring forth the life of a particular individual. What is there other than the *Prāṇa* which is responsible for the set pattern of breathing?

We know it is the sap which constitutes the tree. The sap received by the tree from the surrounding area constitutes the trunk, leaves, flowers, and fruit. In essence, the whole tree is nothing but the expression of this nourishment. The sap comes from the area surrounding the tree in a natural process of evolution. But any amount of sap present in the earth will not be able to produce any specific pattern of the tree unless the seed of the tree is available. It is the seed of the tree that determines the pattern of the tree; without it, the sap does not receive any basis to express itself.

As an example, let us take the sap to be transcendental Being of the absolute Cosmic Life and the tree to be the individual stream of life. Being is eternally present there, but, in order to have a specific pattern of individual life, Being needs the seed of that pattern. Without a specific seed, no specific individual life could manifest out of unmanifested omnipresent Being. Now, what is the seed of the individual through which the omnipresent by Its own nature, *Prāṇa*, manifests into an individual life stream?

The seed of individual life is like the seed of a tree which is nothing but the sap in its most highly evolved expression. Passing through all the cycles of evolution, the sap reaches the highest state of evolution in a fully grown tree and appears as a seed. Thus the seed signifies the most highly developed state of the tree and is the most highly concentrated state of sap. Then that seed becomes the cause of attracting the sap and growing into a tree again.

Being expresses Itself as *Prāṇa*, on which is based the sprouting of a thought which in its turn develops into a desire leading to action. And, when the action is completed, the fruit of action marks the full growth of the tree of thought or desire. The impression of the experience of the fruit of action is like the concentrated state of a seed which is capable of giving rise to future desires and action. Thus, we find that the case of the cycle of seed and tree is like the case of the cycle of thought, desire, action, fruit of action, and its impression. Here the seed is like a thought, and the soil from which the sap is drawn for the nourishment of the seed is Being which lies at the basis of thought. Thus it could well be said for the sake of understanding that Being sprouts or manifests as a thought and evolves to the state of action and, having further evolved as the fruit of action, becomes concentrated to become the impression and then reaches the state from which it started to manifest. This account helps us to visualize the stream of individual life sprouting from universal life by virtue of *Prāṇa*.

The seed of the individual life is nothing but the expression of unmanifested Being in the most highly evolved state of manifestation. Omnipresent Being of unmanifested nature having manifested as a thought, and having gone through all the cycles of evolution, reaches the climax of the evolution of the thought in the fruit of the action, and the impression of the experience of the fruit of the action becomes the seed for future thought. By virtue of the seed-thought Being begins to express Itself in the stream of an individual life of set pattern.

Thus, we have seen how Being expresses Itself in different degrees of manifestation and passes through the different cycles of evolution to arrive at a point where It is capable of being the seed for the future life of the individual.

We have seen that *Prāṇa* is the vibratory nature of Being. Unmanifested Being does not need any outside instrumentality to vibrate; It does so by Its own nature. As a matter of fact, to maintain eternally absolute Being while vibrating and maintaining the transitory levels of life, life after life, is the true nature of Being. Its true nature is to maintain Its status quo as absolute Being and also to maintain the ever-changing aspects of manifested relative existence. So, when *Prāṇa* manifests, Being vibrates, and, by vibrating, It assumes the role of a particular pattern of breathing or life stream in accordance with the individual life.

The individual seed of life is the unfulfilled *Karma* of the past life of man. The sum total of all the unfulfilled desires of the previous life is the seed of the individual that molds vibrating Being into a specific life stream of an individual. So the *Prāṇa*, in conjunction with the desire, forms the mind. And *Prāṇa*, devoid of its association with the mind, forms matter. This is how the subjective and objective aspects of the individual life come into existence. Essentially it is Being; but, as in the life of a tree, it is the sap which expresses itself in different aspects of the tree. Similarly, it is Being which expresses Itself as different aspects of the individual. Just as it is the seed which shapes the pattern of the sap into a tree, in an individual life it is the impression of the experiences of the past life that shape Being into a specific pattern of individual life force or *Prāṇa*.

Thus we find that *Prāṇa* or its gross aspect, breathing, is the fundamental aspect of the life stream of the individual, and that it is the link between the individual life stream and the ocean of Cosmic Life energy. It is by virtue of mind in conjunction with the *Prāṇa* that the whole stream of individual life is set into a specific pattern.

The art of Being with regard to breathing lies in the maintenance of the value of Being in the nature of the mind, because breathing is the result of the combination of *Prāṇa* and mind, and *Prāṇa* and mind are not arbitrarily two different things.

Mind includes within its role the feature of *Prāṇa*; without *Prāṇa* the mind could not be, and without the mind *Prāṇa* is just the nature of Being, something of absolute value beyond the relative life. Therefore, in order to maintain Being on the level of breathing it is primarily necessary to bring Being into the level of the mind. When, with the practice of Transcendental Meditation, the mind becomes saturated with Being, breathing is on the level of Being. Breathing is found in harmony with the rhythm of Nature, and the individual life whose breathing has been transformed on the level of Being breathes in the harmony and rhythm of Cosmic Life. The breathing then gains the subtle state of vibrating *Prāṇa*.

The breathing of the individual is thus the nature of cosmic Being; the breathing of the individual then is the vibrating *Prāṇa*. The art of Being and breathing is the art of raising the status of the individual to the state of eternal cosmic Being. And the fulfillment of this art is found in the regular practice of Transcendental Meditation.

Experiencing and the Art of Being

The experiencer experiences the object when the object connects itself through the senses and is reflected upon by the mind. The object coming in contact with the senses of experience leaves an impression of the object on the mind, and the essential nature of the mind of the experiencer is overshadowed. This shows that the process of experience is a process which throws Being out of sight. This is called identification. It is as if the subject within becomes identified with the objects outside and loses its essential nature, its Being. Thus we find that an experience brings the experiencer out of his own Being.

The art of Being on the level of experience means that the experience of an object should not be able to overthrow the status of Being from the mind; that is, the mind should be able to maintain Being while experiencing the object. In the part on "Mind and Being"[18] we have dealt in great detail with how, by the practice of Transcendental Meditation, the mind begins to maintain the pure state of Being along with the experience of an object.

We have also seen how, by the practice of Transcendental Meditation, Being begins to be maintained at the level of experience or perception, and the experiencer remains unbound by the impact of the experience. The experiencer lives in the complete freedom of fullness of Being and at the same time experiences the outside world around him. In a state where Being is fully maintained, the process of experience becomes powerful and the experience of the object becomes much deeper and fuller than before.

The experiencer also lives the experience in complete freedom of its Being. This art of Being on the level of experience is the skill of fully inte-

18 See page 19.

grated life where one is able to live all values of the transcendental absolute Bliss Consciousness of Being along with the experience of various aspects of the relative creation of material and physical value. It is the art of Being at the level of experience that holds the life of the individual in an integrated state with Cosmic Life. The purpose of the individual life is found fulfilled in the art of Being at the level of experience.

Without the art of Being on the level of experience, when the process of experience brings the subject in contact with the object, then the subject, without the state of Being, becomes so fully identified with the object that the impression of the value of the object becomes very strong in the mind. This impression of the experience is held fast in the mind as a seed for future desire for the same experience. This is how the cycle of experience, impression, desire — experience, impression, desire — continues to be, and the cycle of birth and death is thus continued.

In order to understand the cycle of birth and death caused by the impression of the experience, it should first be understood that the cause of rebirth is the unfulfilled desires of past life. If a man wants to accomplish this or that and fails to do so before the body ceases to function, he dies unfulfilled. Because of this unfulfillment the inner man (mind) goes to create another body through which that unfulfilled desire of the past life may be fulfilled.

Thus it is one's own desire that is the cause of rebirth. When a man is born, he is born with the impressions of the experiences in the past which have laid down deep impressions of their values. These impressions become the seed for future desires, and this cycle of experience, impression, desire, takes the man from birth to birth, and the cycle of birth and death continues until the cycle of experience and impression is broken.

The maintenance of Being at the level of experience does not allow a deep impression of the object on the mind; the impression is just enough to give the experience of the object, just enough to allow the perception to be. Because the mind is full of the value of Being and Being in Its nature is Bliss Consciousness, the impressions of the experience of the transitory nature of the objects naturally fail to make a great impression in the mind. The impression is not deep enough to work as a seed for future action. It is like the tongue saturated with the taste of saccharin is unable to register the impression of other varieties of sweetmeats because the joy of the sweetmeat is not as great as the sweetness of the saccharin. Similarly, the mind, having been full in the bliss of Being, feels so contented that, although it experiences the objects, the value of the object fails to register a deep impression in the mind.

When Being is maintained, then the impression of the object on the mind is not very deep. It is like the impression of a line on water which is drawn but simultaneously erased. Likewise, the impression of the objects on the mind that is full with Being is just enough to give the experience of the object. Without Being in the mind, the impression of the object is like the impression of a line drawn on stone, difficult to erase.

A mind without the value of Being is always under the bondage of experience giving rise to the cycle of impression, desire, and action. It is the technique of Transcendental Meditation that establishes Being in the mind and naturally allows it to live the value of Being along with the values of the outer experiences. Thus we find that the art of Being on the level of experience finds its fulfillment in the regular and steady practice of Transcendental Meditation.

Behavior and the Art of Being

Obviously behavior depends upon the state of one's mind, senses, body, surroundings, circumstances, upon the *Karma*, or the action that one does, upon his way of thinking, breathing, speaking, and experiencing.

All these constitute different levels of behavior. We have dealt with the art of Being and behavior on all levels except that of circumstances. Surroundings and circumstances go together and, therefore, as far as the art of Being at the level of behavior is concerned, we have already understood that it lies in the practice of Transcendental Meditation.

While dealing with the problem of social welfare we will discuss in great detail how, if the mind of the man is contented in the state of Bliss Consciousness of absolute Being, his behavior with others will not only be in harmony with them but will also help them on all levels of their natural process of evolution.

Since the art of Being, on the level of behavior with other people in society, will be dealt with in the part on "Art of Behavior,"[19] let us consider here the art of Being on the level of behavior of man with the natural flow of evolution.

We have seen that the mind established on the level of Being behaves in conformity with the Cosmic Law and all the Laws of Nature. The natural stream of life is certainly in accord with the Cosmic Law and all the Laws of Nature, and, therefore, when one's mind is established on the level of Being or on the level of the Natural Laws, its behavior at all levels is in conformity with the natural stream of evolution.

Thus we find that when one's behavior is set up on the level of Being or when one's Being has been established on the level of behavior, then one's life has naturally established a harmonious relationship with the natural stream of evolution.

The behavior of one who meditates is very natural with other people because Being naturally creeps into the nature of the mind. It is unstrained natural behavior alone that will help Being to grow in the field of activity. Any unnatural manner of behavior only strains the mind, but when one behaves innocently and naturally on all levels the stream of life flows smoothly and in accord with the Laws of Nature.

If a man plans how to behave, then the behavior ceases to be natural and is no longer in conformity with the Laws of Nature. So when we conclude that the art of Being on the level of behavior lies in the regular and steady practice of Transcendental Meditation, then we should also add that, along with the practice, the aspirant has to be very natural and innocent in his behavior with others.

It is not necessary to plan how to behave; it is not necessary to think much about how to behave, what to do, how to speak, or how to handle a situation. Let the situation come, handle it innocently and naturally. If the practice of Transcendental Meditation is regular and sustained, all behavior on all levels will naturally be rewarding.

It is absolutely a waste of energy and time to think about the manners of behavior with others. When the situation arises, take it as it comes and behave

---

19 See page 174.

in a natural way. The art of Being on the level of behavior finds its fulfillment in the regular practice of Transcendental Meditation along with the very natural, innocent, and easy manner of behavior and activity in the outside world.

Health and the Art of Being

Health is Being. Good health is the state of Being and evolving at the same time. Ill health brings disharmony in the state of Being and in the evolutionary process as well.

The fact that Being is the never-changing eternal phase of existence and the fact that It pervades and maintains the diverse forms and phenomenal creation gives us hope of establishing an unbreakable harmony in all the diversified phases of our life by coordinating their values with the absolute value of Being.

All the suffering in life would be alleviated if there were a way to establish Being on the conscious level of life, where discord, dissension, disharmony, and disunity prevail. If there could be a way to establish Being on the conscious level of the mind, the body, and the surroundings, the result would be perfect health on all levels of life.

The all-permeating eternal existence of Being is the basis of the body, mind, and surroundings of the individual, as the sap is the basis of all the branches, trunk, leaves, and fruit of the tree. But when the sap fails to reach the surface levels of the tree, then the outer aspects of the tree begin to suffer and wither away. Likewise, when Being is not brought onto the conscious surface level of life, the outer aspects of life begin to suffer.

If health and harmony are to be enjoyed in life, somehow the transcendental value of Being must be brought out and infused in all aspects of life — body, mind, and surroundings. In addition to bringing the value of Being on the surface of these aspects of life, it is also necessary to establish a healthy coordination between them.

The only thing that is common to all these aspects of life is Being. If there could be a way to bring Being on the surface level of the mind, body, and surroundings, and if there could be a way to establish coordination between them by the link of Being, that would be the way to establish permanent harmony and health on all levels — the way to integration of life and the way to the art of living; for that would establish all phases of life in good coordination with each other and in perfect health.

Now we shall consider how the value of Being could be brought to the surface level of the mind, body, and surroundings; or, how the values of the mind, body, and surroundings could be brought to the level of Being. Either way the purpose of health would be served.

Mind and the Art of Being

The art of Being with regard to the mind means that the value of Being is retained by the mind under all circumstances. When the mind thinks or experiences something, the thought or the experience does not overshadow its essential nature. The mind naturally holds Being while engaging itself in thinking or experiencing. Not allowing the mind to be overshadowed by any thought or experience is said to be the art of Being on the level of the mind.

Another aspect of the art of Being in relation to the mind is that even when the full mind is acting, the overshadowing influence of the thought and experience is minimum; even when the mind is deeply engaged in thinking and experiencing something, the experience or thought does not overshadow its essential nature.

There is yet another factor which is important with regard to Being and the mind. When Being is on the level of the mind, the flow of the mind in thinking or experiencing is in accordance with the Laws of Nature. This we have dealt with in "Cosmic Law"[20] when discussing how the natural flow of the mind, in thinking and experiencing, could be brought into accord with the Laws of Nature. Thus, while the thought is forceful and the experience is complete and deep, the influence of the thought and experience in the surroundings and the individual is in the natural stream of evolution, and both the individual and the universe gain.

The art of Being on the level of the mind also means that the mind has the full value of Being under all circumstances. The mind has three states of

20 See page 10, "Being, the Plane of Cosmic Law."

consciousness: wakeful consciousness, consciousness of the dreaming state, and consciousness of the deep-sleep state.

The art of Being on the level of mind means that Being is in the status of the mind in whatever state of consciousness it is placed. If the mind is in the wakeful state, Being should be lived along with all the experiences; if the mind is in the dreaming state, Being should not be overshadowed; if the mind is in the deep-sleep state, Being should not be lost. Being should permeate the mind in every state. This is accomplished through the art of Being on the level of the mind.

In order to have Being in the state of mind during the activities of the day, it is first necessary for the conscious mind to become acquainted with the state of Being. The state of Being is of transcendental nature; it is transcendental, absolute consciousness. By the practice of Transcendental Meditation the conscious mind fathoms the deeper levels of the thought process and eventually transcends the subtlest thought to arrive at the state of Being. The conscious mind reaches transcendental Being and becomes acquainted with that state.

This is how Transcendental Meditation is the art of bringing the conscious mind to the level of Being or bringing Being within the range of the conscious mind. When, with continued practice, the mind becomes more and more familiar with Being and eventually becomes rooted in Its very nature, even when the mind is engaged by the outside surroundings, Being remains permanent on the level of the conscious mind. This is how the practice of Transcendental Meditation maintains Being on the level of the mind.

This art of bringing transcendental Being to the level of the mind simultaneously enlarges[21] the conscious capacity of the mind and enables the full mind to function. It has the advantage of bringing to action all the potentialities of the mind; nothing remains hidden, nothing remains subconscious, everything becomes conscious. This makes every thought a very powerful thought. Again, while dealing with the Cosmic Law, we have seen that when

21 See page 29.

the mind comes to the field of Being, it is naturally set in rhythm with all the Laws of Nature and is in tune with the process of cosmic evolution.

Another advantage is that, because the nature of Being is absolute Bliss Consciousness, the mind becomes full with Bliss Consciousness, and everlasting happiness comes to the conscious level of the mind. Being is eternal and permanent, imperishable, unchanging. Therefore, the imperishable, eternal, unchanging aspect of Being is found infused into the very nature of the mind. Such a mind is stable, unwavering, steady, and one-pointed, while it is also blissful, contented, self-contained, and sharp. The value of bringing the mind to the field of Being is that the mind becomes both sharp and contented, joyful and peaceful, at the same time.

Because absolute Being is the source of all thought and of all creation, when the conscious mind comes to that level, it comes in contact with the unlimited creative intelligence of absolute Being. Great creative intelligence enters into the nature of the mind; constructive imagination, the power of creative thinking, increases along with joyfulness and contentment.

The mind coming in tune with the field of Being gains the source of unlimited energy. Such a powerful, energetic mind naturally has very powerful thoughts. Every thought stimulates the nervous system with great vitality and vigor and the nervous system is thereby put to sustained and powerful activity so that it stimulates its end organ, the body, with such great force and fixity of purpose that the materialization or the success of the thought in the outside world becomes a positive reality without delay or strain. The chance for materializing a thought is so great that the action becomes forceful. This is what the art of bringing Being to the level of the mind does to the individual in his day-to-day practical life.

Another very great advantage of Being coming to the level of the mind is that, although the mind experiences the thought and action and all that goes with it, nothing is able to overshadow Being which has taken deep root in the very nature of the mind. This enables the mind to behave freely in the perishable and ever-changing field of thought and action and yet remain established in the eternal imperishable nature of absolute Being. The state is said to be a state of eternal freedom in life.

Thus the mind remains in freedom even while it engages itself in the field of thought, speech, and activity. The art of bringing the mind to the level of Being is the art of bringing eternal freedom, contentment, and fulfillment to the mind under all circumstances.

The technique of the art of Being lies in the practice of Transcendental Meditation, which readily brings the mind out of the thinking process to the field of Being and brings Being out of the transcendental into the field of activity.

While we are considering the infusion of Being into the nature of the mind through the technique of Transcendental Meditation, it is also necessary to note that because the whole process of meditation is a process of experiencing subtle states of thinking, and because thinking primarily depends upon the physical state of the nervous system, any factor that influences the physical condition of the nervous system indirectly influences the process of meditation.

The processes of eating, drinking, and breathing nourish and maintain the physical state of the nervous system; the factors of activity and rest also have an influence. Therefore, it is obvious that if all factors are properly adjusted to maintain the ideal physical state of the nervous system, the practice of Transcendental Meditation will be ideally successful. If one eats improper food and breathes improper air,[22] creating dullness in the nervous system, and engages himself in activities subjecting it to fatigue and tension, then naturally the mind will not be able to fathom the deeper levels of the thought process and meditation will become less effective and the infusion of Being into the nature of the mind will be unduly delayed. Therefore it is highly important that care be taken in the selection of the type of food and drink and air.

Regarding discriminatory practices in the matter of food and drink, it is obvious to those who have made a study of this subject that wrong eating and drinking of alcoholic beverages is very detrimental to the overall well-being of a person. This does not mean that one should suddenly make a radical change of dietary habits, but, rather, one should aim toward the rectification of improper dietary habits.

22 For example, breathes the smog of London or Los Angeles.

The Influence of Food

Food has a very great influence on the mind because it is what we eat and drink that goes to make the blood which sustains the nervous system. Therefore the quality of food has a great deal to do with the quality of mind.

Apart from the quality of material in the food, it is important how that food has been earned. When a man earns his livelihood by righteous means, then the food has a good influence on the mind. If, for example, a man commits a theft or earns his living by illegal or unrighteous means, the quality of the food that is bought from that earning produces those qualities in the mind.

The tendencies of the cook who prepares the meals also affect the food; likewise, the tendencies of the mind or the quality of thoughts at the time of eating the food affect it and have a corresponding influence on the quality of mind that is produced by that food. It is therefore highly advisable that while he is eating, a man should either be silent in pure thoughts, or have good conversation with those at the table. It is always best to say a prayer before we begin to eat; one such as the following sets the attitude:

> In Thy fullness my Lord
> Filled with Thy grace
> For the purpose of union with Thee
> And to satisfy and glorify Thy creation
> With thanks to Thee with all our hearts
> And with all our love for Thee
> With all adoration for Thy blessings
> We accept Thy gift as it has come to us
> The food is Thy blessing and in Thy service
> We accept in all gratitude, my Lord.

The Influence of Activity

The factor of activity and inactivity also plays an important role in the state of the nervous system. Overactivity makes it dull and so does lack of activity. A balance of activity and inactivity maintains the nervous system in a state of alertness, which is highly essential for the success of the art of Being on the level of the mind. If the body is fatigued, the nervous system becomes dull and the mind begins to be drowsy, losing all capacity of experience. In such a state the ability to experience the subtle states of thinking is not possible. This leaves no chance of success for meditation.

We have seen that the state of Being is the most normal and self-contained state of mind. When the mind is all in itself, it is the state of Being. We have seen in "How to Contact Being"[23] that the state of Being lies in bringing the conscious mind out of even the subtlest state of experience of a thought. When the mind transcends the subtlest state of thinking, it is left all by itself. This is the state of Self-consciousness, or, the state of pure Being. This shows that in order to produce the state of Being the mind has to be devoid of any experience of the object, yet it should not lose its ability of experience as it does in deep sleep.

In order to give rise to this state of Being, the nervous system has to be in a particular state of activity where the nervous system has to be suspended in such a way that it is not subjected to activity, nor is it allowed to be nonactive. This will be the state of Being.

When the nervous system is functioning, it is giving the experience of the objects through the senses of perception, and it engages itself in activity through the organs of action. When functioning in this manner it becomes fatigued, it is subjected to a condition in which it fails to perceive the world around it. If the fatigue is of a lesser degree, the perception becomes dim and one begins to feel drowsy. If the fatigue is greater, the perception becomes nil and the mind fails to experience. This shows that the state of mind depends upon the physical condition of the nervous system, and we find that fatigue has control of the state of experience. This leads us to conclude that if the nervous system is passive with fatigue, it is not possible to arrive at the state of Being, and if the nervous system is active then also it is not possible for the mind to gain the state of Being.

Thus the factor of fatigue is an important factor to be considered in the art of Being, and we are led to think that the art of Being lies also in not subjecting the nervous system to great fatigue. That is, the activity during the

---

23 See page 27.

day should be such that it does not leave the body tired or the nervous system fatigued. If the body is tired, the nervous system is put to tension and fatigue, and that state of suspension, the state between activity and no activity, will not be cultivated. Therefore, the pure state of Being will not be.

In addition to excessive activity, wrong eating and drinking also cause a great amount of dullness in the nervous system. This, too, is not conducive to the state of Being. Therefore, whereas the art of Being lies basically in the system of Transcendental Meditation, this meditation, in its turn, is highly dependent on the state of the nervous system. It is therefore advisable that one should have regular habits of proper diet and activity. One should neither exert oneself unduly, nor should one remain inactive.

The practice of Transcendental Meditation, in bringing the mind to transcendental Being, infuses an unlimited source of energy into the conscious mind and thereby helps the field of activity to be normal. Even then, one has to be cautious that the increased energy due to meditation is not overspent, otherwise it will again be the cause of producing strain and fatigue to the nervous system which will hamper the effectiveness of meditation. Therefore, we are in a position to conclude that the art of Being also basically depends upon the habits of activity and rest.

Unregulated habits of diet, activity, rest, etc., are due to an unbalanced state of mind. To bring the nervous system to the right conditions of rest, activity, and nourishment, it is necessary that a balanced state of mind be cultivated. The mind will be balanced only when it has a chance of being contented due to the experience of great happiness. The experience of Bliss Consciousness alone can create a state of balanced mind and this is automatically achieved through the system of Transcendental Meditation.

Therefore, the art of Being eventually, in all its different aspects, finds its fulfillment in the regular practice of Transcendental Meditation along with regular habits and a proper way of life.

Thus we find that, whereas the art of Being on the level of the mind finds its fulfillment in the regular practice of Transcendental Meditation, its success depends upon maintaining a regulated life.

The Senses and the Art of Being

There are five senses of perception and five organs of action. The senses of perception are sight, smell, hearing, taste, and touch. The organs of action are the hands, feet, tongue, and the two organs of elimination. Through the five senses the mind perceives, and through the five organs of action it acts. For perception the mind is brought to bear upon the external world through the senses, and for action, it is brought to bear upon the world through the organs of action.

The art of Being on the level of the senses exists when the senses and the organs retain Being under all circumstances. To make this clear, the senses should always be senses and organs should always be organs in the fullness of their respective values. This means that they should always be ready to function and always succeed in functioning with their full capacity.

The art of Being, on the level of the senses, will be achieved when the full value of the senses and organs is used so that there will be full perception of an object and full accomplishment of the action.

The senses of perception should always be strong, fresh, and free from tension, delusion, malice, and narrowness of vision, so that they naturally produce full perception of the object. The organs of action should be energetic, strong, and in good coordination with the senses of perception, so that they may act with precision and success and bring fulfillment to the action.

The art of Being, with regard to the senses, is that, while they remain saturated with the essential nature of Being — bliss of Being — they experience the object. The result is that the object is thoroughly perceived but fails to overpower the senses to the extent that they become slaves to the object.

When the intense sweetness of saccharin is on the tongue, the taste of other sweets does not make an impression. Similarly, when the senses are saturated with the bliss of Being, the small transitory joys of objects fail to bind the senses and do not make a lasting impression on them. Being, on the level of the senses, means that the senses receive their full contentment in Bliss Consciousness, and, even while experiencing the variety of joys of the objects, they are not bound by them because they are bound in the eternal value of the unlimited bliss of the Absolute.

In such a state of contentment, the senses do not lure the mind to wander in search of greater happiness. This is because the bliss of Being is already permeating the level of the senses through the mind's saturation with Being.

In such a state, when the senses are experiencing the outside object, the result of the experience is completely harmonious in the surroundings, and for the body and mind of the individual as well. When the eyes see a beautiful scene, the sight is pure, the vision is full; one is free from any malice or sinful perceptions. All is right on the level of perception, all is virtuous, moral, and is in the natural stream of evolution.

If the bliss of Being has not permeated the level of the senses, the senses are not in a state of contentment. The nature of the senses is to want to enjoy more. This is a legitimate desire. But only by bringing the bliss of Being onto the level of the senses do they succeed in becoming established in that level of contentment which is unshakable and irresistible. Remaining in contentment they remain in freedom from the bondage of impressions of experiences. This is the result of the practice of the art of Being on the level of the senses.

How is this state of infusion of Being on the level of the senses achieved?

It is achieved by the regular practice of the system of Transcendental Meditation. We shall explore the mechanics of Transcendental Meditation and see how this comes about.

First, it is necessary to know the full range of the senses. Ordinarily, when we see, our eyes are open, the mind associates itself with the open eye and comes into contact with the object facing it. This is how perception occurs. But we also know that the sense of sight is not limited to seeing with the open eyes. Even with closed eyes it is possible to perceive an object with the mind. This mental perception or cognition of an object (with closed eyes) will also be by means of the sense of sight. This gives us to understand that the sense of sight ranges in its ability of cognition from the gross level of perception to the subtle.

For example, in the diagram below, A, A_1, and A_2 represent the gross and subtle levels of the sense and objects.

The mind, associating itself with the gross level of the senses — A — perceives the corresponding gross level of the object A; the mind associating itself with the subtle level of the senses — A_1 — perceives the corresponding subtle level of the object A_1; the mind associating itself with the subtlest level of the senses — A_2 — perceives the corresponding subtlest level of the object A_2.

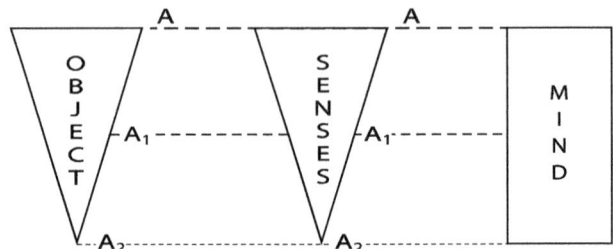

Naturally, the open eyes represent the gross level of the sense of sight. Similarly, when a word becomes audible, that is the perception of the gross sound as a result of the mind associating itself with the gross level of the sense of hearing.

When one speaks within oneself and the mind hears the sound, it is because the mind associates itself with the subtle level of the sense of hearing. When during the process of Transcendental Meditation the mind perceives very refined states of thought, it is due to the mind's associating itself with the very subtle states of the sense of hearing.

Thus, we find that during meditation the finest ability of the sense of perception is put to use, whereas ordinarily in our daily life we continue to use only the gross levels of the senses.

When the mind makes use of the finest level of the senses, the whole range of the senses becomes alive. In this manner, on the way to transcending during meditation, the mind enlivens all the levels of sense through which Transcendental Meditation is carried on. When the full range of the whole field of the senses is made alive, Being comes to the level of the senses. The resulting increase in strength and power is capable of gaining the highest level of happiness, but as long as a small portion of the sense is utilized for the purpose of experiencing the objective world, the faculty of the sense of experience is not fully used. In such a state, the senses are captured by the small joy of the object.

In the gross level of creation, the contact of the sense and the object does not produce great joy. The degree of joy increases as the sense appreciates the subtler levels of creation. During the process of Transcendental Meditation, when the organ of speech experiences subtler levels of thought, the charm increases at every subtler level of experience. As the charm increases, the organ becomes more capable of experiencing increased happiness, and, eventually, when the direct perception of the subtlest state of thought takes place, it has become capable of experiencing the highest degree of happiness in the relative field.

When the mind transcends that happiness and goes completely beyond the realm of sensory perception, the bliss of the Absolute is a direct experience and the mind completely becomes It. When a mind fully saturated with Being comes back into the field of objective experience, the sense which had, through the process of meditation, tasted the greatest degree of happiness in the relative field, becomes saturated with the bliss of absolute Being and remains contented. This is how the transcendental bliss of Being comes to the level of the senses.

The art of bringing the level of Being, the art of bringing eternal contentment to the level of the senses, is the art of Transcendental Meditation. This is the art of enabling the senses to experience the object in its unbiased and unprejudiced states.

This is how, by making use of the subtler levels of the senses, the mind is able to experience the subtle states of creation. Generally, the conscious mind uses only the gross level of the senses. Just as the mind is like an ocean of great depth, the field of the senses also has great depth. With meditation, the mind begins to make the deepest level of the senses active.

This is how the whole range of the senses becomes alive. Eventually the senses reach their source, and from there they are as though fed into the value of transcendental absolute Being. This system of Transcendental Meditation is a way to bring the level of Being into the senses, enabling them to work with their full capacity and at the same time to be free from the binding influence of experience. Thus we find the art of Being on the level of the senses.

The Body and the Art of Being

The body is the end organ or the external expression of the nervous system. Therefore, the art of Being with regard to the body means the art of Being with regard to the nervous system to an even greater extent, so that the body functions to its fullest capacity without losing the level of Being.

The art of Being, with regard to the body, also means the technique of maintaining it so that the nature of Being is infused into the nature of the body — the permanent, never-changing, undying nature of Being is infused into the impermanent, ever-changing, ever-dying nature of the body.

We will see in the next part on "The Nervous System and the Art of Being"[24] that through the practice of Transcendental Meditation a state of nervous system is created such that the entire nervous system is brought to a level of no activity and no passivity. By bringing the nervous system to this level between activity and no activity, Being comes to the level of the body. This is the art of Being with regard to the body. The entire nervous system and the body rise to that state of suspension[25] which knows no change and allows the body to exist in the fullness of life. The study of the art of Being with regard to the body will be complete when we have dealt with the art of Being with regard to the nervous system, senses, and the *Prāṇa*, all of which are essential parts of the body.

When we go into the details of this study, we should have clearly in mind that Being in Its essential nature is pure Bliss Consciousness, the unmanifested Absolute. As a matter of fact, looking at Being from the absolute point of view, we see that It cannot be qualified by any attribute whatsoever; It is attributeless. On the other hand, from the relative point of view it can be seen that all the attributes of relative life have Being at their basis; all the attributes of the different phenomena in the relative field of existence have their basis in Being.

When we consider the art of Being with regard to different aspects of the body, we must be clear in our minds that the art of Being in any aspect of the

---

24 See page 113.
25 It is up to the experimental physiologists to discover the details of the physiology of an evolving man. This is possible now with the advent of Transcendental Meditation where subjects for research are available. In almost every part of the world people who are practicing the system of Transcendental Meditation are naturally allowing their nervous systems to be conditioned in this laudable state.

body means bringing more permanence, more stability, more health, more joyfulness, more creativity, and more life energy. It must be based in a state of greater attunement with the Laws of Nature so that the influence in the surroundings strengthens the purpose of Natural Laws and creates greater harmony in the universe. The art of Being, then, for any particular aspect of the body would mean that the aspect is strengthened for its life, for its value, for the individual, and for the universe as a whole.

Through the art of Being, with regard to the body, the body is maintained in such a manner that it lasts longer, is energetic, lively, free from diseases, and its different parts function in good coordination with one another. The body's coordination with the mind through the nervous system is always strong, and its relationship with the outside surroundings is firm and useful to both the body and the surroundings. The influence that the body produces in the surroundings is harmonious, peaceful, joyful, and healthy.

In order that such a condition of the body may be created, it is necessary that the mind be brought to the level of Being, so that the nervous system, along with its end organ, the body, is simultaneously established on the level of Being. We have seen that through the system of Transcendental Meditation the body is brought to a state of activity and no activity[26] — the level of Being. Thus the art of Being with regard to the body finds its fulfillment in the regular practice of Transcendental Meditation.

The Nervous System and the Art of Being

The art of Being with regard to the nervous system means that the nervous system should function to its fullest capacity under all conditions without losing Being.

Before we proceed further it will be of interest to note that for any experience to be possible the nervous system is required to set itself in a particular state or condition. Whatever be the experience in any state of consciousness — waking, dreaming, or sleeping — it is possible only by virtue of a corresponding setup of the nervous system. The vision of a flower is possible only

26 See page 289, "Physiological Approach to God-Realization."

because the nervous system sets itself in a specific condition which makes it possible for the eyes to remain open and for the image of the flower to enter upon the retina of the eye and the necessary impulses to reach the cortex. If the nervous system does not condition itself in the required manner, then the experience of the flower will not occur. This conditioning of the nervous system holds true for all experiences.

The art of Being with regard to the nervous system is such that whether the nervous system is subjected to the conditions of the wakeful, dreaming, or deep-sleep states, it should never deprive itself of that state which it gains during the experience of pure Being. This is the art of Being with regard to the nervous system.

At first, this retention of the state of pure Being seems impossible because experience shows that the nervous system cannot be subjected to two different conditions simultaneously for two different states of consciousness to be experienced. It can only be subjected to one state at a time, either wakeful, dreaming, deep sleep, or transcendental. But a close scrutiny will reveal that it is within the capacity of man to subject the nervous system to a state which will for all time maintain the level of Being as the very basis of all the conditions responsible for giving rise to the experiences of any of these states — wakeful, dreaming, or deep sleep. The human nervous system is the most complete in the Almighty's creation.

The skill that accomplishes such a permanent state of nervous system — the state which maintains the level of Being and yet allows the experiences to occur — is the art of Being with regard to the nervous system.

What is this art in practice?

To give rise to the experiences of the wakeful state, the mind is brought to express itself in the outside world through the machinery of the nervous system. It stimulates the senses and the body, brings the mind in contact with the world around it, and produces the specific experience. When, due to sustained activity like this, the senses and the entire nervous system connected with them become fatigued, the mind loses contact with the senses and the outside world. This puts an end to the experiences of the wakeful state.

As long as the mind is discontented it continues to be active. But, when the nervous system on the level of the senses is tired, it fails to experience the outside world of the wakeful experiences; yet, because of the mind's desire to be active, some other part of the nervous system receives the mind's commands. The other part of the nervous system then becomes active and stimulates the subtler regions of the senses which are not commonly used for the experiences of the wakeful state. This gives rise to the illusionary experiences of the dream state. When they function on this illusionary level for some time, the subtler regions of the nervous system become tired and the ability of perception of the illusionary experiences is lost and gives rise to a state of no experience, that of deep sleep.

During Transcendental Meditation, however, the nervous system is naturally subjected to a condition which is unlike the conditions which give rise to the experiences of wakeful, dreaming, or sleep states. In this condition it is capable of giving rise to the experiences of pure Being. This experience of pure Being is said to be the experience of Transcendental Consciousness or, to be more exact, the very state of Transcendental Consciousness.

This is how, through the practice of Transcendental Meditation, the nervous system, which is commonly fluctuating only between the conditions of wakefulness, dreaming, and deep sleep, receives a new status. This status, if closely scrutinized, could be located at the junction of any two of the three states of consciousness.[27] Here, at this point, lies the hope for attaining the art of Being on the level of the nervous system.

Because the state of the nervous system which gives rise to the experience of Being is a state unlike those which give rise to the experiences of the waking, dreaming, or sleeping states, because it is located between any two of the three states, because it is a state where the entire nervous system is suspended between activity and inactivity, and because in none of the three states is the

---

27 Refer to "The Main Principle of Transcendental Meditation" on page 30, where it is explained in detail how, by following the thought in its infant states, the conscious mind arrives at Transcendental Consciousness. This explains that the state of this transcendental Being is located in its purity between the rising of two thoughts. Using similar steps it is easy to find that at the end of the subtlest aspect of the wakeful state, prior to the beginning of the subtlest aspect of the dreaming state, lies the transcendental state of pure Being, or, between the consciousness of the wakeful state and that of the dreaming state, lies the state of pure consciousness.

entire nervous system subjected to one type of conditioning, it is possible to maintain the state of the nervous system necessary for the state of Being in a permanent way by allowing the activity or inactivity in certain parts of the nervous system to give rise to the experience of the usual states of waking, dreaming, and sleeping, one after the other. This is the art of Being with regard to the nervous system, which finds its fulfillment in the sustained practice of Transcendental Meditation.[28]

The Surroundings and the Art of Being

While discussing "How to Make Full Use of the Surroundings,"[29] we have seen that by the system of Transcendental Meditation, when the mind is brought to the level of Being and then comes out to behave in the outer world, the atmosphere radiates in the value of Being.

The art of Being, with regard to the surroundings, means that Being maintains Itself whatever the surroundings or circumstances. This means the fullness of life is maintained irrespective of the value of the surroundings — whether the surroundings are good or bad, favorable or unfavorable, harmful or useful, virtuous or sinful. Under all circumstances, Being, the fullness of life, of intelligence, love, joyfulness, and energy is maintained. This is the maintenance of Being in relation to the surroundings, which results in the improvement of the surroundings in every way. It makes the surroundings useful for the individual for the purpose of cosmic evolution and for the universe. This is what is meant by improving the quality and status of the surroundings. This is the art of Being.

If the individual maintains his Being under all circumstances and in all surroundings, his actions definitely improve the surroundings should they need improvement. Because to be established in Being means to be established in great contentment with great intelligence and creativity.

---

28 See page 29.
29 See page 69.

Karma and the Art of Being

The philosophy of *Karma*[30] is a simple philosophy of action and reaction. "As ye sow, so shall ye reap." The law of conservation of energy supports the theory of *Karma*. Every action that one performs has its results or reaction for the doer and for the surroundings.

When one thinks, the process of thinking is the performance of the action of thinking. Similarly, speaking, acting, behaving, or experiencing something are all different levels of performance of action.

When we throw a stone in a pond, the stone sinks but leaves waves in motion on the surface. The waves travel until they reach the shore, where they strike against the sand particles and produce an influence on them, either by pushing them away or bringing them into the pond. The influence is everywhere, all over the pond and on the shore. This is how the action produces reaction, influence, or effects in the doer and in the surroundings.

Through every thought, word, and action, a man produces waves of influence in the surrounding atmosphere. The quality of the influence depends upon the quality of the action performed; the degree of reaction spread in the surroundings depends upon the strength of the action performed. Thus we find that every moment of life produces some influence in the atmosphere by the actions of breathing, thinking, speaking, and behaving in the world.

We now shall see how far the influence of an action spreads. As in the case of the pond, the influence of a wave, however small it may be, extends over the whole pond. Similarly, the vibrations set forth by the performance of an action travel around the doer, striking against everything in the surroundings, traveling far and wide. They strike against everything on Earth, on the Moon, the Sun, and the stars, and keep on traveling in the entire field of the universe, influencing everything that they come across. How

---

30 *Karma* is a term which has its varied meanings according to context, such as: action, force of action, fruit of action, or impression of the experience or action. Generally, in the West, *Karma* is associated with bad action and the results of bad action. But the word "*Karma*" has no evaluation of good or bad; it simply pertains to action or activity. Good *Karma* means good action, and bad *Karma* means bad action, but *Karma* itself means action.

they influence depends upon the quality of the action and the force of performance.

The reaction created by the striking of these vibrations against different things in the universe travels back to the doer as a rubber ball thrown against a wall bounces back to the player. Obviously, a reaction returns to the doer more quickly from the nearby surrounding area but takes a longer time to come back from great distances.

For example, a man says a word. By saying this word he produces vibrations around him. These vibrations go out and strike against a tree and, producing some influence there, they return to the speaker. They go out and strike against a mountain. To return to the speaker from the mountain it takes more time. They strike the Moon and their return takes an even longer time; likewise, reaching the Sun and returning to the doer will take much more time. There are stars in the heavens whose light takes millions of years to reach the Earth. Therefore, for the influence of an action to reach those far distant stars in the galaxies and to return to the doer will take millions of years. This shows how an action performed has its reaction on the doer. It spreads its influence in the entire cosmos, and, in return, the doer is influenced by the deed performed by him.

The question arises then, how can the fruit of an action reach the doer after thousands or millions of years? The life of man is only a few years of time, perhaps one hundred years. How does the reaction produced in the atmosphere return to the doer when he is no longer in this life?

A letter sent by a man a long way from home to his father reaches the home, and if, when it reaches the home, the father has gone on to another town, it is redirected to him there. If the father has traveled still farther to yet another town, it is again redirected to him. The letter is repeatedly redirected as long as the father is traceable. If the father is no longer traceable, and if his son or nearest relation could be traced, the letter will go to the heir. Blood affinity is the agency through which the reaction reaches the doer.

If an action is performed now of which the influence will reach the doer in a thousand years, that influence will reach that soul wherever in the universe it may be. Those who do not understand the philosophy of rebirth and continuity of life after death will not be able to understand this philosophy of *Karma*. How can an action performed now continue to yield results or reactions for millions of years and its influence keep on coming to the doer wherever and in whatever life he may be?

As long as the soul is not liberated, as long as the individual soul has not merged itself into Cosmic Existence, so long will the individuality be held by the soul in whatever world or body it may be. The individual will continue to exist as an individual and will continue to receive the fruits of the *Karma* that he has done in the past.

When a man is liberated and when the individuality has merged into Cosmic Existence, then the influence of the *Karma* done by him in the past will be received by his son or grandson or by those who have blood affinity with him. But the reaction will never become nil; it will be carried on. And if there is no one left in his family, then the influence will reach those who are nearest to his blood relations — their friends and connections.

The *Karma*, the reaction, or the fruit of action, unfailingly reaches the doer just as a calf reaches its own mother in a herd of a thousand cows. Even if there is a large number of cows in the herd, the calf will go only to its own mother. Just as a letter addressed to a man reaches only him and no one else, the fruit of action reaches the doer and no one else. That is why the proverb: "As ye sow, so shall ye reap."

This philosophy of *Karma* explains that whatever a man is, it is the result of his own past. If he is happy, it is the result of good doings in the past. It is the result of his having produced good, happy, and harmonious vibrations in the atmosphere in the past by his virtuous deeds. If a man is suffering in the present, it is a result of his own actions which had at one time spread an influence of misery, ill health, and suffering in the atmosphere.

None other than himself is responsible for a man's happiness or suffering. If a man enjoys, he enjoys out of his own doings; if a man suffers, he suffers out of his own doings.

If a man — call him Mr. X — comes to us and is very happy and good-natured and brings us much joy, we think he is nothing but a bundle of happiness. But the philosophy of *Karma* says that Mr. X is only a bundle of happiness to you because he is at that time delivering to you the happiness that you once spread in the world. The reaction of your good *Karma* is coming through him. He is only making a delivery to you, just as a postman delivers a letter addressed to you. Had Mr. X actually been a bundle of happiness, then he would not be an unhappy companion to some others on some other side of his life.

If a man seems to be good to some and bad to others, he could not be all good or he would be good to everyone. If he is all bad, he would be bad to everyone. But no one is all bad and no one is all good. Everyone is part good and part bad. So, the man becomes the carrier of the good or bad *Karma* of other people. If he is the carrier of good to you, he comes and brings happiness. The same man the next day may become a means of unhappiness to you. He is creating unhappiness when he becomes the carrier of your bad deeds, and he brings joy to you when he becomes the carrier of the influence of your good actions. Therefore, when misery comes we do not blame others, and when happiness comes we should for all time maintain equanimity, which is the state of harmony in divine Nature.

Knowing this philosophy of *Karma*, one should always be intent on good. How may we determine what is good and what is bad? Roughly speaking, society tells us this is good and this is bad; there is a common understanding among the people regarding good and bad to guide their actions. The laws governing one's country provide one criterion of good and bad; one might at least follow the law of the land in order to be right in one respect.

If we want to go a little deeper into the value of good and bad, then we should study the scriptures of our religions. If we belong to Hinduism, the scriptures of Hinduism tell us what is right and wrong. If we belong to Christianity, the scriptures of Christianity tell us what is right and wrong. And if we belong to Buddhism, the scriptures of Buddhism tell us what is right and wrong.

We should not go into the details of how the religious scriptures differ from one another; we should rather confine ourselves to the religion to which we belong. The great truth is present in the scriptures of all religions. Therefore, the followers of one religion may read the scriptures of other religions, but it is better not to become confused with the issue of the value of religion. It is better to follow the scriptures of one's own religion.

So the scriptures may be taken to be the criterion of what is good and what is bad. Sometimes it may be found that the statements in the scriptures appear contradictory. This is quite possible because, in the relative field of life, values change according to the time, circumstances, and surroundings. When we talk in terms of good and bad in the relative field, perhaps the good at one place at one time may be declared bad at another time. In this way the understanding of good and bad, even in the scriptures, may be found to be different pertaining to the difference in the doer, in time, in circumstances, and in surroundings. But a great deal of wrong would be prevented if we followed the scriptures even according to our limited understanding. It is better to follow the scriptures according to our understanding rather than not follow them at all.

We would live the absolute good in our life, but where will the criterion of absolute good be found? Who will tell us how we should mold ourselves, our surroundings, and our associates in order to live a life of absolute good?

If we want to have an absolute standard of right and wrong, it is available to us. There is a way to it that also is in accordance with the philosophy of *Karma*. We shall see how *Karma* or action may be based on the level of absolute good.

Before trying to find a *Karma* through which the whole stream of life may be put on a level of all good, we shall try to understand what we mean by good or bad. What do we mean by virtue or by evil?

Any action that produces a good influence for the doer in the present and secures good in the future, along with a good influence in all fields of the surroundings, is certainly a good action. Any action through which a life-supporting influence is produced for the doer in the present and future and which has the same good influence for the surroundings will certainly be an act of virtue, a good action, a virtuous deed. Any action which produces life-damaging influence for the doer either in the present or in the future, or for the surroundings or for any level of life in the surroundings, will be called bad, wrong, sinful, and immoral.

Thus we have the criterion of right action and wrong action. The action should result in all good to the doer and to the universe for the present and for all times. This is the absolute definition of good and bad.

We have seen that the influence of an action is not restricted to the doer and the present time alone. It influences the present and future of the doer and the whole universe. Then who is able to decide what influence is produced by an action of a man at a particular time? Who can know which particular stratum of the universe it will affect and what reaction it will have at any particular time in the future, at any particular level of creation? The range of the influence of an action is fathomless. It ranges between all limits of time, space, and causation. Therefore, the influence of an action goes beyond the range of the human mind. No one can say what action performed by a man at a particular time in a particular place will produce an effect in any level of creation at a particular time.

To fathom the whole influence of *Karma* is beyond the scope of the human mind. If this is the case, who can say what is right and what is wrong? Who can say what action is worthy of performance and what action is worthy of rejection?

Certainly it does not seem possible to know precisely and understand on an intellectual basis what is right and what is wrong, and even if the right or wrong were known, it would be highly complicated. But it seems to be possible to adjust the whole stream of life in such a way that every action performed by the doer is naturally a good or right action. We shall analyze this and discover how the whole stream of life could be conducted in such a manner that every thought, word, and action of a man will naturally be good for the doer and produce a good and life-supporting influence for the entire cosmos.

The life of the universe means its maintenance and steady growth in evolution. All the maintenance and evolution of innumerable beings on all the innumerable strata of creation are carried on by a natural, automatic process governed by Natural Laws. We have seen, in the part on "Cosmic Law,"[31] that on the basis of the eternal, never-changing Cosmic Law, all the

---

31 See page 10, "Being, the Plane of Cosmic Law."

Laws of Nature, rigid in their character, continue to function on different planes and maintain and evolve all beings. The whole cosmic process of evolution is carried on by the Laws of Nature, which ultimately are based on the Cosmic Law.

If there were a way to channel the life stream of an individual to the plane of Cosmic Law, then the entire process of maintenance of the individual life and all its progress and evolution would be carried on in a very natural and automatic manner. If there were a way to systematize and regulate one's life to make it run in accordance with the Laws of Nature, then all thought, speech, and action of the individual would produce an influence according to the Laws of Nature working for the maintenance and evolution of all beings.

We have seen in the part on "Cosmic Law" that, by the regular practice of Transcendental Meditation, the mind of the individual can be brought in tune with the transcendental, absolute pure consciousness which is the plane of the Cosmic Law. We have also seen that the process of Transcendental Meditation is a simple process which may be practiced by any man, anywhere, at any time.

This brings hope to every man in the world that he might attune his life with the Natural Laws which maintain life and sustain the individual's regular progress and evolution. He then produces through his thought, word, and action, an influence of good for himself and for all others, for the present and for all times.

This is the philosophy of *Karma* which reveals to us the unlimited scope of *Karma*, the ever-increasing influence of *Karma* for the doer. It reveals to us that, even though the range of the fruit of action is far beyond the reach of human understanding, by the performance of the action (*Karma*) of Transcendental Meditation we can put ourselves on a plane of life where anything done by us will naturally be in harmony and in rhythm with Cosmic Life and will be helpful to the maintenance and evolution of all beings all over the universe. This is a way to be able to *do* all good by *being* all good.

So when, by the practice of Transcendental Meditation, Being is brought out from the transcendental field to the field of relative existence (by Its becoming infused into the very nature of the mind), *Karma* becomes a *Karma* of absolute righteousness.

Here is a direct and practical way revealed by the philosophy of *Karma* to do all good for all times for all beings and yet live a life in absolute freedom from the binding influence of *Karma*.

Now we shall deal with bondage and freedom with regard to *Karma*. How can the doer be free from the binding influence of *Karma*? Before we deal with this, however, we should understand clearly what it is.

Being is unmanifested in Its nature, and *Karma* is manifested. It is *Karma* which makes Being manifest, and therefore unmanifested Being in Its essential nature, being transcendental, absolute, is opposed to the nature of *Karma*. *Karma* is temporary, perishable. Being is eternal, absolute. Being is pure consciousness of absolute nature. *Karma* is based on conscious mind. By virtue of *Karma*, the pure consciousness of Being is transformed to conscious mind. Being is eternal unity in Its nature; *Karma* makes the unity diversified by creating multiplicity in the unity. Thus we find that the nature of *Karma* is opposed to the nature of Being. Being is the source of *Karma*, and *Karma* challenges the validity of Being. This is the fundamental relationship between Being and *Karma*. Previously we have seen that the nature of the mind is overshadowed by the experience, the doer is overshadowed by his doing, the thinker is overshadowed by a thought, and this overshadowing of the essential nature of the mind is said to be the binding influence of action or *Karma*.

With the practice of Transcendental Meditation, however, the mind of the doer is fully infused with the value of Being and the doing fails to overshadow the nature of the doer. The doer then maintains his Being, his essential nature, and the doing is done in such a way that it fails to overshadow the nature of the doer. Then the doer is said to remain unbound by the doing, and the action is said not to bind the doer. This is how, by gaining Being, *Karma* fails to bind.

It is not possible to do away with *Karma*. Action has to be performed because life means activity: the very nature of life is dynamic. Thus, it is not physically possible to deter *Karma* or to escape from the action. We have seen that unless Being grows into the nature of the mind it is impossible to not be bound by action and its fruits.

Freedom from *Karma* is gained by gaining the status of eternal Being. Thus we see that by the action of Transcendental Meditation it is possible to create a situation within ourselves so that naturally we shall be always doing good for ourselves and producing good influences on the entire universe. At the same time, it is also possible to rise above the binding influence of action and live a life of eternal freedom on Earth. This is the philosophy of *Karma*. It not only deals with right and wrong and the far-reaching influence of action but also suggests a technique to rise above the binding influence of *Karma*. Over and above this, the philosophy of *Karma* also deals with weak and strong states of action and provides a technique to make *Karma* strong for more powerful and successful results. This we shall consider now.

Naturally a weak action will produce a weak effect, and a strong action will produce a strong effect. The strength of action depends primarily upon the strength of thought. We have seen that when the source of thought comes within the conscious capacity of the mind, the thought force becomes infinitely great. This shows that the technique of making an action forceful is to direct our attention to the source of thinking, which is the field of Being.[32]

Based on infinitely powerful thought, an action will likewise be infinitely powerful, and the influence or the fruit of such an action will naturally be powerful. Therefore, in order to produce a powerful result and enjoy the great fruit of our actions, it is necessary to take the mind to the field of Being, or by the practice of Transcendental Meditation, to infuse Being into the nature of the mind so that the conscious mind is always full with the value of Being. When the mind is infused with the power of Being, the creativity of the mind is infinitely great and, at the expense of very little energy, very powerful actions may be performed to bring in the desired fruits.

This is a technique which permits the doer to enjoy the fruits of his action at the expense of the least possible amount of energy and to produce an infinitely great influence of peace and harmony and life-supporting effect

---

32 See page 88, "Thinking and the Art of Being."

on the entire universe. This is the skill of action which lies in bringing our attention to the source of thought, or, by regular practice of Transcendental Meditation, infusing Being into the nature of the mind and working from the level of Being.

Karma, or action, from the level of Being or at the level of Being, has infinite value. Obviously, it is done at the least expense of one's energy and the result is the maximum for the doer and for the world. The doer, enjoying the results and living in the plane of Being, remains ever free from the binding influence of *Karma*. This skill in action is what the philosophy of *Karma* teaches us. This naturally develops in the individual through the simple system of Transcendental Meditation, which brings our conscious attention to the field of Being. So when *Karma* is done on the level of Being, then *Karma* helps to fulfill the life's purpose, which is evolution of the highest degree.

The purpose of life is to be in Bliss Consciousness, to evolve to the eternal state of liberation. Accomplishing, achieving, and enjoying the maximum in life, and doing the most good to oneself and to others while rising to a state of eternal freedom is the way of individual life. The philosophy of *Karma* teaches us how, by doing the *Karma* of taking our attention to the field of transcendental Being, we can fulfill our life's purpose and play our part in the cosmic purpose of evolution.

Karma done by the mind which has not practiced Transcendental Meditation is motivated by selfish desires which may or may not be right for the doer and may or may not be right for the entire universe. Certainly the mind which is not on the level of the universal Cosmic Life of Being will be motivated by selfishness and the actions will not be absolutely right for the doer or for the universe. Such a *Karma* produces a strain on the functioning of Natural Laws conducting the process of evolution of all beings. Such a *Karma* is weak; it needs great effort for its accomplishment and brings great tension into the individual life and the surroundings. Above all, it binds the mind; the mind remains bound by this *Karma* and by its fruits.

Therefore, whatever the aim of *Karma*, only one technique of successful *Karma* is able to produce the most effective, most powerful, and best results. That is to draw the mind within, let it reach the field of transcendental Being, and, after returning, think of doing the action and come out to perform the action. The action will thus be strong and good, and its fruit will be gratifying on all levels. At the same time, neither the performance of action nor the fruits of action will bind, and the doer will be eternally free, performing the action in freedom, enjoying the results in freedom, and producing the maximum good for himself and for others.

This is the philosophy of *Karma*, which finds its fulfillment in the simple practice of Transcendental Meditation.

The art of Being with regard to *Karma* lies in maintaining the state of Being irrespective of the type or state of *Karma*. Whatever be the activity, whatever be the *Karma* performed by the mind, senses, body, or the surroundings, Being is eternally maintained. This is the art of Being with regard to *Karma*.

It is the art of Being in the field of *Karma* that, even though *Karma* by nature is opposed to Being, *Karma* itself is brought to the level of Being. Being is maintained in Its status and *Karma* fails to challenge Its validity. When both *Karma* and Being are maintained at the level of the mind, then this is the art of Being and the art of *Karma*, simultaneously. *Karma* and Being find their fulfillment simultaneously in the regular practice of Transcendental Meditation.

Art of Thinking

The art of thinking should mean that the manner of thinking is such that the least amount of mental energy is consumed, whereas the thought expressed is the most powerful thought. The thought is expressed in such a way that it is fulfilled without strain or tension; that is, the energy required for thinking is less, the thought is powerful and its fulfillment is certain. This will be the aim of the art of thinking: the least amount of exertion and the maximum results.

The thought should not only be powerful but it should be right as well. The art of thinking also means that no useless or wrong thought should occupy the mind. By nature, only virtuous and moral thoughts should fill the mind, thoughts that will help evolution. If one knows the art of thinking, such will be his state of mind. Another aspect of the art of thinking is that thoughts should come in such a way so that they do the greatest good for the thinker and spread harmony for the surroundings.

Thinking without art will mean that any thought could come at any time: a useless thought, a wrong thought, a weak thought, a misleading or degenerate thought; these are barriers to evolution.

Evolution will be secured only when the process of loose thinking is replaced by the art of thinking. Then only will thinking be in harmony with the Cosmic Law, the Law of Nature coupled with the purpose of evolution.

The art of thinking should mean that the thought, although it sets the mind in action in the relative field, is able at the same time to leave the mind free from bondage or attachment.[33] The art of thinking will mean that while the thought is made more powerful and more realistic to result in fulfillment, it is simultaneously used to make the mind free. The mind should be in freedom while engaged in the activity of thought. First, it should remain free from the binding influence of thought; second, it should be used as a means for eternal freedom in God Consciousness.

The art of thinking, in its practical application, lies in bringing the mind to the source of thought, picking up the seed of thought in a conscious manner so that while the mind picks up the seed of thought it brings along with it limitless life energy from the field of transcendental Being as well. On one side the thought becomes saturated with Being, and on the other side it becomes a means of bringing transcendental Being of absolute nature into the relative field of multiple phenomenal creation. This is the art of thinking. It becomes a means for transcendental Self-consciousness to grow into Cosmic Consciousness.[34] While the thought brings pure consciousness, Being of the mind, into the relative field of activity, it enables the mind to rise to Cosmic Consciousness, where, along with the activity of thinking, Being will constantly be.

---

33 See page 96, "Experiencing and the Art of Being."
34 See page 36, "How to Live Being."

The art of archery is to draw the arrow back on the bow as far as possible and then to release the arrow, sending it ahead with great force. Likewise, the mind should be drawn back to the source of thinking and, from there, released to bring the thought out in a forceful manner supplemented by the power of Being. It will bring out a powerful thought that will succeed in the relative world, bring the infusion of Being into outside activity, and make possible the state of Cosmic Consciousness. The art of thinking enables a man to be more powerful and more efficient in the field of thinking and action. At the same time it relieves him from the bondage of action, from the bondage of the fruits of action, and from the bondage of the seed of action — the thought.

Thus it is the art of thinking that is the most vital aspect of life because it connects transcendental absolute eternal Being with the outside relative phenomenal phase of existence and secures for man the most highly evolved state of human consciousness — Cosmic Consciousness.

The art of thinking also includes clear thinking. Clarity of thought depends upon the state of mind and the nervous system. The nervous system should not be tired, and the mind should be such that the full mind may act upon the nervous system and express itself in the outer world. Clear thinking is the result of a full mind using a strong nervous system; then thoughts are clear, and thinking is effective.

It is essential that one should be well trained in the art of thinking. All the efficiency of any kind of action depends upon the efficiency of thinking, which in turn depends upon the ability of the mind to catch the thought at its subtlest state. If the thought is picked up at the source of thinking, it is picked up where it is strongest and most vital. The art of thinking lies in drawing the mind back to the source of thought; this is the process of Transcendental Meditation.

Thus the art of thinking lies in: having right thoughts; having useful creative thoughts; having powerful thoughts; having thoughts in such a manner that the thinker is not bound by the influence of thoughts and remains in freedom established in Being. We shall deal with these four points separately.

Right Thought

In the field of thinking, it is extremely necessary that the mind entertain only right thoughts. A right thought will be that which will produce a good, harmonious, useful, and life-supporting influence for the doer and for the entire universe in the present and for all times.

A right thought is a thought which is in accordance with the natural process of evolution and which produces no harmful effect ever, for the doer or for anyone else.

What is the art of thinking that will enable the mind to entertain only constructive thoughts?

We have seen, while dealing with Cosmic Law,[35] that when the mind is in the state of transcendental Being it gains a level of consciousness which is the basis of all the Laws of Nature. Thus we find that the art of bringing the mind to the field of Being or the technique of Transcendental Meditation is that art which will naturally establish the mind in such a state that it will entertain only constructive thoughts.

It does not seem possible to entertain thoughts which are always right by *trying* to think rightly. Any conscious attempt on the part of the mind to entertain only right thoughts will only mean straining the mind on a plane over which there can be no control. In order that the mind succeeds in entertaining only right thoughts, it should be cultured so that by nature it picks up only a right thought. If the mind is not established on the plane of Cosmic Law, then the discontented mind, hindered by shortsightedness, will not succeed in having only right thoughts.

First, there is no way of intellectually ascertaining what thought is absolutely right. Second, even if the rightness of a thought could be judged intellectually, it could be judged only after the thought has already arisen. The thought could then be scrutinized and it could be found out whether it is right or not; but by that time, the thinker and the atmosphere have already been influenced according to the quality of that thought.

Thus it is not possible to be able to entertain only right thoughts unless the mind develops a state within itself whereby it will entertain only right

---

35 See page 10, "Being, the Plane of Cosmic Law."

thoughts. We have already seen[36] that such a state of mind is not only possible but easy for everyone to achieve.

Useful and Creative Thought

Every thought, in the process of its origin and development, needs life energy; this is consumed while the thought is created, and, as it develops, it is appreciated at the conscious level of the mind. So, if the thought is not useful, the life energy consumed is wasted. Because some energy has been consumed, it must produce some influence in the surroundings, and if it is not a useful and creative influence, it will be useless or even harmful. Therefore, it is very necessary that only useful and creative thoughts be entertained by the mind.

People who continuously think, often having a long chain of thoughts which has no bearing upon practical life and only serves to exhaust the mind, are just daydreamers. They are left to become impractical and wasteful thinkers who lose precision and the power of decision in life, to remain in that state of indefiniteness which is a total waste of life energy. Therefore, it is highly important that the thought the mind entertains be useful to the thinker and produce useful influence for the whole creation, both present and future.

A useful thought means that it should be creative and have a constructive purpose in life. A thought is entertained by the mind in order that it may be developed and made use of in the fulfillment of some desire. Thought is only a previous state of action. If the thought is useful, then the action will be useful and there will be a positive gain from it. It would be far more beneficial for the mind to remain contented in the bliss of its own Being rather than to entertain useless thoughts. For, if the mind is established in the state of contentment in the field of Being, then the thought that is right and useful, either for the thinker or for the surroundings, will naturally arise in the mind. To have one such useful thought is by far more valuable than to waste mental energy in entertaining innumerable useless thoughts one after the other.

36 See page 88, "Thinking and the Art of Being."

The art of such thinking lies in the regular practice of Transcendental Meditation, which cultivates the state of Being in the very nature of the mind so that it is always contented in the Bliss Consciousness of absolute Being. Remaining thus contented, the mind only entertains useful thoughts, thoughts that will spring to fulfill the need of the hour for the doer and for all in the surroundings, thoughts that will fulfill the purpose of evolution of the doer and of the entire Cosmic Life.

Powerful Thinking

The art of thinking produces powerful thoughts. In order that the thought may be most powerful, two things seem to be necessary. First, the mind should entertain the thought with its full potential; that is, the power of the full mind should be used in creating and developing a thought. Second, all the forces of Nature should add their strength to that thought; that is, a thought will be the most powerful only when both the thinker and his world put the greatest amount of power available at both ends.

If a thought makes use of the full potential of the mind and is not cherished by the surroundings or atmosphere and is not welcomed by Nature, then the power of thought, even though based on the full potential of the thinker, will not succeed in maintaining its force for its ultimate fulfillment. In order that the mind thinks the thought with its full potential, it is necessary that the mind should be conscious of the thought at its very origin.

We have seen[37] while dealing with the expansion of the conscious capacity of the mind, that when the source of a thought comes within the range of the conscious mind, only then is the conscious capacity of the mind enlarged to its maximum and the full potential of the mind can come into its full use. If, at every stage of the development of the thought, the mind holds the process of development on the conscious level, then the development will be on the basis of the full potential of the mind. This is how, by the practice of Transcendental Meditation, the whole field of the process of thinking is made familiar to the conscious mind.

37 See page 27, "How to Contact Being" and page 29, "Transcendental Meditation."

With regular practice, a state of mind is created so that every thought that originates is supplemented by the full potential of the mind at its origin and at all stages of its development. And along with that, we have seen that the practice of Transcendental Meditation also enables the mind to pick up only right and useful thoughts — thoughts that are the need of Nature, thoughts whose influence will produce good, harmonious, life-supporting influence in accordance with all the Laws of Nature in the whole of the universe.

Therefore, the practice of meditation not only enables the mind to use its full potential naturally in order to make the thought force powerful, but also adds to it the power of all the Natural Laws. This is how a situation might be created by the practice of Transcendental Meditation, wherein every thought is a powerful thought and is therefore naturally accepted by all the Laws of Nature working out the process of evolution.

The practice of Transcendental Meditation creates a natural situation in the mind so that the mind entertains right thoughts, useful thoughts, powerful thoughts, thoughts that are cherished by Nature and whose fulfillment is worked out by all the Laws of Nature.

Thoughts to Liberate the Thinker

The art of thinking also demands that the thoughts should not bind the thinker, but should instead prove to be the means of liberation from bondage.

While considering "Thinking and the Art of Being,"[38] we have seen that when the mind thinks a thought, it identifies itself with the thought. This identification of the mind with the thought overthrows the validity of Being. Such a mind possessed by the thought and devoid of the value of its own Being is said to be in bondage. This mind in bondage is a mind devoid of the value of Being. Therefore, the art of making the mind completely free from the binding influence of a thought or of thinking, lies in the infusion of the state of Being into the nature of the mind, which we have seen is brought about by the practice of Transcendental Meditation.

When the mind, or the thinker, entertains a thought at its origin, the thought becomes a means of liberation. When the thought is ignored at its

38 See page 88.

origin by the thinker until it has developed to a stage where it can no longer be ignored, then it captures the mind, and the mind comes under its influence, becomes bound by it. It is like a child who is properly taken care of in his infancy by his mother and naturally grows up to serve and respect the mother. But if the child is ignored in his infancy, he grows up and ignores his mother, troubles her, and becomes a means of bondage to her.

Thus we find that the art of thinking a right, useful, powerful, and liberating thought of creative value finds its fulfillment in the regular and sustained practice of Transcendental Meditation, through which the mind is freed from the binding influence of action and attains a state of liberation in eternal Being.

Art of Speaking

The art of speaking obviously consists of: speaking with a minimum consumption of energy; speaking rightly; speaking harmoniously; speaking pleasingly; speaking powerfully; speaking usefully; and speaking in such a manner that the speaker remains free from the binding influence of speech.

Now we shall discuss these one by one.

Speaking with a Minimum Consumption of Energy

Speaking with the least consumption of life energy is possible only when thinking is clear and powerful, when there exists a good coordination between the mind and the organ of speech, and when the surroundings and circumstances are favorable to the nature of a thought.

When thinking is clear and powerful, the thought finds no resistance in developing itself into speech; it flows naturally out into speech without requiring any extra effort or energy for its expression. If on the other hand a thought is weak it needs more energy to reinforce it and transform it into speech.

Clarity of mind obviously results in precise thinking, which, in turn, results in precision and clarity of speech. Clear and precise speech certainly consumes much less energy than is needed by loose speech, which is exhausting and exasperating to both the speaker and the atmosphere. Apart from the advantage of consuming minimum energy the precision and clarity of speech has the great advantage of creating a good impression and achieving the purpose of the speaker.

We have seen in the part on "Thinking and the Art of Being"[39] how the process of thinking could be easily made more clear and powerful in order to accomplish the desired goal of precision and clarity of speech, with the minimum consumption of energy.

The coordination between the mind and the organ of speech is another vital factor for minimum consumption of energy while speaking. This necessitates a clear and powerful mind and a normally functioning powerful nervous system capable of bringing the full potential of the mind to bear upon the external world. While dealing with "Mind and the Art of Being,"[40] and "The Nervous System and the Art of Being,"[41] we have seen how it is practically possible to achieve this in a simple way.

The influence of surroundings is another vital factor for minimum consumption of energy while speaking. If the surroundings and circumstances are not favorable to the nature of the thought, then there will be a great deal of hesitation to put the thought into speech, and a great effort will be needed to restrain the thought from bursting forth as speech; this will unnecessarily consume great energy. And again, when it is necessary to give expression to thoughts in unfavorable surroundings, the transformation of thought into speech is a great strain, unnecessarily consuming great energy.

On the other hand, if the surroundings and circumstances are conducive to the thought, the process of transference of thought into speech results in the resurgence of life energy, causing joyfulness and creative intelligence, and becomes a means of gaining energy instead of consuming it — it serves as a regenerating and rejuvenating force. Thus, the art of speaking with min-

39 See page 88.
40 See page 101.
41 See page 113.

imum consumption of energy lies in giving expression to thoughts conducive to the surroundings and circumstances.

The practical formula will be:

Speak according to the time.

Speak in accordance with the surroundings — to the level of conscious receptivity of your surroundings.

Speak in accord with your own circumstances.

Do not speak as and when you feel.

If the surroundings and circumstances at the outset do not seem to be in accordance with the thought, or your own circumstances are not favorable to the thought, the art of speech lies in using such words that will first suit the surroundings and circumstances and then gradually express the purpose. In this manner, the chances may be that, without much extra use of energy, the speech will achieve its purpose in a graceful manner.

Such a manner of speech, however, cannot possibly be cultivated on an intellectual basis, because if one strains himself in trying to adjust the way of speech — measuring and gauging his expressions all the time — he will continuously be straining within himself and will appear unnatural to the surroundings. This will be another means of loss of great energy which will defeat the very purpose.

While dealing with the art of thinking, we have found that a forceful thought from a clear mind in accordance with the surroundings and circumstances is naturally entertained by the mind which is established in the state of Being; moreover, the thought from such a mind very naturally finds its expression in proper speech, with the minimum expense of energy.

The fulfillment of this principle is to be found in the regular practice of Transcendental Meditation, which readily brings the value of Being into the mind while making the surroundings and circumstances favorable.

Speaking Rightly

While dealing with "Right and Wrong,"[42] it will be made clear that a correct evaluation of right and wrong is found in its absolute value only on the plane of Being. Therefore, the art of speaking rightly necessarily has its basis in the plane of Being.

However, the basic considerations of the relative nature of the art of speaking involve the projected art of thinking; so all that is valid for the art of thinking is valid for the art of speech. Right speech has its basis in right thinking.

Speech is the expression of both the heart and mind together. Therefore, for the speech to be right, it is necessary that the man be right in his heart and mind.[43]

Speech is the expression of one's state of evolution. One word from the mouth of a man reveals his inner quality. The softness of speech gives an expression to the culture of the heart, and the logic, imagination, or creativity expressed through the speech reveals the culture of his mind. A man could be screened for his whole state of evolution and development through one word of his speech.

Speech is a very delicate medium between the man and his surroundings. It is highly important for the well-being of the individual and his surroundings that all the people should cultivate the art of speech, because one wrong word spoken gives wrong impressions in the atmosphere. The man may change his attitude, his decision, or his course of behavior, but the word that has gone out of his mouth can never be withdrawn. The influence that he has created in the audience and in the atmosphere around him can never be withdrawn. Therefore, it is highly important that one should know the art of speech and should know how to speak rightly.

Speech is a projection of a thought, and, while the art of speech fundamentally lies in the art of thinking, it is much finer than the art of thinking itself, because every thought that arises in the mind need not be expressed as speech.

---

42 See page 219, "Right and Wrong."
43 See page 101, "Mind and the Art of Being."

Take the example of a businessman who is sitting with a friend in the evening, when suddenly an idea comes to his mind regarding some matter that he had to speak to his manager about the next day. It would be very odd if he began to give expression to his thought right there. This is what is meant by the art of speech being much finer and thus a more advanced art than the art of thinking.

Speech has to be in keeping with the atmosphere. (This point we have also dealt with in the art of thinking.) The thought and its expression as speech should be such that they are welcomed by the surroundings. Hundreds of words unsuitable to the atmosphere will prove futile against one word of value.

Thus the art of speaking rightly gains fulfillment in the art of thinking, together with the skill of proper expression suitable to the atmosphere. This, as has already been said, depends upon the man being right in his heart and mind, and this, as we have seen, is only possible by the infusion of Being into the nature of the mind, which is easily accomplished through the regular practice of Transcendental Meditation.

Speaking Harmoniously

For speech to be harmonious, appropriate, and suitable, thinking has to be clear, sharp, and, at the least, harmless — and, at the best, life-supporting to the whole of the environment.

The greatest art of speech lies in clear thinking and an innocent, simple way of expression. One should express what one feels, provided the thought is suitable to the occasion. If one feels a certain way and if the surroundings will be hurt by the expression of that feeling, then it is better not to speak. It is not right to hide one's feelings; it is right to speak exactly how one feels, but it is the art of speech that demands that a thought not be spoken if it will displease anyone, disturb the surroundings, or produce disharmony in the atmosphere.

Even if "no" is to be said at any point, the art of speech demands that it should be expressed in words that will not be apparently abusive or harsh.

The art of speech lies in truthful speech; yet, at the same time, the truthful expression should not hurt anyone.

Many people think truthfully by nature, and they believe that truthfulness lies in speaking out just what they think. It may be truthful speech, but it is also tactless and displeases the listener and results in a disharmony which mars the very purpose of speech. Even if you have to give a ruling against something, express it in decent words. This quality of kindness and delicacy of the heart develops when the heart begins to melt at the experience of bliss and great happiness of transcendental Being. The heart becomes softer and then, by nature, a man cannot be harsh or displeasing to anyone. Speech will naturally flow in all harmony.

Speaking Pleasingly

This is the technique of the art of speaking: that, although we are truthful in our thinking and speaking, the words that come out must be pleasing, soft, and of good quality. For this, simplicity and an affectionate nature must be developed. It is no use to try to be polite, or soft and kind. No amount of trying will really bring the art of pleasing speech to a man.

The habit of speaking pleasingly lies in cultivating that nature, that politeness, that softness and kindness of heart that will not at any time produce harshness of speech. The speech must be spontaneously truthful and pleasing to those who hear it. This quality can be naturally developed only by regular practice of Transcendental Meditation. Any attempt to try to unnaturally shape the speech so as to sound pleasing makes it artificial and will not produce a smooth and harmonious effect on the listener. Affectation on the part of the speaker results in inner strain for himself and for his listeners.

There are at present many wise teachers training people how to speak. Their teachings bring out some effect in improving the quality of the voice, but these teachers themselves know that there is no way of improving the speech until the tensions of the mind and muscles are released.

The art of the manner of speaking pleasingly does not lie in speaking less or more. It lies in speaking in a simple and natural way, neither trying to minimize nor maximize speech unless it be for political reasons (in politics it is common practice either to speak less or more without any meaning); but even in the field of politics the technique of speaking pleasingly lies in truthful, simple words of expression which will produce the desired effect. Short or lengthy expressions do not have much to do with the impression that they create; it is the sincerity and truth of the speech and the intelligence behind it that make an impression and accomplish the purpose of speech. If the speech is pleasant while it is also purposeful, then such manner of speaking is the fruit of the art of speech. Speech that is pleasing could even make an enemy work for us. Blessed are those who speak sweet words.

The art of speaking pleasingly lies in making the mind and heart full with happiness. This we have seen is effectively possible only by infusing the bliss of Being into the nature of the mind, which is easily accomplished by the regular practice of Transcendental Meditation.

Speaking Powerfully

The power of speech depends on the power of thought, on thorough knowledge of the subject of speech and on purity of heart and mind. It has been seen that purity of heart and mind are gained by increasing the purity of consciousness through the regular practice of Transcendental Meditation.[44] That also helps to increase intelligence and thereby makes a man more capable of a thorough knowledge of the subject of speech.

Speaking Usefully

Speaking usefully is an art belonging naturally to the contented mind and heart; these are easily gained by the development of Bliss Consciousness.

---

44 See page 127, "Art of Thinking."

Speaking in Such a Manner That the Speaker Remains Free from the Binding Influence of Speech

The art of gaining Self-consciousness and rising to the state of Cosmic Consciousness[45] is the art of remaining free from the binding influence of speech.

ART OF ACTION

There is a common proverb in India which says that the success of the work of great men depends upon the purity of their hearts and not so much upon the accessories. This is a proverb of the Sanskrit language; there is much of substance in it.

While dealing with Cosmic Law it has been made clear that when the mind is established in the absolute purity of consciousness, it comes into full coordination with the Laws of Nature. The secret of success is in gaining a favorable influence from the Natural Laws carrying out the process of evolution of all beings. So the art of action would basically be found in the art of Transcendental Meditation, which readily washes away all the impurities of the mind and leaves it in purity and in conformity with the Laws of Nature. Basically, this is the art of action for all success.

In explaining the philosophy of action while dealing with "*Karma* and the Art of Being,"[46] it has been made clear that the art of Being underlies the art of action because the gravity and the power of action depends upon the gravity and power of thinking; that, in its turn, depends upon the gravity and power of Being. If Being is powerful, thinking will be powerful and action will be powerful. If Being is not in the conscious mind, thinking will be lifeless and action will be poor and less effective.

For more effective action, more effective thinking is required, and for more effective thinking, more effective Being is required in the nature of the

---
45 See page 36, "How to Live Being."
46 See page 117, "*Karma* and the Art of Being."

mind. So the basis of the art of action is in the art of Being, the technique of which lies in the practice of Transcendental Meditation.

The quality of any action depends upon the quality of the doer, the circumstances, and the receptivity of the action by the nature surrounding the doer. The doer may be of good quality and possess neat habits and purity of life, be strong in mind and clear-thinking; but if the circumstances and surroundings are not favorable to the action, it will not be fruitful. In "How to Make Full Use of the Surroundings,"[47] it has been considered in detail how, through the practice of Transcendental Meditation, the surroundings and circumstances are made harmonious and conducive to the fulfillment of desire and action.

Another aspect of the art of action is performance of the action with the minimum amount of energy expended and with the maximum amount of work achieved; thus, the efficiency in work is greater. So the quality and quantity of the output of work is greater, while the energy consumption is less.

The least strain and the maximum amount of gain to the doer and to the surroundings is the art of action. Both the individual and universe are amply rewarded by the art of action.

Another aspect of the art of action is the skill in action. Skill in action means that the doer gains great pleasure out of the action but, at the same time, remains free from the binding influence of the action and from the binding influence of its fruits. The skill in action is that the mind of the doer is placed on the level of the bliss and the unlimited creative intelligence of Being so that it remains contented all the time, does more work and accomplishes more in the day-to-day life. By "more" we mean a more efficient and greater amount of work for better and more results. If this is performed while the doer remains in freedom, it is the skill in action or the art of action.

The art of action is such that, although the doer is fully identified with the thought of the work, the process of action, and the enjoyment of the fruit of his action, he yet remains in the state of eternal freedom, saturated in Bliss Consciousness of absolute Being. So the art of action requires that Being be

---

47 See page 69.

saturated into the nature of the mind and, through it, be brought to express the world of forms and phenomena.

Thus, in short, the art of action lies in first fathoming the deeper levels of the ocean of mind and then taking the mind to the source of thinking, the field of Being where the action of thinking starts. This process enables the full potential of the mind to engage in the thought process and, at the same time, fathom the field of Being.

In this way the whole field of thought and action becomes a means for transcendental absolute Being to come into the field of relativity and vibrate through the thought and action. The entire field of thought and action, and its fruit, becomes a pleasure, because the Laws of Nature and all the surroundings are conducive to the fulfillment of desire. It is as if the entire creation takes it upon itself to fulfill the thought and action that arose. The thought becomes a thought of the Divine. Action then becomes a means to fulfill the divine purpose while, at the same time, the purpose of the individual is served to maximum capacity. In the fulfillment of the divine purpose, the purpose of individual life gains a glorious phase.

This is the art of action. It only necessitates diving deep within oneself before the action starts, and the entire process of thought and action thereafter automatically comes out of the mold of the art of action, whereby the action is beneficial for the doer and for the universe and leaves the doer in eternal freedom.

The action should be done for all good to the doer. In this consideration, the safety of the doer should be the first concern; in other words, the doer should not be bound by doing an action. Neither the binding influence of action nor the binding influence of the fruit of action should touch the doer. There is very little conception about the binding influence of action in the world today. The action is done just for the sake of satisfying the sensory level of life. This is because there is very little conception of Being. That is why the action is never thought of in terms of the level of Being and is only taken to exist on the level of the mind, senses, body, and environment. We find that the whole sphere of life today is on a very superficial level.

When we consider the art of living we have to take into account the whole field of life. When we do this we consider Being, thinking, doing, and the atmosphere — all the fields of life. Therefore the range of action has to be considered not only in terms of its completion and fruitfulness, but also in terms of what impressions and influence it creates in the doer and in the outside surroundings.

The main points of the art of action are the following:

1. The art of performing an action with the least amount of energy expended
2. The art of performing an action in the least amount of time
3. The art of performing only useful action
4. The art of performing an action to produce the most effective and desirable results
5. Fixity of purpose in performance of action for the most effective and desirable results
6. The art of performing and completing the action without harming anyone
7. The art of performing an action to yield maximum results
8. The art of performing an action so that the performance remains pleasant and does not become a tiring or tedious task
9. The art of proper planning of action
10. The effective execution of the plan

We shall take the items one by one and deal with them thoroughly, because the art of action is the primary constituent of the art of living.

The Art of Performing an Action with the Least Amount of Energy

In order to perform an action with the least amount of energy, it is first necessary that the thought of the action be powerful. A weak thought will necessitate a great amount of exertion to accomplish the action, whereas a powerful thought will easily find its way to materialization. A highly developed power of thought, as we have seen while dealing with "Thinking and the Art of Being,"[48] comes through the process of Transcendental Medita-

48 See page 88.

tion. So, in order to be successful in the field of action, it is first necessary that the power of thought be great. For this, one must regularly practice Transcendental Meditation.

The surroundings and circumstances should also be favorable for its performance. That is, the surroundings should also feel the need of the action and hope to receive something useful. The surrounding atmosphere then becomes favorable for the performance of an action and its performance becomes easy and harmonious.

The action should be harmless. If it is meant to harm someone, then certainly there will be opposition to its performance in the surroundings, and it would therefore become necessary to exert extra energy to meet this resistance.

The doer should also be powerful and energetic. In the part on "Being, the Plane of Cosmic Law,"[49] we have seen that the practice of Transcendental Meditation takes the mind to the source of all creation, which is the field of limitless life energy. The conscious mind coming directly in tune with the field of limitless life energy gains such a great amount of vitality that any action can be easily handled and performed quickly, without strain, and with great success. If a man is not energetic when he performs an action, he lacks confidence in what he has done and at every moment of the action he is afraid to step forward.

The Art of Performing an Action in the Least Amount of Time

For quick disposal of work, self-confidence, preciseness of decision, and exact thinking are necessary. A great amount of time is lost when one acts without being sure of the results and tries to undo the act again and again in the hope of improving it. This lack of confidence is a great barrier for performance of actions in the least amount of time.

The increasingly fast tempo of modern life necessitates great presence of mind, developed intellect, and an energetic and vital personality. A slow-going process of action does not fit in with the nature of things today.

49 See page 10.

Speed marks the tendency of this age. Anything slow or dull does not belong to the modern times. Those who are not able to keep pace with the fast tempo of modern life create tension in themselves because success in life today demands quick disposal of work. If these qualities are not present in a man by nature, then he does not belong to the modern age and is not able to keep pace with the times. Speed in action is a must for a joyful life in the world of today.

The aspiration of modern man is to live on Earth when the Sun shines during the day and to fly to the Moon at night when it shines on the Milky Way. Success of action demands that man should be energetic, intelligent, quick, and self-confident.

The factor of time is very vital in life. Those who have accomplished great things in the world have been those who valued time in their life. The time of life is limited and a great amount of evolution has to be accomplished for fulfillment of life. Therefore, the factor of time must be valued above everything. Certainly time is the most binding factor in life. It is said that "time and tide wait for no man." Experience shows, however, that if we gain ground in the timeless eternity of absolute Being, then the time serves us most because the absolute existence of unbounded eternity is the source and basis of all time — past, present, and future.

In the part on "Being, the Plane of Cosmic Law,"[50] it has been seen that the life of the individual supplemented by Being becomes free from all types of resistance, inner and outer. Great self-confidence, clarity, and power of mind dawn in the individual and all harmony and favorable influence in the surroundings naturally create a basically congenial atmosphere for an action to be performed in the least amount of time. Thus, the art of performing an action in the least amount of time finds its fulfillment in the infusion of Being into the nature of the mind through the regular practice of Transcendental Meditation.

---

50 See page 10.

The Art of Performing Only Useful Action

The ability to perform only useful action is a very great part of the art of action. If a man has learned the art of action but does not select a useful kind of action, he will meet with a variety of results which may be wrong and painful. Therefore, before one may successfully practice the art of action, it is first necessary to acquire the ability to select proper action. This is the first step to useful and beneficial action.

When we consider the fields of useful action, we come across the different states of consciousness wherein different types of actions are supposed to be useful.

The usefulness of an action differs from man to man, depending upon the state of his consciousness. No action in life can be said to be absolutely useful unless it is performed on the level of absolute consciousness. Every action in the world may be regarded as useful from some angle, but, from other points of view, it may be considered completely useless. When we are considering the ability to perform only useful action, we can only think in relative terms of usefulness to the doer and to his surroundings.

Thus, it seems that a man normally has the ability of performance of only right action, only useful action. But a deeper consideration of the usefulness of an action for the doer and the surroundings leads us to the conclusion that there could be an action which the doer likes, the fruit of which may be cherished by him, but yet may be harmful or antagonistic to some others in his vicinity or far from him. When the action is only partially useful, it cannot be called a really useful action.

For example, a thief commits a theft and quickly collects great wealth. This is apparently an action whose results the doer enjoys. In a minute the thief is able to put another man's money in his pocket, but this means of collecting money is certainly not cherished by the surroundings. Such an act is called a selfish act, sinful, and wrong; it is useful for the doer, but only useful on the gross considerations of life. But, considering the subtle aspects of the issue, this action is not useful even for the doer.

The ability to perform only useful actions means that the individual will perform only such actions that will be useful to himself as well as for others.

The selection of such actions will depend upon the heightened consciousness of the individual. If the individual has the vision to distinguish between right and wrong, to foresee the results of his action, that vision alone will make him select a proper action which will be useful to the doer and whose effects will also be enjoyed by all others.

We have seen in the considerations of "The Surroundings and the Art of Being"[51] that it is only by the system of Transcendental Meditation, when the individual mind is set in tune with the Cosmic Law, that one's action and behavior come in tune with the stream of evolution. Only then is the ability to perform useful action attained by the individual.

We have also seen that it is not possible to determine the absolute usefulness of an action on the intellectual level. What action will be permanently useful for the doer and produce a good, harmonious, life-supporting influence in the surroundings? As we have seen, this is difficult to know on the level of the intellect. Therefore, the ability to perform only useful actions lies basically in attuning oneself with Cosmic Law. Everyone has this ability, and it is easily put to use through the practice of Transcendental Meditation.

The Art of Performing Action to Produce the Most Effective and Desirable Results

For proper ability to perform action to produce the most effective and desirable results, a man has to have the following:

1. Strong thought force
2. Great energy
3. Favorable surroundings and circumstances
4. Ability to perform right action
5. Self-confidence

We shall deal with these one by one and see how one can develop these qualities within one's self and one's surroundings in order to perform action to produce the most effective and desirable results.

51 See page 116.

Strong Thought Force

A strong power of thinking depends upon four factors: the ability to use one's full mental potential; the ability to concentrate; the capacity of conserving mental energy; and a good coordination of mind and nervous system. We shall see how these can be cultivated.

Full Mental Potential. In "How to Live Being,"[52] we have seen that through the practice of Transcendental Meditation it is easily possible for anyone to use his full mental potential.

Concentration. The ability to concentrate depends upon the nature of the mind. It is the general conception that the ability to concentrate depends upon the quality, power, or strength of the mind. However, the ability to concentrate in actuality depends upon the degree of joy or happiness which the point of attention is able to provide the mind. If a rose is beautiful, the mind will be concentrated on that in a natural way. If the rose is for some reason not fascinating and attractive, the mind will not remain concentrated on it. Anything that is charming attracts the mind. It remains concentrated longer if the point of attention is capable of providing greater charm and greater happiness. Everyone's mind has the power of concentration to any limit. It is not necessary for the mind to *acquire* it because it is already there in the mind. No one's mind will rest on something that is ugly or that does not provide any happiness. But everyone's mind will be attracted to something which is charming and joyful. Therefore, everyone has the power of concentration to any extent.

It is the common experience, however, that the mind does not remain concentrated at any particular point. The reason for this is that, wherever the attention goes, the point of attention fails to provide great happiness to the mind and the mind wants to go to another field of happiness. Because there does not seem to be a point of such great joy in the world that can always satisfy the mind's thirst for happiness, the mind does not seem to remain concentrated at any point. It is always seeking something — some variety, something of greater happiness. When such is the situation that nothing is

---

52 See page 36.

able to satisfy the mind's thirst for happiness, is it possible for the mind to remain one-pointed and concentrated? The answer is, yes. It is possible only when the mind can be based on something which satisfies its thirst for happiness. If the mind could find the greatest happiness of a permanent nature it would stay concentrated.

From the time of birth the mind has been flickering about in transitory joys; this is the reason it seems that, by nature, the mind is wandering. In general, it has been thought that the mind is like a monkey, jumping about from branch to branch. Since wandering has been accepted as being the nature of the mind, to effect a change in its nature from wandering to steadiness has been thought to require that the mind and desires be controlled. However, wandering is not the nature of the mind, and it is not necessary to control it in order to make it steady. It would be right to say that the nature of the mind is to remain steady.

If a honeybee is flying here and there in search of a honeyed flower, it should not be thought that flying is its nature. It is flying with the purpose of remaining steady at a flower; it will wander as long as it does not find a flower containing honey. But as soon as the flower is found, the bee immediately will alight on it.

There is a purpose to the flying. It is not the nature of the bee to fly; rather its nature is to be at a flower and to draw out the honey.

Similarly, the mind wanders, but it is not wandering by nature. It wanders because it does not find a place to rest or a medium of happiness. The mind is not like a monkey; rather it is like a king. Everyone's mind is like the king of kings. It will go to a place it likes to go, it will do the job that it likes, it will stay where it likes to stay. If a king is found wandering about in his country, it is wrong to conclude that wandering is his nature. He is wandering only in the absence of a throne to sit upon. In the absence of the proper seat — a throne — the king keeps walking about.

No respectable man will sit in an untidy place not worthy of him. So, although it is not the nature of the king to keep wandering, he will do so even though he feels tired. He will not sit until he can sit on a seat that is worthy of him.

Similarly, the mind, like the wandering king, will not rest in any place not worthy of it, and will not want to remove itself from a place that is worthy of it and which provides greater charm, joy, and happiness. Such a place is where the mind rests, sits, enjoys, and remains enjoying. Thus, it is wrong to conclude that wandering is the nature of the mind.

Any work done in accordance with our nature pleases us. Anything done against our nature displeases us. If our nature is to run about then we feel better when we are allowed to run about. If our nature is to sit, we feel happier when we are allowed to sit. If our nature is to sit and we are asked to run about, naturally we become miserable and tense.

We find in the case of any mind which does not have a place to rest, which does not have a medium of enjoyment and is made to run about, that it begins to feel miserable and tense. If wandering were the nature of the mind then it would feel happier if it were allowed to wander about more and more. Contrary to this, however, we find that when anyone's mind does not have a place to rest, when it does not have its desires fulfilled, it begins to feel restless. Since we have seen that wandering is against the nature of the mind, the true nature of the mind is to remain steady. In order to make the mind remain concentrated in one place it is only necessary to provide it with something it likes. When something charming is given to it, the mind remains steady; the state of steadiness of the mind is the concentrated state of the mind.

Thus, we find that it is not the ability of concentration that has to be acquired by the mind, but that the mind has to be led to a place of great joy and happiness where it naturally will remain. The mind generally seems to have lost the ability of concentration because it has been searching for something for a long time. But it is not actually a question of losing the ability to concentrate, because even in the world we find that the mind is able to concentrate on something that is pleasant and joyful while it is not able to concentrate on something which is ugly. This is because it is ugliness that is against the nature of the mind.

Nothing in the field of gross creation is so joyful that it will satisfy for all times the thirst for happiness of the mind. Experience shows that the subtleties of creation are much more charming than the gross. So, if the attention could be led to the subtle fields of creation, and if they could be experienced by the mind by being more charming than the gross strata of creation, they will naturally attract the mind. If there could be a way to lead the attention from the gross to the progressively subtler strata of creation, the mind at every step would find increasing charm. If there were a way of transcending all the relative states of fine creation and getting to transcendental Bliss Consciousness, there the mind would find that great joy which transcends the greatest joy of relative existence and achieve eternal absolute bliss. Having gained this absolute eternal bliss the mind never comes out of it. It holds it to such a degree that Bliss Consciousness becomes infused into the very nature of the mind, and then the mind is Bliss Consciousness. This happens through the practice of Transcendental Meditation, as we have discussed earlier.

When the mind is thus established, it remains steady in itself. It does not need anything else because there is nothing in the relative field of existence that could challenge the validity of absolute Bliss Consciousness. Therefore, once the mind becomes rooted in Bliss Consciousness, that state of eternal contentment becomes the very nature of the mind, and the mind remains steady in itself even when it associates itself with the outer experiences and activity.

The mind is able to remain concentrated only in the state of Bliss Consciousness. Any attempt to cultivate the ability to concentrate amounts to hard work without achievement. The practice of Transcendental Meditation, which is so simple, and which readily brings Bliss Consciousness into the very nature of the mind, is the practical and most suitable way to concentrate.[53] As we have seen, it is not that the ability of concentration is to be gained; a state of Bliss Consciousness has to be created in the mind so that by nature it remains steady and concentrated.

People go into the ascetic way of life thinking that, in the busy life of the world or the life of the householder, the senses are too attracted by the joy of their objects. They believe that, in order to control the mind, the joys of the senses must be sacrificed and that the senses should not be allowed to come in contact with these objects. This belief has led to controlling the mind and

---

53 "When the mind remains concentrated in its own Self, by nature it does not wander about, and, wherever we put the mind, it remains concentrated there" (see page 153).

has given rise to asceticism for all the seekers of truth who want to increase the capacity of the mind. That is not necessary. Straining and controlling the mind become necessary only when we accept the principle that wandering is the nature of the mind. We have seen that the practice of control is not necessary because the mind will be found naturally steady and concentrated if the experience of absolute Bliss Consciousness is brought to it.

There are two ways of keeping a dog at the door. One way is to run after it, forcibly bring it to the door, and tie it with a chain. But this is a difficult job. Even if the dog is tired, it would be pulling against the chain trying to run away. It would be difficult to keep it quiet at the door. The second way of keeping the dog there is not to run after it or tie it, but place some good food for it to eat. The dog will eat the food and choose to remain at the door.

In like manner, it is not necessary to try to control the mind. The best, easiest, and most practical way of allowing the mind to remain concentrated by nature is to put it to the practice of Transcendental Meditation and let it acquire Bliss Consciousness. When the mind remains concentrated in its own Self, by nature it does not wander about, and, wherever we put the mind, it remains concentrated there. In such a state the full mind is applied, and whatever thought comes, it comes out forcefully; whatever action is taken is a forceful action. This is the way to perform an action to produce the most effective and desirable results.

Conserving Mental Energy. We have seen in our consideration that when the mind remains concentratedly established in Bliss Consciousness it does not wander about. This is the way to conserve mental energy.

Mental energy is consumed in great amounts when the mind keeps on thinking and wandering. Every thought, in order to be a thought, consumes quite a lot of mental energy. If thoughts arise one after another, mental energy is being consumed all the time; if fewer thoughts come, less mental energy is consumed. If the mind is established in Bliss Consciousness, it remains contented in itself and does not wander here and there thinking useless thoughts. If one thousand thoughts were being entertained every hour before the mind was established in bliss, and, after it was established, only ten thoughts came in an hour, then every thought would have gained one hundred times more power. Thus, the only way of naturally not wasting mental energy and conserving it for something constructive is the practice of Transcendental Meditation.

Coordination of Mind and Nervous System. In order to have a strong thought force it is necessary that the coordination between the mind and nervous system be well maintained; for this it is necessary that the nervous system should be strong physically and that the mind should also be strong. The physical nervous system is material; the mind is abstract. Concrete physical nervous system and abstract mind. For a strong thought force, the physical as well as the mental aspect should be strong. We have seen[54] that the mind naturally becomes strong with the practice of Transcendental Meditation when the whole of the subconscious becomes conscious.

The physical strength of the nervous system depends upon the food that we eat. The proper functioning of the nervous system depends upon its physical condition, which is controlled by food and exertion. If the food we eat is proper, it keeps the physical state of the nervous system energetic and lively under normal conditions of functioning. If the nervous system of the body is not strained, the nervous system functions normally. But if the body is strained by the flickering attitude of the mind and by a lack of fixity of purpose on the part of the mind, then the nervous system becomes exhausted and stops functioning. In order to maintain a good coordination of body and mind, it is simply necessary that food should be right. If we eat spoiled and stale food, the nervous system becomes weak. If we drink alcohol, for example, the nervous system becomes inactive and dull. If we work too hard, the nervous system becomes tired and does not function normally. This lack of normal functioning makes the coordination of body and mind weak. Therefore, for good, healthy coordination of body and mind, it is necessary that the mind be healthy, and the mind becomes healthy by the power of Being.

The physical state of the nervous system should be intact; right food and drink and regular habits of eating, rest, and activity will make it so. Life

54 See page 27, "How to Contact Being" and page 29, "Transcendental Meditation."

should be regulated in comfortable and regular habits of sleep, food, and rest. The time for eating should be regular, the time for going to bed should be regular, and activity should be moderate — not so much as to make the body exhausted. If the body is exhausted, then the nervous system does not function; when the coordination between body, nervous system, and mind breaks down, the mind is disconnected from the body and the nervous system, and the whole charm of life is lost in deep sleep.

So, here also we find, as in the part on "Key to Good Health,"[55] that the practice of Transcendental Meditation helps to strengthen the physical condition of the nervous system as well as the mind. Therefore, Transcendental Meditation enables the mind to remain concentrated, to use its full potential, to conserve its energy, and to establish a good coordination between itself and the body. By the regular practice of Transcendental Meditation a strong thought force is cultivated whereby it becomes possible to perform an action in such a way as to produce the most effective and desirable results.

Great Energy

In order to perform an action to produce the most effective and desirable results, it is very necessary that along with the increased thought force there should be enough energy in body and mind.

How is it possible to be filled with life energy all the time?

It is extremely necessary that every man, for the sake of himself, others, and the whole world, make contact with the unlimited source of life energy by the practice of Transcendental Meditation. In the part on "Individual and Cosmic Life,"[56] we have seen that the individual life is like a wave on the ocean of Cosmic Life, and that every wave has the possibility of drawing any amount of water from the ocean; the whole ocean could rise in one wave. Likewise, every individual has the chance of communicating with the unlimited ocean of Cosmic Life energy to gain the strength so that he will perform an action which will produce the most effective and desirable results.

The energy we derive from what we eat and drink and breathe is limited. Many things we eat and drink produce energy, but there are many elements

---

55 See page 180.
56 See page 53.

in that food and drink that also help to produce dullness in the mind. That is the reason why, when we work for some time, the energy produced by the food is exhausted, and by evening we begin to feel hungry and exhausted. Thus, in order to perform action to produce the most effective and desirable results, we should have some additional source of life energy.

When we are considering how to add life energy to our capacity of action, we should also know that life energy appears as power of thinking, intelligence, creativity, and joyfulness. So the life energy is the same but appears to have different types of functions.

Obviously, if we want more life energy than what we ordinarily get from food and drink, it will be necessary to find a means to draw more energy from the atmosphere. Apart from that, it is necessary to know how to draw more life energy through the power of thinking and being.

We find that the source of all creation, the source of all the atmosphere, the source of all food, drink, and air, and the source of all thinking ability and thought is Being. If there could be a way of communication between our conscious mind and the ocean of Being, that will be the way for conscious attunement with the limitless source of energy. This, as we have seen repeatedly, can easily be accomplished by the regular practice of Transcendental Meditation.

There are many practices of drawing more energy from the air. There are saints in the Himalayas who live on life energy drawn from the atmosphere, but they are accomplished Yogis who can draw, in the early morning hours, enough life energy to sustain them throughout the day. These methods are not for the common people.

This system of Transcendental Meditation, however, is the most effective way of bringing the mind to the field of transcendental Being, where it naturally acquires a great deal of life energy to be used for performing any amount of hard work with efficiency to produce the most effective and desirable results. This drawing of energy from the field of Being is the greatest art of living, for it brings the active life of the day-to-day world into communion with eternal Being, the limitless source of life energy, power, intelligence, creativity, and bliss.

If this message of drawing limitless life energy from the field of transcendental Being could reach the people of the world so that they could start the practice of Transcendental Meditation, everyone's life would be free, joyful, full of creativity, intelligence, peace, and happiness. And when the people of the world rise to this high state of consciousness, the world will be a paradise to live in.

Fortunately, the present time is the most suitable time for the propagation of the ideology of Transcendental Meditation, because the need for such a formula is felt more than ever in the present generation, when man has virtually lost the anchorage that, in the past, religions and metaphysical studies offered him.

The alert intelligence of the scientific age has contrasted with the futility felt in the promises of religion and different schools of philosophy and psychology. Tensions are fast increasing on all levels of life all over the world. On one side, the individual feels lack of energy and an increase of tensions, and, on the other hand, the fast tempo of modern life does not allow him a moment of real silence. The individual is torn between pressing activity and lack of energy to cope with it. The result is an increase of heart disease and suffering. Every man is seeking something which will help him to cope with the increased speed of living which modern civilization demands.

At this perilous hour of human civilization the technique of Transcendental Meditation is a gift to humanity and a boon from the heavens to improve man in every way. It directly brings the energy of the individual in tune with the energy of Cosmic Life.

Favorable Surroundings and Circumstances

When we are considering the art of performing an action for the most effective and desirable results, it is also important to consider the factor of surroundings, because the surroundings of the doer have a great deal to offer for the success of the performance and its results.

The surroundings must either be favorable so that the doer will have enthusiasm and fervor, or the doer must have great strength of mind which will lead him to effectively persist in performance of the action under any circumstances.

The effect of the surroundings on action is very great. It is a part of the action itself that the surroundings should be maintained in harmony with the work to bring greater effectiveness and facilitate the performance of the action. Therefore, maintenance of the harmony of the surroundings should be part and parcel of the efforts that are made to bring success to the work.

The greatest force that man can ever have, in order to keep the surroundings harmonious and in conformity with the purpose of his actions, is to maintain the purity of his soul, mind, and body, and the purity of the purpose of action and sincere devotion to activity.

We have seen while dealing with "Being, the Plane of Cosmic Law"[57] that by the practice of Transcendental Meditation the individual becomes harmonious with the surroundings, or the surroundings become harmonious with the individual. Therefore, the greatest force that a man can use to this end is maintenance of the purity of Being in the very nature of his mind. For that, the regular practice of Transcendental Meditation is imperative.

Other attempts to maintain harmony in the surroundings are not as effective as this practice. Good behavior toward others, kindness, compassion, and helpfulness all have their value, and on the surface of behavior one has to be guided by these high principles of life. One has to be helpful to his neighbor, kind to his friends, and compassionate to his surroundings; but all this kindness and compassion and help to others will be more fruitful and valuable if the inner life of the individual is pure.

Fortunately, for our generation there has come to us an easy method to make the life pure. The realization of transcendental pure consciousness amounts to gaining absolute purity of life. So in order to have the surroundings and circumstances favorable for the performance of action to produce the most effective and desirable results, it is primarily necessary to have Transcendental Meditation included in one's daily routine.

---

57 See page 10.

Ability to Perform Right Action

In the section on "Life," we have seen how it is possible for the individual mind, through the practice of Transcendental Meditation, to contact the cosmic mind and draw from it an unlimited amount of energy, intelligence, and creativity in order to make an action yield desirable results.

Performance of right action is a great art. Right action comes from a platform of contentment and from the natural need for action. That a man entertains only right action should be his natural state. Right action is the action which fulfills the legitimate need of man. By "legitimate," we mean that the doer is justified in his need and in the manner of action that he adopts to fulfill his need.

The question of right and wrong in the relative field of life is a very complex question, with which we have dealt in the part on "*Karma* and the Art of Being."[58] There we have seen that right action can only be determined on the functioning level of the Laws of Nature, based on Cosmic Law. We have seen that a man who is naturally established in the state of Being moves in accordance with the Laws of Nature. Only on that level of heightened pure consciousness is it possible for the mind to lean toward righteousness. Right action is always based on moral laws. Any lack of morality, any deviation from the integrity of the purpose of life, results in deviation from righteousness.

It is ordinarily difficult for a man to know what right action is. The law of the land, however, provides one criterion. In that sense, right action is that which is at least not against the law of the land. Lawful action is right action. In general, it could be said that the law of the land is based on the Laws of Nature. In countries whose civilization is old and where tradition has value, the law of the land is fundamentally derived from the Laws of Nature. Therefore, as a guide in selecting the right action, it is imperative that the action should not be against the law of the land, and, if possible, it should be in accordance with the Laws of Nature.

The law of the land and the traditions of the country are general guides to what is right and wrong. The consideration of the Laws of Nature is very delicate. The Laws of Nature govern the process of evolution on all levels of

---

58 See page 117.

creation; they either complement or contradict each other, depending on the stratum of creation on which they are functioning.

While discussing right and wrong thoughts in the part on "Thinking and the Art of Being,"[59] we found that the mind, when infused with the nature of Being, functions naturally, in accordance with the Laws of Nature. Therefore, it is only a mind which is infused with Cosmic Consciousness that can possibly determine an action which is in accordance with the Laws of Nature. At that level, however, it is not a matter of determining the rightness of an action; at that level the mind, by its very nature, knows only the right action. Therefore, the state of Cosmic Consciousness affords an absolute criterion of right and wrong in the field of action. Earlier we have said that the law of the land and its traditions provide criteria of right and wrong. These are criteria in the relative field and are not a perfect guide for those who have not yet attained Cosmic Consciousness.

Many people have the ability to choose the right action naturally because the structure of society is such that from childhood one is brought up to know, roughly at least, what is right and what is wrong. Deeper criteria of right and wrong are established when the individual grows older and comes to know the law and tradition of the land more thoroughly. A more and more exact sense of judgment between right and wrong comes naturally, as one's consciousness grows, but when the consciousness is highest and Being is infused into the nature of one's mind to the fullest extent, the mind knows without doubt what is right and wrong. By natural inclination and natural taste, wrong actions and wrong thoughts are not even considered. So, the real art of performing right action lies in having a mind which is right at all times. To be right, the mind has to be in that state of lasting contentment and purity which belongs only to the state of pure consciousness. Thus, the art of doing right in the world has its basis in the regular practice of Transcendental Meditation and the acquisition of the highest purity of consciousness. That purity of consciousness will in itself induce and maintain in the mind a natural tendency for only right action, and thus it is essential that it be cultivated.

59 See page 88.

The true knower of "skill in action" knows that action is a means of joy in the life and liberation from its bondage.

We have dealt with liberation from the bondage of action in the part "*Karma* and Being."[60] Here we will only recall that right action should be the natural tendency of man. The mind should be so trained and developed that it tends only toward right action, because right action alone is useful to the doer, the surroundings, and all concerned everywhere. Any action performed results in overshadowing the natural state of the mind. In such a state the mind is said to be in bondage; that is, the mind is not able to maintain its status of pure Being. The experience that results from the performance of the action has obscured the essential nature of the mind. Right action will be performed when the mind, while engaged in the activity, is able to maintain its Being without the impression of the action overshadowing the mind.

This means that the full value of the mind, or the subject, and the full value of the object — full value of the absolute state of Being along with full value of the activity, both maintained simultaneously — is the state of freedom from the bondage of action.

Self-Confidence

Self-confidence is a very necessary ingredient for performance of an action to produce the most effective and desirable results. We have seen that self-confidence depends upon the state of mind. The word "self-confidence" obviously means confidence in oneself. In order to have confidence in the Self, the Self has at least to be known, and has to be brought to the conscious level.

One who is unaware of his Self cannot possibly have confidence in himself. Any attempt to improve self-confidence without a way of gaining familiarity with the Self will always be ineffective.

Gaining familiarity with the nature of the Self is the first step to gaining self-confidence. When the familiarity with the essential nature of the Self has been gained to such a profound degree that the nature of the Self is never out of conscious level of awareness, then the state of profound self-confidence is gained.

60 See page 23.

Unless one is firmly grounded in an unshakable state of Bliss Consciousness of eternal Being, unless one has developed Cosmic Consciousness, which alone is capable of establishing the absolute status in the relative field of day-to-day life, it is not possible to have a natural state of unshakable self-confidence.

Thus, we find that regular practice of Transcendental Meditation is the direct way for attaining self-confidence.

Fixity of Purpose in Performance of Action for the Most Effective and Desirable Results

For any action to start, it is first necessary that the mind have a purpose to serve through that action. It is obvious that if an action is started and the purpose is forgotten, the action will not be continued.

For success of the action, it is necessary that the process of action be sustained, and, for this, a fixity of purpose should always be held by the performer. If the mind wishes to conduct the action most effectively and arrive at the most desirable results, it is extremely necessary that the mind not deviate from its purpose.

This fixity of purpose, which is the backbone of action and acts as a driving force for the process of action, is the most important factor in gaining the most effective and desirable results from any action.

There cannot be two opinions on the importance of fixity of purpose in performance of action for the most effective and desirable results.

The main question is how that ability may be acquired. The answer lies in cultivating a state of mind that is by nature not wavering and that remains concentrated and fixed on action. It is the wavering of the mind that tends to distract it all the time, and it is this condition of the mind that is always a threat to the continuance of action and thus a threat to the fixity of purpose.

Maintaining a fixity of purpose requires a habit of the mind to start on an action only after having considered all the points for and against the results of the action. But most necessary is the ability to put oneself steadfastly in one channel of action until the action is completed.

In the life of a man, naturally it is not just one thing that must be performed for all time. It is not just one condition of life that has to be lived for all time. It is not one kind of aspiration to be cherished for all time. From the beginning of the day until the time for sleep there are hundreds of fields of activity and experiences, all of which have their value in life. All these different fields of activity serve as the different components of the one machinery of life.

When we speak of having fixity of purpose in performance of an action, we also have to take it for granted that, along with the ability of fixity of purpose in the performance of one action, there has to exist, simultaneously, the ability of shifting from one type of action to another, from one field of activity to another. It is not that the mind must be fixed on one thing constantly. This shifting from one platform of activity to another should also be as natural to the mind as the ability to remain fixed on the performance of one action. Thus, the mind must have a dualistic ability in order to have spontaneous fixity of purpose in performance of action, so that this steadfastness does not keep a man from participating in the multiple activities and experiences of other spheres of life.

If one wants to build a house, the fixity of purpose in the performance of the action to build a house should not be to such a degree that a man becomes blind to everything else in life. He should go on conducting a normal life: eating, resting, lighting the lamp, performing whatever his normal activities are. All these go along with the fixed purpose of building the house.

Therefore, when we aim at cultivating fixity of purpose, we should not forget that we must not get absorbed in the performance of action to such an extent that we lose sight of other aspects of life. Often, when a person such as an artist, musician, or scientist is engaged in an activity very well-suited to his nature, he becomes very much absorbed in his work to the exclusion of other activities. It is a very good habit to have a fixed purpose for an action which they like and enjoy, but it makes other aspects of life suffer.

For example, if a man with a family is a devoted scientist who spends all his time in the laboratory, his wife begins to suffer, the children do not get the love of their father, the house is not well taken care of. The habit of remaining fixed on the purpose of action is a desirable quality of the mind, but if it is overshadowed, always remaining on one aspect of life, it may become a means of misery as well, by unduly overshadowing other aspects. Therefore, when we want to cultivate the ability of fixity of purpose in action, we should, at the same time, cultivate it in a balanced manner.

This leads us to the conclusion that cultivating fixity of purpose in action, devotion to work, and all that goes with it, is important, but this must not rob a man of other values in life. The culture of the mind should be on a broader scale, on an all-around basis. In order to gain the ability of fixity of purpose in action, the whole of the mind has to be cultured, and its ability must be improved on all levels.

We have seen in a previous part[61] that it is the practice of Transcendental Meditation that enlarges the conscious capacity of the mind and makes it more profound and sensible on all levels. It is through this practice alone that it is possible to cultivate the great ability of remaining fixed on the purpose of action; however, at the same time one must not be bound with it so much that it robs him of the charm of other aspects of life.

Thus, the art of cultivating the ability of fixity of purpose in the performance of an action, for the most effective and desirable results, lies in the regular practice of Transcendental Meditation and in conducting all aspects of life in a normal and easy way.

The Art of Performing Action Without Harming Anyone

The art of performing an action without harming anyone lies first in selecting an action which will bring the maximum good to oneself and to all others in the surroundings. Second, it lies in adopting legal ways and means of carrying out the process of action.

If the action has been selected so that its results are useful to the doer and to the surroundings but the process selected for the performance of action is not legal, it will create tension in the surroundings. Therefore, it is necessary that, along with the choice of useful action, the choice of means for carrying out the process of action should be harmless. The ability to

61 See page 27, "How to Contact Being" and page 29, "Transcendental Meditation."

select only the right action in order to act without harming anyone is also very important.

This again leads us to conclude that, without having attained the state of Cosmic Consciousness, no one can claim that he performs action without harming others, because which action at which time produces that good or this bad influence in which strata of creation? This cannot be judged or justified by human intellect. The effects of action in the universe are so complicated and far-reaching that it is beyond the range of human intelligence to assign accuracy of performance of an action in terms of harm or good done in creation. This we have already seen in the part "Individual and Cosmic Life."[62]

Therefore, the only way to perform action without harming anyone is to raise the level of intelligence and consciousness to absolute divine consciousness. And when the doer is established on the level of Cosmic Consciousness, the undertaking will naturally be harmless to him and to the entire creation. All the activity will be in accordance with the upgoing stream of evolution, which alone could be a means to institute harmless action in the true sense of the word.

Therefore, we may conclude that the ability to perform action without harming anyone lies basically in the regular practice of Transcendental Meditation, which also succeeds in establishing the individual intelligence as Cosmic Consciousness.

The Art of Performing Action to Yield Maximum Results

The art of performing action to yield the maximum results rests in two factors. The first pertains to the ability of intelligence, energy, fixity of purpose, preciseness of thought and action, and the state of concentration of the mind of the doer. The second is the ability to control the surroundings in favor of the performance of an action.

In order to gain maximum results from an action, it is necessary that the action be performed to the best ability of the doer, and for this the doer

---

62 See page 53.

should have maximum ability. The maximum ability requires the most highly developed intelligence and energy in the doer.

We have seen[63] that the greatest energy and intelligence is gained when the individual consciousness is brought to the level of Cosmic Consciousness, and, at the same time, the individual energy is brought to the level of cosmic energy. We have also seen that, when this occurs, great contentment, the ability to concentrate, and the faculty of perseverance naturally develop in the mind along with the unfolding of latent potentialities. With these qualities, a man is able to act with great precision — with maximum results at the least expense of energy.

Therefore, by improving one's consciousness and tuning oneself in with the cosmic life energy, it is possible to gain the ability to handle the work so that it will yield maximum results.

However, something more than the inner ability and efficiency of the man is needed to bring maximum results from the performance of an action. That is the ability of controlling the circumstances and surroundings. If the surroundings could be made favorable to the performance of an action, certainly the action would bring maximum results, and there would be no limit to the results that an action could yield.

The results are restricted (aside from the restricted ability of the doer) by the resistance offered by the surroundings and circumstances. If one had the ability to perform an action in such a manner that the surroundings and circumstances automatically became congenial and favorable to success, one would certainly succeed in producing maximum results from an action. And the art of gaining this ability lies in the regular practice of Transcendental Meditation.

An innocent simple approach to the action, in accordance with the Laws of Nature in line with evolution, naturally succeeds in producing maximum results. It is wrong to think that one has to put out great labor in order to produce maximum results. No, it is not on the hardship of performance on the part of the doer that an action succeeds in bringing maximum results. And, again, it is not only due to the great energy and intelligence on the part

---

63 See page 36, "How to Live Being."

of the doer that an action succeeds in bringing maximum results; mainly and basically, it is the purity of the heart and mind of the doer and his innocent and faithful approach to action with the purpose of all good to everyone that really succeeds in yielding maximum results.

We have seen that the state of Cosmic Consciousness, where the mind is in complete harmony with the surroundings and with the natural process of evolution, is able to produce maximum results out of the least doing.

We have also seen previously, in detail, how the purity of the heart and mind of the doer influences the results of his actions. We could say that this result of an action depends upon the purity of the mind of the doer. If the mind is one hundred percent pure, that is, if one is evolved to Cosmic Consciousness, then the result will be one hundred percent maximum. If the purity is fifty percent — that is, if the evolution of man is fifty percent, if the man is fifty percent evolved on the way to Cosmic Consciousness — then the result of each of his actions will be fifty percent of the total possibility.

Generally, the people in the world, for the success of their actions, count upon their ability of performance of an action, and they count upon the intelligence that they have, upon the creative mind that they possess, and upon the energy that they have. But all these factors are of a secondary importance. The main factor for success and production of results is the purity of the doer.

One more factor plays an important part in producing results from one's actions. It is the element of *Karma*, the fruits of actions performed in the past. A good, virtuous man of the past has been doing good, virtuous deeds which were in accordance with the process of evolution. The result of those good deeds now adds to the success of the action which is being performed in the present. Thus, we find that the present ability of mind and body, the ability of intelligence and energy of the man in the present, brings success of the action in proportion to the influence of good or bad *Karma* of the past influencing the present action of the doer.

The influence of the good of the past *Karma* results in more energy, clarity of thought, and right decisions in the doer and also produces good influence in the surroundings, which thus become favorable for the performance of the action at hand.

The bad influence of the past *Karma* likewise brings in dullness, inefficiency, loss of energy, weakness, and even tension and suffering in the doer and adverse influence in the surroundings, which begin to provide obstacles for the successful performance of action and hinder progress toward any substantial results.

This aspect of the *Karma* of the past is something beyond the control of the doer. The best the doer can do in the present in order to neutralize the influence of past *Karma* is to engage in the practice of Transcendental Meditation, which will readily raise the consciousness of the doer and produce favorable influence in the surroundings; when the consciousness is raised, energy and intelligence are increased. Then, whatever is the influence of the past, that influence will not be able to nullify present action. Certainly the influence of past *Karma* will be there, but it may not completely guide the destiny of the present action.

If a businessman loses five hundred dollars, the loss is a loss for all times. Although this loss will always remain a loss, if two thousand dollars are earned the next day, the gain overshadows the loss.

This is how, by due amount of performance of Transcendental Meditation, supplemented with the power of charity and virtuous deeds of helping others, the negative influence of the past *Karma* can be counteracted in order to smooth the path of the present *Karma*. And then the action will be performed without resistance or obstacles, yielding maximum results.

So, the formula to produce maximum results is not to mind the obstacles and negative influences trying to offer resistance to the performance of action. The doer should put himself into action and continue it until the desired results are achieved. The process of meditation, of bringing the conscious mind in tune with transcendental absolute eternal Being, which is the source of all life energy and intelligence, raises the standard of consciousness. When the standard of consciousness is raised, the action performed from that raised level of life energy and intelligence will certainly have an over-riding influence over the *Karma* of the past to produce maximum results.

This is how, by the power of present action on *Karma*, the destiny is improved. Herein lies the full meaning of the proverb, "Man is master of his own destiny."

The Art of Performing an Action So That the Performance Remains a Joy and Does Not Become Tiring, Tedious, or a Boring Task

The process of any action will remain joyful for the doer and for the surroundings only when the doer has very great energy and intelligence and he encounters no resistance on the way and receives all cooperation from everywhere. The action must not become taxing to his ability. He must have self-confidence, efficiency, and the ability to concentrate, so that he feels that the action is not beyond his capability.

When a businessman has a great amount of wealth, he does not feel concerned about what he spends in the market. The whole field of business remains a joy to him because it does not much matter whether he loses or gains; he already has more than enough for his purposes. Likewise, when the doer has much more energy than is required to perform an action, the action is easy and remains a joy.

Anything that is done in accordance with the nature of the mind pleases it, and anything done against its nature displeases it. So, if an action undertaken by a man is in accordance with the nature of his mind and within his capacity, that action cannot be taxing or wearisome. Only an action which suits the temperament of the man provides a means of joy during its performance.

For example, a boy is told to take a football to a house two miles distant. If there is a chance for him to keep kicking the football toward the house, then the boy gets it there in a very pleasant and joyful manner. The delivery of the football to the house does not become a burden because he has been playing with it all the time. If, however, he is asked to carry it on his shoulder or in his arms rather than being permitted to kick it, the delivery of the football will become a burdensome task. It ceases to be a joyful action; it begins to cause tension and worries.

If there could be a way for all the actions in life to be brought on the level of joy, that would be the technique of gaining the ability to perform an action so that its performance was done with joy and did not become trying, tedious, or boring.

If a mother is very loving to her child and has given her great love to him, and he has made her very happy, the child is saturated with great joy. If the mother asks the child to run an errand for her, the will of the mother becomes an added wave of joy for the child. He jumps up and does what he is asked in a very playful and joyful mood. But if the mother has beaten the child, making him cry, and then orders him to do the errand, her order becomes an additional wave of misery to the child. He will do the action, but under great pressure, and thus the whole thing becomes a burdensome and tedious task for him.

This shows that if the mood is joyful, the performance of any action will be joyful. If the mood is miserable, tense, and worried, then any action will become a means of added tension. Therefore, the technique of making all actions joyful is to bring joy to the mind. Fill the mind with that great happiness which knows no end, let the mind be saturated with absolute bliss, and then the undertaking of any action, whatever it may be, will be performed in all joyfulness.

Thus, the ability to perform an action with joy lies in saturating the mind with bliss, cultivating that absolute Bliss Consciousness. That alone is the state of eternal happiness which knows no misery. This we have seen is easily gained by the regular practice of Transcendental Meditation.

If the mind is not in a natural state of happiness, then any attempt to try to be joyful and happy while performing the action will not succeed. Only when the very nature of the mind is saturated with joy can any action be joyful. This is possible only when the mind has gained the status of pure consciousness. Only when the conscious mind has become so familiar with the bliss of transcendental Being that it never leaves, is it possible to have all action in joyfulness.

Thus, we have seen that the performance of an action can be joyful only when there is spontaneous joyfulness in the very nature of the mind; otherwise, any attempt to be happy while performing an action will just add tensions because the energy is divided between the performance of an action and the need to feel joy.

The modern tendency of playing music in the factories to bring happiness to the workers has two effects: one is that the attention of the workers is divided, and the other is that although the work is there and has to be completed under pressure from authority, it is the natural tendency to listen to the music. The performance of the work is thus against the normal tendency of the mind, which is to enjoy the music. Therefore, on the one hand, tension is created in the minds of the workers, and on the other, the work begins to suffer. The employer provides music in the workshop to make the mood of the workers happy, but the net result is that the work becomes a means of tension in the mind and divides the attention, making the worker less efficient.

Any artificial attempt to produce joyfulness in the field of activity results in minimizing the efficiency of the activity and, at the same time, makes the activity become a means of overtaxing or tension. Therefore any unnatural method of producing joyfulness only results in disaster on the side of activity and tension on the side of the doer. The only way to make the whole field of action joyful is to fill the mind with joy. Let the very nature of the mind be transformed into a joyful nature; this can be readily achieved through the system of Transcendental Meditation.

The Art of Proper Planning of Action

Planning of an action depends upon the clarity of the mind. This, as we have seen in the part "Thinking and the Art of Being,"[64] is readily gained by the regular practice of Transcendental Meditation. Unless the action is properly thought of and the steps of performance are properly planned, the whole process of action remains in all probability indefinite for the doer and for all those who are concerned with it.

In modern times, when there is pressure for rapid completion of action, it is all the more necessary that proper planning be done for effective execution of the work. "Look before you leap" is a common saying. For proper action, proper planning is vital. Effective planning depends primarily upon the state of the mind and secondarily upon the circumstances and resources at hand. One should always consider thoroughly one's resources before commencing an action. A survey of the resources and estimation of the possibilities

64 See page 88.

of gaining more resources, or of completing the work with the resources already at hand, is a necessary part of planning.

If the undertaking comes through a pure and expanded consciousness, then the resources come according to the need. In the case of highly evolved consciousness, there is hardly any need for planning. In such cases, what comes to the mind leads the course of action, and Nature provides resources for its fulfillment. The evolved souls do not think what they are saying, they speak as they feel; their feeling finds concrete expression in results, and success follows their aspirations. Nature provides fulfillment for their desires. There is no plan. It is only necessary to start the work, and the work itself will take care of itself, and success naturally follows. The force of the whole of Nature is behind such an undertaking.

Thus, we see that the best way for automatic planning is the raising of one's consciousness to the level of Cosmic Consciousness, where all the forces of almighty Nature will be conducive to the fulfillment of desire. This is the most effective technique, although it is without any obvious planning at all. The ability of such an automatic planning during the course of execution of the work lies in gaining a state as near to Cosmic Consciousness as possible, through the regular practice of Transcendental Meditation.

The plan of being regular in performance of meditation, morning and evening, will result in automatic planning for the proper and effective execution of every undertaking.

But, for all practical purposes in life, until the consciousness has been raised to a sufficiently high degree, it is necessary, before starting the work, to look into the surroundings and circumstances and gauge the possibility of successful performance in view of the resources at hand. The factor of time also is an important factor in the mechanics of planning for an action. But, although such planning seems a waste when seen from a highly evolved state of consciousness, it is necessary to be practical and realistic on one's own level of consciousness. "Being realistic," for one thing, requires that we must live within our means. If we have a certain amount of resources, we start the action after planning to complete the action with these resources.

When we consider the importance of planning, we should also mention that it is automatic machinery which produces the ideal product free from error, but, if it is not automatic, the finish of the product may not be even. If we could adopt a system of automatic planning, achieved by raising our consciousness to a state where planning and execution of the work occur simultaneously in an automatic manner, then, of course, the chances of variation and error would be much less. But as long as we have not gained such a state of mind, it is to our advantage that we spend some time in proper planning.

If the planning is very efficient, the action will certainly take much less time and it will be performed with the least amount of energy, yielding maximum results under the circumstances. But there should be a limit to planning.

Certainly there must not be a great amount of time spent on planning, because not much else will be accomplished in life. Planning should be done properly, but the factor of time, which is the most valuable factor in life, should not be lost sight of either. Through the regular practice of Transcendental Meditation, higher consciousness should be cultivated as soon as possible to develop a broad angle of vision, foresight, clear thinking, intuition, power of imagination, and precision in thinking, along with the unfoldment of all mental faculties which form the basis for proper planning. To gain mastery in planning, however, the achievement of Cosmic Consciousness should be aimed at, which will create conditions suitable for "automatic planning." This provides the master key to successful economics in all fields of life, which is the main purpose of planning.

The Art of Effective Execution of the Plan

Once the action has been planned, it is highly important that the plan be executed in the most effective manner.

All that has been said regarding performance of action to yield maximum results will also be true for effective execution of the plan.

Over and above this, it is necessary that, from time to time, one review the plan, what has been accomplished, and what remains to be done, according to the plan. The review or survey of the progress of work adds to the effectiveness of execution of the plan. All these abilities are the natural qualities of a clear and powerful mind.

We have seen that the art of performing action to yield maximum results and the art of clear and powerful thinking, foresight, tolerance, persistence, and concentrated attention are gained through the regular practice of Transcendental Meditation, wherein lies the fulfillment of the art of effective execution of the plan.

Art of Behavior

The art of behavior means acting in such a way that both parties involved enjoy the behavior and it brings satisfaction to both. They gain from the behavior to the utmost degree, they gain energy and joyfulness; the quality of love increases and evolution is helped. This is the art of behavior. Both parties, as the result of behavior, should find their life fruitful, find their life fulfilled, and find their behavior a means to evolution.

It is the art of behavior that not only influences the surface values of life and makes both parties happier and better in all ways, but also touches the inner core of life and makes it advance on the higher levels of evolution.

The purpose of social behavior is to give and take help for mutual benefit. One should meet the other either to give or take. No, mainly to give, and when the two meet to give the best of themselves to each other, then both gain the maximum. On the contrary, if both meet and expect the maximum from each other, each in his attempt to gain from the other has closed his door to giving, and thus no one gains from the relationship except disappointment, resulting in tension on both sides.

The basic fundamental of behavior should be to give. When you are going to meet someone, think what you are going to give him, whether it be a concrete gift of a beautiful object, words of greeting, warm sympathy, praise, adoration, love, elevating advice, or good news for his body, mind, or soul. There must be something for you to give when you meet someone. Just a "hello" and "how do you do" cannot produce a wave of love and joyfulness at the meeting. The art of behavior is such that the first moment of the meeting should have a real value of the meeting of the two hearts.

Thus, we find that the first fundamental in the art of behavior is: meet with warmth, and meet to give. Behavior should be on the level of giving. "In giving, you receive" is a common saying: it has great truth in it. If all the people in a society behaved on this level of giving, social behavior could only result in the advancement and glorification of everyone's life. Giving is the basic formula of the art of behavior.

This sincere sense of giving can only arise on the level of contentment. The contented hearts and minds alone can think in terms of giving. This eternal contentment can only come through the development of Bliss Consciousness, which can only be developed quickly through Transcendental Meditation.

The art of behavior is becoming of growing concern in today's society. How one should behave with another — the problem of social relationships — is a growing problem in the world today, because the qualities of heart and mind are not given a fair chance to develop. Social relationships should always be a means of joy. They can become a problem only when the very fundamentals of life are not understood. In order to behave properly with others, one has to think clearly and have clear and good intentions, a decent way of life of one's own. One should have qualities of tolerance, love, kindness, and joyfulness in one's own nature.

If tolerance is not there, ill-feelings and disharmony result. Take the example of someone making an ill-humored remark. If one is not able to withstand the remark without reacting to it, in the repercussion that follows, ill-feelings spring up and the social relationship is spoiled. If a man does not have the quality of love, if his heart is hard, he begins to hate the person who has offended him.

It is the love of a mother for her child that makes her look kindly upon his mistakes. In fact, a mother enjoys the mistakes of the child because, when he commits a mistake, she is able to give him more of her love. In that love, the child grows to be better able to overcome the weakness of committing mistakes. This is how, by the tolerance and love of the mother, the child improves and the art of behavior is naturally infused in him.

Joyfulness is a quality that cultivates and spreads love. And again, that is the result of the overflowing love of the heart. Joyfulness, love, kindness, and tolerance should be cultivated. With all these qualities comes the contentment and overflowing love of the heart and mind which is the basis of good social relationships.

What is the shortest way to the art of behavior? Language is one expression of behavior; we could polish the language. Good manners are part of the art of behavior, but good manners come only from the method of raising the children. Children of good families are trained in better behavior. But the root of the art of behavior lies in the polished state of one's mind. The refined state of mind depends, as we have seen, upon the system of Transcendental Meditation, wherein the conscious mind is brought into communion with the bliss of absolute Being. Thus, the basis of the art of behavior is that technique of bringing the mind to the Bliss Consciousness of transcendental Being. This leaves both parties in added joyfulness, energy, love, and harmony, while, at the same time, it creates an influence of peace, harmony, joyfulness, and freshness in the atmosphere. The individuals gain and the universe gains through the art of behavior.

Really good behavior will be possible only when the minds of both the parties are broadened, when they are able to see the whole situation, understand each other more thoroughly in their true perspective, and succeed in locating the needs of the other and formulating their behavior on the basis of attempting to fulfill these needs. This naturally necessitates expanded consciousness and right sense of judgment and all the qualities that only a strong and clear mind possesses.

Small minds always have a very narrow vision and they fail to perceive the total situation; in their narrow vision they create imaginary obstacles and close themselves in their narrow scope of imagined forms, which are useful neither to themselves nor to anyone else. Then their behavior with others only results in misunderstanding and increase of tension. This shows that the fundamental of good social behavior is the strong, clear, and contented mind of the individual, which as we have seen in the part on "Mind and the Art of Being,"[65] easily develops through the simple system of Transcendental Meditation.

The minds of both parties should be established on the level of Being, or Being should be established on the level of both parties, so that the bliss, contentment, and joyfulness of Being are in the heart and mind of each. Then behavior becomes a means of adding to joyfulness, love, kindness, tolerance, and all other virtues. Such behavior produces radiations of peace and harmony in the surroundings. The art of behavior is best expressed when not only the two parties that engage in behavior gain, but the entire atmosphere is thrilled with the influence of love, kindness, harmony, and peace.

Behavior and the Surroundings

Once established in Being, one is able to make the best use of the surroundings. What they are does not matter; they are made conducive to the fulfillment of the desire of the individual.

No set of surroundings could be said to be absolutely bad or completely useless or damaging. If a mind is not able to take advantage of the surroundings, it is its own weakness that makes it unable to do so. For example, a man is sitting in a room that is filthy, full of dust and dirt. If his mind is grounded in contentment, joyfulness, peace, and happiness, he radiates those qualities around him and does not pay attention to the dirt and dust.

It is the inner status of the mind that is responsible for making a man joyful or miserable. In the man's joyfulness and contentment he begins to sweep up the room and wipe off the dust and, in doing so, he takes delight because he is in such good harmony with the surroundings.

If a man is sad and tense, however, and finds the room dirty, he just adds to the tension and his mood grows worse. He becomes more and more tense because of the condition of the room, and he thinks that it is its filthiness that has made him more miserable and tense. But it is not so. It is the misery of his mind that has multiplied itself while being reflected from the particles of dust in the room. Had he been joyful, the joyfulness would have reflected from the dust of the room.

65 See page 101.

If someone makes an ill-humored remark, a joyful mind that is fully developed and full of love and contentment responds to it with forgiveness. The joyful man does not mind the wrong, because his is a strong mind. A strong mind has the ability of tolerance; a weak mind takes upon itself all the insult and all the ill-humor of the utterance.

Another point may be made in this connection: If someone has already had doubts regarding another man's behavior, even if that man expresses something of love and joy, the doubter keeps on having doubts because his doubts were present before the conversation started. So a doubting or unkind mind, even if there have been reasons for the doubts in the past, fails to enjoy the joyfulness and sincerity of the other. Thus, it is not the present behavior of the man that is causing the other to be doubtful; rather it is the state of his own mind.

So as far as the influence of the atmosphere upon the individual is concerned, the state of mind is of primary value. The nature of the atmosphere turns and takes shape according to the state of mind of the individual. If one puts a red glass to his eye, he sees everything as red; if he looks through a green glass he sees everything as green. Whatever the individual's state of mind, it reflects itself. But due to ignorance, generally, the atmosphere is held to be responsible for it.

The individual is responsible for the atmosphere. True it is that the individual creates the atmosphere and the atmosphere in turn has its influence on the individual. But when the mind of the individual is strong, functioning at its full potential, then he is able to make the best use of the surroundings and circumstances. This is the art of behavior with others. The art of action and the art of behavior lie in making things favorable for us and in not making them unfavorable. The atmosphere is there for us to use and not for making us miserable. If someone has said something, it is his action, his responsibility in saying it. If it is useful to us, we enjoy it, accept it, think about it, act on it, and derive benefit from it. But if it is not useful and not elevating or favorable to us, then we do not think of it again and again; we do not attend to it. If it happens to be an expression of something bad, and if we are not responsible for it, and the speaker thrusts the responsibility for the wrong on us, then he is in the wrong. We do not bring that wrong to mind and mull it over and over. If we do so, we are putting a bad thought in our mind, which was not our own fault in the first place.

Therefore, once and for all, we must make our mind such that it becomes a principle of life that we naturally think and act in a way that is elevating and beneficial to us. This way we derive great benefit and advantages for ourselves and others. We do not go for damaging or malicious thoughts, either to reject or accept them; indifference is the weapon to be used against any negative situation in life.

This is the art of behavior. If someone has done us an injustice, we do not harbor it or think about it. Perhaps it was a mistake. If we permit it to affect our future actions toward him, we are not giving him the opportunity to improve in his relations with us, and we also suffer. Even if he *does* harbor ill-feelings toward us, we will benefit him and ourselves if we still behave toward him with love and tolerance. In this way, we help the atmosphere to improve, and, with an improved atmosphere, we are better served.

Therefore, the first principle that will make us live the art of behavior is to make our mind blissful, peaceful, harmonious, fresh, and intelligent by the practice of Transcendental Meditation. As we have seen in "Art of Being,"[66] when the mind is brought to the level of Being, the body is also brought to that level. Thus, by our thought, word, and action — and even by our very presence — we vibrate a good influence of life and peace, harmony and joyfulness, around us.

To improve relationships we must improve our own minds first; then we begin to behave well. It is true, of course, that on the gross level of behavior we should be conversant with good polished language and manners of behavior, but the art of behavior lies in much more than that. It lies in the art of Being; that is the technique which places our life in a state of harmony, joyfulness, peace, and intelligence, so that we naturally and innocently behave well and on a high level. We, therefore, do not have to be unnatural in any way. Such natural behavior on a high level demands that the individual should be well-grounded in himself and maintain an unshakable status

---

66 See page 112, "The Body and the Art of Being" and page 116, "The Surroundings and the Art of Being."

of his Being, so that, whatever comes in the outside world, he is able to love and enjoy it; he is not upset by any antisocial or wrong type of behavior.

If all people would begin to meditate a few minutes, morning and evening, and contact transcendental Being, the whole field of social behavior would reach an ideal state. The technique of behavior, as we have already discussed, not only improves and satisfies in the individual life, but it improves the atmosphere, brings it more harmony, and reduces fear, hatred, tension, cruelty, and antagonism. The art of behavior makes the life of the individual happy, brings greater harmony to family life, produces more love, kindness, and harmony in the society, and improves the social relationships in the international world.

In the absence of the art of behavior, quite the contrary effect is produced. Tensions grow in the family, in society, and in the international relationships. Eventually, the threat of world war and annihilation arises. This aspect is dealt with in the part on "World Peace"[67] in more detail. Suffice it to say that by improving Being in the minds of the individuals, social relationships improve in the most automatic and natural way, and thus great harmony is produced in the atmosphere, tension is released, and the world is made better for people to live in.

Key to Good Health

The problem of health is the most vital problem of life. Everything depends upon health. The peace and happiness of man within himself, his accomplishments in different spheres of life, his attitude and behavior with others, and, above all, the very significance of his existence depend upon health.

In order to consider health fully we should take into account the health of the individual and that of the cosmos — man and his atmosphere.

Consider the details presented in the following table.

---

[67] See page 237.

ART OF LIVING

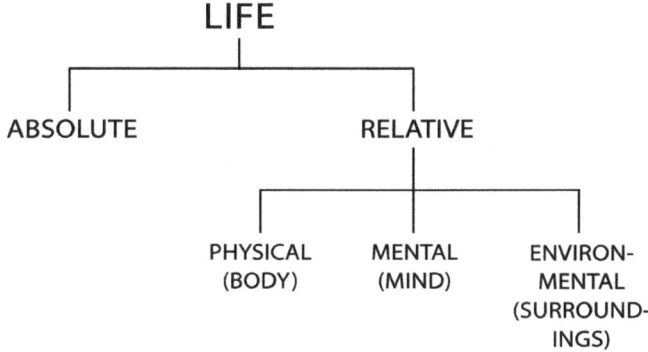

The two main aspects of man's life are the relative and the Absolute. The relative aspect of life is perishable; the absolute aspect is imperishable. The relative life has three aspects: physical, mental, and environmental; or, body, mind, and surroundings.

Thus, we find that man's whole life has four different components: Being, mind, body, and the surroundings.

A healthy Being, a healthy mind, a healthy body, and healthy surroundings, along with a healthy coordination between Being and mind, between mind and body, and between body and surroundings will constitute the state of perfect health of an individual. Therefore, in order to determine the nature of good health, we must consider:

1. Being
2. Mind
3. Body
4. Surroundings
5. Coordination of Being and mind
6. Coordination of mind and body
7. Coordination of body and surroundings

Unless all these seven points are taken into account, the consideration of health will always remain incomplete and cannot provide a complete solution to the problem. In order that a correct and complete solution be brought to light, it is necessary to consider all seven aspects of the individual life.

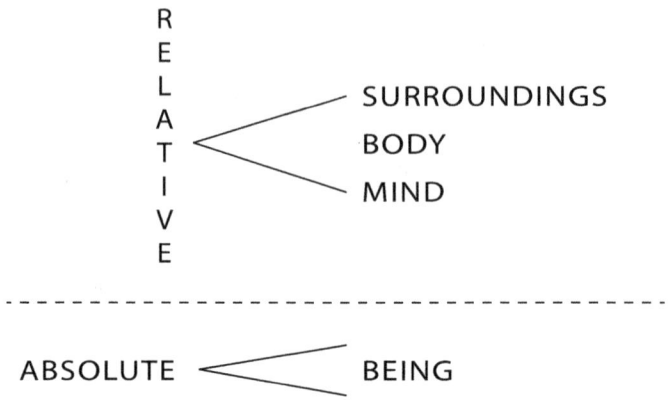

Here is an invitation to the various health organizations of the world to look into this and do what is needed to solve the problem of health and alleviate man's suffering.

It is rather sad to note that for centuries past the problem of health was considered primarily on the physical level. Thanks to the recent advances in scientific medical treatment, inquiry and research into the cause of diseases have revealed that for a great majority of ailments, although the disease may be of a physical nature, its cause is not physical. Such medical research findings have brought to light the validity of mental phenomena as the cause of disorders on the physical level of the body.

Psychology then stepped forward in answer to the call from the medical profession to deal with the mental phenomena to alleviate physical suffering. Psychiatry developed to remove mental stress and thereby eradicate the mental cause of physical diseases, while the rest of the medical profession continued to treat the diseased part of the physical body.

How far medicine helps to restore physical health and how far psychoanalysis and psychiatry succeed in helping man to overcome the mental causes of psychosomatic diseases is a question to be considered by the wise men who are presently guiding the destiny of medical science, psychiatry, and psychology.

The least that could be said about the problem of health in the world today is that the measures adopted so far are insufficient to maintain the health of the people. Even in countries where medical science is most advanced and psychiatrists and psychoanalysts are the fashion of the day, the record of health shows that a large number of people live with weak hearts and die of heart failure and that the number of mental patients is fast increasing. It is a serious situation which can only be completely resolved on the governmental level. But before this can be achieved, it is necessary that those individuals who constitute the governments add something more to their present knowledge. Something more than what is already known has to be discovered in order to maintain the health of the people all over the world.

But before new findings may be effectively and advantageously applied to the cause of health, it is first necessary that the heads of the medical associations of the various different countries adopt a sympathetic attitude to new suggestions for health programs from all responsible quarters. Secondly, it is essential that they put them to scientific test on the experimental level. If they prove the validity of a new idea, it should openly be accepted as a new method of medical treatment or as an aid to it.

If a leaf has begun to wither and dry up, it may be either because the particular leaf has been affected by undue heat or because the supply of nourishment from the root has lessened. If the case is excessive heat, attending to the individual leaf and protecting it from this heat will remove the cause and save the leaf from dying. But even when the leaf is being attended to individually from the outside, it is necessary to see that a supply of nourishment is reaching the leaf from the root. In any case, it is essential to maintain a good supply of nourishment from the root to all parts of the tree.

When a boil rises on one's finger, a good doctor tries to investigate in what subtle part of the body the cause lies. Whether the cause lies in the blood or only on the surface of the skin, a good doctor will start treatment from the level of the cause, even though he also attends to the boil on the surface.

This brings out a certain principle — that one who is interested in prevention or cure of diseases should have a knowledge of all the aspects of the body, both gross and subtle, because there are many gross and subtle levels of the individual constitution. They range from the body, the end organ of the nervous system, to the field of the mind, which itself again ranges from gross and subtle levels of thinking and touches the field of Being.

Therefore, it is advisable for the medical profession to have knowledge of the whole range of life right from the outside cosmos to the body, through all the subtle fields of the body to the mind, and through all the subtle regions of the mind to the state of pure consciousness, Being. In addition to this knowledge, it would be most fortunate if the health authorities had the formula[68] to successfully handle ultimate Being, which is the very basis of all the different levels of individual life.

A gardener who knows how to take care of the tree and see that it receives the nourishment it needs will certainly succeed in maintaining the health of all the different levels of the tree. A medical man having the knowledge of all the different aspects of individual health, knowing how to take care of the basic stratum of life — the field of Being — will certainly succeed in restoring and maintaining good health on all levels.

It is fortunate for the health of the world that one formula has been developed to take care of the very root of individual life, to maintain and restore good health on all levels of mind, body, and surroundings.

In this part we shall deal with all the different aspects of individual life and suggest one simple formula which will serve as a preventive measure for good health and also as a means to restore and maintain perfect health on all levels of life.

This is offered not in any spirit of competition or challenge to the medical men and all those engaged in the problem of health, but in all love for man's life and with all goodwill and appreciation for those who are helping people in all parts of the world with whatever they have found useful for health.

It is logical that, unless all the seven aspects mentioned previously are taken into account, the problem of health will always remain unsolved.

To build more hospitals in order to remove the sickness and suffering when people have already fallen ill is a laudable act of charity. But a far

---

68 See page 29, "Transcendental Meditation."

greater responsibility lies in finding ways and means whereby people would not fall sick and will always enjoy good health. If there could be some means found whereby people would not become sick, it would be a much greater act of charity to introduce it to the people all over the world.

We shall see how this new goal of good health may be achieved.

We note that preventive medicine is always an established and important part of health programs in every country. Progress in this field depends upon the application of new findings from time to time.

The following pages present something new which has proved its value for the preservation and betterment of the health of the body, mind, and surroundings.

Mental health depends upon the state of the mind, which is obviously an abstract factor, and upon the state of the nervous system, which is concrete. The nervous system is the vehicle for the functioning of the mind, for it serves to connect the subjective nature of the man (the mind) with the objective world around him. Thus, to consider mental health we have to take into account both the state of the mind and the state of the nervous system.

Before dealing with mental health, let us have a clear conception of what the mental health aspect of the personality is — what mind is — for we cannot consider the health of an aspect about which we do not have any clear conception. So, let us understand what mind is in relation to the body and in relation to the whole personality.

The mind lies between Being and the body. It will be better to first look into the relationship of the mind with the body and with Being. Mind is just a link to connect Being of the unmanifested nature with the body and the manifested aspects of the relative world. It is a link to coordinate the absolute and relative aspects of one's life. On the one hand, the finest aspect of the mind touches the core of the absolute existence, Being, and on the other, it touches the gross levels of relative existence. In terms of Being, mind could be defined as vibrating consciousness.[69] In terms of the body,

---

69 See page 19, "Mind and Being."

mind might be defined as the fountainhead of the nervous system and, as such, the source of the body.

This gives the mind the status of the root of the tree, with the function of the mind like the dual function of the root. On the one side it has to draw nourishment from the ground, and, on the other, it has to pass on that nourishment to the outer tree. Likewise, the mind, by virtue of its status in between Being and the body, has a dual function to perform. It has to draw in life energy from absolute Being and pass it on to the body and other fields of relative existence. If the root successfully maintains the process of drawing in and giving out, then the health of the tree is ideally maintained. Any failure to maintain this process results in ill health to the tree. Likewise, failure on the part of the mind to draw sufficient life energy from Being would naturally result in the weakness or ill health of the body or personality. Thus we find that good coordination of the mind with Being and with the body is the key to good health.

Now we shall deal with the different aspects of health — mental, physical, and environmental.

Mental Health

Mental health depends upon the normal functioning of the nervous system, so that the full mind is brought to bear upon the external world. The normal functioning of the nervous system results in physical good health so that the body is able to carry out the dictates of the mind, fulfill its desires, and fulfill the purpose of existence.

As long as the coordination of the mind with the nervous system is intact, mental health is maintained. When this coordination breaks down, either because of some failure on the part of the mind or of the nervous system, ill health is the result. Such failure of the mind is brought about by a continued inability to fulfill its desires.

The main reason for this is weakness in the clarity and power of thought, which thus fails to stimulate the nervous system to the extent that it can successfully carry out the activity needed for fulfillment of the desire. For the most thorough coordination and the most perfect functioning, a profound power of thought on the part of the mind, together with a correspondingly efficient executive ability in the nervous system, is required.

The integrity of the organic nature of the nervous system is certainly as essential as the power of the mind. As far as their functioning is concerned, they are interdependent. It has been found that while the nervous system remains unchanged, an improvement of the state of the mind results in an improved state of thinking and better coordination between the mind and the world around it. When the full mind is brought out to express itself in the external world, the subject comes into a more perfect and rewarding relationship with the object. Happiness is clearly the result of the fulfillment of the needs of the mind. A mind that is happy and contented produces health.

It has also been found that, if the physical state of the nervous system is improved by means of medicine, while the state of mind remains the same, the thinking becomes more profound and the mind functions more energetically and more efficiently. Thus, we find that the mind and the nervous system are interdependent, but, since the mind is obviously of a more subtle nature than its organ, the nervous system, it seems wiser to assume that the mind is primary.

Any number of factors might interfere with the growth of a tree, but weakness in the seed itself would overshadow them all in importance. In the same way, any number of factors might prevent the fulfillment of a need, but weakness of the power of thought must certainly overshadow the rest. A strong seed will produce a tree even in a desert, while no amount of nurturing will help a weak seed. If the basic power of thought is strong, it will find its way to fulfillment.

If, because of the failure to satisfy the needs and desires of the mind, discontent begins to produce tension within it, then the way to remove these tensions will be to strengthen the mind by increasing its power to think — the force of thought. This is achieved by enlarging the conscious mind through the practice of Transcendental Meditation, as has already been explained.

When tensions build up in the mind, they are reflected through the nervous system upon the body. The anxious mind, constantly flitting back and forth amongst its problems in its discontented state, exhausts and irritates the nervous system and the body. As a servant whose master constantly gives indecisive and confusing orders becomes tired and irritable and eventually fails to do anything, likewise the nervous system and the body become tired and exhausted and eventually fail to function efficiently when the mind is in a state of stress due to confusion and indecision.

In this way, mental stress produces disease, and even organic changes in the body. Obviously the cure of all such suffering is to create such a situation in the mind that it may become and remain unwavering and steady. This is achieved by expanding the conscious mind, thereby making it strong. As a result of strengthening the conscious mind, a better coordination between the mind and the nervous system is established, and smooth and efficient functioning of the body is the natural result. Perfect mental health is maintained because of this coordination of the mind with the nervous system and with its end organ, the body.

It has been seen in hundreds of cases in many countries that worried and tense people naturally lose their tensions within a short time of starting the practice of Transcendental Meditation. We find that this practice of Transcendental Meditation is a boon to mental health. It is a means for preservation of mental health: it serves as a mental tonic and, at the same time, is a natural and effective cure for mental illness.

Physical Health

Medical research has shown that a very large proportion of physical disorders arise primarily from mental tension as a result of the anxieties and failures of life.

While dealing with mental health we have seen how the process of Transcendental Meditation releases tension, and this is why we find that all suffering that could be described as psychosomatic is relieved at its source by Transcendental Meditation. There are, however, purely organic diseases in which there is no evidence of a mental cause — but it is well-known that a sick man has a mental and emotional attitude toward his illness which, while not causal to the illness itself, may still have profound effects upon its course.

Certainly meditation will remove these secondary anxieties. But let us now consider what effects meditation may have upon a purely organic disease. To do this we must consider the physiological effects of Transcendental Meditation.

Physiological Effects of Transcendental Meditation

As the attention is drawn to consciously experience the subtler states of a thought during Transcendental Meditation, it is found that respiration becomes greatly reduced in amplitude: the breathing becomes soft and refined.

Physiologically it is clear that for this to take place there must be a fall in the level of carbon dioxide in the plasma. This can occur only as a result of either forced over-breathing, which washes the carbon dioxide out through the lungs, or by a fall in the production of carbon dioxide through the metabolic process.

Because there is no forced over-breathing during Transcendental Meditation, we can only conclude that the softening of the breath is due to the fall in the production of carbon dioxide by metabolic process.

The production of most of the energy for activity in the body involves, basically, the oxidation of carbon and then its elimination as carbon dioxide.

Greater activity needs greater energy, which is produced by a greater amount of oxidation of carbon, and its elimination as carbon dioxide. Lesser amount of activity needs lesser amount of energy, which is produced by lesser amount of oxidation of carbon and its elimination as carbon dioxide.

This shows that when a lesser amount of carbon dioxide is eliminated by way of softer breathing during Transcendental Meditation, the process of oxidation is lessened, and this naturally produces a lesser amount of energy.

That is why the activity of the body and that of the nervous system is lessened during Transcendental Meditation. This explains why, during Transcendental Meditation, as the mind proceeds to experience finer states of a thought, the whole body becomes calm and quiet.

This quieting of the body naturally allows an unusual degree of rest, which itself stores energy to a considerable degree. It is certain that the activity of the mind and the nervous system is least in this state, and, thus, the mind becomes quiet and calm.[70]

In this quiet state the mind and the nervous system are alertly poised like the arrow drawn fully back upon the bow; they are without activity, but the entire system is alert in stillness. At the same time, all the mechanisms of the body are acutely balanced and steady. It is this restful alertness of the nervous system that is its most healthy state and is the basis of all energy and action.

This restful alertness of the nervous system is a state of suspension wherein the nervous system is neither active nor passive. This state of no-activity and no-passivity is the state of Being. This is how the nervous system is brought to the level of Being, and coming in tune with Being, the nervous system reaches a level of limitless energy and eternal existence of Being. It is like the whole tree coming in direct attunement with the field of its nourishment. The nervous system gains the most normal and healthy state. Here lies the key to good health.

The fall in carbon dioxide output has also another effect — that of a tendency to change the reaction of the blood from acidity toward alkalinity. This, in its turn, has widespread effects upon the blood chemistry — all of which are beneficial to the system as a whole.

These considerations lead us to the following:

That the system of Transcendental Meditation is beneficial in the field of health in two ways. It is both preventive and curative: (1) It is a means of preservation of mental and physical health. (2) It is a means of providing complete rest and relaxation to body and mind, which restores energy and greatly aids medical treatment toward a speedy recovery from ill health.

When we say "body," we mean the entire nervous system and all the limbs that are said to be the end organs of the nervous system. The existence

---

70 If by means of meditation one does not produce this state even for a few minutes daily, then one has no chance of providing any rest to the inner machinery of the body, which otherwise is kept functioning twenty-four hours of the day, for the whole of one's life, as long as the breath keeps flowing.

Obviously, it is to the advantage of health and longevity of life that the ever-functioning inner machinery of the body is allowed a few moments of rest and silence each day through regular practice of Transcendental Meditation.

of the body depends upon the activity of the metabolic process. Activity belongs to the relative fields, whereas Being is of transcendental absolute nature. Maintenance of the body is dependent upon both subtle and gross fields of activity. If the body could be brought to a state where its activity stops, but the nervous system were not allowed to be passive, if it could be in a state where it was neither active nor passive, the activity of the body would then be on the level of Being. If the metabolic process could just remain still without rendering the body passive, it would place the activity of the body on the level of Being.

When we talk of the level of Being, let us first see clearly what we mean. Being is the essential constituent of the individual. It is just there — everything — and Its unmanifest state forms the basis of everything and every phenomenon. It is the basis of all mind and matter, the basis of the entire manifest creation. This state of Being is out of all relative existence; that is why It is called transcendental and absolute: transcendental because It is out of all relative creation, absolute because It does not belong to the relative existence. It is never-changing, eternal existence. Like the sap in a tree, Being is omnipresent in creation. It is the ultimate source of all energy, intelligence, creativity, and activity. It, in Itself, is neither active nor passive. It is the source or the fountainhead of all activity and passivity.

In the relative field of life there is either activity or passivity. Absolute Being, in Its essential nature, belongs neither to the field of activity nor to the field of passivity. Any state of life which could belong to neither activity nor passivity goes out of relative existence and naturally belongs to the field of absolute Being, and that which belongs to the field of absolute Being gains the status of absolute Being Itself. For nothing other than Itself can be It.

Thus the meaning of the words "absolute Being" is clear: In light of our present thesis, it means the state of life which is neither active nor passive.

Thus it is clear that if the metabolic process which keeps the body alive and maintains the coordination of body and mind in the relative field of existence could be brought physiologically to a state of restful alertness, a state where the metabolic process would slow into a state of no-passivity, the state of life could be placed on the level of Being.

Passivity and activity both belong to the relative field of existence. The metabolic process causes the mind to be either active or passive in the waking, dreaming, or sleeping states and thus maintains life in the relative field. If the metabolic process, the inner activity of the body, could be stopped in such a way that it does not become passive, the body will be in a condition that is neither active nor passive.

When the nervous system is active, awareness is in the waking state; when the body becomes fatigued, the awareness is lost and gives rise to deep sleep. Here, in deep sleep, awareness may be said to be in a passive state. It could be said that awareness depends upon the state of the nervous system. When the nervous system is active in the wakeful state the mind has no opportunity to dissociate itself from the world around it; when the nervous system is tired, the mind has no chance of using its conscious capacity, and awareness is lost in deep sleep. If the nervous system could be brought to a state where it is able to hold the mind in such a way that it is not able to use its conscious capacity for the experience of any outer object, and at the same time it does not completely lose its conscious state — that is, if the mind could remain just conscious, without being conscious of anything of the outer world — the mind will acquire the state of pure awareness where the mind is neither active nor passive in its nature. This pure awareness will be on the level of Being.

If the nervous system could be established in a state that is neither active nor passive, but in a state of restful alertness, there would certainly be produced a condition for awareness on the plane of Being.

If such a state could be accomplished by the nervous system, the nervous system in that state would assume the role of a platform for the relative and absolute states of life to meet. The nervous system then, as far as its ability to produce conscious awareness is concerned, would be on the plane of Being, or Being would be brought to the level of the nervous system.

How is this possible? What approach could be adopted to produce such a physiological state of the nervous system?

Physiologically, the functioning of the nervous system depends upon the metabolic process. The metabolic process depends mainly upon breathing.

If by some means the breathing could be slowed down, made softer, or reduced in amplitude, the metabolic process would thereby be reduced. And if the breathing could be brought to a state where it was neither active nor passive, that state of extremely delicate breath where the breath could be said to be flowing and yet not flowing, the metabolism would be established in a state of suspension between activity and no-activity on the level of Being. This would harmonize the body with Being. Life would be sustained, but its expression would be silent in the relative existence. This is the state of the nervous system which would keep the mind awake in itself, and, with reference to this state of self-awareness of the mind, the whole body would be sustained in itself.

A state of no physical change in the body will exist, the whole physical structure and all matter of the body will just be suspended on the level of the pure state of life: a state where the process of evolution or the process of change has stopped building up or deteriorating, where the change has ceased to be. The whole body has thus been placed on the level of Being, as has the mind. Mind and matter both, forming the gross and subtle aspects of the individual, have been raised to one level of never-changing existence, the level of eternal absolute Being. Here they lie together in unity with one another, for both have gained the same level of life. If one hesitates to accept the notion that in this state the mind and body are united in one state of life, let the statement be made that, in this suspended state, body and mind are in perfect coordination with each other. The individual mind is one with pure consciousness or absolute intelligence, and the body in this state of perfect health is resting in full accord with the mind.

This is how, by reducing the breath, it should be possible to set the nervous system in the state of perfect health and at the same time in full coordination with the mind. Such a perfect state with regard to body and mind and their mutual relationship is only possible on the level of Being. And it is possible only when either the mind is brought to the level of Being or the body is brought to the level of Being.

Thus the desired results can be achieved in any of the following ways:

1. Psychological — where only the mind is involved. This, in practice, is the system of Transcendental Meditation.
2. Physiological — where metabolic process is reduced by working on the body or breathing. This practice is achieved through Yogic physical culture and proper breathing exercises.
3. Psycho-physiological — where mind and breathing both are made to function on their levels in order to bring both the mind and body to that state of suspension on the level of Being.

Now we shall see how the breathing can be brought to a state of neither activity nor passivity.

This state of breath has to be created in a very natural way, because any unnatural method will cause strain. This cannot be achieved by attempting to slow the breath, because slowing it will strain the process of breathing. The problem is how to create a natural state of extremely soft breathing in which breathing would almost transcend activity. One possibility for slowing the breath is the extended practice of controlled breathing so that the system becomes used to maintaining itself either when the breath is in or out. This practice does result in maintaining the body with very soft breathing. Eventually a physiological state is created in the system in which the breath is brought to a condition of neither activity nor passivity.

The goal of bringing the body on the level of Being is achieved as a result of such a practice of controlled breathing. But because long practice of a great amount of control is necessary for success through this path, it does not suit the householder's way of life and is even less suited to the busy householder of the modern nuclear age.

There is another way to achieve this state through slowing of the breath. First we shall consider the principle involved in this second way.

Experience shows that breathing becomes faster when we run and it is slower when we sit. It is faster after we have eaten because more oxygen is needed for the digestion of the food. Breathing is slow or fast according to the work to be done by the body. The work to be done by the body depends upon how the mind wants the body to function. That means the activity of the mind — thinking — is at the basis of the activity of the body. Thus we find that the activity of the body, which directly controls the process of breathing, is governed by the process of thinking.

Again, as we have seen while analyzing the thought process, the thought process on the level of the conscious mind is the result of much greater activity than it is at the starting point of thought. Increased activity naturally needs greater release of energy in the system, and this necessitates correspondingly heavier breathing. On the contrary, if the thought can be consciously recognized as a thought right at its source, then the energy required to raise the thought to the ordinary conscious level of the mind would naturally be saved and would cause less production of energy in the system. This would necessitate a fall in the process of oxidation in the plasma, which, in turn, would soften the breathing, and the goal of bringing the breath to a state of neither activity nor passivity will thus be achieved.

This shows that, as the mind begins to experience subtler states of thought during Transcendental Meditation, it engages itself in correspondingly less activity, and, as a result of this, breathing simultaneously begins to be shallower, more refined, and reduced in amplitude. When the mind arrives at the experience of the subtlest state of thought, the breathing arrives at the shallowest level of its flow and, eventually, when the mind transcends the subtlest thought and gains the level of pure consciousness, the breathing comes to that state which is neither active nor passive, the level of pure Being.

Thus we find that the practice of bringing the mind to the level of Being simultaneously brings the breath to the same level and establishes the nervous system and the body in the plane of absolute existence. In this state there would be no release of energy by the metabolic process, no change or decay in the state of the body. The body, then, becomes the fit medium for omnipresent absolute Being to shine through and radiate Being in the relative field.

When a glass of water is placed in the Sun, the Sun is reflected in it. The Sun is always there, but it shows no reflection unless a proper medium is found through which it can be reflected. Similarly, Being is always here, there, and everywhere, but it has no opportunity to radiate itself directly in the relative existence unless a suitable state in the nervous system is created for it.

By bringing the nervous system to this condition, through systematic refinement of breathing or thinking, or both together,[71] the body can be brought to the level of Being to live long in good health.

Having thus considered how the body could be maintained in perfect health, we shall now consider the health of the atmosphere, or environment.

Health of the Atmosphere

The atmosphere of an individual is made up of the radiations from his mind and the body. The quality of the atmosphere around the individual depends upon the quality of radiations set forth by his thinking and his activity.

The atmosphere created by a lazy man is dull and depressing, whereas an energetic man carries with him a dynamic influence.

Every man produces his own atmosphere, and everyone's atmosphere is influenced by that produced by every other man. To produce a healthy and elevating atmosphere, one has to be healthy.

We have seen that health depends upon the state of Being. Therefore, in our attempt to find out a formula for good health of the surroundings, we shall chiefly try to find out how Being could be brought to the level of the atmosphere or how the surroundings could be brought to the level of Being.

In order to produce the influence of Being in the atmosphere it is necessary to have the mind and body established in Being. This, as we have seen, is brought about by taking the conscious level of the mind to the subtlest levels of thinking, to eventually transcend thinking. Then the thinker is left all by himself and the state of Being is created in the individual.

We have also seen that when the mind is established in the state of Being, the activity of the body ceases and the entire nervous system is set on the plane of Being. When the mind and body are established on this plane, the surroundings, by being in contact with the body, naturally receive the

---

71 This is the practice of Transcendental Meditation.

corresponding influence and radiation of harmony, peace, and eternal life, because the nature of Being is eternal life, eternal existence, all purity, absolute bliss, and pure consciousness. This is how, by bringing the mind and the body to the level of Being, the atmosphere is naturally infused with the value of Being.

When the mind emerges from the state of transcendental Being and engages itself in the field of thinking, the entire thinking process has its conscious basis on the level of Being. The vibrations emitted by the process of thinking have the quality of Being; that is, the quality of harmony, purity, and bliss. Thus, by gaining the conscious status of Being, the mind continuously radiates the influence of Being in the atmosphere. This is how the outer activity and behavior of a man become saturated with the quality of Being.

When the mind is brought to the level of Being, it is established on the level of Cosmic Law, and we have seen that such a mind, when it comes out from the field of the Transcendent, comes out infused with Being. When, with practice, the infusion of Being continues to be held on the level of the conscious mind — even when the mind engages itself in outer activity — the mind remains in constant communion with the Cosmic Law, which is the basis of all the Laws of Nature.

In the outer atmosphere such an individual is set in the most natural state of cosmic evolution, because when the mind functions from the level of Cosmic Law, then all the Laws of Nature are as if in complete harmony with the mind. When the Laws of Nature around the individual are completely in tune with the mind which is established in the Cosmic Law, then the entire nature around the individual is set free from any strain and disharmony.

Disharmony in Nature is due to the mind not being in tune with the Cosmic Law. This point should be thoroughly understood. When the mind is attuned to the Cosmic Law, all the Laws of Nature are in perfect harmony with the aspirations of the mind. This leaves the entire surroundings of the individual in perfect harmony in the most natural way and in the most normal state, free from any tension or strain.

When the surroundings are thus completely in harmony with the individual, perfect harmony is established in all the different strata of Nature around the individual. When the body and mind are in tune with Cosmic Law, the entire atmosphere surrounding the individual is set in accordance with the cosmic purpose. Everything is in harmony. This is how, by bringing the mind and the body in union with Being, the influence of life and harmony is naturally created in the surroundings. The surroundings are brought to bear on the influence of Being.[72] When the mind functions while it is established in the state of Being, when the individual has gained Cosmic Consciousness, then every individual emits the vibrations of Being. Being which was at the transcendental level is brought out into the field of relativity. All his thoughts, actions, and words vibrate Being and bring transcendental Being onto the level of the surroundings.

Naturally all the different strata of creation are nothing but different stages of vibrating Being. But when the mind of a man is not in conscious union with Being, the vibrations of the mind may not be in accord with the Natural Laws. Established in cosmic Being, when the individual personally vibrates, Being permeates the atmosphere. Being that is already present in all the different strata of Nature becomes as if alive and vibrates in perfect unison with all the different levels of creation. The different levels of creation are then correlated with each other under the most natural conditions of affinity, with the Laws of Nature functioning at their different levels. This eliminates any disharmony or discord among the different planes of creation around the individual which might have existed when the mind was not in accord with the Cosmic Law. This is a very subtle consideration, but it is the truth of Nature.

When the mind is not in tune with Cosmic Law, in tune with Being, when it is not functioning in the state of Cosmic Consciousness, it is not functioning in complete accord with the Laws of Nature. Such a mind, without any knowledge, even without any intention to do so, is apt to emit an influence of disharmony and discord.

Either the mind naturally functions in such a way that all the Laws of Nature are in perfect accord with Cosmic Law, or the harmony is disturbed

---

72 The surroundings are brought to bear due to the influence of Being. Refer to Appendix A, the *"Maharishi Effect,"* page 369.

because the mind is not naturally established on the level of Being. The ever-active and vibrant atmosphere around the individual is made alive into the value of Being, and all around the individual is created an atmosphere vibrant in the value of Being.

The atmosphere of an individual cannot possibly be made as quiet and calm as his body when the mind transcends and Being is established. The nervous system of the individual is brought to a state which can be said to be a state of activity and no activity, a state which is neither static nor dynamic. This is where the level of Being is gained by the nervous system. This state of perfect equilibrium is not possible in the surroundings because the surroundings of the individual are full of activity caused by the Laws of Nature operating in accordance with the cosmic purpose of evolution.

Nature moves on and on in evolution, and this process of creation is eternal. It is therefore not possible to bring Nature to the level of transcendental Being. But, because the eternal ever-changing field of Nature is eternally permeated by the state of Being, it is possible to make transcendental Being vibrate in the surroundings. This is possible by eliminating the disharmony that might be radiated by the individual who is not cosmically evolved. This disharmony should be properly understood.

Take the case of a man who is not cosmically evolved and acts and thinks according to his selfish desires. The selfish desires may not be in accord with the cosmic purpose because they have no cosmic basis, and, therefore, all that he does may or may not be in harmony with the cosmic purpose.

Whatever thought or activity is carried on by the individual, if it is in accordance with natural evolution, if it is in accordance with the cosmic purpose, it creates an influence that is in accordance with the Natural Laws. But, if it is not in accordance with the cosmic purpose, if it is against the natural way of evolution, the entire atmosphere is strained, and all the Laws of Nature subjected to that influence are strained. This is how the actions and thoughts which are not in accord with the process of evolution cause strain and tension in the surroundings. Discord is created, currents antagonistic to the natural conditions of evolution are set in motion in the atmosphere, and the natural stream of individual and cosmic evolution set by Mother Nature is strained.

Here we find the explanation of why a virtuous way of life should be lived. All that is moral, virtuous, and truthful in life is in accord with the Laws of Nature. And all that is immoral, sinful, and fearful is against evolution.

When a man thinks wrongly, speaks wrongly, and acts wrongly, he strains the Laws of Nature functioning around him and causes discord and disharmony in his surroundings.

And you can feel it. If you enter the room of a bad man you begin to feel his sinful influence. If you enter the room of a good man you immediately feel the influence of harmony. That influence of harmony is, in turn, indicated by your being pleased within yourself. When you are pleased within, the sense of harmony and goodwill that you create in the room of your good friend is in accordance with the process of evolution. It helps your soul to evolve, because harmony is in accordance with the Natural Laws of evolution.

The quality of goodness permeates the very atmosphere and is felt immediately upon entering the room. The influence of the man is held in the walls around him; he is, so to speak, found on the wall, the ceiling, and the floor of his room! If he is in an evolved state of consciousness, a strong influence of harmony is naturally created in his room. This is the value of Being which is harmony, life, and stability.

The value of eternal Being is already there in the entire sphere of creation, but, when a man is not in the state of pure consciousness, his activity produces strain and disharmony.

When the individual has risen to Cosmic Consciousness, all his thoughts and actions are part of the cosmic purpose. Then, whatever he does, speaks, and thinks helps the process of evolution. They help to neutralize the unnatural influence created by those minds which are not integrated.

The integration of the personality, or the evolution of the personality to the level of Cosmic Consciousness, sets forth the atmosphere of the individual on the most powerful and natural state of Being or Cosmic Law. This is how by raising one's consciousness to the level of pure consciousness, one naturally sets the surroundings and circumstances in harmony with cosmic purpose, that is, in accordance with cosmic Being. This means either diffusing the value of Being in the surroundings or bringing the surroundings to the level of Being.

Nothing can be done to bring the Nature, the atmosphere, and the surroundings to the level of Being, because they are ever set on the level of Being.

What do we mean, then, by saying we bring the atmosphere to the level of Being? We mean only that the individual does not emit vibrations or influences which may in any way be opposed to the natural process of evolution or create disharmony in the natural functioning of creation at all the different strata of Nature. So, in order to let Being remain in perfect accord with all the different strata of Nature in the atmosphere of the individual, the individual has only to rise to the state of pure consciousness. This is the way to bring the surroundings and the atmosphere of the individual to the level of Being.

When the breath of the individual becomes the impulse of eternal life, the health of the individual is brought to the level of eternal health of Cosmic Life. When Being is set up on the conscious level of the mind, when the mind has gained Cosmic Consciousness, then the body serves the purpose of cosmic evolution. Such a mind, such a body, with such an atmosphere, breathes perfect health.

Thus, only when Being is established on all levels of individual life is it possible to have a state of perfect health on all the planes of individual life — as when all the different aspects of the tree are saturated with the sap, only then does the entire tree breathe perfect health. If any part of the tree loses its conscious contact with the sap, it begins to dry up. Similarly, any aspect of individual life, when it loses coordination with Being, begins to suffer the influences of non-Being. When the atmosphere fails to receive the influence of Being through the individual, then the atmosphere loses health and becomes strained. This, as we have said, is felt by the individual. It brings him not a sense of harmony and peace, but rather it brings a sense of strain and agitation, fear and tension.

When the body has no opportunity to come to the level of Being, it loses the strength of life. When the nervous system is not brought to that state of restful alertness, the level of Being which we have described, the body becomes strained, as does a machine which continuously functions without stopping. But if the machine is given rest at intervals, then the wear and tear is less and this gives strength and life to the machine. Similarly, when the body eventually is brought to that state of restful alertness where the nervous system enables the mind to experience the state of transcendental Being, the body is not continuously under strain; it begins to maintain its level of normal life, free from strain and tensions. Such a body breathes health.

The mind always wandering in the field of desire, wavering between the path and the goal in the relative fields of life, does not find that great goal of eternal bliss. There is nothing in the world which could possibly give lasting contentment to the mind because everything is perishable and ever-changing and phenomenal. Therefore, the quest of the mind for happiness is not satisfied, and the mind wanders all the time, seeking a point where it can rest in eternal bliss. A man with such a mind gains lasting satisfaction and contentment only when he comes in tune with the Bliss Consciousness of Being.

It is this state of Bliss Consciousness that brings the mind eternal contentment and gives steadiness to the mind. It brings fulfillment to the mind, and this is the most healthy state of mind, for it has acquired the purpose of life, eternal Bliss Consciousness — Cosmic Consciousness.

So we find that by tuning the mind with Being through the process of Transcendental Meditation, which has been described separately in great detail,[73] it is possible to remain in perfect physical and mental health and maintain the atmosphere in such a manner that it is conducive to the health of the mind and body of the individual. This is the way of gaining perfect health on all levels of individual life.

The problem of health is not solved unless we consider it from the standpoint of the individual mind, body, surroundings, and Being. If we do not take Being into account, the purpose of physical and mental health will not be served, just as if we do not take into account the value of the sap, the health of the tree, its branches, flowers, and fruit cannot be maintained. A skilled gardener seeing a withering leaf does not bother to attend to it by itself; through the wilting leaf he only receives the danger signal for the entire tree. So he directs his attention to the root, waters it, and, by his doing so, the sap is again able to reach all the different parts of the tree.

73 See page 29, "Transcendental Meditation."

Similarly, when a man finds that the atmosphere is strained, his mind tense, or his body suffering from some disease, he knows these are symptoms that signal danger to his entire life. A wise man will go to the root of the problem.

Wrong influence emitted from the mind and the body of the individual, be it any type, creates tension in the atmosphere. It is the wrong type of activity of the mind that produces tension in the mind. When the process of thinking is not in accord with the cosmic purpose or the Laws of Nature, it creates strain and suffering in the body and mind and produces strain and negative influence in the atmosphere.

Failure of achievements and unfulfilled desires arise when the individual life stream is not set in harmony with the Laws of Nature. And how can this be remedied? It is not humanly possible to know all the Laws of Nature. Physics, chemistry, biology, physiology, anatomy, and all the different branches of learning are exploring the different Laws of Nature. But innumerable are the strata of creation, innumerable are the Laws of Nature, and varied is the pattern of their interrelationship.

It is therefore not humanly possible to know all the Laws of Nature, but, by bringing the mind to the level of Cosmic Law, it could be brought in tune with the entire course of Cosmic Law, and it could be brought in tune with every law in Nature. When the mind is set on the level of the Cosmic Law, the mind becomes cosmic mind.

Unless the mind is in tune with Cosmic Law, life will not be in tune with Nature, and unless life is in tune with Nature, the individual will always be producing strain in the natural stream of evolution. The strain produced in the atmosphere has its maximum effect upon the individual himself. This is why discord, disharmony, disease, and suffering exist.

Limiting the investigation of the cause of disease and the cause of mental strain to the physical level is due to incomplete knowledge of the entire life of the individual, the entire scheme of creation.

If the health of the individual is to be properly considered, it cannot be considered in segments. The health of one's hand can be successfully considered only in terms of the health of the entire body, and the health of the entire body can be successfully considered only in terms of the entire nervous system, which in turn can be successfully considered only in terms of the mind. The mind can be successfully considered only in terms of Being, because eventually it is Being which is the essence of the individual life. Being is the essential constituent of all the different phases of life. Being therefore has to be taken care of. Only if good coordination between the mind and Being, between the body and the mind in terms of Being, and between the atmosphere and the body in terms of Being is maintained, can the problem of health be solved.

It is unwise to consider the health of man only in terms of physiology or psychology. The problem of health will be solved when the problem of life as a whole is solved.

From research in the field of medical science, the new theories of psychology and the findings in physiology tackle the point of health from a very limited point of view. In this way only a partial aspect of health can be considered, and that is why suffering continues to exist.

It is not our intention to show here what great harm is produced to the entire personality by dealing with the problem of health in a partial manner; however, the medical profession and the psychologists are themselves aware of their great limitations.

When the problem of suffering — physical or mental — is to be tackled, it has to be tackled at the level of the cause in order to produce lasting results. And the cause of all causes in life is Being. And all the causes of suffering — physical, mental, or environmental — are due to the inadequate coordination between Being and the different planes of the individual life. So if sound health is the aim, one formula could be evolved of sound health in all spheres of life. This formula will basically be in coordination between Being and the mind, between Being and the body, and between Being and the environment. How this is brought about is explained in the part on "How to Contact Being."[74]

It is high time that the medical associations of different countries consider the value of Being and put to scientific tests the physiological and psychological effects of Transcendental Meditation in order to bring out the benefit

74 See page 27.

of Being for mental and physical health to the people. This can only result in the eradication of mental and physical suffering. By this time, in almost every country of the world, many people are practicing this Transcendental Meditation and would naturally be good subjects for tests to be carried out to determine the physiological and psychological effects of Transcendental Meditation.

The cause of mental and physical suffering in the world is the lack of knowledge of Being and ignorance of the fact that by infusing the value of Being into the mind, body, and the environment, the very cause of all disease and suffering could be eliminated.

This is an invitation to all medical associations to explore, even on a merely experimental basis, the great possibilities of the good that could be done to alleviate the suffering of the body, the mind, and the whole atmosphere, by the influence of Being through the practice of Transcendental Meditation. This invitation to the health authorities of different countries is being extended not on the basis of theoretical knowledge, but on the basis of personal experiences of many thousands of people who have been practicing the system of Transcendental Meditation and who have found in their lives that their health becomes better, that their behavior with other people improves, and that success in life and peace within themselves and in the atmosphere is thereby maintained at all levels.

EDUCATION

Education aims at culturing the mind of a man to enable him to accomplish all he would like to accomplish in the great field of life. Education should necessarily enable a man to make use of his full potential in the field of his body, mind, and spirit. But it should also develop in him the ability to make the best use of his personality, surroundings, and circumstances so that he may accomplish the maximum in life for himself and for all others. There are tremendous possibilities latent in these fields which are never fathomed nor unfolded by students during their student life, which is the most precious time for building up the career of a man.

When one travels in the world and meets people of different nations, one finds that the public opinion in almost every country is set against the prevailing system of education. In no country of the world are people really satisfied with the existing system of education. There may not be many who could satisfactorily point out what the ideal system of education ought to be and indicate what is lacking in the present curriculum of the schools, colleges, and universities. Nevertheless, it is evident that dissatisfaction with the existing curricula prevails everywhere.

What is lacking is the completeness of the system of education which will give fullness to a curriculum through which students coming out of the educational institutions will be fully developed and completely responsible citizens of their countries, well-grown in the fuller values of life, developed in higher consciousness and understanding.

The subjects taught should be such that they bring home to the students the full scope of life. Whatever subject they choose should contain within it the view of a full life, a complete perspective of the full values of life and living.

In the present, with the advent of new inventions in all the fields of learning, a great number of subjects are creeping into the field of education. The field of specialization becomes one branch of learning in itself. Whatever precise specialization is taught to the students, along with knowledge of that subject, they should also receive the vision of the full value of life.

Obviously each branch of learning ranges from the most elementary to the most advanced study of a particular subject. But no subject of study and no branch of learning has yet reached the pinnacle of investigation in that subject. Every branch of learning presents great findings to a point, but the possibility of still greater findings lies in store for investigation by the oncoming generations. Therefore the highest peak of study of any subject is beyond the present-day sphere of knowledge. This leaves every branch of learning in a very unfinished state.

However, with the study of the Absolute in the higher courses of every branch of study, it seems that a student, along with gaining advanced knowledge of that subject, will also have an idea of the extreme limit of that subject. This is because the study eventually will touch the horizon of the Absolute. The study of the eternal Absolute, therefore, seems to be highly significant. It should be an accompaniment of the study of each branch of learning. The student will thereby find the extent to which life goes. As it is, the study of any branch of learning is limited only to the gross levels of that subject. Therefore, it is for the experts in the field of education to consider introducing the study of the Absolute along with the higher study of every branch of learning. This should at least be included in the curriculum of adult students in the colleges and universities.

The study of the Absolute will reveal to the students the great and hidden values of life lying beyond the obvious phenomenal phase of existence and will bring to them a deeper sense of existence, a broader vision of life and the unfathomable field of wisdom. It also will reveal to them the possibilities of living values of life much greater and higher than those found on the level of relative existence. If the technique of Transcendental Meditation is practiced, along with the study of the Absolute, the purpose of education would really be served. The system of education would thus be complete in the true sense of the word.

Present systems of education in the various countries of the world only give the students informatory knowledge. There is nothing precise in the field of education today which will really develop the inner values of mind, body, and spirit. Therefore, whatever education is received by the people is just on the surface level of information. In every subject certain information is given about that subject, and if a student is able to remember the information, he passes the course. The current system of education prepares the student only for a recognized career in the society primarily for earning a living.

There is no field of inner values of life open to the students. The information about the inner world of the mind and spirit is closed. It is surprising how the more substantial aspects of inner life which form the very basis of all the outer life and existence have been ignored for so long a time all over the world. It is now high time that, along with the outer fields of the different branches of learning, education be provided to the students in the inner spheres of life. Without the knowledge of the Absolute, and without the practice of Transcendental Meditation to unfold the mental faculties, education is incomplete. The responsibility for keeping this generation of students out of contact with the inner values of life and the field of the permanent status of existence lies on the shoulders of those wise men who are responsible for the present curriculum in every country.

When the student is given only informatory education in his subject he has no basis from which to fathom a great range of knowledge in that subject. How much of the world could be physically investigated and known through investigations of phenomena! The universe is so vast and the creation so unlimited that it is not physically possible to analyze and dissect everything in the entire creation.

That is why the present system of education fails to quench the thirst for knowledge. It has the ability of exciting the thirst but has no means to satisfy it. It is almost always true that as a man studies any field, he finds a greater field of the unknown lying ahead. Whatever little is known about a subject, the more advanced study of that subject silently informs the student of a much greater range of knowledge lying ahead, for which at present there is no means of learning. This will always remain the case as long as the system of education is based only upon informatory knowledge.

When, according to the present system of education one finds a greater field of unknown lying before the student, it amounts to increasing ignorance of the subject rather than knowledge of it. Such is the deplorable state of the present system of education. It can only excite the thirst for knowledge and has no way to satisfy it, and it only helps to advance the ignorance of the subject to a greater degree than it provides knowledge of it.

The only way to come out of this deplorable state of education is to find ways and means to culture the mind from within, and make it strong, so that when one studies a particular subject on the informatory level, one is also able to explore the deeper regions of the subject.

If this inner culture were provided to the student of any branch of learning, along with his usual course of informatory knowledge, the education from outside would be supplemented with the development of mind from the inside, and all mental faculties might be developed. A really well-educated man would be the product of such an educational system. This is an education which will not leave any door of knowledge closed for the mind and which will enable every student to have command of the full knowledge of the subject. Then the citizens of the world will really derive benefit from what we call education.

If education is based on inner values along with information of the outer world, education in any branch of learning will not create mere ability to maintain life by means of a job somewhere but will reveal to the growing man the real significance of inner life. His personality will develop a bold character and brilliance in his career. Every man will be found profusely equipped with the ability to gain great knowledge on every subject.

The current educational system, by providing varieties of subjects, only helps the student to make a choice of one of them. Every man has such tremendous mental faculties latent within him that, if there could be a way of properly developing them during the student career, every citizen of the world would be a very highly developed personality and could use his developed potentialities for all good for himself and all others.

Without the technique of unfoldment of mental faculties the great genius present within man is only wasted. We have seen in the part on "How to Contact Being,"[75] which explains the principle of Transcendental Meditation, that in one stroke of inward direction, the conscious capacity of the mind is developed to the fullest extent. In the outward stroke the inner potentialities of man, the spiritual nature of transcendental absolute consciousness, comes out with the mind to be lived in the midst of all relative values of the world of forms and phenomena.

This system of Transcendental Meditation, which is an easy approach to mental development and the unfoldment of all latent potentialities, and a direct way to fathom the spiritual values of inner life and glorify material values by the light of the inner Self, is a simple and a direct technique of education from within. The system is there, it has been evolved, it has been tried, and it has proved its value in every part of the world. Now it is left to the wise men responsible for the field of education to put this in the curriculum of the students in the colleges and universities so that a new humanity

---

75 See page 27.

may be born — free from shortcomings, free from ignorance about the inner values of life, and more developed in their fuller personalities.

This is the need of every country. Any country in which such a program is introduced would soon naturally gain greater advantages over other nations. The citizens of that nation would be much more capable men in all fields of thought, speech, and action because they would be using their full potential in all fields of life. That country will have better businessmen, better technologists, better statesmen, better scientists, better sociologists, better people in all fields of life. The people will be more advanced and integrated in their personalities — happier and more peaceful. This system of Transcendental Meditation is a boon to the student world. Whether it is adopted or not depends upon the educators of the world and on the good sense of judgment of those in whose hands lies the destiny of education in the different countries.

Now we shall analyze the different subjects of study, in view of Transcendental Meditation, and see how the study of the Absolute and the practice of meditation will enrich every subject of study and glorify the whole field of education.

Economics

Economics is the science of production, distribution, and consumption of scarce resources to satisfy human wants. Economics would be perfected if and when it created a state of abundance in life to properly satisfy the needs of the people. Such a state of material abundance can be created, but whether it would satisfy the man and make him contented is difficult to say, because even today those who have abundance in their individual lives are not found to be entirely satisfied. If man's contentment is not achieved, the very purpose of economics would be marred.

With all emphasis it should be stated that unless a man achieves a state of happiness of a permanent nature, he will not be contented and satisfied in life. To bring about this state of permanent contentment is the final aim of economics. Therefore, it appears the field of economics should not be restricted to material production and consumption alone, but should be extended to bring about the means of greatest happiness of a permanent nature in everyone's life.

Transcendental Meditation is a direct means of achieving inner happiness, the great happiness which could be made the very part and parcel of one's nature. Thus we find meditation brings the fulfillment of the highest goal of economics. It is for the advanced economists of today to introduce this meditation in their study. Apart from this, meditation improves the ability and efficiency of men's work and directly enriches the field of economics in the material plane, with which current economics is most concerned. Thus we find Transcendental Meditation is an essential requisite of economics in its present state.

It is suggested to the research scholars in the field of economics that this is a most suitable subject for study and development. This observation alone, meditation in connection with economics, would take the scope of economics beyond the limits of its present theories, extending its scope to its proper limits. If the field of economics is limited to creation of material abundance alone, it would appear to defeat its own purpose.

Humanities

The humanities — philosophy, theology, literature, history — are interested in recording what men have held to be of value and what ought to be of value in different spheres of human life. The basis of all the relative values of life is the Absolute, which is the source and end of everything. Therefore, without a proper knowledge of the Absolute, the progress made in the field of the humanities will remain incomplete.

The scope of the humanities should be extended beyond its present range of the curriculum to include the direct experience of the Absolute. It seems to be necessary that the study of the Absolute be introduced as a part of the study of the humanities.

Philosophy does aim at the study of the Absolute. But the fact remains that without the direct experience of the nature of the Absolute, it remains inconceivable by the fields of logic and discrimination. It is now high time that the practice of Transcendental Meditation be introduced along with the study of the humanities and the allied sciences, so that along with knowledge of relativity, man may gain the experience of the Absolute. Thus the fullest scope of the humanities may be covered.

Without meditation the mind will never experience the finer realms of relative existence, and will never know the nature of the Absolute, and thus the study of the humanities will never be complete. The humanities as taught today do not help a person to have strong convictions of life and its higher purposes. Thus they enervate man by making him feel, since all is relative, that it is not worth struggling for, instead of invigorating him in his search for complete understanding of his subject of study.

The study of the humanities will be complete only with the practice of Transcendental Meditation. This system can fill that pressing need and thus expand the scope of the humanities beyond their present limit, making it possible to fulfill their purpose.

Political Science

The purpose of the study of political science is to learn how to better organize human beings for greater peace and happiness in their lives. This has been the accepted view of the role of political science from the time of Confucius.

To improve the world, one must improve the nation; to improve the nation, one must improve the community; to improve the community, one must improve the individual. As the individual perfects himself, the family tends to perfection; from the family the effect is felt on the community; from the community, thence to the nation and to the world.

The mere comparative study of the political constitutions of different countries and their political parties and customs does in no way help a man to improve *as a man*, and therefore, if the scope of political science is restricted only to this sort of study, the very purpose of political science will be defeated. Meditation uncovers the latent faculties and improves man's ability in all walks of life. Therefore, it seems unavoidable that the practice of meditation should be included within the study of political science.

With knowledge of organizations plus the development of his inner latent faculties, man grows in better qualities and abilities. This will accomplish the purpose of the study of political science, and complete and fulfill its wider scope. Therefore, it is suggested that a few minutes daily of Transcendental Meditation be introduced into the study of political science.

Sociology

Sociology has, as its area of study, group and community behavior. It aims at improving man's lot by perfecting his social institutions. The mutual relations of the members of a community formulate the standard of the society. The social behavior of the members depends basically upon the states of their individual minds. When the individual is discontented from within, he behaves and deals with others while impelled by hidden motives to achieve his ends. This brings artificiality into his relationships with others, which in the long run results in the corruption of these relationships. This breaks the harmony of community life.

Unless sociology aims at improving the inner contentment of individuals and increases the love for others, its purpose remains unfulfilled. Transcendental Meditation makes possible the realization of this purpose. It therefore should be a part of the study of sociology.

The social scientist who has not properly integrated his own personality cannot satisfactorily study human relations and apply the knowledge of the social sciences to improve human relations. Transcendental Meditation leads the mind to inner happiness, bringing inner contentment, which results in right thinking and proper values in life. Inner contentment results naturally in increased tolerance and the capacity to harmonize the two opposite ends of behavior; spontaneous love of others brings mutual harmony.

Improvement of social relations depends upon the willingness and the ability to adjust to different natures and varying circumstances in society. Social relations improve through developed qualities of the minds and the hearts of the people. Spontaneous love goes to awaken the spirit of forgiveness, to create the ability of loving others.

One who does not have good harmony between body and mind will fail to have a complete view of life, of one's surroundings, or of the relationship between peoples. A social scientist's intellect must be so sharp, acute, and comprehensive that he combines the innocence of a child and the wisdom of an elderly father at the same time. Then alone can he understand the fullness and the completeness of the relationship between the father and the son. Furthermore, a social scientist should be able to understand and bring improvement to the behavior existing between the cruel tyrant and the innocent, helpless, oppressed man.

Psychology

Psychology has as its area of study the scope of the human mind. Physiological psychology studies how the functioning of the mind is affected by the nature of the body, while the psychology of personality focuses on individual differences in the field of thought. The purpose of both of these branches of psychology is to understand both abnormal and normal human behavior and to utilize this knowledge to aid individuals to integrate their personalities. The integration process promotes first the normality of the conscious mind and then aims at unfolding the subconscious mind.

The aim is to correlate the conscious and the subconscious states of mind. This purpose is a glorious one and, as far as the practical achievement of the idea is concerned, the method adopted to bring the abnormal minds to the normal state may be justified greatly; but the attempts of present-day analysis to correlate the conscious with the subconscious are greatly disappointing.

Their attempts to bring out the suppressed memories of traumatic experience fathom only the deeper levels of the conscious mind, which may be considered to be the upper levels of the subconscious, called by Freud the preconscious. The mind at the deeper levels of the subconscious has the ability to experience the subtler fields of creation lying beyond the ordinary sense perceptions.

The inner discontent of the great majority of people who are neither neurotic nor psychotic indicates a need for a prescription for inner happiness.

If modern psychology could satisfy this need of everyone's mind, then the study of the mind on modern lines could be considered useful and worthwhile. What is the use of the study of mind which fails either to unfold the latent mental faculties or to quench the thirst for happiness?

The system of Transcendental Meditation is a method of sharpening the mind to its ultimate point of refinement.

This is a process which positively makes active the latent levels of the subconscious mind, develops latent faculties, and brings out in life the inner happiness of the soul, thereby improving the man in aspects of thought, speech, and action, and for all good in life — both individual and social.

Only if Transcendental Meditation is made part and parcel of the study of psychology and is adopted by psychoanalysts and psychiatrists, will the study of psychology be complete and worthwhile. It is true that many advanced psychologists, who are able to see the validity of their science, do find "something wanting" in the field of modern psychology because they have found in the practical field that they are not able to produce effects as intensive as they desire.

The effects of Transcendental Meditation go beyond the limits set by psychoanalysis, which strives to bring to the conscious state only the repressed material in the preconscious area of the psyche, but fails to correlate the conscious mind with the deeper levels of the subconscious and thus fails to uncover the latent faculties — to say nothing of reaching the state of pure consciousness beyond the subconscious, or the relative states of mind beyond all limits of subconscious mind.

Here is a call for all research scholars in the field of psychology to experience for themselves the validity of the system and to work out further theories beyond the scope of the present theories of psychology.

Natural Sciences

The natural sciences — physics, chemistry, biology, geology, astronomy — study the cosmos in its various aspects of organization at the subatomic, atomic, molecular, cellular, and organismic levels of objective creation. They are concerned with the way in which matter and energy operate to bring out the different aspects of creation. Their purpose is to give man some degree of command over these forces to improve his own material well-being. By striving to get at the subtler aspects of creation, and eventually to find the ultimate cause of creation, the natural sciences aspire to use this knowledge of the ultimate cause of creation to control the different phenomena and thus make man the master of the cosmos.

All this is the proper province of the mind. If the mind of man, as scientist, is free from the worries and miseries of life, is peaceful, happy, and contented; if his intellect is sharp, and his discriminating capacity is refined; if he has a developed intuition and an increased sense of foresight — then certainly he will be able to find out much more than has yet been discovered during the many centuries of scientific research.

All of these qualities of the mind are easily developed through this system, in the absence of which the findings of modern scientists are found to be more those of chance or accident, although in the line of what is called a systematic method of research. Such accidental findings in the field of natural forces by immature minds have produced means of destruction for humanity. As a child who plays with anything, even with a burning branch or hot charcoal, so the immature minds of the present scientists all over the world are playing with whatever they find by chance during their experiments with atomic and nuclear forces.

Deeper considerations along these lines will indicate that unless the study of the Absolute supplements the field of education, the very significance of education will forever be incomplete. Let us hope that the educators of this generation will rise to the occasion and pave a way for the complete education of the present and future generations.

Highway to Rehabilitation

The need to rehabilitate the offenders and criminals in society is an age-old problem that has plagued many civilizations. So far there has not been found an effective solution to the problem of making useful people out of delinquents and criminals.

Crime is evidently a shortcut to satisfy a craving — a shortcut which goes beyond normal and legal means. Crime, delinquency, and the different patterns of antisocial behavior arise from a deep discontent of the mind; they arise from a weak mind and unbalanced emotions. A weak mind is one which lacks balance and a sense of proportion.

No approach to the problem of delinquency and crime can be truly effective unless the basic weakness of the mind is remedied.

In the part on "Transcendental Meditation,"[76] it has been made clear that the conscious mind may be enlarged to its fullest capacity and strengthened to its greatest extent by the practice of Transcendental Meditation.

Many with potential talent are among those who are shut behind bars because of their misguided behavior. Instead of being a burden, they could become useful citizens making a genuine contribution to the progress of society, if they could be successfully rehabilitated.

It has been found that all kinds of tensions are released and that the hard, cruel nature of a man changes to one of tolerance and compassion through the practice of Transcendental Meditation.

Therefore, it is necessary to introduce this system of Transcendental Meditation as a speedy and effective rehabilitation of delinquents and criminals.

---

76 See page 29.

Recreation and Rapid Rejuvenation

Continuous activity results in wear and tear on the body mechanism. Rest is a means of staying this process of wear and tear.

A man works throughout the day and becomes fatigued by the evening. He rests during the night and becomes fresh by the morning. But if he is engaged in an activity which provides increasing charm as it is continued, then he does not become fatigued. Such an activity replenishes life energy and revitalizes the body and mind.

The experience of happiness is a direct means of replenishing life energy and revitalizing the mind. The degree of replenishment and revitalization depends upon the degree of happiness experienced. If there could be a way to experience great happiness, the degree of replenishment of energy and revitalization of body and mind will be correspondingly great.

The real purpose of recreation is not only to divert the mind from one type of activity to another. It is not only to provide amusement and entertainment on the physical or mental level, but it should actually "re-create." Re-creation is the sole purpose of recreation. Its real purpose is the re-creation of body and mind, the re-creation of a fresh body and mind, and the re-creation of a healthy body and mind. It should serve to re-create a healthy coordination between body and mind and to re-create healthy surroundings and circumstances and a healthy relationship with all around.

The sole purpose of recreation is rapid and effective rejuvenation of one's personality and body, along with the rapid revitalization of the surroundings, circumstances, and relationships.

We have seen in the previous parts that the state of absolute Being is the field of absolute Bliss Consciousness. Therefore, the purpose of recreation is best fulfilled in the state of transcendental Being, which provides the direct experience of absolute bliss.

We have also seen[77] that the body, mind, and surroundings and circumstances are all subjected to the direct influence of the state of Being. Thus, the purpose of recreation and rapid rejuvenation is best served by gaining direct experience of the Bliss of Being through the regular practice of Transcendental Meditation.

Now that the system of Transcendental Meditation is available to all the people, it depends upon the people to introduce it into their lives for their own re-creation and rapid rejuvenation.

The means of recreation used up to this time — games, sports, and crafts, etc. — for the most part only serve to consume life energy rather than conserve it for the regeneration of body and mind. The commonly used methods of rejuvenation lie solely in the fields of physical manipulations and the use of cosmetics. Experience has shown that all these measures do not produce profound results. On the other hand, experience has shown that marvelous and highly gratifying results for recreation and rejuvenation of the body, mind, and surroundings are found through the regular practice of Transcendental Meditation.

Right and Wrong

Everything is so intimately connected with every other thing in creation that it is not possible to distinguish completely the existence of one from the other. And the influence of one thing on every other thing is so universal that nothing could be considered in isolation. We have already mentioned that the universe reacts to an individual action. Therefore the question of right and wrong is a highly complicated problem. A person who knew all about everything in creation and could determine the influence of any action of any individual on any stratum of existence — he alone would be able to say for certain whether that action was right or wrong.

[77] See page 181.

Right is that which produces good influence everywhere. Certainly right and wrong are relative terms, and nothing in the field of relative existence could be said to be absolute right or absolute wrong, but, even so, the right and wrong could only be judged by the influence of good or bad. If something produces relatively good influence everywhere it would be said to be right.

Human intellect does not seem to be an adequate judge of right and wrong, because reasoning has its limitations, and because the scope of the vision of the human mind is restricted when measured against the vast and unlimited field of influence produced by an action in the whole cosmos.

In the state of Cosmic Consciousness, however, when the individual mind gains the status of cosmic mind, then, of course, the intellect could be taken to be an adequate criterion for right and wrong; this criterion, however, is set on the level of Being and not on that of intellectual understanding, thinking, discrimination, or reasoning. Those whose consciousness is raised to the level of Cosmic Consciousness and function on right levels of life naturally do not take in anything that may be wrong. Thus, in such a case, the question of a suitable criterion to judge right and wrong does not arise.

We have to find an adequate criterion of right and wrong for the people whose consciousness is not raised to the level of Cosmic Consciousness.

Scriptural authority is the supreme criterion of right and wrong in the relative field of life. All that the scriptures say in the right sense of understanding is the criterion of right and wrong for all the people everywhere.

Since there exist scriptures of many different religions, the question may be asked, which one should be the authority for determining right and wrong? In answer to this query, we find that, although the language of the scriptures differ and the exponents of the scriptures have been different and come from different times in the long history of the world, the basic truth of all is the same. It is not necessary to go into great details of the history of scriptures, but it is recorded that the Vedas are the oldest scriptures. It is easy to locate the basic essential truth of life propounded by the Vedas in other scriptures that have appeared from time to time in different cultures to guide the destiny of man and to provide an authentic measure of right and wrong for the well-being of the people. The main point of interest is that the basic truth of life is contained in all religions and, therefore, it is sufficient to note that the followers of any religion may find a criterion for right and wrong according to the right understanding of the scriptures of their own religion.

A man leading life according to the scriptural authenticity of his own religion will certainly find the truth of life without any confusion, without creating any confusion by the comparative study of different religions.

This may be beyond the realm of the topic in hand, but it is timely to record that people, without being grounded in the truths of their own religions, sometimes try to understand the truths of different religions and in so doing become more confused. If a man stands on a platform and measures the different levels of the mountains, it is possible for him to record with precision the difference in the levels of the mountain heights. If he does not, however, make a rigid platform for himself before measuring the various heights, he is sure to be confused, because he has no fixed level of reference.

If one is not living the truth of any one religion, then it is not possible for one to understand or fathom the depth of wisdom of different religions, because religion is a thing to be *lived* — it is not a hypothesis for intellectual understanding. It is not the realm of metaphysics which scrutinizes the status of truth and comes to certain conclusions which are to be intellectually understood. Religion is a practical thing which has to be followed, lived, and the truth of it realized by living the principles laid down in the scriptures. The truths of metaphysics, understood intellectually, are realized in life by living the precepts of one's religion in the routine of daily life. It is necessary to live one's religion and know the truth of it by experience. When the truth of religion has been realized by living it, then there is no harm in reading the texts of other religions. Then one will find that basically the truth of one's own religion is the basic truth of the religions of others. These truths are the proper criterion of right and wrong.

The field of *Karma* — action — is so vast, unlimited, and complex that it is not possible to intellectually understand the proper criterion of right and wrong. But, needless to say, the scriptures are the foremost criterion of right and wrong. Many people talk of inner feelings. They say, "I feel like doing that, so I do it."

But "my" feelings and "my" doing can only be right or wrong according to the standard of "my" consciousness, and who knows whether "my" consciousness is absolutely pure or not?

It is the pure state of consciousness which alone could be unbiased and absolutely right for its inspiration, and this consciousness belongs only to the field of Cosmic Consciousness. The ordinary consciousness of man is motivated by many selfish ends. Therefore, the consciousness overshadowed by selfish motivations cannot possibly bring out a feeling or a thought or words or an action which could be justified as really right or wrong. But, if one's judgment is based on this scriptural authority, he has every right to feel within himself whether the problem at hand is really right or not.

It is true that one always has to feel within himself the right or wrong nature of the situation, but it is always safer to test it in the light of scriptural authenticity. One's inner feeling, however, cannot be taken to be a criterion of right and wrong. But again it may be emphasized that the ultimate criterion of right and wrong in the field of relative existence and behavior should be on the basis of the scriptures.

If one who has no knowledge of the scriptures is not able to decide for himself whether something under question is right or wrong, the problem should be decided by the elderly people in the society. The elderly people have the experience of life, they have gone through the thick and thin of human existence and have dealt with all types of people and have lived all phases of man's life. They know and understand by experience the play of Nature and the influence and effect of right and wrong actions much more than youngsters. They have seen in their lives people flourishing and being useful to themselves and others by right actions, and they have seen hundreds of people in society who took the path of wrong behavior — exhibiting cunning and cruelty, deception and manipulation. They have seen that such people have had repercussions of their own misdoing and that their heirs did not enjoy life. All these things the elderly people in the society have gone through and have seen, either in their own case or in the lives of many others. They are in a position to give advice to the younger generation on the basis of their own experience of life. Thus the verdict of the elders is another aspect of authenticity for deciding the right or wrong of any problem.

Another criterion of right and wrong may be the path of great men. History records the actions, both the successes and the failures, of great men, both good and evil, at different times in different lands. The paths they took, the practical way of life that they lived, and the consequences that they reaped from that particular way of life is again another criterion by which to determine right and wrong ways of life.

Apart from these different levels of criteria of right and wrong, it is common knowledge that it is right not to harm anyone and it is wrong to do harm. It is right to see good in others, and it is wrong to see bad in anyone. It is right to love people, and it is wrong to hate them. It is right to admire people for the good in themselves, and it is wrong to rebuke them for their shortcomings and bad behavior. It is right to advise a man if he is doing something wrong, and it is wrong not to advise him to do good. It is right to do things that will help the doer and help others, and it is wrong to do things that will harm others. It is right to speak truth, but it is wrong to speak words that will harm others, even if they are the truth. It is right to be good to others and wrong to be unpleasant to anyone. This distinction of right and wrong is to help the individual and to help the whole of creation because, as we have seen in the part on "Individual and Cosmic Life,"[78] the whole universe reacts to an individual action. Therefore, the great responsibility of right and wrong lies in the individual himself on the level of his consciousness.

It will be good to scrutinize the value of the points mentioned in the previous paragraph. We said that it is right not to harm anyone and it is wrong to harm others. We have seen that action and reaction are equal. If one slaps a child in anger, then one has slapped or beaten the whole universe and produced an atmosphere of crying and hatred, suffering and discord — not only in the child but all around him and in the universe. Perhaps the influence of cruelty, hatred, discord, and suffering is much greater in the

---

78 See page 53.

child, and is very faint in the surroundings, but the influence, nonetheless, is there. If every day a majority of the people in the world slapped someone and created the same atmosphere, then certainly the intensity of influence of discord, suffering, sorrow, and hatred would be enough to begin to show its effect in the world.

Thus, it is highly necessary that one not harm anyone. This is the least a man can do; the best thing he can do will be to produce an influence of harmony, good, kindness, and helpfulness.

We have seen in the part on "*Karma* and Being"[79] that one's action rebounds to him from all fields of creation, and, therefore, if one has done some harm to someone, that harm will return to him from the innumerable strata of Nature and for uncountable lengths of time, and therefore the best policy is not to do any harm to anyone so that we may not be harmed by anyone, and to do as much good to others as possible, so that maximum good may return to us from the entire field of creation.

It is said that we should love others for the good in them, and that it is wrong to rebuke anyone for any weakness that he might have, or for the bad behavior of others. It is a highly significant point to see good in others. As a matter of fact, no man can be all good or all bad, because human life is the result of a mixture of good and bad. Had it been only good, one would have been in the world of angels where there is no suffering and where dwells only happiness and joy. In man's life, however, one finds happiness and suffering mixed. This shows that human existence is the result of some good and some bad action. Everyone has some good in him and some bad in him, and, if we admire a man for the good that he has, then we have first seen the good in him. When we see good in him we receive the reflection of the good. If, on the other hand, one tries to see bad in someone, one receives the reflection of the bad which pollutes one's own mind and heart. If one sees good points in someone, then naturally some good reflects on him. The very action of seeing good in someone reflects that good on the mind and the heart of the seer and therefore the seer gains good from the good that he sees in the other man. This is a great skill in life, to see the good in others. Everyone has some good.

79 See page 23.

There is a story in India about a learned man living in Banaras, the seat of learning in northern India. The wise man would always admire others, and no one ever heard him speak ill of anyone. The people were all astonished that this man could see good in everything in all fields of life and creation. He would only admire things; he would not allow his mind and heart to become impure from the sight of anything bad in anyone. One day a mischievous man thought he would find something that would be all bad and present it to the wise man to see what good he could find in it. He found a dead and rotting dog lying in the street and invited the learned man to have dinner with him. (In India people take these wise men and saints to their homes for festivities and offer them meals.) He took the learned man along the street on which he had seen the rotting dog. A bad smell was coming from it, and it was an obnoxious sight to see. When they came to it the mischief maker pointed it out and said, "What a horror to come across in the street." The wise man then suddenly said, "But look at the clean white teeth of the dog." As he exclaimed about the great sparkling whiteness of the teeth of the dog, the other man fell at the feet of the wise man, and the wise man said, "If we do not want to ignore it, we will find some good in everything in the kingdom of God." This world is the garden of the almighty God and he has made a variety of flowers. You may pick the one you like, but you have no right to say that another one is bad. Even if you do not like that flower, God has created it for someone who has such taste and who will be happy to have it. Do not go by your own taste alone, but admire the great variety in the garden of God.

It is said that it is right to advise a man to do right and good, which will help him and help others. It is also said that it would be wrong not to advise a man for right or wrong, if we know it. This is a highly significant point in the world today.

A general feeling has overtaken civilized society today that they should not infringe upon the feelings, likes, and dislikes of other people. This has gone so far as to create a widespread belief that even children should not be told what to do. It is said that they should not be told what is right and what is wrong, should not be guided to do good and to steer away from bad. This probably comes from the field of psychology, which brings out the principle of growth in freedom. But it is fundamentally unfortunate to let this criterion of freedom overshadow all the basic fundamentals of advancement of life. If one does not know that the thing that he is doing is going to harm him either now or later, then someone who has that knowledge must tell him, in a spirit of love, kindness, sympathy, and help, that this action is not right.

If a child is going to pick up a burning coal, thinking that it is a lovely bright toy kept there for him to enjoy, it is only right for the parents to stop the child from going to it, even if the child resents not being permitted to jump into the fire. Such a freedom is ridiculous and dangerous to the development of man, to the development of the younger generation, and to the development of the innocent, ignorant people who do not have this wisdom and the experience of life. It is the responsibility of the elderly people to advise the young. Even if the young people resent their directions and do not obey, it is good to tell them. They will find out for themselves the result of not obeying their elders, but if the elders do not speak out at all and leave the child to find out for himself that it was wrong, then they have wasted the child's time and have been cruel to him. Knowing that it was not right for the child and not helpful for his life, they did not keep him from going that way. It is a very wrong tendency in parents that although they believe that whatever they say must be followed by the child, if they see the possibility of the child resenting their advice, they keep quiet and do not give it. It is not kindness; it is not love; it is not right for the parents to take this attitude. The child is young and inexperienced and has not that broad vision and experience of life. In all freedom for the child, the parents should tell him in love and kindness that this is wrong and that is right. If he resents it, the parent should not much insist, because if he does not obey and does that thing, he is naturally going to come across an experience which will tell him that his father or mother was right. That is the way to cultivate the tendency of the child to obey and act according to the wishes and feelings of the parents. If the child is resentful and does not obey, the parents have at least done their duty in informing the child. And then again, it is also their duty to have the child informed of the right action by their friends, teachers, and neighbors — from someone whom the child really loves and obeys. It is the duty of the parents to see that the child is brought up on all levels of wisdom and good in life. The responsibility for not having told the child what is right and wrong and not trying to change his ways if he is going wrong lies with the parents. Children are the flowers in the garden of God, and they have to be nourished. They themselves do not know which way is better for them to go. It is for the parents to make a way for them that is free from suffering. It is also part of the parents' role to correct a child if he does not obey and does wrong, but the children should be corrected in all love.

It is the foremost duty of parents to see that their children are brought up on a constructive scale of wisdom and right action in the society. And the modern tendency of putting the fate of the children completely in their own hands is highly detrimental. It only leads to uncultured growth of the younger generation.

There are schools in some countries which advocate complete freedom for children, but these schools are basically the result of a policy sponsored by those whose sole purpose is to make the nation weak and who therefore want the younger generation to grow up without traditions and without any cultured basis in life, devoid of the strength of character. It is cruel and greatly damaging to the interests of human society not to guide and shape the manner of behavior, thinking, and action of the younger generation through simultaneous love and discipline. The same idea has crept up even in the schools for very young children where the teachers are forbidden to discipline the children. The result is found in the growth of child delinquency, leading to juvenile delinquency and to great uncertainty in the minds of youngsters about the right and wrong of an action, thought, or mode of behavior. Today's youth does not understand and does not have any comprehension of the standards of traditional decent behavior of his nation. This is just the wild growth of undeveloped minds without the background of any traditional culture.

It is a shame that education in many countries has been influenced in such a manner, in the name of growth in freedom. There have been disastrous results from not shaping and directing the modes of thinking and behavior in the lives of the younger generation.

It is up to the statesmen, the patriots, and the intelligent people of the various nations to look into the disastrous results of such a pattern of education, perpetrated in the name of child psychology, and to amend the ways of education and the raising of the children. Children should be loved and they should be disciplined. They have to be loved for the growth of their life, and they have to be corrected if they are wrong. This is just to help them to succeed in life on all levels. Each nation has a tradition of its own, and its people have their religions and faiths. The children should be given the understanding of their tradition, their religion, and their faith.

It is a great mistake on the part of educators today to find an excuse in the name of democracy not to give any traditional understanding to the children. Such ideas necessarily originate with those whose motive is to weaken the nation and rob the people of their national traditions and dignity. And to root out the traditions of the society is the greatest damage that can be done to the welfare of a nation. A society without tradition has no basic stability or strength of its own; it is like a leaf left to the mercy of the wind, drifting in any direction without any stability and basis of its own.

In the name of modern education, the societies of many countries are drifting away from old tradition. The result is a wild growth of faithless people, without tradition, whose society exists only on the superficial gross level of life.

Without the benefit of established culture, it is highly important that the give and take of wisdom should exist between youth and the matured generation. And it is only right to tell the people of something that is good and not to tell them to do something that is wrong. It is necessary to say the right things and to express the right feelings on a dignified level and in a moderate manner. If an expression of right and wrong is not given by the man who has the ability to discriminate between right and wrong, then he is guilty of not sharing it with others.

It is said that it is right to speak truth, but wrong to speak words of a nature or in such a manner that they will harm others. Any harmful words spoken by an individual will certainly have repercussions on that individual. The harm is spread in the entire universe and will return from many sides to the doer. The speech should always be on a very high level of love, admiration, and forgiveness for others.

If the expression of truth damages the surroundings and atmosphere, it should not be spoken. The truth is to glorify the creation of God, and, therefore, its expression must necessarily be on that high level which is the level of the truth. It is not good to be displeasing, even in the expression of truth, because truth is the Light of God; it is most precious and pure, and it should not be brought down to the level of harm or hatred in life. It should be preserved on the high level of purity of consciousness, the great height of purity of love and godliness.

The whole field of life of the individual is a field of give and take. It is always mutual behavior that helps to sustain the life of the people and to help their evolution. Therefore the behavior is always right for those who know the truth. There is no greater act of charity than in providing a man with something that will directly elevate him and help his evolution. This is in the interest of both.

There would be no virtue greater than creating a means for the people to naturally rise to a state of life where the streams of their life would flow only in the right channel. All the virtues have to be imbibed in the very nature of the mind, so that they may be properly lived in life, and so that all right may be naturally lived. For this, as we have seen in "Art of Behavior,"[80] the only direct way is to make available the technique of Transcendental Meditation to all the people.

A great effort should be made by responsible people everywhere to see that the technique of Transcendental Meditation is given to all young people, so that the consciousness of the people may be raised. Greater energy, clarity, and purity of mind and unfoldment of mental faculties are available to all. If Transcendental Meditation is given to all students, they will grow in a right sense of values and be citizens of their country with a broad vision of life and a right, true sense of judgment of right and wrong.

LIFE IN FREEDOM

Life is lived in freedom when all the different components of life function in full coordination with each other, fulfilling their ultimate purpose of gaining a state of eternal absolute freedom in divine Bliss Consciousness.

80 See page 174.

Freedom in life means that life in all its planes of physical, mental, and spiritual existence should be full, unrestricted, unbounded, and complete for all values. Completeness of life on the physical plane means that the surroundings should be conducive to the fulfillment of life.

The body should be perfectly healthy, with all its components functioning in perfect coordination with one another so that it does not distract from the purpose of life and does not obstruct the flow of individual life. The whole wave of individual life will then be able to enjoy its state of eternal freedom and remain in the fullness of its values at all levels, if the individual is free on the plane of physical body.[81] We have seen that the state of freedom from bondage is gained by the mind, body, and surroundings with the regular practice of Transcendental Meditation.

When one produces an influence of wrong in the atmosphere, the smooth functioning of the Laws of Nature sustaining the natural process of evolution is disturbed. This resistance to the natural process of evolution restrains the growth of things and keeps them as though bound in lesser evolved states. This is the binding influence of the wrong action on the surroundings. The doer of wrong thus binds himself and the surroundings to the lower states of evolution.

It is evident that freedom on the level of mind should mean that the individual mind should be capable of doing what it likes and be able to materialize its desires without encountering any difficulties or obstacles. This would assign the status of freedom to the mind, or, freedom to life on the level of the mind.

As long as the mind is not functioning with its full potential and is not in a position to use all the faculties that it has, latent and conscious, the freedom of the mind will be restricted. Therefore, the first important aspect that could put the mind on the plane of freedom would be the state of mind wherein all its potentialities are unfolded. A state of full unfoldment of the latent potentialities of the mind is the first step toward gaining the status of freedom for the mind. We have seen in the "Science of Being" that the ability of the mind to function with a fully developed conscious capacity

81 See page 289, "Physiological Approach to God-Realization."

is achieved by the regular practice of Transcendental Meditation. Another important point regarding the freedom of the mind is freedom from the bondage of experience. On this point the whole philosophy of bondage and liberation of life turns.

This point of liberation from the bondage of experience has been very widely misunderstood for many centuries, and this misunderstanding is responsible for the loss of the direct path to freedom. The phenomenon of experience is the main field of metaphysical study, and it is the correct understanding of this phenomenon of experience that provides a direct way to eternal liberation of life. A little misunderstanding in this field results in strengthening the bondage of life in the name of gaining freedom. This long-standing misconception has led to the failure of students of metaphysics to locate the essential nature of divine Being and thus liberate themselves from the tight clutches of bondage.

We shall deal with this phenomenon of experience in detail and see where the key to liberation in life lies. It will also be interesting to discover what was the key point that has been lost by the different schools of metaphysics for the past centuries, whereby the direct path to liberation was not made clear to the students of philosophy.

Let us analyze the phenomenon of experiencing the flower. The process of experience is that we open our eyes and see a flower. This process of experiencing the flower entails the image of the flower traveling to the retina of the eye and reaching the mind. The image of the flower coming onto the mind gives the experience of the flower. The result, apart from the sight of the flower, is that the mind, as it receives the impression of the flower, is overshadowed by that impression. The mind's essential nature is as if lost and therefore only the image of the flower remains impressed on the mind. The seer, or the mind, is as though lost in the sight.

The essential nature of the subject or the experiencer within is lost in the experience of the object, just as though the object had annihilated the subject, and the subject misses the experience of its *own* essential nature while engaged in the experience of the *object*. Only the object remains in the consciousness. This is what the common experience of people is.

When the experience thus holds the object in predominance, and the subject as if loses itself in the object, the subject is said to be in bondage as if gripped by the object. The values of the object have bound or overshadowed the nature of the subject and have become predominant, leaving no trace of the essential nature of the subject. This is bondage of the subject; in the metaphysical field it is termed as the identification of the subject with the object.

From the point of view of the logic offered, it seems quite correct to conclude intellectually that identification is the nature of bondage. But this conclusion is incorrect and highly damaging. Led by this wrong conclusion, thinkers and philosophers who have guided the destiny of metaphysical thought for many centuries advocated practices for gaining freedom which have proved damaging to the lives of seekers of truth. It has been the conclusion of metaphysicians and great thinkers of the past that identification is the nature of bondage. This conclusion is incorrect, but, in order to investigate the wrong done by it, we shall, for the time being, take the statement to be true and analyze it more thoroughly.

When it was thought that identification was bondage, naturally freedom was thought to be in terms of non-identification. It was thought that if one does not identify oneself with the object of experience, then one is in the state of freedom. This metaphysical understanding (which really is misunderstanding) has given rise to various practices of gaining freedom. It has advocated that maintenance of self-awareness is the technique which would not permit one to fall into the bondage of identification. Those who attempted to gain freedom by trying to maintain self-awareness started practices which involved the remembrance of God while they were engaged in the process of experiencing things in the world or during the activity of daily life.

Another method was the attempt to be conscious of one's own self while engaged in the field of experience and activity. By trying to maintain awareness of the self while looking at the flower, the aspirant began to think that "I am looking at the flower." The emphasis of his thought was on "I am." Those who tried to maintain God Consciousness held the idea of God in their minds, remembering God while engaged in action. It was thought that if one is identified with the idea of God then his mind, engaged with God, will be free from identification.

Such practices of trying to maintain self-awareness or trying to maintain God remembrance or God Consciousness, as it was called, were undertaken with all sincerity by the aspirants of truth. The net result, however, was fatal. Trying to maintain self-awareness or God Consciousness on the level of thinking and, at the same time, engaging oneself in activity only divided the mind. While half a mind was engaged in maintaining self-awareness or the remembrance of God, the other half was engaged in the outward activity. This practice of dividing the mind only made the mind weak. Work suffered because it did not receive full concentration of the mind, and self-consciousness or God Consciousness remained only an act on the gross conscious thinking level of the mind. The aspirant was found to be neither fully in the field of activity nor fully in the state of God Consciousness.

The long practice of dividing the mind in this way resulted in weakening the personality. Those who did so neither cultivated self-consciousness, nor God Consciousness, nor were they successful in the world. The reason for this is obvious. When practical people in the society found that the life of those people devoted to God or to metaphysics was found to be half in and half out in the world, this created a peculiar condition in the society. Practical people began to be afraid to start such practices of spiritual unfoldment, because those who were devoted to those practices were found not practical in life and were found weak and less dynamic.

A thought of freedom, although it seems to be good, is only a thought, and not a state. A thought of freedom is as much binding as any other thought. Thought, by its very nature, is out of one's self. When the mind begins to entertain a thought, it comes into the field of duality, and the thought overshadows the essential nature of the mind. Therefore, any thought causes identification. This problem of identification was thus not at all solved by the thought of the Self or of the Divine or of God. That is why such practices failed to give freedom to the people and the quest for freedom remained unsatisfied and became muddled by such practices of cherishing the idea of the divine Self or God on the thinking level.

The fundamental error in these practices was that the identification itself was thought to be bondage. As a matter of fact, identification is *not* bondage. What *is* bondage is the inability to maintain Being along with identification. What is bondage is the inability to maintain Being while indulging in the field of experience and activity.

If identification were bondage, freedom would be possible only in the state after death, in which one ceases to experience and ceases to be active. As long as one is alive, one continues to experience and act, and so it is impossible to avoid identification during one's lifetime.

Identification is not bondage, because freedom has to be lived in the world, and living in the world means identifying oneself with everything for the sake of experience and activity.

Identification should not be a horror to the seekers of truth and to the aspirants of reality. It is only that a state of mind has to be cultivated so that the mind engaged with outer things does not overshadow the pure state of Being.

The maintenance of Being can never be achieved by the practice of thinking about Being. Being can be spontaneously lived on the level of thought only when the very nature of the mind is transformed into the nature of Being. Then all experiences will be on the level of Being. Only then is it possible that experience will not be able to overshadow or overthrow the validity of Being. Being will be lived along with identification.

If one thinks about Being, it is just a thought of Being, not the state of Being. In order that Being may be established in the very nature of the mind, so that during the wakeful, dreaming, or deep-sleep states, through all experience of activity and inactivity in life, Being is not obstructed and continues to be, it is necessary that the mind be transformed into the nature of Being.

For this it is necessary that familiarity with the state of Being be gained by the mind to such a degree that the mind lives Being through all conditions and situations of life. This is possible by bringing the conscious mind through the subtle states of experience of thinking to eventually transcend the subtlest thought and arrive at the transcendental state of Being. Coming out into the field of relative existence, the mind emerges familiar with the state of pure Being. Through the regular practice of Transcendental Meditation the nature of Being becomes steadfast in the very nature of the mind to such an extent that it can never be overshadowed by anything of relative order.

This permanent infusion of the absolute Bliss Consciousness establishes the mind in the state of everlasting freedom, and, when the mind identifies itself with the objects of experience or with the activity, Being and the freedom continue to exist along with the experience and activity. This is the state of eternal freedom which cannot be obstructed or overshadowed by any state of experience, activity or passivity, of the relative existence.

Thus, freedom in life belongs to the field of Being. It can be established only through the practice of Transcendental Meditation, which establishes pure Being in the very nature of the mind by taking the mind to the field of the Transcendent.

This state of eternal freedom can never be established by the practice of maintaining a thought of Being or a thought of God.

Being, or the Divine, or God, is something to be lived; a mere fanciful thought of It does not much help in practical life. A thought of God could be cherished in the mind, but, apart from providing a psychological satisfaction, it does not provide the advantages of contact with the almighty God. Thought is just abstract imagination, it is not a concrete state. This is the fundamental difference between really succeeding in establishing eternal freedom in life and remaining hovering in the thought of freedom.

Such misunderstanding in the field of metaphysics for the past many centuries has only helped to mislead the genuine seekers of truth and has created a great gulf between the spiritual and material aspects of life.

The whole conception of freedom, as well as the way to establish it in life, is so delicate and fine that it is easy for it to be lost by the passage of time. Once the fine thread is lost, the whole field becomes confused as far as reality is concerned.

Freedom in God Consciousness is gained by leading the mind to the field of Bliss Consciousness, not by thinking about Bliss Consciousness and making a mood of it. Unfortunately, realization of God or eternal freedom on Earth has remained only on the ordinary thinking level. That is why mystical practices in the name of enlightenment and God-Realization have only left aspirants in a state of suspension in the mere thought of the Divine.

With the thought of God, the mind takes a deep swing into the abstract. The thought envelops the mind and the aspirant loses a clear conception of the outer surroundings and feels that it is the state of Cosmic Consciousness that he has experienced. This is sheer delusion. By being intent on the idea of being a king, one can never attain the state of a king. By thinking he is a king over and over, no one can really attain kingship. In order to be a king, it is necessary to have oneself enthroned and actually enjoy the status of a king. To achieve God Consciousness and to live God Consciousness in life, it is necessary to put ourselves in the state of the Divine.

God is omnipresent — the Divine is present everywhere. This is the common understanding. So, unless the mind is brought to the level of omnipresent Being, the omnipresence of God cannot be lived. This thinking of God and the Divine has created a great barrier in the fields of metaphysics and of religion. It has only helped the people to remain as though suspended in the air in the name of God.

God-Realization is a positive concrete experience on the level of pure existence. It is more real, more substantial, and more sublime than the existence of anything on Earth. The existence of divine Being is absolute and can very well be lived if the mind is led from the field of relativity to God Consciousness in the transcendental field, which is omnipresent, omniscient, and omnipotent. Through Transcendental Meditation the mind is actually brought to this level, and, as we have seen in the part on "How to Contact Being,"[82] the process is simple. It is only necessary that one put his mind in the process, transcend, and then come back to the relative field. This occurs over and over again, morning and evening. Within a short time a state of mind will be gained in which Being is not lost, even while the mind is engaged in the field of experience and activity. This is the state of real freedom in life.

We have also seen that during the process of transcending, the conscious capacity of the mind increases, and, when one comes out of meditation and engages oneself in the field of experience and activity in the world, the experience of objects becomes deeper, fuller, and more substantial. One engages in the activity with greater energy, more intelligence, and improved

82 See page 27.

efficiency. This is the glory of divine realization: that, on the one hand, the state of Being is cultivated to remain for all times infused into one's very nature, and, on the other, the field of activity becomes more substantial and more rewarding on all levels. This brings harmony between the inner, spiritual, and outer material glories of life.

This state has been the object of a great quest for man from time immemorial because it glorifies all aspects of one's life. The material life of man is brightened by the light of the inner Self. That is why the emphasis of all the scriptures of religions and of the whole field of metaphysics is that the state of Self-Realization or God-Realization is the goal of man. Because, on the way to achieving this goal, the world is made better, efficiency improves, and the man becomes more capable in the world. He enjoys the world more on all levels while enjoying the divine. The individual enjoys the world to the maximum because the nature of his mind is now Bliss Consciousness, and the Bliss Consciousness is the basis of all experience and activity. This is the state of a God-realized man. This is the state of a man successful in the world. These states go hand in hand. Success of the divine quest brings the height of success in the world in a most natural way and the individual life is fulfilled. Then, under all circumstances, he virtually lives the life in eternal freedom.

We have seen in all the parts on the "Art of Living" how this eternal freedom in life glorifies all fields of thinking, speaking, acting, and behaving, along with the whole field of *Karma* — the past and the present. The way to eternal freedom is also the way to success in the world, and the key to it is the regular practice of Transcendental Meditation.

The Problem of World Peace

The problem of peace is only solved fully and finally in the state of divine consciousness or God Consciousness in eternal freedom. The way to peace has become a great problem in the world today in all its aspects: peace of the individual, peace of the family, peace of society, and peace in the world.

The basis of peace is bliss. Unless one is happy, he cannot be in peace. Peace without real lasting happiness is only passivity. When one sleeps in the night he feels absence of activity. This is called peace. But when he wakes up in the morning and comes into the field of thought, speech, and activity, he begins to feel miserable again. The peace felt by the absence of activity is not lasting.

The peace gained by emptying the mind of thoughts, holding the mind in suspension, is due only to the lack of pressure of thought. When such a mind returns to the field of thinking and acting, it again begins to feel the pressures of thought and action. Then the individual begins to feel unpeaceful. All such practices of silencing the mind are wrong. Such practices continued for much time result in making the mind dull.

There are many groups in the world who sit in silence and try to hear their inner voice or the voice of God, as they term it. All such practices make the mind passive and dull. Those who practice silencing the mind begin to lack in brilliance. Dullness can be seen on their faces. They are not energetic in the field of action. They look peaceful, but they are passive in life. Peace at the cost of activity is at the cost of life.

Such an experience of peace is at the cost of efficiency in life and at the cost of life itself. An attempt to silence the mind in the hope of experiencing pure consciousness is pursuing a mirage. When one keeps the thoughts out of the mind, it becomes passive because it remains on the conscious thinking level without a thought. This practice makes the mind dull. What is necessary is not the attempt to vacate the mind, but that the conscious mind be led on to the subtle states of thinking to eventually transcend the subtlest state and arrive at the positive state of Being. Holding the mind on the conscious level is only taking it out of the field of activity and allowing it to be passive or inactive. This only helps to diminish the brilliancy of the mind and brings dullness and passivity to it.

People who practice this do feel peace in life because they are practicing suppression or negation of thoughts. When a mind that has gained the quality of sluggishness and dullness through such practices does not have a thought in a very energetic manner and does not engage itself energetically in the field of experience and activity, peace is felt because of the innate dullness of the mind. But, whenever some serious problems in life arise, the mind feels a strain because it has been trained to remain dull and passive. When the individual must become active to accomplish some work in a very precise and energetic manner, the mind feels the strain.

Such practices have also done great damage to the progress of the individual and society.

Thus we find that practices to silence the mind in the first place produce dullness in the mind, and, in the second place, the peace that is felt is not lasting. As we have said, peace can be lasting only if the mind could be made happy forever. Only if the very nature of the mind could be transformed to Bliss Consciousness could peace be lasting. The quest for peace should be directed to bringing the mind to the field of the Transcendent, the source of all happiness, through the practice of Transcendental Meditation.

When one is not peaceful, fear, lack of self-confidence, and all the pettiness in life arise and the consciousness of man becomes so abjectly miserable that he cannot think and cannot accomplish anything worthwhile. Fear is just lack of self-confidence, and the basis of confidence is in contentment which can only result from the experience of bliss. There is nothing in the world which can really bring lasting contentment to the mind because everything in the world, although it provides some happiness to the mind, is not intensive enough to satisfy the great thirst for happiness of the mind. The only field of contentment is the transcendental field of Bliss Consciousness. Unless one arrives at that state, one's peace will always be threatened by everything in the world because of lack of contentment.

The only golden gate to peace in life is the experience of transcendental Bliss Consciousness, and this great glory of life is easy for everyone to achieve and live throughout life.

We have seen in the part on the "Individual and Cosmic Life"[83] that the life of the individual in its every thought, word, and action influences the entire field of the cosmos. Therefore, someone with peace at heart naturally vibrates peace and harmony to influence the whole universe. Those who are restless, worried, and troubled in life and have no experience of Bliss Consciousness are continually producing an influence of adverse nature in

83 See page 53.

the surroundings. The tensions and worry in the individual produce a tense influence around him and contaminate the atmosphere. All unrighteous, immoral, and sinful activity produces a degenerating and bad influence in the atmosphere. When large numbers of people in the world are miserable and tense, the atmosphere of the world also has that quality. When the tensions in the atmosphere extend beyond a certain limit, the atmosphere breaks into collective calamities.

It has been brought out by Charak and Sushrut, the great exponents of medical science in ancient India, that as long as people behave in righteousness, the atmosphere remains full of harmonious vibrations. The crops are good, the Sun shines, it rains at the proper times, and the whole life in creation enjoys everything in the atmosphere. But when people lose righteousness and act against the moral codes of life, the balance of Nature is disturbed, and the atmosphere breaks into collective calamities like famines, floods, accidents, and all that damages life in the world. This is the diagnosis with regard to the health of the world.

Thus we find from every angle that in order to produce a good, harmonious, and healthy atmosphere for the good of all creatures in the world, it is necessary that man live in happiness, peace, and abundance. Every man has a chance to live this way.

The problem of world peace can only be solved by solving the problem of peace of the individual, and the problem of peace of the individual can only be solved by creating a state of happiness in the individual. Therefore the problem of peace in the individual, family, society, nation, and world as a whole, is solved by the practice of Transcendental Meditation, which is a direct way to establish Bliss Consciousness in the life of the people.

Where there is disagreement and dissension in families and in the circle of friends, the disharmony appears to be occurring in small circles. Individuals hardly realize that they are contributing to an influence that disrupts and destroys the peace of the world through the ill feeling, malice, bad behavior, harsh words, and suffering they are creating.

All international conflicts are caused by the collection of great tensions in the atmosphere that have been released by the individuals. And the individual hardly realizes that constantly through his thought, speech, and action he is gathering the influence of hatred and tensions in the atmosphere that will sometime break and bring back to him all the results of what he has been storing around him.

In the part on the "Individual and Cosmic Life,"[84] we have seen how the life of an individual is responsible to the life of the cosmos. We have seen in the part on "*Karma* and Being"[85] how a man through his every action is responsible to the whole world.

It is now high time for all those interested in world peace to start from the individual units of universal life. Trying to solve the problems of international conflicts, while ignoring the level of the individual problems, is not an adequate attempt to establish world peace.

If a crisis is created in Berlin today, the minds of all the statesmen rush to Berlin. If something happens in the Congo, their whole attention goes to the Congo. If there is fighting in the Himalayas, the attention of all is directed there. Trying to solve these problems individually is just like trying to make a leaf healthy by watering it instead of watering the root. By now, man should be wise enough to know that only by watering the root can the leaf be helped. By now, the statesmen of the world should be wise enough to adopt ways and means to bring happiness and creative peace in the life of the individuals in their attempt to create world peace.

All the laudable aims of the United Nations are only scratching the surface of the problem of world peace. If the minds and resources of the statesmen of all the countries could be utilized to popularize and effectively bring to the individuals the practice of Transcendental Meditation, the face of the world and the world situation could be changed overnight.

It is a shame that, with all the intelligence and sincerity in attempts to help people, hardly enough is being done to improve the life of the individual. As long as the statesmen in power remain ignorant of the possibility of improving the life of individuals and bringing abundance of peace, happiness, and creative intelligence to them through the simple system of Transcendental Meditation, the problem of world peace will always be dealt with on the surface and the world will continue to have cold wars and hot wars.

84 See page 53.
85 See page 23.

History records the attempts of statesmen of all times to establish a state of lasting world peace, but, because all the attempts have been made on the surface of international life and not on the improvement of the life of the individual, the problem of world peace is a problem for every generation.

UNESCO[86] is trying to improve the individual but all their attempts again are on the surface value of life. The attempts to develop cultural relationships between nations and to bring literacy to the lesser developed areas of the world are again just scratching the surface of the problem of world peace.

Here is an opportunity for all the great minds engaged in the work of UNESCO to take it upon themselves, with their vast resources, to bring this simple system of Transcendental Meditation to every individual everywhere. If this is done there will be established a natural state of lasting world peace. There will be love, kindness, sympathy, gratitude, and mutual admiration on all levels of international life. Here is something of practical value, which can really change the face of the world from the state of suffering, misery, doubt, hatred, and fear to a state of happiness, peace, creativity, kindness, and love.

Any generation whose leaders sincerely start to widely apply the system of Transcendental Meditation to the life of the people will succeed in creating a state of lasting world peace. If the statesmen and influential leaders of public life of the present generation do this, the credit will be theirs and they will cherish the satisfaction of leaving a better world for the oncoming generations.

A solid foundation of permanent peace and happiness in the world can be laid down in the present generation. Success depends upon the undertaking by those who have the ability and resources to do something of practical value. If the fortunate ones of the present generation lay a proper foundation, and the fortunate leaders of the oncoming generations maintain the regular practice of this Transcendental Meditation in the lives of their people, there will be all glory of life enjoyed on all levels for all the generations.

Be it so, is the sincere prayer to the Almighty of people of goodwill everywhere.

---

86 United Nations Educational, Scientific and Cultural Organization

Section IV

FULFILLMENT

- FULFILLMENT OF LIFE 245
- FULFILLMENT OF RELIGION 250
- FULFILLMENT OF PSYCHOLOGY 256
- FULFILLMENT OF PHILOSOPHY 264
- PATHS TO GOD-REALIZATION 267
  - God 267
  - Impersonal Aspect of God 267
  - Personal Aspect of God 272
  - Intellectual Path to God-Realization 278
  - Emotional Path to God-Realization: Path of Devotion 285
  - Physiological Approach to God-Realization 289
  - Mechanical Path to God-Realization 295
  - Psycho-physiological Approach 298
- GENERATION AFTER GENERATION 300

Fulfillment of Life

Fulfillment of life lies in gaining the status of divine life and living the life of eternal freedom in fullness of all values of human existence.

Fulfillment of human consciousness lies in the attainment of divine consciousness, God Consciousness, which brings together the absolute and relative values of life.

The Bliss Consciousness of absolute Being and the relative joys of the variety of creation should be lived hand in hand. This means the fulfillment of life in Cosmic Consciousness.

For the sake of clarity we shall consider what Cosmic Consciousness is.

We have seen that during Transcendental Meditation[1] the conscious mind arrives at the transcendental field of absolute Being of unmanifested nature. Here in this field, the mind transcends all relativity and is found in the state of absolute Being. The mind has transcended all limits of the experience of thought and it is left by itself in the state of pure consciousness. This state of pure consciousness, or state of absolute pure Being, is called Self-consciousness.

When this Self-consciousness is not lost, even when the mind comes out of the Transcendent and engages itself once more in the field of activity, then the Self-consciousness gains the status of Cosmic Consciousness. The Self-consciousness is then eternally established in the nature of the mind. Even when the mind is awake, dreaming, or in deep sleep, the Self-consciousness is naturally maintained and is said to be Cosmic Consciousness.

Cosmic Consciousness means that consciousness which includes the experience of the relative field along with the state of transcendental pure Being. This state of Cosmic Consciousness is a state where the mind lives in eternal freedom and remains unbounded by what it experiences during

1 See page 29.

all the activity of the outside relative world. This state of freedom from the bondage of experience gives the mind the status of Cosmic Consciousness, the state of eternal freedom in any of the relative states of life — waking, dreaming, or sleeping.

Perfect mental and physical health is the key to fulfillment of life, where the Divine Intelligence speaks in all the phases of life, where God Consciousness permeates all the experiences and activities of daily life, and where universal love flows and overflows in the heart; Divine Intelligence fills the mind, and perfect harmony in the behavior results. In such a state of integrated life, where all the planes of living are infused with divine consciousness, and when the universal love overflowing for everything becomes concentrated in devotion to God, then life finds fulfillment in the unbounded ocean of divine wisdom.

The world is the active Divine; everything rises as a wave on the eternal ocean of Bliss Consciousness. Every perception, the hearing of every word, the touch of every little particle, and the smell of whatever it may be, brings a tidal wave of the ocean of eternal bliss — in every arising of a thought, word, or action is the arising of the tide of bliss.

In every static and dynamic state of life the divine glory of the unmanifested is found dancing in the manifested field of life. The Absolute dances in the relative. Eternity pervades every moment of transitory existence. The life is then ultimately fulfilled when Cosmic Consciousness is centered in devotion to God. Such is the condition of perfection of life where a cosmically evolved man rises to the realm of devotion.

Fortunate are those evolved, cosmically conscious men who have the chance of a devotion which brings the value of infinite Bliss Consciousness to a concentrated state. In comparison with this state of devoted life, the life of Cosmic Consciousness is spoken of in terms of "mere Cosmic Consciousness." It is as if gaining Cosmic Consciousness is not actually attaining the ultimate fulfillment of life, but it is merely gaining the ability for acquiring real and ultimate fulfillment.

Unless one is cosmically evolved, unless one lives the eternity in the day-to-day transitory activity of life, it is not possible to overflow on the level of universal love. Unless one overflows on the level of universal love, where is the possibility of having that universal love in a concentrated manner?

The personal love for mother and father and for husband or wife is just symbolic of the concentrated state of universal love which a cosmically evolved soul attains in the state of devotion to God. The level of love in the heart of a child for his toys, games, and studies is spread out over those objects, but the concentrated state of his love is for his mother. This is an analogy to make clear the degree of love when one is devoted to God, having attained the state of Cosmic Consciousness. A child's innocent fancy has a certain amount of love, and that love is concentrated in the love for his mother. A student has a certain amount of love in his heart for the various branches of learning, but all this love is found concentrated in the love for his teacher. Similarly, a husband has a certain amount of love flowing in his heart in the whole field of life, but he finds the concentrated state of all his love in the love for his wife.

In the same way, a man with Cosmic Consciousness has the unbounded, unlimited amount of love overflowing in all directions for everything. When this overflowing, unlimited, unbounded cosmic universal love becomes concentrated in the devotion to God, then that concentrated state of universal love is of such a degree that it brings ultimate fulfillment of life.

Much more concentrated is the state of Cosmic Consciousness in devotion to God than any love that could ever be in any sphere of existence. To live this state of concentrated universal love is the ultimate fulfillment of life. Here is the unbounded flow of love — at the sight of everything, at the hearing of everything, at the smelling of anything, at the tasting of anything, at the touch of anything. The entire life in its multifarious diversity is nothing but fullness of love, bliss, and contentment — eternal and absolute.

The ability for fulfillment comes with the constant practice of Transcendental Meditation in order to acquire Cosmic Consciousness and then by a turning to devote oneself to God. Unless the state of Cosmic Consciousness is achieved, devotion in the real sense of the word does not begin, it does not mean much. A man whose heart does not flow in universal love does not gain much from devotion, because devotion results in surrender, and surrender means loss of one's identity and the gaining of the identity of the beloved. The path of love, the path of devotion is successfully traversed only by the cosmically evolved souls.

A man who has not risen to Cosmic Consciousness, who is shrouded by selfish individuality and who is only awake in the identity of his individual self, cannot have a clear and significant conception of love or devotion. Although people on all levels of consciousness feel love in their hearts and feel devotion to God, the charm of devotion in the state of Cosmic Consciousness is a charm beyond the limits of imagination.

Devotion and love belong in full value only to the life of Cosmic Consciousness. Below that standard of Cosmic Consciousness, devotion and love have not much significance and value on the ordinary human level. The devotion of an unrealized man is just an attempt, an effort, a strain. At best it leads to an imagination of the greater and more intensified states of love. But the love and devotion of a cosmically evolved man has a significant and substantial value of love and devotion that reaches eternity, and that love and devotion binds eternity into one single individuality. That is the power of love, that is the power of devotion.

Below the level of Cosmic Consciousness the power of love and devotion is limited and insignificant, and therefore all those who want to follow the path of devotion are invited to start the practice of Transcendental Meditation, which enables the individual to rise to a state of Cosmic Consciousness without much struggle and strife.

The individual then comes in tune with the Cosmic Life, the movements of the individual are in accord with the movements of the entire cosmos, the purpose of the individual is found in the purpose of the entire cosmos, and the life of the individual is found established in Cosmic Life. Such a state of the individual is a part of the cosmic state of life. The will of man, then, is the will of God; the activity of man, then, is the desire of God; and man, thus, fulfills the purpose of God. When a man accomplishes the purpose of God, when he breathes the desire of God, then the son of God is the word of God. Then the Father in Heaven and man on Earth are united in the same goal of eternal good. Man, through all his thoughts, words, and actions, produces an influence which serves the purpose of creation, and on all levels of his individual life he gains fulfillment in the purpose of Cosmic Life.

The selfishness of man, then, is the selfish end of God; the individual mind of man is the cosmic mind of God; the individual breath of man is the cosmic breath of God; the individual speech of man is the expression of cosmic silence.

The Lord speaks through him, the omnipresent Cosmic Life gains expression in his activity, the omniscient is expressed in the limitations of the man's individual personality, the Cosmic Intelligence finds expression in his individual mind, the thought of Cosmic Life is materialized in his process of thinking, the immutable silence of eternal Being finds expression in the man's thought, speech, and action. The man's eyes behold the purpose of God, his ears hear the music of Cosmic Life, his hands hold on to cosmic intentions, his feet set the Cosmic Life in motion; he walks on Earth, yet walks in the destiny of Heaven; he sees, yet sees the glory of God; he hears, yet hears the silence; he speaks, yet speaks the word of God; he speaks, yet speaks the intention of God; he speaks and draws out the purpose of Cosmic Life; he speaks and gives expression to the cosmic purpose; he speaks yet his words speak eternal Being. The man is the living expression of the omnipresent, omniscient, Cosmic Existence.

Here is he who can speak for God, here is he who can speak for the Cosmic Law, here is he who acts for God, here is the image of God on Earth. His life is the stream of cosmic Being. His individual life stream is a tidal wave of the eternal ocean of cosmic Being, a wave which holds within itself the entire ocean of Cosmic Life. He is the expression of the inexpressible eternal Being. He moves in the ever immovable status of the Absolute; his activity of relative existence expresses the eternal silence of the Absolute. In the radiance of his relative life, the Absolute finds in him an expression of its Being. Angels and gods enjoy his being on Earth, and the Earth and heavens enjoy the existence of the bliss of eternal Being embodied in the form of man.

The formless appears in form, the silence becomes vibrant, the inexpressible is expressed in a personality, and the Cosmic Life is breathed by the individual.

This is how, when the breath of the individual becomes the impulse of eternal life, the individuality breathes universal existence, and then is gained the fulfillment of life.

Fulfillment of Religion

The fulfillment of religion lies in gaining for man a direct way to God-Realization and all that is necessary for making him a complete man, a man of fully integrated life, a man of great intelligence, creativity, wisdom, peace, and happiness.

The fulfillment of religion lies in gaining for man that for which the word "religion" itself stands. "Religion" comes from the Latin root "religare," meaning "re," back; "ligare," to bind: or, that which binds one back. The purpose of religion is to bind man back to his source, his origin.

If religion succeeds in bringing a man back to his source, in bringing the mind back to its source, in bringing the body and mind's activity back to the source of all activity, religion succeeds in fulfilling its purpose. Mind is the pivot of life. If the mind could be drawn back to its origin, the whole of life would thus be drawn to its source and the purpose of religion would be fulfilled.

Religion is a way, or at least it should be a way, to raise the consciousness of man to the level of God Consciousness, to raise the human mind to the level of Divine Intelligence or universal cosmic mind.

The purpose of religion is to set the life of the individual in tune with the Laws of Nature and set it so that it naturally flows in the stream of evolution.

Religion should coordinate the individual life with Cosmic Life and improve all values of human life. Religion provides a practical way to the realization of the supreme reality brought to light by philosophy. Philosophy is descriptive, whereas religion has practical value in providing a direct way to God-Realization. It is a direct means of enabling human beings to evolve to the level of the Divine. Religion dictates the do's and don'ts of life in order to channel the activity of the individual to attain the high purpose of human existence. All these do's and don'ts of religion are meant to provide a direct way to the realization of the ultimate reality, or, freedom in God Consciousness. Religion serves a practical purpose.

Without enumerating the details of the deplorable state of religions in the world today, it will suffice to say that it is found only in body; it is devoid of the spirit. Only the rituals and dogma are found; the spirit has departed. That is why the followers of religion do not find fulfillment.

This does not mean that religious rituals have no value. The dogmatic aspects of religion are certainly necessary because, for the soul to be, the body has to be. They have the value of constituting the body of religion for the main purpose of providing a proper field for the spirit of religion to guide the destiny of the people.

All the rituals of the various religions are like the body, and the practice of Transcendental Meditation is like the spirit. Both are necessary; they should go hand in hand. One will not survive without the other.

When the spirit leaves the body, the body begins to disintegrate. This is the case of religions today. They seem to be in a state of disintegration because they lack spirit. Religion today is like the corpse of a man without the man. The rites and rituals remain without elevating the consciousness of the people.

The inner spirit of religion does not seem to exist. If it does exist at all, it fails to appeal to the people. Because of its ineffectiveness, it has practically ceased to capture the fancy of the modern man. There is hardly any religion in the world today which has, in the conscious level of its scriptures, the description of the practice of Transcendental Meditation. That is why all over the world religion has lost its effectiveness and fails to fulfill its purpose.

The purpose of religion should not only be to indicate what is right and what is wrong, but its direct purpose should be to elevate man to a state of life so that he will only go for that which is right and by nature will not go for that which is wrong. The true spirit of religion is lacking when it counts only what is right and wrong and creates fear of punishment and hell and the fear of God in the mind of man. The purpose of religion should be to take away all fear from man. It should not seek to achieve its purpose through instilling fear of the Almighty in the mind.

Religion should forward a way of life, where the life is naturally established in tune with the cosmic purpose of evolution, and every thought, word, and action of the individual may be guided by a higher purpose in a natural way. It is not that a man is required to strain in order to do right and to aspire for higher values of life, but, by nature, all his thoughts, words, and actions should be placed not only on the level of the highest purpose of life, but on the level of the goal of the highest purpose of life. Religion should be strong enough to bring to the individual that state of fulfillment in life in a natural manner, without strenuous practices or long years of training. If it is fully integrated in itself, a religion should enable man to live fulfillment naturally.

A really alive and integrated religion should be able to induce in man a spirit of fulfillment. By the time a man comes out of the limitations of life as a minor and attains his majority, his nervous system is the fully developed nervous system of a man. By this time he should have gained, by following his faith, the status of fulfillment of life. The rest of his life should be lived in such fulfillment.

A fully alive and integrated religion will be that in which every man is a man of realized God Consciousness, a man of full values of life, a man of God — the Divine in the form of man on Earth.

The possibility is now at hand for the peoples of all religions to start the practice of Transcendental Meditation and acquire within themselves a state of integrated life by the direct experience of absolute consciousness of divine Being.

A religion that delivers to the people a message of doing good but fails to develop their consciousness and fails to elevate them to live a life of all good in a natural manner is merely a religion of words. A religion worthy of the name should be of real practical value. It should directly put man on a way of life full of all good and free from evil.

It is the responsibility of religion that all good should shine on the faces of its followers. If religious teachings fail to inspire the people to live a life of good in God Consciousness, it should be for the preachers of religions to review their strength and do justice to their teachings. The inner light of religions is missing from the religious teachings, and this is the case all over the world. The result is absence of peace and happiness in the lives of the people, and increasing tensions everywhere. Those religious people who seem to have peace in their lives are often found to be men of passive attitude, lacking dynamic life — which is not a feature of true religious life. This passivity springs from the misguided application of religious idealism.

The life of a religious man should have all right and dynamic activity on the surface of life, and underneath, should have the unshakable eternal peace that lies at the depths of the ocean.

Life should be such that the religion is naturally lived with its purpose accomplished. It should not be a struggle to live or to fulfill. Life should be lived in fulfillment for all its values. The man on Earth, a man of a real, lively, and integrated religion on Earth, should be a moving God, the speaking Divine — not a struggling man with faith in God, yet still searching for the meaning of the Divine. The substance of God, the status of God, the existence of God, the experience of God Consciousness, the life of divine consciousness — all these should be the natural life of man. Faith in God and faith in religion is supposed to have a purpose in life. Any faith for the sake of faith alone is just a draw on the energy of the people.

"Faith moves mountains" is a common saying, but, if faith is not able to relieve a man from suffering and bring him all good, then that faith needs something more to make it productive. The people belonging to different religions do have faith in their religions, and it is admirable how they endure in their faith through the thick and thin of life. So it is for the preachers of religion to provide them with something of practical value through which their faiths will lead them to the goal of life.

The ministers are the ministers of God standing between man and God. Their responsibility is that of a link between humanity and divinity. Likewise, the priests in the temples stand as mediators between man and God, and, as such, their responsibility is great. Their life must be an integrated life in God Consciousness, and, if they fail to live life in God Consciousness, then they cease to be a link between man and God.

It is high time that the custodians of religions were awakened. Here is something offered to them in all love of God, and in all love for what they stand for. It is high time that Transcendental Meditation be adopted in the churches, temples, mosques, and pagodas. Let all the people who are proud of their religions, who are living their own ways of life in their own faiths, enjoy the fulfillment of life — the divine life in the life of man.

Here is the fulfillment of every religion in the simple practice of Transcendental Meditation. This belongs to the spirit of every religion; it has existed in the early stages of every faith; it is something which has been lost. It has been lost in practice. Certainly no one can be held responsible for that. The responsibility for the loss of the spirit of religions lies with the eternity of time. But now is the time for revival.

Fortunately this technique has come to light in the present generation. Let it be adopted by the peoples of all religions, and let them enjoy it while being proud of their faiths. Let the intelligent minds of all religions and the custodians of the various faiths delve into the deeper essence of their scriptures, find Transcendental Meditation in the textbooks of their own faiths, learn the practice, and adopt it in the light of the teachings of their religions.

The basic premise of every religion should be that man need not suffer in life. Any man belonging to any religion should have no place in his life for suffering, tension, immorality, vices, sinful thought, speech, or action. All these negative aspects of life should not exist for a man following religion.

It is not necessary to take an account of the deplorable state of the followers of religions today: increasing tension in life, suffering, disease, and incapacities of human values in all faiths. These failures on the part of religions are the reasons why modern life is drifting away from religion. Even though the people carry the name of religion, they fail to live the values of a religious life.

A religious life should be a life in bliss, joyfulness, peace, harmony, creativity, and intelligence. The stream of religious life should flow on the level of common sense at least. It should be a life of love, kindness, tolerance for others, and an innate desire to help one's fellow man. All these qualities should make up the natural state of mind of a religious man. If these qualities — these virtues, morals, and the state of God Consciousness — are not naturally found in a religious man, then he is merely carrying the burden of the name of religion.

Religion should not only provide a solid foundation, but also should be able to build a high edifice of divine life in the life of man, and this can be accomplished only by transforming man's nature into divine Nature. It will be difficult for religious ritual in the churches or at home to transform the inner tendencies of the people into the essential qualities of the divine Nature. Yet, unless this is done, life on Earth can never be virtuous, moral, and dignified on all levels.

Suggestive teachings on the surface of the conscious mind do not have much to do with the transformation of the inner mind. In teaching truthfulness, kindness, love for others, and fear of God, the religions have virtually failed to provide any significant degree of evolution of human life, because a practical technique of bringing the human mind into divine value has not been used.

Unless the mind rises high in its values and attains a fair degree of Divine Intelligence, the man will continue to err. To err is human, to be free from error is divine. Thus, so long as man remains in the field of humanity, he is apt to err. It is necessary, therefore, to take him above the field of error, bring the Divine Intelligence within the range of the conscious mind, and thereby infuse the divine Nature into the nature of man. Raise humanity into divinity — then it does not matter what rituals are followed and which are ignored on the gross level of religion and life.

As long as the spirit of religion dominates the life of the people, it does not matter what name they give to their religion, or what rituals they follow in their churches, temples, mosques, or pagodas. As long as they are established in the spirit of religion and have risen to the state of God Consciousness, as long as they live the Divine in their day-to-day life, as long as the stream of life is in tune with the cosmic stream of evolution, it does not matter whether they call themselves Christian, Mohammedan, Hindu, or Buddhist — any name will be significant. On the gross level of life these names carry significance, but on the level of Being, they all have the same value.

What does matter is that man should live a life in God Consciousness in freedom and should live an integrated life of completeness. The key to the fulfillment of every religion is found in the regular practice of Transcendental Meditation.

Here is an invitation to the custodians of all religions, to the masters of philosophies, to the leaders of metaphysical movements all over the world, to test for themselves the validity of Transcendental Meditation and to bring out to their followers the fulfillment of life.

This meditation should not be a threat to the authority of the priests in the temples, maulvies in the mosques, ministers in the churches, or monks in pagodas. Let it be known to them all that this is something that does belong to their religions and that it has been forgotten for the past many centuries. This is something that will restore to them their followers. Let them know that this will again bring and establish in society the value of temples and churches, mosques and pagodas, and will bring to the priest and maulvi, monk and minister, the status that should be theirs.

Transcendental Meditation is the practice to live all that the religions have been teaching through the ages; it is through this that man readily rises to the level of divine Being, and it is this that brings fulfillment to all religions.

Fulfillment of Psychology

The fulfillment of psychology lies in:
1. Making the mind strong
2. Enlarging the conscious capacity of the mind
3. Enabling a man to use his full mental potential
4. Bringing out techniques whereby all latent faculties of the mind might be unfolded
5. Bringing greater contentment, peace, and inner happiness, with greater efficiency and creativity in each individual
6. Bringing the power of concentration, increased willpower, and the ability to maintain inner poise and peace, even while busily engaged in outside activity
7. Developing self-confidence, power of tolerance, clear thinking, and greater power of thought

8. Establishing the mind in eternal freedom and peace in God Consciousness under all circumstances in the midst of all the activity and silence of relative existence

The ultimate fulfillment of psychology lies in enabling the individual mind to tune itself and remain tuned with the cosmic mind, in bringing a fast coordination of the individual mind with the cosmic mind, so that all the activity of the individual mind is in conformity with cosmic evolution and with the purpose of Cosmic Life.

Psychology should enable a man not only to overcome the stress and strain produced by the failures or pressures of work in his day-to-day life, but should also give such strength to the mind that it never falls under stress and strain and never falls victim to what are called psychosomatic diseases.

The purpose of the study of psychology should be to enable man to overcome the obstacles in life and live without any suffering. It should provide that strength of thought force and clear thinking which will enable his desires to be fulfilled so that he lives the life of fulfillment.

The goal of psychology, the study of the mind, should be to enable a man to live all values of life, to enjoy all phases of existence, and create more, understand more, live the maximum of life, and live life in eternal freedom in God Consciousness.

When we consider the great possibilities in the field of psychology and review the achievements so far made by that science, we find it discouraging.

It should not be the act of psychology to remind a man that his past was miserable, or that his surroundings and circumstances were unfavorable, or that his associations were depressing and discouraging, or that there was lack of love and harmony with dear and near ones. Such information delivered to anyone only results in suppressing one's consciousness.

It should be considered a crime to tell anyone that his individual life is based on the inefficient and degenerate influence of the environment of his past. The psychological influence of such depressing information is demoralizing. The inner core of one's heart becomes twisted by such information. On the other hand, information regarding the greatness of one's family traditions and the glory of one's parents, friends, and environment helps to elevate one's consciousness and directly encourages one to surmount and rise above one's weaknesses.

Analyzing an individual's way of thinking and bringing to the conscious level the buried misery of the past, even for the purpose of enabling him to see the cause of the stress and suffering, is highly deplorable; for it helps to strengthen directly the impressions of the miserable past and serves to suppress his consciousness in the present.

It is the blessing of God that we normally forget the past. The present is born of the past certainly, but the fact remains that the past has been through lesser developed states of consciousness, and that the present belongs to a more developed state of life. Therefore it is only a loss to overshadow the more evolved present with the memories or reviews of the less evolved past.

The whole of one's past is less mature and tends toward the life of animals, and the result of digging out the buried impressions of lesser developed states is that the lesser developed states of animal life overshadow the brightness and brilliance of the developed human consciousness in the present.

By looking back into the past, one's vision gets expanded, but, even though it expands, it expands to bring to the conscious level the lesser developed states of life. It enlarges one's vision, but, at the same time, overshadows one's genius and brightness of intelligence.

If there could be a way to expand one's consciousness in the direction of more evolved states of consciousness, and if there could be a way to enlarge the present stage of consciousness to the unbounded universal state of Cosmic Consciousness, then the subjects of psychoanalysis would certainly be saved from the unfortunate influence of overshadowing their consciousness by digging into the mud of the miserable past — which suppresses their consciousness.

It is for the statesmen of the various nations of the world to realize the degenerating influence of modern psychoanalysis and to try to replace it with the practice of Transcendental Meditation, which directly elevates the consciousness of the people and, thereby, not only strengthens the mind of the individual, but also enables him to use his full potential, making him definitely better and more powerful, peaceful, happy, and creative.

Let us not, however, consider the failure of modern psychology to live up to its purpose. Let us not dwell on the slow progress of the development of the science of psychology, and let us not remark that the science of psychology is yet in its infant state of development. Let us be more constructive and bring to modern psychology the key to its long-cherished aim to glorify man's life in all fields of existence.

It will be interesting to record here that Prince Alliata di Montereale, a Member of the Italian Parliament, while giving his experiences of Transcendental Meditation to fellow members of the various parliaments of the world at an international parliamentary gathering at Paris, stated as follows: "The study of psychology has shown that whatever a man is able to express of himself is only a part of his whole.

"The greater part of man does not find expression in his behavior and activity in life, because the conscious mind is only a part of the total mind that a man possesses. So what we need is to make available to every man in our country a technique of enlarging his conscious mind, a technique of enabling him to use his full mind.

"For example, if a man is using only a fraction of his mind, by enabling him to use the whole of his mind, he will become infinitely greater as a man. He will think much more deeply and more fully than he does now.

"Suppose that the conscious mind of man is only one-fourth of his total mind, then whatever he thinks and does is only a quarter of his real potential. If we want him to use his full potential, then his full mind should be made conscious, and only then his thought force will be four times more powerful, and he will be four times stronger and four times more sensible and happier than before.

"His love for his fellow man and the harmony in his home and his surroundings will increase four times. In the field of science, in the field of industry and commerce, on the level of civilization as a whole, great improvement will be found.

"For this purpose we propose adopting *one simple method* which will enlarge the conscious mind and thereby simultaneously improve man on all levels — physical, mental, and spiritual — and also increase his creative intelligence and improve his relations with his fellow men.

"This *one simple method* of improving each man as a whole is available in the world today..."[2]

The technique[3] of gaining Transcendental Consciousness brings to the conscious level the subtle levels of thought. This is how the whole of the thought process comes within the range of the conscious mind. The conscious capacity of the mind increases to the fullest scope of the mind. This is how it is possible to enable a man to rise up to his full mental potential in thought and action.

When the mind becomes familiar with the deeper levels of the thought process it becomes aware of the subtle levels of creation. And when the mind becomes familiar with the subtle regions of creation, the ability is gained to stimulate those regions for all advantage. This amounts to unfolding the latent faculties of the mind. Gaining Transcendental Consciousness through the practice of Transcendental Meditation is a direct way of making the mind familiar with all levels of creation, subtle and gross. It thereby gives the mind the ability to operate in the subtle regions in such a way as to bring advantages from the entire field of creation into the everyday life.

This unfoldment of latent faculties of the mind by Transcendental Meditation may be clarified by an example.

When a man takes a dive into a pond, he passes through the surface levels of water to the deeper levels, reaches the bottom, and comes up. A second and third dive take him through all levels of the water in the same way. The practice of diving makes the man familiar with all the levels of the water, and, as the familiarity with the deeper levels grows, the diver is able to remain longer at the bottom of the pond. When he is able to remain at the bottom for some time, with more and more practice, he gains the ability to move around at any level of the pond at will.

This is the result of gaining familiarity with the deeper levels of water. With a little more practice, he could make himself comfortable at any level and produce activity there in order to produce some desired activity on the

---

2 See Appendix I for full text of the speech.
3 See page 29, "Transcendental Meditation."

surface of the pond. Eventually it will be quite possible for him to comfortably stay at any level of deep water and produce a desired activity at any level of the pond he chooses. When this ability has been gained, the diver becomes the master of the pond. This mastery over the entire field of the pond is only due to his making himself familiar with the deeper levels of the pond by constant practice.

When by practice of Transcendental Meditation the mind becomes familiar with the deeper levels of consciousness, or, when the mind becomes familiar with transcendental pure consciousness, or when transcendental pure consciousness is found within the conscious capacity of the mind, then the mind gains the ability to work from any subtle or gross level of consciousness. Then it comes within its power to stimulate any stratum of creation for any advantage.

This opens the door of mastery of creation for man. This is how we find that Transcendental Meditation is quite enough to enlarge the conscious capacity of the mind to the greatest extent possible. It unfolds the subconscious and brings to conscious capacity the entire field of the ocean of mind. At the same time it brings a chance to every man to unfold all the latent faculties and arrive at the mastery of Nature.

Now we shall see if this Transcendental Meditation succeeds in tuning the conscious mind of the individual with the cosmic mind, and if it will succeed in putting the mind of the individual in a state where it would naturally function in accordance with the cosmic mind and in conformity with the cosmic purpose of evolution.

The practice of Transcendental Meditation takes the conscious mind directly to the transcendental state of consciousness. The absolute field of transcendental Being then comes within the range of conscious mind. When this field of Being is reached, the individual conscious mind takes the form of pure consciousness. Because that pure consciousness is an experience in itself, we can frame the expression that in the transcendental state of pure consciousness absolute Being comes within the range of conscious mind.

When absolute Being, which is the plane of Cosmic Law,[4] comes within the conscious capacity of the mind, the mind is naturally in tune with Cosmic

4 See page 10, "Being, the Plane of Cosmic Law."

Law. All the Laws of Nature are based on Cosmic Law, and, when the individual mind becomes tuned with that and remains in its attunement, it is in tune with all the Laws of Nature which are responsible for the progressive stream of evolution. Then the flow of the mind is in accordance with the natural stream of evolution, quite in conformity with the cosmic purpose of life. This is how the practice of Transcendental Meditation succeeds in establishing the mind in the state of cosmic mind.

Transcendental Consciousness is Bliss Consciousness. When Bliss Consciousness comes within the range of the conscious mind, the mind is contented. On the platform of contentment, based on the positive experience of bliss, all the virtues flourish. Love, kindness, compassion, tolerance, appreciation of others, all naturally take hold of the mind and the individual is the center of Divine Intelligence. The field of absolute Being, the field of pure consciousness, is the source of all intelligence, all creativity, all peace and happiness. When that field comes within the conscious range of the mind, the mind naturally becomes highly creative, greatly intelligent, filled with peace and contentment. These are the faculties that make a man accomplish all that he could possibly aspire for in life.

For the information of the students of philosophy and psychology it may be mentioned that the practice of Transcendental Meditation is the key to open the gates of the most advanced science of psychology developed in ancient India and found in the teachings of the Bhagavad-Gītā.[5]

Psychology as exemplified in the Bhagavad-Gītā presents the study of the development of the mind from a pitiable state of anxiety and depression to that most highly developed state in which the intelligence is established in the consciousness of eternal Being, the most evolved state of human evolution.

The Bhagavad-Gītā describes the psychologies of the individual and the cosmic minds, and marvelously succeeds in bringing about their correlation, so that the status of eternal life may become infused into the temporal phase of the phenomenal existence of man. If this does not take place the individual remains forever subjected to the phenomenal aspect of his nature and it

---

5 The Bhagavad-Gītā is the cherished scripture of universal nature which presents in essence the wisdom of integrated life as brought out by the Upanishads of the ancient Vedic Wisdom (see Appendix C).

is as a consequence of this that suffering overtakes him.

The way in which the surroundings and circumstances influence the individual mind is demonstrated at the very beginning of the text, where the most highly evolved man, the greatest archer of his time, Arjuna, the hero of the Mahābhārata, although awake to a most complete knowledge of right and wrong in the world, is unable to rise to the occasion before him and falls into a state of utter dejection. The surroundings have so strong an effect upon his mind that all persuasion and suggestion are powerless to help him.

The Bhagavad-Gītā teaches that the effect of the surroundings and circumstances upon the mind depends upon its strength — that the intensity of the effect of an impression is in inverse ratio to the strength of the mind. At one time Arjuna is found in a perilous state of indecision, but, after having put into practice the psychological teaching of the Gītā, it is not long before he is found in his full power of confidence and decision, although the circumstances remained quite unchanged. A close study of Lord Krishna's discourse reveals a great depth of psychological insight; it shows that the individual mind, however intelligent it may be on the superficial conscious level, can be overcome by its failure to understand and encompass a situation which obviously lies beyond its control, unless it is in tune with the unlimited cosmic mind. The establishment of conscious coordination between the individual and the cosmic mind is the only way to ensure that the individual becomes entirely free of the possibility of failing to understand a threatening situation and of successfully rising above its adverse effect. A pond is apt to dry out in the heat of summer, but for the ocean the question does not arise. The psychology of the Bhagavad-Gītā presents one master technique for bringing out this coordination of the individual mind with the cosmic mind; the attention is to be brought to the field of the transcendental absolute existence. This is to transform the weakness and limitation of the individual mind into the unbounded strength of Cosmic Intelligence. This great achievement is so simple to achieve that any and every individual on Earth can easily succeed in it, and in this way make unnecessary all the petty complexities and innumerable sufferings in life.

Thus we find that the technique of Transcendental Meditation is the golden key to the wisdom of psychology, the study of the mind. The key is something of practical value. It has a scientific basis that could satisfy any intellect. Here is the fulfillment of modern psychology, this technique which readily opens the gate of absolute wisdom to supplement all fields of relative existence and makes a man not only free from tension but a master of the universe, whose mind, being an individual mind, acts in conformity with the cosmic mind. Here is a boon to humanity in the field of the mind. Here is the fulfillment of psychology which is capable of bringing to a man all the points which were mentioned in the beginning of this part.

Fulfillment of Philosophy

The fulfillment of philosophy lies in:
1. Unveiling the mystery of Nature
2. Revealing to man the reality of life
3. Fulfilling the quest of human mind
4. Providing the direct experience of the ultimate reality of life and thereby bringing to the level of direct experience all the various levels of life and creation

The fulfillment of philosophy lies in making a man realize that the transitory values of day-to-day life coexist with the permanent and imperishable values of eternal life.

The student of philosophy should be the knower of reality of established truth of life, free from any doubts regarding anything in the field of creation. He should not only be the knower of reality, but above all should live reality in life with fully integrated values of life. He should be an eternally contented man in divine consciousness, living the fulfillment of life. The student of philosophy should be the master of the art of living, the knower of the Science of Being.

What the modern study of philosophy does to students of philosophy is pitiable. Again, we shall not go into the details of the failure of philosophy to reveal the truth to the peoples of the world. Rather than taking account of the inefficient and deplorable state of the study of philosophy for the past centuries, we shall step into a field of fulfillment of philosophy, and explore and bring to the level of common intelligence the great values of the study of philosophy on the day-to-day practical life.

Fortunately for the present generation of mankind the fulfillment of philosophy is found in a technique to explore the unseen regions and the ultimate reality of life. It makes available for everyone the nature of transcendental absolute Being on the level of actual experience. We have seen in "Fulfillment of Psychology"[6] how the field of transcendental absolute Being comes within the range of the conscious mind by the practice of Transcendental Meditation.

This absolute Being is the ultimate of creation, the ultimate reality, the Truth of life. By Truth we mean that which never changes. Transcendental absolute Being is eternal in Its nature; It remains the same. It is the ultimate constituent of creation; It never changes, for change belongs to the relative field.

All the different strata of creation are made of that substance which is called absolute Being. We call It a substance in order to understand more clearly that all this creation has come out of that pure consciousness of absolute Being. It is as if absolute Being is the material from which all this creation is made. That in Itself never changes, and yet It gives rise to the ever-changing diversity and multiplicity of forms and phenomena in creation. In the part on "Cosmic Law,"[7] we have dealt with this principle and have made it clear how this is true.

The experience of absolute Being leaves no doubt about the essential constituent of the whole structure of creation, for, in diving deep within, the mind passes through all the subtle strata of consciousness, which are different strata of creation. That is why, in the practice of Transcendental Meditation, not only does the inner field of consciousness unfold, but the entire field of subtle creation also is traversed. Between the gross strata of

---

6 See page 256.
7 See page 10, "Being, the Plane of Cosmic Law."

consciousness, on the level of the ordinary conscious mind, and the Transcendental Consciousness of pure Being, lie all the different strata of creation. When the mind unfolds and activates the deeper levels of consciousness it transcends all these strata of creation. This is how the mind gains more and more ability to cognize the entire universe.

All these inner mechanisms of the entire creation come to the conscious experience of the mind only by the practice of Transcendental Meditation. This practice unfolds the mysteries of Nature and reveals to man the truth of creation and the entire field of life. Nothing remains hidden, everything becomes clear to the mind on the way to the transcendental state of pure consciousness.

Here is the fulfillment of the age-old quest for the experience of reality, of the age-old quest of the seekers of truth. Philosophy is fulfilled in this simple system. For now is available to every man in the world this simple technique of unfolding the inner realms of life and cognizing the essential nature of the ultimate reality. Every man is thus able to know for himself the truth of creation by first-hand personal experience and by a systematic understanding of it. The experience and understanding of eternal reality set a man free from the subjugation and authority of his own inner thoughts and desires and the influence of the outer ideas, surroundings, and circumstances.

The fulfillment of philosophy lies in making it clear to the understanding on the intellectual level and also in bringing the reality to the positive, direct, and personal experience.

All the great expressions of the Vedic Wisdom of India found in the Upanishads declaring the ultimate oneness of life in the expressions "I am That," "Thou art That," and "All this is That," remain a fanciful imagination, or, at best, an intellectual mood, without the actual cognition of ultimate absolute Being. The study of philosophy leaves a man in the uncertainty of the nature of the supreme reality without the direct experience of transcendental Being. Actually it is experience which succeeds in eliminating the confusion caused by the study of the different schools of philosophy.

We give thanks to the great glory of His Divinity Brahmananda Saraswati, Jagadguru Bhagavan Shankaracharya, devotion to whom has revealed the key to the fulfillment of philosophy and has made the path of the seekers of truth easy of accomplishment. The path of the seekers of truth has been reduced to almost no path; it has been reduced to the achievement of the goal. The path now lies in learning the technique of Transcendental Meditation, practicing it every day, and arriving at the goal many times during the daily practice. This is the fulfillment of philosophy.

Paths to God-Realization

The conception of the word "path" indicates a distance starting from one point and ending at another. The paths to God-Realization mean the methods or practices adopted by man in order to reach God. To understand the path clearly, it is first necessary to clarify what we mean by God and how far He is from man.

God

"God" is the most highly cherished word for hundreds of millions of people of the world. The idea of God is the most highly cherished idea in human life for those who understand it. The conception of God is a reality greater than the reality of any conception that the human mind has developed at any time. The idea of God is not a fanciful thought, a thought to hide, or a thought to serve as a shelter or refuge. God is a reality more concrete than any of the realities of the entire cosmos. The existence of God is an existence more permanent and more substantial than the ever-changing temporary existence of the forms and phenomena of creation.

God is found in two phases of the reality: as a supreme Being of absolute eternal nature, and as a personal God at the top of phenomenal creation. Thus, God has two aspects, the personal and the impersonal. They are the two realities of the word God.

Impersonal Aspect of God

The impersonal aspect of God is formless, supreme; It is eternal and absolute Being. It is without attributes, qualities, or features, because all attributes, qualities, and features belong to the relative field of life, whereas the impersonal God is of an absolute nature. It is absolute, impersonal, and attributeless, but It is the source of all relative existence. It is the fountainhead of all the different forms and phenomena of creation. All the attributes of relative existence have their source in the attributeless absolute Being of impersonal nature. This Absolute is of unmanifested nature; It manifests in different degrees and forms in the various strata of creation. Everything in creation is the manifestation of the unmanifested absolute impersonal Being, the omnipresent God.

The impersonal, omnipresent, absolute God is by Its very nature progressive.[8] It manifests into the different aspects of creation, but even when found in the varieties of forms and phenomena of manifest creation, It maintains Its status as the unmanifested Absolute. So the impersonal, omnipresent God, remaining always impersonal and omnipresent, appears in the relative field in the form of creation, guided by Its own nature.

In order to understand how the unmanifested Impersonal takes the form of the manifested forms and phenomena of creation, let us take again the example of hydrogen and oxygen. Remaining as hydrogen and oxygen, the substance takes on different qualities and appears as vapor, water, and ice. Similarly, omnipresent impersonal almighty Being, while remaining as the Absolute, manifests into different qualities of forms and phenomena of creation. This is the ultimate reality of life. It is life eternal; It knows no change in Its character. It is the ultimate of creation, the source, the be-all and end-all of the entire creation. It is because of the power of the impersonal God that the world was, is, and will be. Just as there is only one essential constituent H_2O in vapor, water, and ice — the ultimate constituent of the entire creation, the impersonal absolute God, is one; It appears as many, however. The appearance of the one as many is only phenomenal. The reality of the one impersonal God is still eternal and absolute.

All the ever-changing forms and phenomena are grounded in never-changing eternal absolute Being. It is the creator, maintainer, and sus-

---

8 See "*Prāṇa* and Being," "Mind and Being," and "*Karma* and Being" on pages 17, 19, and 23 respectively.

tainer of the world. It is called the creator because It is the basis of all creation; all creation comes out of It. To create is Its nature, to be is Its nature, to expand is Its nature. So, creating, being, and expanding are the different aspects of the nature of the almighty impersonal God.

It is the maintainer of creation in the sense that It is the essential constituent of creation. Being the very basis of all creation, all beings naturally dwell in It; their ever-changing existence has its basis in unchanging, unchangeable, eternal Being. Thus we find that the world is the creation of the impersonal, absolute God. It is sustained by It and eventually dissolves into It. To understand how the world dissolves into its source, consider again the example of hydrogen and oxygen taking the different forms of water and ice. As the qualities of water dissolve into oxygen and hydrogen, the qualities of ice dissolve into oxygen and hydrogen, and the qualities of vapor are dissolved into oxygen and hydrogen; so, all the forms and phenomena of relative existence dissolve into their essential constituent, which is the Being of the impersonal absolute eternal God, the Almighty.

The Absolute is said to be almighty, but not in the sense that It is able to do everything. This is because being everything, It cannot do anything and cannot know anything. It is beyond doing and knowing. It is almighty in the sense that without It nothing would be. All that exists is in Its absolute status of Being. In this sense, the impersonal God is creator, maintainer, and sustainer of the world, remaining eternally in Its unmanifested state, and only in that sense It is almighty.

We have seen in the parts on "Breathing and the Art of Being"[9] and "Transcendental Meditation,"[10] how the absolute, impersonal, transcendental Being vibrates and comes into the relative phases of existence as the thought, the thinker, and the *Prāṇa*. We have seen that, as the process of evolution of a thought is carried on, the subtle state of thought becomes the gross state, and is then transformed into speech and action. So it is Being, pure consciousness, the impersonal almighty God that appears both as the subject and the object.

9 See page 92.
10 See page 29.

The individual in all his various aspects of life is the Light of God, impersonal absolute Being. That is why, in the section on "Life,"[11] life is defined as the Light of God, the radiation of eternal absolute Being.

This impersonal absolute Being, or God, as the essential constituent of creation, is pervading all fields of existence. It is omnipresent, It is of transcendental nature beyond everything of relative existence. It is beyond belief, thought, faith, dogma, and ritual. It lies beyond the field of understanding, beyond mind and intellect. Being transcendental, It cannot be comprehended by thought; It is beyond contemplation and intellectual discrimination and decisions. It is the state of Being. The Being of all is the omnipresent, impersonal God.

It is beyond knowing: It is knowingness itself. Because It is the Being of all, to realize It means just to be what one is. Being is realization of the impersonal, omnipresent God. For anyone to be, it is only necessary to be. No path to one's own Being could be thought to exist, no path of realization of the impersonal God, omnipresent Being, could be shown, because the very conception of "path" takes one's self out of one's own Being. The very idea of a path introduces the conception of something far away, whereas Being is the essential *oneself*. A path means a link between two points, but, in omnipresent cosmic Being, there cannot exist two different points or states. Omnipresent means "present everywhere"; It pervades everything, and, therefore, there is absolutely no question of a path. It is just a question of Being, and, even when one is established in the different states of manifested creation, one is established in the state of Being, but in a different form. So Being can never be different from what one already is, and this leads us to conclude that the question of a way for the realization of the Absolute just does not arise.

Therefore, the realization of the omnipresent almighty impersonal God is the natural state of one's Being. If a way to realize the impersonal omnipresent could be expressed, it could only be said to be a way of coming out of what one is not. To be is of an impersonal nature, so, in order to be one's Self, it is only necessary to come out of the personal nature, come out of the field of doing and thinking, and be established in the field of Being. Being

11 See page 43.

is the realization of the Impersonal. It has been made clear in the part on "Transcendental Meditation"[12] that it is only necessary to gain the habit of arriving at Being by coming out of the gross into the subtle levels of thinking and eventually transcending.

Thus it is clear that the realization of the Impersonal is merely arriving at one's own Being. And this shows that there exists no "path" between the experiencer and the Impersonal. What exists is the eternal existence of the omnipresent Impersonal. The Impersonal is permeating the entire field of creation as butter permeates milk or oil permeates a seed. A practical way to reach the level of the oil in the seed is to enter into the subtle status of the seed and reach the field of the oil. Likewise, if the level of the butter is to be reached in milk, it is necessary to enter into the subtle strata of a particle of milk.

The only way to realize the almighty impersonal God is to enter into the subtle strata of things and transcend the subtlest experience. There will be found the field of the Impersonal, the field of pure Being, the state of pure consciousness. It lies in the transcendental field of everything. Transcendental Meditation is a way to consciously arrive at the state of the impersonal, transcendental absolute Being, the almighty transcendental God.

The world today has a very vague conception of God. There are those who like to believe in God, those who love God, and those who want to realize God. But even they do not have a clear conception of what God is. The word "God" has remained for the most part a fanciful, pleasant thought and a refuge during the suffering and misery in life. And, for the custodians of many strange religions, the word "God" is a magic word, used to control the understanding and religious destiny of many an innocent soul. God, the omnipresent essence of life, is presented as something to fear.

God is not the power of fear; it is not anything from which fear could emanate. God is the existence of the Bliss Consciousness of absolute and eternal life. No fear of the name of God should have been perpetrated in the life of the people; no religions should have survived on the fear of God.

Unfortunately, there are religions existing in the world today whose main platform is the fear of God, and this fear is instilled in the children of God. It is cruel and detrimental to life to spread fear in the name of God. God is

---

12 See p. 29.

life eternal, purity, and bliss. The kingdom of God is the field of all good for man. God is to be realized, not to be feared.

The impersonal God is that Being which dwells in the heart of everyone. Every individual in his true nature is the impersonal God. That is why the Vedic philosophy of the Upanishads declares: "I am That," "Thou art That," and "All this is That." No one need be afraid of his own Self, no one need be afraid of the result of bliss, no one need be afraid of the Kingdom of Heaven, where there is all bliss and fulfillment.

The God almighty, impersonal unmanifested Being, is the eternal reality of life. It is imperishable, It is abundance, It is life, It is fulfillment. It is at hand for anyone to realize It. One has only to be, and the technique to be lies in Transcendental Meditation.

Personal Aspect of God

God in personal form is the supreme Being of almighty Nature. It is not "It." It can only be He or She. The He or She God has a form, a specific nature, certain attributes and certain qualities. To some, the personal God is He and to others it is She. Some say it is both He and She, but certainly it is not It, because of the personal character. It, we have seen, belongs only to the impersonal aspect of God.

The personal aspect of God necessarily has form, qualities, and features, likes and dislikes, and the ability to command the entire existence of the cosmos, the process of evolution, and all that there is in creation.

God, the supreme almighty Being, in whose person the process of evolution finds its fulfillment, is on the top level of creation. In order to understand how the process of evolution and creation find fulfillment in the personal God, we should review the whole range of creation.

We find that there are grades in creation. Some forms, some beings, are less powerful, less intelligent, less creative, less joyful; others have greater degrees of these attributes. The whole creation is composed of different strata of intelligence, peace, and energy.

At the lowest end of evolution we find the inert states of creation. From there, the life of the species begins, and the creation changes in its intelligence, power, and joyfulness. The progressive scale of evolution continues through the different species of vegetable, the egg-born, the water-born, the animal kingdom, and rises to the world of angels. Ultimately, on the top level of evolution, is He whose power is unlimited, whose joyfulness is unlimited, whose intelligence and energy are unlimited. All knowing is He, all powerful is He, all blissful is He, almighty is He who dwells on the top level of evolution.

What do we mean by saying He has an almighty nature? Almighty means having the power to do, to be, and to understand everything. This one supreme personal Being would have a nervous system so highly developed that His ability on every level of life would be unlimited. His senses would be the most powerful senses. His mind would be the most powerful mind. His intellect would be the most powerful intellect. His ego would be the most powerful ego.

When we see different levels of evolution in the fields of life below the species of man, right down to the inert creation, we can intellectually conceive of some stratum of evolution on the highest level of creation where the life will be perfect. Perfection of life would mean that the senses are perfect, mind is perfect, and intellect, ego, and personality are perfect. Between this highest state of evolution where the life is perfect and the lowest state of evolution, where the life begins to be, lies the whole range of creation.

So this supreme, almighty God is as though controlling the entire creation. All the Laws of Nature are controlled by His will. He, being almighty, has set the entire creation and the whole field of evolution in an automatic manner; or, we could say that He is in complete harmony and conformity with all the laws of creation. With the dissolution of creation, the almighty, personal God on top also merges into the impersonal absolute state of the Supreme and, with the creation, comes back again to dwell on the highest stratum of creation. This is how the personal God, along with the whole of creation, keeps on eternally maintaining the cycle of creation, evolution, and dissolution.

The whole field of relative existence is governed by the Laws of Nature automatically functioning in a perfect rhythm of life. That rhythm, that harmony of life, is maintained by the almighty will of the almighty God at the highest level of creation, controlling and commanding the entire process of life. He is God, She is God, almighty He and almighty She. At least intellectually we can hold Him or Her to be the supreme Being, God. Thus we find that we can understand intellectually the possibility of the existence of some supreme Being in the form of a personal almighty God.

In order to have a clear conception of the almighty nature of personal God, let us make it clear that the almighty nature lies in the perfection of the senses, the mind, the intellect, and the ego. When we say perfection of the senses, we mean that if He has eyes, His eyes should be perfect in the sense that they would be able to see all things at one time. If He has a nose, the almighty nose should be able to smell all the varieties of smells at one time. If He has ears, the almighty ears of the personal God should be able to hear all the sounds of the entire cosmos at one time. His almighty mind would naturally be aware of anything, of any grade, at any time. His almighty intellect should be able to decide everything at any time. All the innumerable decisions that are apparently the results of Natural Laws in the process of evolution are the innumerable decisions of the almighty personal supreme God at the head of creation. He governs and maintains the entire field of evolution and the different lives of innumerable beings in the whole cosmos.

All this about the personal God we can intellectually understand and can see the possibility of such an almighty supreme Being as the head of creation. If we can conceive of this, then we should also be able to intellectually understand that, if there could be a means of communion with that almighty, supreme power, then the life of the individual could be greatly benefited by the blessings of such a communion. We can intellectually understand that if He or She is a personal Being, certainly He or She would have a particular nature of His or Her own, and that the way to achieve His or Her blessings would be to get the individual life in tune with His or Her nature. Such an attempt would improve life at any level of creation. This would hasten the progress of evolution and permit an individual life to arrive at the highest evolution as soon as possible. If the individual can, by molding his thought, speech, and action in accordance with the nature of the supreme God, succeed in tuning himself with Him or Her, then certainly the unevolved, insignificant life of the individual will be blessed with the all-powerful, merciful nature of the almighty, supreme God. Thus the height of evolution could be gained by any man.

It would seem to be the result of poor understanding if the existence of the supreme, almighty personal God could not be intellectually conceived of. Anyone who could see the inert or most unevolved creation at one end of existence and recognize the different grades of creation, should be able intellectually to conceive of the almighty, supreme Being at the top level of evolution of relative existence and, having done so, could aspire to the great realization.

The inability to appreciate the conception of personal God and the inability to realize the personal God is understandable. But to refute the existence of the personal God can only be the result of an undeveloped state of mind.

"God" is the holiest of holy words because it brings to consciousness the supreme state of existence, the almighty status of the supreme Being. God-Realization has been said to be the aim of life. An individual at any level of evolution in human existence can well be said to have God-Realization as his ultimate goal because if and when he is in tune with the almighty, supreme Being, that will be the state of fulfillment, abundance, unlimited energy, creativity, intelligence, and bliss.

Now we shall see the possibility of God-Realization and analyze the different ways to realize the personal and impersonal God.

In our consideration of the two aspects of God — impersonal omnipresent absolute Being and the personal supreme Being — we have seen that realization of God could mean realization of the impersonal God or the personal God. We shall discuss the realization of the personal and impersonal aspects of God separately, because realization of the impersonal God will naturally be on the transcendental level of consciousness. Anything in the relative field cannot be omnipresent; relative means bound by time, space, and causation, whereas the plane of the omnipresent is unbounded by time, space, and causation.

The realization of the personal God, then, by necessity, will be on the level of human perception, on the level of the sensory experience. Realization of the personal God means that the eyes should be able to see that supreme Person and the heart should be able to feel the qualities of that supreme Person. The realization of the personal God has to be in the relative field of life. Thus, the realization of the impersonal God is in Transcendental Consciousness, and the realization of the personal God is on the level of consciousness of the waking state.

While dealing with the nature of the impersonal God, we have seen that It is absolute Bliss Consciousness of transcendental nature. In order to realize It, our conscious mind should transcend all the limits of experience in the relative field and should enter into a field beyond relative existence, where the conscious mind would be left to remain conscious all by itself. This necessitates the realization of the transcendental field. It is necessary for the conscious mind to be brought from the present level of experience to the subtler levels of experience and eventually transcend the subtlest level of relative experience to consciously arrive at the transcendental field of existence. Let us consider how many possible ways could bring the conscious mind to the field of transcendental Being.

Obviously the machinery, the body or nervous system, is the physical mechanism which is responsible for the abstract mind having an experience. For any experience to be, the nervous system has to adapt itself to certain specific conditions. Knowledge of the nervous system has revealed that when a man sees, a particular part of the brain functions in a particular manner. Likewise, when he hears, thinks, or smells, different parts of the brain function for each activity. So, according to the activity in the mind, a corresponding activity is set up in the nervous system. Thus, in order to produce a particular experience in the mind, the nervous system has to be brought to a state of specific activity.

Let us suppose that the mind is thinking of the Sun. The thought of the Sun could be experienced only when the particular part of the brain functions in a particular manner. This leads us to conclude that a thought of the Sun could be experienced by the mind in two ways. Either the mind starts the process of thinking and correspondingly stimulates the nervous system so that the progress of the process of thinking keeps on stimulating the nervous system until the particular portion of the brain comes to that level of activity which makes the mind experience the thought of the Sun; or, if such activity were produced in the brain physiologically, the mind would certainly experience the thought of the Sun.

Since a thought could be experienced in two ways, it shows that an experience could be had in two ways. Either the mind starts on the process and stimulates the nervous system for a particular experience, or the nervous system is stimulated in a particular fashion to create an activity which would naturally enable the mind to experience the desired object.

The realization of transcendental Being is an experience, and so the realization of the impersonal God means a positive experience of transcendental reality of life. Realization means experience. The experience of transcendental reality would establish the nervous system in a particular state because for any experience it is necessary that the nervous system be brought to a specific type of activity. The experience of the transcendental impersonal God necessitates a particular condition of the nervous system. If this activity in the nervous system could be produced by physiological means, then this would be the physiological approach to realization of the impersonal God. We will see in detail how this could be possible.

Having established the path of God-Realization from the physiological consideration, we find the possibility of God-Realization: (1) through the process of understanding, (2) through the process of feeling, and (3) through the process of action or perception.

Perception is also an action of the mind — we could say, a mechanical process. We see a thing and in order to see it, we just open the eyes and see; perception is just a mechanical thing. In order to see, we need not stimulate the intellect nor excite the emotions. Thus, the process of perception is just a mechanical process which does not include within its range any quality of the emotion or of the intellect. Thus we find the path to realization of the impersonal God could be mainly divided into five different groups:

1. Psychological or intellectual approach
2. Emotional approach
3. Physiological approach
4. Mechanical approach
5. Psycho-physiological approach

In consideration of these five paths to God-Realization, we find that any of the approaches would suffice for any man. Certainly the intellectual approach to God-Realization will suit only those who are cultured intellectually, those whose intellectual capacity is high. The emotional approach to God-Realization will generally suit those whose qualities of heart are highly developed. Those who are cultured neither emotionally nor intellectually are left two approaches to realization: physiological and mechanical. The physiological approach to God-Realization necessitates bringing the body and nervous system to a state which will establish the mind on a level of cognition of the transcendental nature of existence. The physiological way will suit those people who are physiologically normal, whose nervous system is as near normal-functioning as possible. Regardless of their intellectual or emotional culture, if their nervous system is normal, the physiological approach will raise their level of consciousness.

In order to produce a particular state of nervous system without the training of mind or heart would require a great amount of sustained physical or physiological training.

The psycho-physiological approach is a way which will suit the people who would prefer to approach the problem of God-Realization from both ends, physical and mental — training the mind and training the body simultaneously. The mechanical path, however, will suit any man, no matter how weak his mind, heart, and nervous system might be.

Intellectual Path[13] to God-Realization

Discrimination, or the power of intellect, is the vehicle which enables a man to advance on the path of knowledge. The intellectual approach to God-

13 In dealing with the omnipresent state of the impersonal God, a statement was made that the transcendental, omnipresent Divine, by virtue of Its being omnipresent, is the essential Being of everyone. It forms the basic life of one and all, It is not anything different from one's own Self or Being. Therefore, no path to realize It could be conceived of. Certainly, to talk in terms of "path" of realization of one's own Being seems to be unjustified, but because all the time in our life the attention is left outside in the gross relative field of experience, we are as if debarred from the direct experience of the essential nature of our own Self, or transcendental Being. That is why it is necessary to bring the attention to the transcendental level of our Being. This bringing of the attention is said to be a way to realize. Thus, although we find the idea of a path to realization absurd metaphysically, it is highly significant on a practical level.

Realization is that of knowledge. On this path, only the intellect functions; the qualities of the heart, the path of mechanical perception, and physiological means to realization have no place. On this path everything has to be scrutinized and understood through discrimination based on logic. Everything has to be exact and precise on this intellectual path to enlightenment; the intellect must be wide awake. It is a very delicate path to realization.

One hears about the nature of the world and reality from a teacher who has come to the cognition of divine Nature through the path of intellect, through the path of discrimination. Three steps are necessary on this path.

First, it is necessary that one hear from a realized man about the nature of what one finds in life. One has to delve deep into the nature of the experiences of the world. And what one hears from the realized soul is the natural conclusion that creation is perishable, everything is changing; time-space-causation-bound manifested creation of forms and phenomena forms the perishable aspect of life. Having heard this, one is required to distinguish one state from the other and, eventually, to assimilate the fact of the futility and impermanence of creation.

The discrimination between the different phases of life, leading to the conclusion that the whole field of life is a field of perishable nature, is the first lesson on the intellectual path of enlightenment. It must first be known that the world is not real, even though it seems to be. The mind concludes that these things are always changing and that which is always changing has no lasting status of its own.

On the sensory level, however, the world seems to be real. Through the intellect we decide that because the world is ever-changing, it cannot be real; the real is described as that which will always be the same. But the world cannot be dismissed as unreal, because we *do* experience it.

We experience that the wall is here, that the tree is there. We cannot say that the tree is not there. If we say that the tree is unreal, we will have to say that it does not exist, and we are not in a position to make such a statement. We acknowledge that the tree is there, but we must also say that it is always changing. Because it is always changing it is not real, but, because it is there, for all practical purposes, we have to credit the tree with the status of existence.

What is that status between real and unreal? We call it "phenomenal existence." The phenomenon of the tree is there, even though it is not real. So the tree has a "phenomenal" reality. In Sanskrit it is called *Mithyā*. The world is "*Mithyā*," phenomenal, not really existing. The conclusion is, thus, that the world is neither real nor unreal.

A strong cultured mind analyzes his life in the world with discrimination and eventually comes to the conclusion that the world is *Mithyā* — or, only a phenomenon.

For the aspirant, discrimination between the temporary values of the world in the quest of finding something permanent eventually reveals to him the perishable nature of the entire creation. Contemplation on the perishable nature of creation begins to take his mind to some deeper reality underlying the ever-changing phase of existence.

When he gains some insight into the reality of inner life, he is able to contemplate the abstract metaphysical reality of imperishable nature and realizes hidden secrets of existence that lie beyond the ever-changing phenomenal phase of life.

In a tree he finds its different phases — the trunk, branches, flowers, and fruit. The tree changes every day: New leaves come out, old leaves decay, branches fall, and new ones grow. The whole existence of the tree seems to be set up in an ever-changing pattern. But behind these ever-changing phenomenal phases of the tree there is one that does not change — the nourishment or sap that is drawn from the root is the same all the time. It is the sap which appears as the branches, leaves, flowers, and fruit. The different aspects of the tree change, but the sap remains unchanged in its value. The transformation of the sap into the different aspects of the tree reveals the hidden mystery of Nature.

Beyond the ever-changing phases of phenomenal existence, there seems to be some reality of unchanging character, some phase of existence which does not change and which gives rise to all the changeable aspects of phenomenal creation. When the power of discrimination reveals to the aspirant the possibility of the existence of some never-changing reality at the basis of the ever-changing phenomenal creation, he enters into a second phase on the path of knowledge. He is set to contemplate upon the never-changing permanent phase of life, the unchanging aspect of existence which is the reality of life. When he has thoroughly assimilated the idea of the impermanence of creation and the phenomenal nature of the world, when his intellect has been established firmly in the idea that the world is perishable, ever-changing, and phenomenal, then he begins to dwell on the permanent never-changing sphere of life. Like the example of the sap in a tree, analogies in the material world of creation help the aspirant to discover the metaphysical truth lying beyond the phenomenal phase of existence.

The science of physics tells us that beneath the phenomenal existence of water, there is the reality of oxygen and hydrogen. The water changes in its form, becoming vapor, snow, and ice, but the essential constituent does not undergo any change. The truth of the permanent value of the element gives rise to various kinds of perishable values — of water, snow, and ice — ever-changing values of different forms and phenomena. The subtle findings of physics have gone far beyond the realm of elements, but our example is just to indicate that underlying the different levels of creation is a substance that remains integrated in its value, even when, on the surface, it continues to give rise to qualities of an ever-changing nature.

Contemplation on the inner value of life eventually reveals to the aspirant that the ever-changing world is based on a never-changing element of no-form and no-phenomenon. All forms and phenomena belong to the relative field of existence, whereas that which lies beyond all form and phenomena necessarily belongs to a field that is out of relativity.

For the aspirant, the value of the world in terms of phenomenal existence was established on the intellectual level of discrimination, as was the value of the permanent element underlying the phenomenal phase of life. This is how the seeker of God, treading the intellectual path to enlightenment, finds his mind firmly established on the impermanence of creation and the permanence of the transcendental nature of life. Certainly the intellect is able to come to a point where it could hold the idea that the essential nature of the transcendental reality is permanent, of never-changing eternal nature, and is absolute in its value. Now what remains is to realize it.

When the aspirant has succeeded in contemplating the reality of transcendental absolute Being as underlying all the ever-changing phases of relative life, it is then left for him to directly experience the nature of transcendental Being. Because he is on the intellectual path to realization, he tries to see the reality of the transcendental absolute Nature that underlies the phenomenal existence of creation.

As his practice of contemplation continues, his mind begins to be established more and more in eternal Being as his own Self. He contemplates in terms of "I am That," "Thou art That," "All this is That." The ideas of "I am That," "Thou art That," and "All this is That," become so deeply rooted in his consciousness that with prolonged practice of contemplation, he begins to live this understanding through all the thick and thin of daily life.

In having gained the oneness of life, he begins to have his mind held in the oneness of existence in the midst of all the relative, phenomenal experiences and actions in his daily life. Such a state of mind is created in him, that it is as if he has been deeply hypnotized by the notion, "I am That, Thou art That, and All this is That." His consciousness is captured by the idea of the oneness of life, and the obvious diversity of existence and phenomenal creation begins to lose its hold. This is the beginning of the experience of the transcendental reality on the level of intellectual understanding.

Thus, we find that the first step on the intellectual path of God-Realization is discrimination between the real and the unreal, and contemplation on the transient, futile, ever-changing, perishable nature of the world.

The second step is to contemplate upon the oneness and eternal nature of the never-changing existence that lies at the basis of all the ever-changing phases of life.

The third step is to ponder over and assimilate that oneness of life in terms of one's own Being through the practice of establishing in the depth of consciousness the oneness of eternal life, in terms of the first person, second person, and third person: "I am That," "Thou art That," and "All this is That."

This path of enlightenment is, we could say, a path of self-hypnotism. Discrimination of the ever-changing phenomenal existence and the attempt to locate an unchanging underlying feature is one thing, while attempting to associate one's Being with the Being of the entire creation is another. But this is the intellectual path of enlightenment, where only the intellect functions. Unless the understanding of the oneness of life goes deep in consciousness and begins to be lived in the midst of all the multiple and diverse experience and activity of life, it will not be a state of realization. Therefore, the aspirant on the intellectual path of realization understands, assimilates, and tries to live the unchanging, imperishable oneness of absolute Being in terms of his own Being.

The idea of the oneness of life goes so deep into the aspirant's consciousness that the association of his mind with the experiences of the wakeful state, the dreaming state, and the deep-sleep state does not weaken the conviction that he is imperishable, unchanging, eternal, absolute Being. When this becomes fixed in the consciousness, he begins to live that oneness of life through all the diversity of the wakeful, dreaming, and sleeping states. When he rises to a state of eternal Being while yet remaining in the field of relative experience, then is his consciousness complete, then is his life fully realized. This is realization of the omnipresent, impersonal God by way of the intellectual path to divine realization.

The nature of this path of enlightenment is such that it cultures the mind so that it gradually loses interest in the practical life and the experiences of day-to-day living. This is because the mind is of a contemplative nature. The mind is engaged first in thinking in terms of negation of creation, the futility and the evanescent, perishable nature of phenomenal existence of the world; and, second, in contemplating the imperishable Nature that lies behind the obvious phase of life. The mind is always thinking, contemplating, trying to assimilate the transcendental reality in contrast to the perishable outside world, and, in trying to live it, it loses the charm of the outside world. Such a mind necessarily becomes useless and hopeless for all practical purposes in life and therefore, certainly, the intellectual path of God-Realization through contemplation is not a path for practical men. This is not a path for the householder. No man, remaining active in the world, having the responsibilities of family and society and the pressure of business, can possibly succeed in infusing the divine Nature into his mind through this method of contemplation.

This intellectual path of divine revelation suits those who have nothing to do with practical life, those who have kept themselves away from the responsibilities of life, who have shunned business activities in life and have chosen the way of a recluse. The silence which a recluse enjoys is such that it keeps him away from work. He is in silence most of the time, contemplating, discriminating, and assimilating the divine Nature as his own. The aspirant who leads this type of contemplative life can succeed in realizing only through the path of contemplation.

Take the example of a man who says again and again, "I am a king, I am a king." By concentrating on being a king, he could eventually produce within himself a state of mind in which even if he is walking on the street he would continue to feel that he is a king. So firm and effective a state could be created that, even if he has to beg on the street, he feels within himself that he is a king. So, irrespective of any circumstances or surroundings, he could create such a state of mind that he will feel he is a king.

Such is the plight of the contemplative seeker of truth treading the intellectual path of realization. One point to note here is that the success of this type of contemplation depends upon a long-time devotion to one path. If a man has much time at his disposal to dwell on the idea that he is a king, then of course it will be possible for him to establish deep in his consciousness that he is a king. But, if he does not have an opportunity for lengthy contemplation upon the idea that he is a king, that idea will not become firmly rooted in his mind.

In order to establish oneself in the oneness of life through contemplation, it is necessary to be contemplative during most of one's life. Much time is needed to sway the aspirant in the idea of oneness and permanence of life. This is certainly not the path of a householder, because a householder has great responsibilities on many levels of life. This type of contemplation will either make the householder resign from the responsibilities of his way of life, or will make him an irresponsible man in the world. Execution of responsibility requires attention and devotion to work, whereas this type of contemplation requires negation and abstinence from work.

The practice of *Rāja Yoga*[14] also belongs to this type of intellectual approach to God-Realization and is, similarly, accomplished through contemplation. Certainly this is not the way of a householder. For God-Realization, the householder needs a path through action, not through contemplation. It is impractical for a man of the world with responsibilities of family life and social obligations to think of everything in terms of evanescence, futility, and impermanence. The intellectual method of discrimination, along with behavior in the world, disturbs the coordination of body and mind and prevents the possibility of any development of higher consciousness.

Unfortunately, many seekers of enlightenment have for centuries past been the victims of this state, which results in failure in the world and failure in the divine quest as well. True enlightenment through the intellectual path means intellectually rising above the field of the intellect and arriving at the field of the transcendental divine consciousness. This certainly will mean bringing the conscious mind to the transcendental reality of Being. Intellectual mood-making of any type does not succeed in bringing anyone to this state of realization.

Emotional Path to God-Realization: Path of Devotion

The path of devotion leads through the qualities of the heart. All the paths of devotion are emotional paths to God-Realization. The qualities of the heart are the qualities that enable a man to feel. They differ from the qualities of the mind, which enable a man to know and understand.

On the intellectual path to God-Realization the predominant factor is knowing and understanding. Here on the path of devotion the main factor is feeling. The feeling of love is the vehicle which enables man to advance on that path. The increasing capacity of love, emotion, happiness, kindness, devotion, and surrender are the qualities of the heart which sustain the path of devotion. Love increases, and, as it advances, it leaves behind fields of lesser happiness and gains ground on more stable, more important, more valuable fields of happiness. The path of devotion is a path of happiness, the path of love, the path through the qualities of the heart.

14 *Rāja Yoga* is a path to God-Realization through contemplation.

Love of God is the greatest virtue that a man can ever cultivate, and through that develops the love for the creation of God, for the children of God; kindness, compassion, tolerance, and helpfulness to others emanate when the love of God grows in the heart.

Fortunate are those whose hearts melt in love of God, who feel abundance in the love and devotion to God, whose hearts flow and overflow with the remembrance of God, with the thought of love for God, and with the name of God. Fortunate are those whose life is dedicated to the almighty God and to the doing of good to His creation. Increased devotion means increased love, and this amounts to increased happiness, contentment, glory, and grace.

Certainly one on the path of devotion finds himself more and more aware of greater degrees of happiness. The path of love is like the relationship of a child with the blissful heart of his mother. As the child advances, his mother's heart swells. Her happiness radiates and reflects on the child, so that at every step he enjoys a greater degree of happiness. And that again reflects in the heart of the mother. The mother's joy increases and reaches a summit when the child finds himself one with his mother's heart.

With the increase of love in the heart of the devotee, he gains a greater degree of happiness. His heart finds its goal when his love rests in the eternal existence of God. The devotee and God become one. The drop of water finds itself in the fullness of the ocean; the two unite. The unity is full, and that alone is; here is the one, leaving no trace of the other. The two are there no more, the path of union is extinct, and only the union stands.

The lover of God is drowned in the ocean of His love, and God is drowned, too, in the ocean of his love. This is the great union in all simplicity. There is no discrimination, there is no elimination, there is no negation, there is no understanding. The path of love is the path of bliss. The path of love is a one-way march from the field of lesser happiness to that of greater happiness. Love increases. The stream of love begins to flow, and, as it advances, it leaves behind fields of lesser happiness and gains ground on more stable, more important, and greater fields of happiness. Certainly one on the path of devotion finds himself more and more awake in greater and greater degrees of happiness.

The river of love flows one way on the steep slope of God Consciousness. It runs rapidly and quickly loses itself and, in losing itself, gains the unbounded status of the ocean of love. Loss is a victory on the path of love. It is a blessed loss that marks the gain of fulfillment in life, and blessed are those who lose themselves in this path of love, and more blessed yet are those who lose the path too, and gain the goal and live it.

The beauty is that here on the path of love the loss of the self is incurred for the sake of love. The lover knows only to lose, and this loss, the process of losing, has no motive for gain. It only knows to be without any aim. The love begins, and he takes it upon himself as it comes, and, as it comes, it becomes greater. He keeps on losing himself, but he does not know that he is losing himself and does not know even when he is completely lost. For, when he is lost, he is God; not even that he is God, but that God is God. Oneness of God Consciousness, one eternal existence, oneness of eternal life, oneness of absolute Being; only the One remains. And then, the varieties of life are like the varieties of the waves in the eternal ocean of love of God.

The multiplicity of life finds itself in the oneness of God Consciousness. The many forms and phenomena of the world around are like the ripples and the waves, a mirage that only appears to exist in the unbounded existence of God. The waves of love come up on the surface of life just for life to be felt and known and lived in variety. This is so that the path of love may continue to be found on the surface of life, and the love may continue to be for everyone who comes to life. It is so that the lovers of life may find life in losing it and may find God in losing themselves in God Consciousness.

The purpose of all this is that again and again the devotees continue to need and find God and that God may continue to descend on them, and God may rest in the devotees, and the devotees rest and live in God. The path to God is only one way, a one-way path of love, moving from lesser degrees of happiness to greater degrees of bliss, to bliss eternal; from lesser degrees of intelligence to absolute and eternal intelligence.

Speaking of the increase of intelligence on the path of love seems to be inconsistent, because love is the quality of heart and has little to do with intelligence. It does not seem to be fair to say that intelligence grows as love grows. With the increase of love, the Light of God increases, and what remains is the light of love. The Light of God increases, and through it is nourished intelligence and all that rests on it. Yet there is left no place for intelligence in the influx of love. Not that it is annihilated, but it is only as if the light of intelligence merges into the light of life. As different colors of light merge together to give rise to a powerful beam of white light, so the light of intelligence, happiness, creativity, all join together to produce a forceful stream of love.

The light of love is the blinding light of love alone, and all the greatness of intelligence and power and everything else is present there, but in latent form. They are all lost in the light of love — nay, not actually lost — they forget their identities in the love of God. Love and intelligence, power and intelligence, and all that there is in all the variety and vanity of life, merge in the oneness of God, leaving God in love of devotee and devotee merged in the ocean of love of God. All the qualities of life and multiplicity of the forms of phenomenal existence sink to leave the fresh waters of eternal life, to remain full in the ocean of God Consciousness.

On the path of love the variety of the universe finds fulfillment in the unity of God. In love, God is found in the world, and the world is found in God. And for the glory of God to be experienced, happiness has to increase. What is there on the surface of life to make happiness increase? The attention has to go to the finer fields of life, to the subtler levels of creation, to the deeper levels of consciousness. Bringing the attention to the deeper levels of consciousness is the key to the experience of greater happiness; it is the method of Transcendental Meditation. This is what rows the boat of love and brings fulfillment to the path of love. The path of devotion without the practice of this Transcendental Meditation, without greater experience of great happiness, is not practical.

Transcendental Meditation fills the heart of man with great happiness, certainly greater than before — but surely not great enough to be called unbounded and eternal in itself. Yet the heart may feel completely filled. This will mean that the reservoir is felt to be full even when it is not yet full. The practice of Transcendental Meditation constantly increases the ability of experience of greater happiness in the heart of the devotee and thus enables him to continue while he feels the fullness of eternal bliss, and to go on until the ocean of love is full to the brim of the absolute glory in grace. It makes absolute love a real, significant, personal experience in impersonal and eternal God Consciousness.

Physiological Approach to God-Realization

It may seem strange to speak of a physiological approach to God-Realization. But we are of a scientific age, and, in order to explore completely the paths to God-Realization, we should explore them from all sides. We have the physical universe of multiple experiences before us.

Could there be a physical means of God-Realization? Could there be a way to rise to Cosmic Consciousness from the physical plane? Could there be a way to rise to the fulfillment of life from a physical plane? How can we produce a state of all-tranquility in the midst of all-activity? How can we reach that pinnacle of human development from the physical side of life?

To understand this we should know that the state of divine existence, or divine life, or God-Realization, is a state of positive experience; it is an experience — it is not a fanciful thought, it is not a mood, it is not on the thinking level. It is the state of life, it is Being.

For anything to be an experience, there has to be a specific activity created in the nervous system. The nervous system has to be set in a particular order. The machinery of the nervous system has to come to a specific status in order to give rise to a specific state of experience.

For any experience, there has to be a specific activity in the nervous system. If we hear a word, this hearing is the result of much activity in the nervous system and the activity is responsible for providing the experience of the word. If we see a flower, and its image falls through the retina on the mind, there is a highly complicated activity in the nervous system which gives rise to the perception of the flower. If we smell something, there is much activity in a specific part of the nervous system that produces that particular experience of smelling. If we touch something, the experience of the touch produces a particular activity in that particular part of the nervous system in order to give the experience of touch. So, whatever experience is there, it is based on a particular activity of the nervous system.

Those who are meditating know that during meditation they experience the subtle states of the thought. In order to experience a very subtle state of the thought, there has to be a correspondingly subtle activity in the subtle part of the nervous system. When the thought has been transcended and the meditator reaches the transcendental — that state of suspension, silence, and full awareness, of pure consciousness, where the experiencer is left all by himself — that state is also a positive experience. Although it is not an experience of an outside object, it is an experience of its own kind, where the experiencer is left all by himself. This is the state of pure consciousness, the experience of pure Being. The experience of pure Being and the state of Being mean the same thing.

In order that this experience may be possible, there has to be a particular type of setup of the nervous system in which it is in a particular state of poised alertness, where the nervous system is not passive. It is active, but it has no activity because there is no experience of any outside matter. Certainly the nervous system is not as completely passive as in deep sleep. In the state of the transcendental, the mind does not become passive.

When the brain does not function during deep sleep, that state of no-function deprives the mind of the ability to perceive. But when some word is spoken — for example, during meditation, when the word[15], or *Mantra*, is repeated — a particular state of the brain mechanism is created. At every level of subtle experience of the word the brain functions at different levels of activity. In the state of transcending there is a specific state of the brain mechanism which gives rise to the experience of transcendental pure consciousness. Just as with any other experience, the brain has to come to a specific state for the experience of the transcendental. It comes to a state of suspension, of activity and no-activity. This, however, is not the common state of the brain.

The brain is either functioning while in the wakeful state, not functioning while in deep sleep, or functioning in an imaginary manner during the dream state. But because the state of transcendental Being is not the common experience, the setup of the brain to give rise to this transcendental

---

15 Word — "thought."

experience is therefore not a common setup. It does not take place during the wakeful state, the dream state, or the deep-sleep state.

One way to bring about that setup of the brain is by experiencing the subtle states of a thought, by reducing the thought until its subtlest state is experienced and the experience of the transcendental is gained. By this process the setup of the brain, which is responsible for giving rise to the experience of Transcendental Consciousness, is brought about, step-by-step, through the process of experience. It is brought about by the agency of the mind.

This is the mental approach to God-Realization. The mind is brought from experience to experience, from the experience of gross nature to the experience of subtle nature, in order to have the particular experience of Transcendental Consciousness.

When the body functions for a long time the nervous system becomes tired and sleep follows. It wants rest and ceases to function because of strain and fatigue. This fatigue is a physical state of the nervous system created by continuous functioning without rest so it gets to a state that gives rise to no experience.

In some way it should be possible to create physically a particular state of the nervous system that will correspond to the state of the nervous system when it is responsible for the experience of Transcendental Consciousness. Just as when the nervous system is tired a state is created in which the brain does not experience anything, similarly, by stimulating the nervous system physiologically, it should be possible to create a particular state of the nervous system to give the brain mechanism the particular setup that will enable the mind to experience the transcendental.

If this is physiologically possible, this would constitute the physiological approach to God-Realization.

In *Hatha Yoga*[16] we find that there has existed since ancient times in India a physiological approach to God-Realization whereby the nervous system is brought to a state which gives rise to a particular setup of brain functioning. In this setup, the brain enables the mind to experience Transcendental Consciousness.

---

16 *Hatha Yoga* is a path of enlightenment by forcefully controlling the body and bringing about forced control over breathing in order to control the mind to cultivate God Consciousness.

The body is always functioning because breathing is continuous. Sleeping, dreaming, waking — through all experience, breathing goes on. This activity must go on because the activity of the body depends on the activity of the brain. We have seen that in order to have the experience of Transcendental Consciousness the activity of the brain has to cease, but the brain should not be allowed to become static. The brain is held in a state of no activity yet is not passive. It is awake and alert in itself. If the brain has to be held in a state of suspension, then the entire nervous system has to be held in a particular state — presumably in a state of neither activity nor inactivity. In order that this may be, the breath has to be held in a state of neither breathing out nor breathing in. The breath has to be between flowing and not-flowing, but it has to be there.

In order to bring the body to that state of suspension, the body has to be trained, because the habit of the body has been to move about in activity in the waking state or to be static in the sleeping state. This is the ordinary condition of the body. It must therefore be trained to be still, yet not to go into a passive state.

If a body is normally functioning, the general experience is either that of being awake or asleep. To some extent we are aware when sleep comes by the gradual dullness which overtakes us. The ability to experience becomes less and less, and we do not know when sleep actually comes. We do feel when we are about to sleep, and we do feel that our consciousness gradually becomes fainter, and then we do not feel anything. Consciousness fades to nil, but we do not experience the actual fading of consciousness. This shows that the body or the mind is not purely normal. If the whole nervous system were just normal, then we should be able to experience the subtlest state of awareness, the state of awareness which is almost one with deep sleep and at the same time almost one with the subtlest state of the wakeful state.

Because we are subjected to outer experiences constantly, this habit has as though contaminated the system. Normally we should experience the start of the thought. This should be one's normal experience if the body is perfectly pure; that is, if the brain is perfectly pure physically.

To be physically pure means to be free from dullness and tension. The constituent of the brain matter should be such that it enables the brain to be normal in its physical nature and in its functioning.

In the ordinary state of the mind, when a thought arises, it overshadows the mind. The mind is then engaged in that thought. After translating itself into action, and the purpose of the thought is achieved, the desire is fulfilled. If we want to smell a flower the thought arises, and, later reaching the conscious level, our mind dictates to the hand to grasp the flower, bring it to the nose, and smell it. Now the desire to smell the flower is complete, that is, the desire has come to an end.

If the brain is functioning normally, once the desire is fulfilled, and before another desire arises, the mind will experience the state of pure Being or pure consciousness. This is what happens in the case of a realized man when he has a desire. His mind is functioning, but when the desire is fulfilled and before another desire arises he enjoys the natural state of Being. This is because there is no activity in the brain. Being free from activity the brain does not go to a state of passivity. It cherishes the state of Being, or pure consciousness.

In between two thoughts is the state of pure Being. Every thought arises from the state of pure Being, and between two thoughts there is a gap. The gap should not be a gap of no experience. If the brain is functioning normally, if the mind is pure, if the nervous system is pure, then between every two thoughts the state of Being will be experienced. This is not generally the case, however.

When we become tired, the mind becomes dull and ceases to function. Impurity would then mean the inability of the brain to function. This could be due to physical reasons. For example, the intake of alcohol affects the brain and causes dullness of the mind. The effect of activity also makes the mind tired and dull, exhausts the nervous system, and makes the mind unable to experience even the gross — not to speak of the subtle.

The ability of the nervous system to cognize very subtle states of experience is marred when the brain matter is contaminated by impure physical matter, through fatigue, or through wrong thinking, all of which exhaust mental energy. Fatigue is the main factor. It does not allow the mind to experience subtleties. Another factor is the quality of matter which makes the mind dull, puts one to sleep, or makes one irritated. These are all tendencies in the mind produced by impure physical matter. We eat and drink, and whatever we eat or drink may contain some impure element which affects the mind and puts it in a state of no function.

If a material factor could influence the mind to become dull, then a material factor could also influence the mind to become sharp and acute. If exhaustion could make the mind dull and produce sleep, then freshness and energy could revive the mind and make it alert.

The physiological approach is meant to relieve the physical condition of the nervous system from being dull. Therefore it should attack the impurity in the body and the reasons for fatigue. It is the physical approach. We want to purify the nervous system to such a great extent that eventually it will create the exact setup of the nervous system which will be able to give rise to the experience of Transcendental Consciousness. We are creating such a physical condition of the nervous system that it will cause the body to be in the most normal condition.

The makeup of the human nervous system is such that it is perfect; it has the ability to experience Transcendental Consciousness. But the wrong food eaten, the wrong liquids consumed, and the wrong air breathed cause the system to become physically unfit to give rise to the natural experience of the transcendental state. Thus we find the physiological approach to divine consciousness consists of: (1) selecting the proper quality of food; (2) selecting the proper type of activity; and, (3) eliminating from the system the influence of wrong food and wrong activity.

All these naturally require much discipline on all levels of life. Therefore such an approach can only be suitable to the hermit's way of life. They can afford to spend time under the personal supervision of a teacher. Certainly it is not the path of the householder, whose pattern of life is such that he cannot be put to laborious and time-consuming practices. This fact should not cause disappointment, however, because there are other ways which are available to bring enlightenment more suitable to the householder of modern times.

Mechanical Path to God-Realization

It is unusual to consider a path of God-Realization proceeding and succeeding in a mechanical manner. But a close scrutiny of the process of perception will reveal that God-Realization is possible in a mechanical way.

Perception is the result of the natural radiation of consciousness from the center of pure Being in man onto the object to be perceived. An example will illustrate this more clearly.

The current from a battery cell reaches the bulb and through the process of projection it comes out as a beam of light. As it proceeds, the content of light diminishes until eventually a limit is reached where the light may be said to be nil. Likewise, from the inexhaustible battery of Being the radiation of consciousness starts and, through the nervous system, reaches the senses of perception and passes on to the object of experience. As it proceeds to radiate outward, the content of consciousness, the degree of bliss, diminishes. The whole process is automatic and mechanical.

The nervous system is the means through which consciousness manifests and projects itself to the outside world, resulting in the phenomenon of perception.

The process of perception is automatic and mechanical. If we have to see an object we open the eyes and the sight of the object results automatically without the use of the intellect or the emotions. In order to see an object, in order for the perception to take place, it is not necessary to implicate the intellect or emotions. This is what is meant by the statement that perception is a mechanical process.

The radiation of consciousness starts from the abstract, absolute pure state of bliss and carries the bliss content in a diminishing degree as it proceeds outward. The oneness of Being appearing in its infinite variety is an automatic projection of consciousness.

Perception in the outside world, as we have seen, results mechanically from the diverging process of consciousness. The degree of bliss decreases as we proceed to the outward gross levels of experience, and it increases as we move toward the subtler levels approaching the source, Being. So, whether we experience on the levels of outward-projecting consciousness or experience on different levels of inward-projecting consciousness, the process of perception remains mechanical and automatic. Perception remains automatic, whether it is directed outward or directed inward — whether it is perception of the gross fields of life or of the subtler fields, or whether it is the perception of the transcendental state of Being. This is how realization of Being is found on the mechanical plane of perception. This justifies the mechanical process of perception as a means to God-Realization.

Now we shall analyze the process of perception that brings about this realization.

The process of perception of the outside world starts from the unmanifested field of pure consciousness and is carried on through the instrumentality of the mind and the nervous system to the manifested field of gross creation. This means that the process of perception results by virtue of the inner consciousness projecting outward. If, however, the perception of pure consciousness is sought, it will be necessary that the above-mentioned process of perception be reversed. The consciousness must then be gathered from the outward gross field and directed inward. The perception of pure Being, therefore, necessitates stopping the activity in the gross and appreciating successively less activity until the least activity can be appreciated and transcended. This gives rise to the state of pure consciousness, or the perception of transcendental Being.

The appreciation of subtler fields of activity starting from the gross is obviously the path in the inward direction. Whether the perception is outward or inward, it is automatic and mechanical. Perception in the outward direction is the result of a progressive increase of activity of the nervous system. And perception in the inward direction is the result of diminishing activity of the nervous system, until the entire nervous system ceases to function and reaches a state of stillness, a state of restful alertness. This brings the realization of "Be still and know that I am God."

This stillness is ideally achieved when the activity of the nervous system is brought to that state of restful alertness, when even the activity of the mind is reduced to nil, when the thinking process has been reduced to a point at the source of thinking. At this point, perception remains in the state of absolute consciousness, the state of enlightenment is gained, absolute Being of the transcendental nature comes to be on the conscious level of life, or, the conscious level of the mind reaches the transcendental level of Being.

The inward march of the mind, thus, mechanically brings the mind to the state of full enlightenment. This mechanical process of perception in the inward direction, causing the nervous system to arrive naturally at the state of restful alertness, is the mechanical path to God-Realization. In its practical form it is known as Transcendental Meditation. It is called a "mechanical" path to indicate that the process of inward perception is very innocent and does not need any intellectual or emotional help. It does not proceed through discrimination or feeling. This mechanical path of perception succeeds independently, without intellectual or emotional interference.

The activity of the mind in the inward direction brings it to the field of the transcendental Absolute and fills it with the power of eternal Being. Then, during the outward stroke, the activity of the mind brings the light of transcendental absolute Being into the outer world, thereby increasing the intensity of bliss in the perception of the gross manifested fields of creation.

This is how the innocent path of mechanical perception quietly serves to take the mind to transcendental absolute Being, or, to take the man to the field of God, and from there bring him out with the glory of God to brighten all the fields of life in the world.

This explains the significance of action and justifies its status as a path to enlightenment. This innocent, natural, simple process of perception and experience — from the outward gross to the inward subtle and Transcendent, and, from there, again returning to the outward gross — comprises the path of action[17] for enlightenment.

This is how the mechanical path of perception succeeds in harmonizing the values of eternal Being into the transitory field of activity in the world. Because the realization of Being entails perception in the inward march, and because infusion of Being in the outward activity entails outward perception, we find that it is the glory of mechanical perception that fills the whole field of life with the glory of divine Being and brings individual life to

17 The Bhagavad-Gītā calls it the Path of Action, or *Karma Yoga*.

the state of Cosmic Consciousness. This is how we find that the mechanical path of God-Realization lies in the simple process of perception.

Therefore, any man is able to realize God through this path, irrespective of his intellectual or emotional state of development. It remains only to know how to use one's ability of experience or the mechanics of perception. The knowledge of how to make use of one's ability of perception opens the highway to God-Realization.

The mechanical path of God-Realization, as found in Transcendental Meditation, is so simple and so comprehensive in its results that it remains a temptation for all the lovers of God and seekers of truth proceeding on any of the paths of God-Realization — intellectual, emotional, physiological, or psycho-physiological. It is so graceful that anyone treading any path of life finds it comforting and elevating. It supplements and reinforces any path to fulfillment.

Psycho-physiological Approach

The psycho-physiological approach to God-Realization, as is clear from the name itself, involves the simultaneous use of the body and mind.

We have seen in the previous parts how the body and mind are closely interrelated.[18] The state of mind directly affects the body, and the state of body influences the mind.

In the "Physiological Approach to God-Realization,"[19] we have seen that by culturing the body and breath, the state of restful alertness could be created in the nervous system so that the individual may have the experience of Being. This brings hope that it may be possible to accelerate the pace of progress of any path of God-Realization, intellectual or emotional, by supplementing it with the features of the physiological approach.

This combination of the aspects of physiological and intellectual or emotional paths constitutes the psycho-physiological path to God-Realization.

It may be said that culturing the body and mind simultaneously to produce the state of Transcendental Consciousness with regard to the mind,

18 See page 180, "Key to Good Health."
19 See page 289.

and the state of restful alertness with regard to the body, is the main feature of the psycho-physiological path. The purpose is to provide help from the physical plane to culture the mind and from the mental plane for the culture of the body. The sole intention is to arrive at the goal with greater ease and facility in the least amount of time.

Seen from this point of view, the psycho-physiological approach seems to be fascinating because there is no lover of God or seeker of truth who would not be lured to follow the path of greater ease and comfort for quick realization. But, as has already been made clear, the physiological path, necessitating rigorous practices of physical control and breath control, does not suit the householder's way of life. This restricts the scope of the psycho-physiological path from being universal.

As we have seen, culturing the body and breath needs close personal supervision by a teacher so that the health of the student may be safeguarded. There are, however, some suitable, light exercises for the body and breathing which may be practiced simultaneously with the intellectual or emotional paths that do not require strict personal supervision. These certainly would help to accelerate the progress toward God-Realization on these paths.

The psycho-physiological path to God-Realization, however, finds its fulfillment in the practice of Transcendental Meditation, which, as has already been made clear, simultaneously influences the body and mind. Without any sort of control on any level it automatically places the mind in the state of Transcendental Consciousness and brings the body and the nervous system to that state of restful alertness which is most suited to the state of enlightenment.

The mental and physical aspects of the psycho-physiological path are simultaneously fulfilled by the practice of Transcendental Meditation.

Generation After Generation

Generation after generation, man is born anew. Every man in every generation is born a new man with a new quest for fulfillment, with a new aspiration in life, with a new standard of fulfillment of life. It may be that his aspirations are in common with those around him, but for him they are new and they are his own aspirations to bring fulfillment to his own life.

There should be established a solid foundation for all men in all generations to gain fulfillment in life on all levels. The responsibility lies on the shoulders of the great men of the present generation.

Only the great hearts and the great minds of our present generation could rise to establish a solid foundation for all men of all generations to find a way to fulfillment in life, and this will be a boon for man, generation after generation.

Every man needs sound physical and mental health, greater ability of action and greater capacity to think clearly, greater efficiency in work, more loving and rewarding relationships with others, greater accomplishments in life on all levels, with freedom from suffering and misfortunes in day-to-day living. He needs enough intelligence and vitality to satisfy the desires of the mind along with contentment in his life. With all these is aimed a life of permanent freedom in God Consciousness.

We have seen in all the parts of this book that all these are gained by the regular practice of Transcendental Meditation and taking life easy in the day-to-day routine. Simplicity and innocence of natural behavior with other people and regularity in the practice of this meditation accomplish all these in the individual life for the present and for the future. Therefore, measures have to be adopted and a firm system has to be created so that every man in the world will naturally receive this system of Transcendental Meditation to fulfill the mission of his life and create an atmosphere conducive to the fulfillment of life for others.

In order to formulate a proper plan for the emancipation of the entire human race, generation after generation, we must give primary consideration to the factor of purity. Purity is life. Absolute purity is eternal life. Survival depends upon purity. The basis of the plan should be purity.

When we deal with the factor of purity, let us make it clear that in the state of highest evolution, in the field of Cosmic Consciousness, when the mind is brought to the fullest degree of the infusion of absolute Being, by nature the mind functions on the plane of purity in accordance with the Natural Laws engaged in carrying out the eternal process of evolution of everything in creation. This we have seen in the part on "Cosmic Law."[20]

We find that any system or principle of life which could be based on the level of natural evolution in creation will certainly survive all the ages to come, because it is the process of evolution which conducts the march of time through all the thick and thin of life.

The sole purpose of the plan is to maintain continuity of the teaching of Transcendental Meditation, generation after generation. For this, a system has to be evolved that is based on the Natural Laws of evolution.

In view of the foregoing consideration, the plan for the emancipation of all human beings, generation after generation, should contain the following points:

1. In order that the teaching of Transcendental Meditation be imparted on the level of the Laws of Nature governing the process of evolution, it is necessary that the teachers who impart this knowledge should be established on the plane of Cosmic Law, or at least be sincerely working toward this end in their own lives.

For this it is necessary that an ideal setup be created so that the teachers of meditation may be trained thoroughly in the practice and the theoretical understanding of Transcendental Meditation.

For this, an Academy of Meditation in the foothills of the Himalayas on the bank of the holy river Ganges has been planned, where people from all over the world will be trained under ideal conditions for meditation. But it would be still better if similar academies could be built on each continent.

---

20 See page 10, "Being, the Plane of Cosmic Law."

2. In order that the teaching may be imparted on the level of the natural process of evolution of the individual, it is necessary that the teaching be imparted according to the natural tendency of the individuals. Whatever the natural inclinations of the people, they should not be disturbed, because that is the path of their evolution. It should allow them to be what they are, allow them to do what they like, allow them not to do what they do not like. If the teaching could be such that it brings to every individual the fulfillment of his desires, tendencies, inclinations, and ways of life, through Transcendental Meditation, then it will not only be readily accepted by the people, but would certainly improve them and bring them greater momentum on the path of their evolution. The technique of imparting Transcendental Meditation to the people is to find out what they are aspiring for in life, find out what they want to accomplish, what their desires are, and then tell them of the gains of Transcendental Meditation in terms of their desires and needs and aspirations in life.

If Transcendental Meditation is taught to the people in terms of their aspirations in life, then certainly it will be in accordance with the level of their evolution and will regulate their life in accordance with Natural Laws. It will thus set the whole stream of their life in tune with Nature, and, without much delay, the harmony of life will become the harmony of the entire Nature, the universe.

3. The purity of the system has to be maintained, generation after generation, at any cost, because the effect lies in the purity of the teaching. Whereas it is necessary to train the teachers thoroughly in the practices and the theory of Transcendental Meditation, it is also necessary that it be passed on to the people in its pure state. To maintain the purity of this system it seems necessary that teachers be found in all parts of the world and that they have their own premises from which to work. Centers of meditation, temples of human evolution, should be constructed everywhere in the world, in order that the teachers dedicated to the spreading of Transcendental Meditation continue to function, generation after generation, with ease and facility.

4. To maintain the teaching, generation after generation, for all times to come, it seems also to be necessary that the practice of this meditation should somehow be made part and parcel of the daily routine of the people. It should fall in the pattern of life, it should be a way of life. For this it seems necessary that sanctuaries of silence be constructed in the midst of noisy marketplaces of big cities, so that people, before going to their business, and after completing their business of the day, may enter into silent meditation rooms, dive deep within themselves, and be profited by undisturbed, regular, and deep meditations. Apart from the silent meditation centers in the noisy areas of towns, it seems to be necessary that such silent meditation centers also be constructed in the holiday resorts where people go on weekends to stay for one or two days. There they may have long hours of deep meditation and come home renewed in spirit, intelligence, and energy.

Actually, the practical aspect of the plan for the emancipation of all mankind, generation after generation, lies in the construction of a world center for training spiritual leaders and the construction of silent meditation rooms in the midst of business areas of cities and towns of the world and at holiday resorts.

It is hoped that the lovers of life and well-wishers of humanity will rise to the occasion and start on a program of constructing these silent places to bring a practical message of harmony and peace in life throughout the world.

To maintain the purity of the system it is highly necessary that the organizations have their own premises. The history of different religions shows that it is the temples, churches, mosques, and pagodas that have retained the voice of wisdom of the mastery of the various religions. If it were not for these great edifices, the message would have been lost long ago. Certainly the structures themselves do not have any significance in the maintenance of the purity of the tradition, but they are a strong safeguard. It is not the buildings that will carry on the message, but they will be fixed places from which the message will be given to the people, generation after generation. In time of need, especially if some of the teachers begin to become weak in their understanding, and the teaching becomes loose and is not able to maintain the great effect of the method, then these permanent buildings will stand as a symbol of the message. And, although they themselves are not able to carry the message effectively from generation to generation, they do silently speak of the existence of a useful method to liberate mankind.

It is as if the buildings serve as the home of the ideology. Both body and spirit are needed to have an effective personality. Without the body, the spirit will not be found; and, without the spirit, the body will not function. So the spirit of the message will be the realized or evolved state of the teachers and the purity of the system; the body of the message will be these buildings and the books that will stand and help to preserve the spirit of the message.

5. If the message is to be carried from generation to generation, it should be placed on the mass tendency of each generation. It is found that the general understanding and tendencies of the people keep on changing from time to time. There was a time when religions guided the destiny of the people, but when the message of religions failed to provide a means to peace and inner harmony and a direct way to God-Realization, then the people lost faith. When religion is reduced to ritual and dogma only, the human mind, in its attempt to find a true understanding of life, turns to philosophy, the quest of truth on the intellectual basis, and dogmatic religions lose their importance and naturally go into the background of mass consciousness.

Until about fifty to one hundred years ago, the religions held sway over the people, over the mass consciousness. When the religions lost their hold, metaphysical movements, or the comparative study of different religions, became predominant, and the mass consciousness leaned on metaphysical studies. When metaphysics, in all its endeavor to describe the reality, could not offer any practical formula for the realization of the abstract metaphysical truth, the human mind wanted to turn to something else.

The study of philosophy remained the interest of some in the society, but the mass consciousness rose to political awakening. With the advent of the democratic ideology, the mass consciousness was caught up in the day-to-day events of political affairs in the respective countries. In a democracy each man is supposed to rule himself, and, as the democratic governments became more and more predominant, political consciousness came to dominate the life of the people. People began to look to the fulfillment of life on the platform of politics. Politics is not a field to provide an adequate formula for the fulfillment of life of the individual. Yet today is the time when politics seems to have the upper hold of mass consciousness. Anything that happens in the field of politics receives wide publicity, people talk about it, it attracts the attention of all nations. Certainly the times are fast changing, and the day is not far off when political consciousness will be replaced by economic consciousness.

Economics has already begun to influence the destiny of politics in many countries. This shows that the teaching of Transcendental Meditation should be based according to the consciousness of the masses at any particular time. In view of all these changing phases of mass consciousness at different times, it seems logical that the level of teaching of Transcendental Meditation should not be rigid and restricted to any specific level for all times. The policy of its propagation should accept the change in the level of mass consciousness at any time so that it could be easily imparted to all the people in every generation.

Whenever and wherever religion dominates the mass consciousness, Transcendental Meditation should be taught in terms of religion. Whenever and wherever metaphysical thinking dominates the consciousness of society, Transcendental Meditation should be taught in metaphysical terms, openly aiming at the fulfillment of the current metaphysical thought. Whenever and wherever politics dominates the mass consciousness, Transcendental Meditation should be taught in terms of and from the platform of politics, aiming at bringing fulfillment to the political aspirations of the generation. Whenever and wherever economics dominates the mass consciousness, Transcendental Meditation should be taught from the level of economics, with the aim of bringing fulfillment to the economic aspirations and goals of the time.

Today, when politics is guiding the destiny of man, the teaching should be primarily based on the field of politics and secondarily on the plane of economics. It will then be much easier to spread it in all countries and make it not only popular but practically available to all the people everywhere. When, after a few years, economics takes the upper hand, the main platform of teaching should be the field of economics; politics should then be a secondary platform, and the field of metaphysics and religion, a third.

Therefore, basically, the teaching of meditation should be based on that phase of life which at a particular time is guiding the destiny of mass consciousness.

What is suited to the present generation?

It seems, for the present, that Transcendental Meditation should be made available to the people through the agencies of government. It is not the time when any effort to perpetuate a new and useful ideology without the help of governments can succeed. It is the governments of the democratic countries that hold the faith and goodwill of their people. The leaders of governments are the representatives of the peoples of the countries, and every leader naturally wishes to do something good for those whom he represents. Therefore this meditation, which is a means for all good to every individual, will certainly be accepted for its truth and value by all the leaders in different governments, and, through them, it could be easily and effectively propagated throughout the world.

In view of the great benefits of Transcendental Meditation in the fields of health, education, and social welfare, and for the lives of prisoners in jails and in the misguided lives of the delinquents, it is highly useful that Transcendental Meditation be given to the people through the governmental agencies of health, education, social welfare, and justice. It should be a practice adopted by the medical profession, by teachers and professors in schools and colleges, by social workers working to improve the behavior of the people within a society, and for all the well-wishers of life in every field.

Thus, the proper plan for the emancipation of all mankind, generation after generation, lies in training evolved teachers of Transcendental Meditation, constructing suitable, silent sanctuaries for the meditation, bringing it to every individual on the basis of his need and his nature, and finding various ways and means for its propagation according to the consciousness of the times.

The maintenance of the purity of the teaching will help the people of all times by alleviating suffering, shortcomings, and ignorance, and will usher in a new era for a new humanity developed in all the values of life — physical, mental, material, and spiritual — and enable man to live a life of fulfillment established in eternal freedom in God Consciousness. The peace and prosperity of people everywhere will be secured in their evolved consciousness and status in higher values in life. The accomplishments on the level of family, society, national, and international planes will be the maximum possible, and man will naturally live in fulfillment, for generation after generation.

APPENDICES
and AFTERWORD

APPENDIX I: A Proposal to the World Parliament Association, Paris,
October 1962 — *Speech by Prince Giovanni Alliata Di Montereale, M.P. (Italy)* 311

APPENDIX II: Timely Call to the Leaders of Today and Tomorrow —
*An appeal made by Members of Parliament from all the States of India,
in the Spring of 1963* 329

AFTERWORD: Sequential Unfoldment of Maharishi's Teaching,
by Dr. Bevan Morris 333

APPENDIX A: Overview of the Scientific Research on the *Transcendental
Meditation* and *Transcendental Meditation Sidhi* Programs Including
Yogic Flying 363

APPENDIX B: Human Physiology — Expression of Veda and the Vedic
Literature: *Modern Science and Ancient Vedic Science Discover the Fabrics of
Immortality in the Human Physiology* — A Textbook of Life for Everyone,
by Professor Tony Nader, MD, PhD, MARR 376

APPENDIX C: Introduction to the Bhagavad-Gītā — *A New Translation
and Commentary, Chapters 1–6,* by Maharishi Mahesh Yogi 380

APPENDIX D: Maharishi's Master Plan to Create Heaven on Earth:
Reconstruction of the Whole World 382

APPENDIX E: A Glimpse of Maharishi's Achievements
1957–2008 Continuing 384

APPENDIX F: Maharishi's Books — Enlightenment for Everyone and Every
Nation: The Literature on Natural Law That Offers Freedom from
Problems in Every Field of Life — *the Guiding Light of Today's World
and the World of Every Tomorrow for All Time* 388

APPENDIX I

A Proposal to the World Parliament Association
Paris, October 1962

Speech by
Prince Giovanni Alliata Di Montereale, M.P. (Italy)

Dear Colleagues:

In my contact with parliamentarians for the last fifteen years, ever since the birth of this World Parliament Association, I have come to the conclusion that something has to be done by us to improve the peoples of our countries.

On the international scale our aim is to establish unity among the nations and for this high purpose we have been working and our efforts will continue.

On the national scale, all of us are directly concerned with the integrity of our own nations. We want our industry and commerce to grow; we want our technology to develop; we wish our scientists great success in their undertakings; we want our agriculture to be better; we want our nation to be more integrated and more powerful in every way.

In order to achieve all these aims we should plan for our people to be healthier, more intelligent, and more creative. This could certainly be achieved by developing the power of each man within himself and unfolding the faculties latent in his mind.

The study of psychology has shown that whatever a man is able to express of himself is only a part of his whole.

The greater part of man does not find expression in his behavior and activity in life, because the conscious mind is only a part of the total mind that a man possesses. So what we need is to make available to every man in our country a technique of enlarging his conscious mind, a technique of enabling him to use his full mind.

For example, if a man is using only a fraction of his mind, by enabling him to use the whole of his mind, he will become infinitely greater as a man. He will think much more deeply and more fully than he now does.

Suppose that the conscious mind of man is only one-fourth of his total mind, then whatever he thinks and does is only a quarter of his real potential. If we want him to use his full potential, then his full mind should be made conscious, and only then his thought force will be four times more powerful, and he will be four times stronger and four times more sensible and happier than before.

His love for his fellow man and the harmony in his home and his surroundings will increase four times. In the field of science, in the field of industry and commerce, on the level of civilization as a whole, great improvement will be found.

For this purpose we propose adopting one simple method which will enlarge the conscious mind and thereby simultaneously improve man on all levels — physical, mental, and spiritual — and also increase his creative intelligence and improve his relations with his fellow men.

This one simple method of improving each man as a whole is available in the world today. We have only to incorporate it in our system of education, health, and welfare.

To accomplish this I propose that we, the members of the Parliaments assembled here from all over the world, unite in presenting to our respective governments the bills incorporating these ideas, the details of which are available for your examination.

I propose that we present four bills in our parliaments to cover the scope of the ministries of education, social welfare, justice, and health.

I trust that you will certainly examine this matter carefully and that you will be one of those who will introduce this in your Parliament.

As I previously remarked, a simple method of improving each man as a whole is available in the world today. I can, with confidence, say something about it, because of my own experience. The method is known as "Transcendental Meditation." Its practice has been introduced to people throughout the world by Maharishi Mahesh Yogi.

APPENDIX I

I have personally practiced Maharishi Mahesh Yogi's simple system of Transcendental Meditation for enlarging the conscious mind.

On the basis of my own personal experience, and on the basis of my observations of some hundreds of people from England, Germany, and Italy who are also following this practice, I urge you most earnestly to practice it yourselves.

In the name of peace and happiness of the individual, in the name of the solidarity of our nations, and in the name of world peace, I urge you, my friends, to introduce this tried and proven method to all the people of your countries through your Parliaments in a systematic and effective way.

All our peoples will be healthier, happier, more intelligent, and more creative.

By improving our peoples we will be improving our civilization on all levels. Our present generation will be better and will leave a better world for the oncoming generations. This, I am sure, is an effective way of creating a natural situation for lasting world peace.

Now I take this occasion to propose a theme for our next conference. As the aim for our World Parliament Association has always been the peace and progress of mankind, and in our past meetings we have been discussing the legislative, economic, and other topics of national and international importance, for the next year, I propose we meet to discuss: The Development of Man as a Means to National Harmony and International Peace.

The Main Principle of Maharishi Mahesh Yogi's Simple System of Transcendental Meditation for Expansion of the Conscious Mind[1]

Maharishi explains his principle of expansion of the conscious mind by the analogy of a wave on the sea:

> When the wave makes contact with the deeper levels of water, it becomes more powerful. Likewise, when the conscious mind expands to embrace deeper levels of the subconscious, then the conscious mind becomes more powerful.

1 Please also refer to page 29 for a detailed study of the principle.

In order to achieve this, Maharishi uses a technique whereby the subconscious area of the mind is made conscious. This is done by consciously experiencing the thought in its infant state in the subconscious.

The correctness of the process is verified directly by the results — the man begins to feel instantaneous release of mental fatigue and tension. Increase of compassion, feeling of increased energy, clarity of thought, along with increase of self-confidence are some of the obvious experiences that justify the expansion of the conscious mind.

To picture this principle more thoroughly, let us examine the process of thinking.

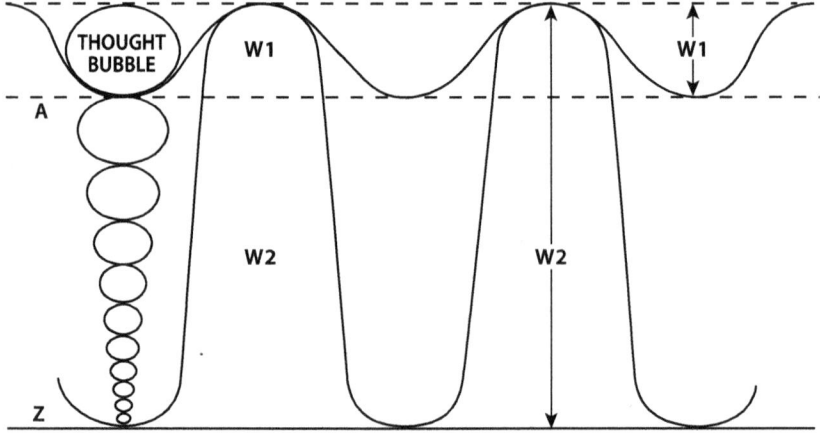

The Main Principle of Transcendental Meditation

Thought Process

The origin of thought is in the deepest level of the subconscious, from which it rises to pass through all levels of the subconscious to reach the conscious level of the mind. It is here, at the conscious level, that the thought is appreciated as a thought.

A thought starts from the deepest level of the subconscious as a bubble starts from the bottom of a pond. As the bubble comes up it becomes bigger. Only when it reaches the surface does it become large enough to be perceived.

The bubble of thought arising from the level Z becomes bigger (*see illustration*). By the time it has reached the surface level A, it has developed enough to be appreciated as a thought. This is the level of the conscious mind.

The subtle states of the bubble of thought below the level of the conscious state are not consciously appreciated. If there could be a way of conscious appreciation of the bubble of thought at all levels of its development, and at the source Z, then the small area of the conscious mind represented by W1 will become a bigger area, represented by W2.

If the bubble of thought could be consciously appreciated at the level below A and at all levels of its subtlety from A to Z, then it would be possible to bring the level Z within the range of the conscious mind. In this way, the depth of the conscious mind represented by W1 would become greater, as represented by W2, and the power of the conscious mind would be increased manyfold.

Application of the Principle

The Technique: Bubbles of thought are produced in a stream one after the other, and the mind is trained to experience the oncoming bubble at an earlier and earlier stage of its development, from A to Z, in sequence (*see illustration*). When the attention has reached level Z, then it has traversed the whole depth of the mind and has reached the source of creative intelligence in man.

The source of thought, the source of creative energy, thus comes within the scope of the conscious mind and fills it with strength over and above the strength gained by the conscious mind in fathoming the deeper levels of the subconscious. The depth of the conscious mind represented in the diagram by W1 has thus been transformed into greater depth represented by W2. This is how the conscious mind is enlarged to its maximum capacity, embracing within its fold the source of creative intelligence and thus becoming infinitely powerful.[2]

2 This finding of Maharishi Mahesh Yogi is unique and has no parallel in the findings of modern psychology.

It is noteworthy that this technique of enlarging the conscious mind is so simple that it can be practiced by anyone. It does not need any preparation to start, nor does it depend upon the power of concentration on the part of the practitioner. It is not dependent on the intellectual or emotional state of one's mind.

Although the technique has become famous as "Transcendental Meditation," it is nonsectarian in its character. It is purely a scientific[3] method of enlarging the conscious mind. It does not conflict with any religion or faith. It is already practiced by over fifty thousand people in twenty-five different countries.

This simple technique of enlarging the conscious mind has been found beneficial in the various fields of:

1. Education
2. Delinquency and Crime
3. Social Welfare
4. Mental Health

This is the reason why it is intended that this technique be made available in a systematic and effective way to all the people through government departments concerned with education, social welfare, justice, and health.

Education

Development of Mind by Transcendental Meditation

As it is, our present system of education is lacking in a technique to enlarge the conscious mind by developing the potentialities of the subconscious. It has the capacity of exercising the conscious mind, but it fails to develop the potentialities of the subconscious.

---

3 This technique of enlarging the conscious mind is scientific because:
   1. It is systematic.
   2. It is not opposed to any methods of scientific investigation.
   3. It is universal in its application.
   4. It is open to verification by personal experience.
   5. The end results are found to be the same by everyone.

It has been made clear, while dealing with "The Main Principle for Expansion of the Conscious Mind," that the conscious mind is only a small portion of the total mind that man possesses, and that through Maharishi Mahesh Yogi's system of Transcendental Meditation, the whole mind becomes conscious, and the potentialities develop. This is highly important in the career of students.

That is why we propose to introduce this system into the curriculum of our schools and universities.

This is the unique approach to improve our present system of education. The introduction of this simple principle of Transcendental Meditation will vitalize modern education and will usher in an educational renaissance all over the world. It will develop the potentialities of the minds of students to their fullest extent and enable dull minds to become bright.

It will develop balance in life and understanding of right values. It will improve the memory and power to retain knowledge. It will increase self-confidence and self-reliance. It will develop creative intelligence. In fact, it will supply that which is needed to make modern education complete.

It is therefore proposed that this simple system of Transcendental Meditation should be introduced into the curriculum so that the students may start practicing it from about the age of fifteen years (in Italy this is the last year of the compulsory education). It is also proposed to introduce it into the curriculum of university classes, so that before the students enter the full responsibilities of life they develop the full capacity of their minds.

The following is the outline of the way in which this aim could be achieved:

Teachers could be fully trained to give the technique of Transcendental Meditation for the development of the conscious mind to the students for whom they are responsible. This can be accomplished in three ways:

1. Several teachers could be sent to Maharishi Mahesh Yogi's Academy of Meditation in India for three months, so that they could return and train others.
2. Some of our teachers could go to participate in the Meditation Guides' Training Courses, which Maharishi Mahesh Yogi conducts

annually in different parts of Europe, America and India.
3. Arrangements could be made so that a large number of our teachers could be trained in their own countries. For this, arrangements could be made by contacting any of the centers of the Spiritual Regeneration Movement.

Delinquency and Crime
Rehabilitation of the Delinquent and the Criminal Through Transcendental Meditation

The need to rehabilitate offenders is the age-old problem of society. Crime, delinquency, and the different patterns of antisocial behavior arise from the deep discontent of the mind. A weak mind loses its balance and sense of proportion.

Crime is evidently a shortcut to satisfy a craving — a shortcut which goes beyond the normal and legal means.

No approach to the problem can hope to be truly effective unless the basic weakness of the mind is remedied.

While dealing with "The Main Principle for Expansion of the Conscious Mind," it has been made clear how the conscious mind is enlarged to its fullest capacity and strengthened to its utmost extent by the practice of Maharishi's simple system of Transcendental Meditation.

Therefore it is necessary to introduce this system of Transcendental Meditation for the speedy and effective rehabilitation of delinquents and criminals.

Many with potential talent are among those who are shut behind bars because of their misguided behavior. Instead of being a burden they could become useful citizens, making a genuine contribution to the progress of society, if only they could be successfully rehabilitated.

It has been found that all kinds of tensions are released, and the hard and cruel nature of man changes to one of tolerance and compassion, through the practice of Transcendental Meditation.

The following is an outline of the way in which this aim could be achieved:

Social welfare workers, prison officials, and others who are engaged in the rehabilitation of delinquents and criminals could be fully trained to give the technique of Transcendental Meditation to develop the conscious mind to the offenders with whom they are concerned.

This can be accomplished by utilizing trained meditation guides of the Spiritual Regeneration Movement, who are conducting meditation centers in the country. In addition to this, any of the following methods may be employed:

1. Some of our welfare workers could be sent to Maharishi Mahesh Yogi's Academy of Meditation in India for three months, so that they could be trained to teach the method.
2. Some of our welfare workers could go to participate in the Meditation Guides' Training Courses which Maharishi Mahesh Yogi conducts annually in different parts of Europe and America.
3. Arrangements could be made for training courses to be held in the country. For this, arrangements could be made by contacting any of the centers.

Social Welfare
Development of the Mind Through Transcendental Meditation

The need to improve the quality of human relationships is deeply felt in every country in the world. Within the family, within larger spheres of industry, and on the international scale, the need is there.

There can be no improvement on a larger scale until harmony is established on all the smaller scales within it. Everything is finally dependent upon the individual mind, for the only actuality of any group, however large, is the individuals of which it is composed.

The basis of all disharmony is the inability of man to satisfy his needs. This may be due to loss of energy or to lack of intelligence, to poverty of imagination or to his inability to make the best use of the situation in which he finds himself.

These are the human incapacities which must be overcome in order to improve the whole man and thus improve his total situation and his accomplishments on every scale.

To achieve this end, it is necessary to develop and strengthen the individual mind.

Maharishi Mahesh Yogi's work in all parts of the world during the last six years has proved that this is precisely what his simple system of Transcendental Meditation does achieve, and in this way the whole man is improved.

It is within the easy reach of every human being to improve the quality of his mind and of his heart. This meditation enlarges the mind's conscious capacity and enhances its ability to perceive and respond significantly to its situation.

Generally, a man does not use his whole mind, and therefore he perceives only a part of his situation. Responding to that alone, his behavior remains inadequate to his total position.

Transcendental Meditation brings into conscious activity areas of the mind which before were active only below the level of conscious mind, and so the conscious mind is made larger, and therefore more alert and powerful. A fully developed mind succeeds in perceiving the total situation and is thus enabled to respond fully and successfully to that situation.

Maharishi illustrates this by describing how a wave on the surface becomes powerful when it includes within itself the deeper levels of the ocean that lie beneath the surface. Likewise, when the conscious mind embraces the deeper levels of the subconscious, it becomes more powerful; all the latent faculties of the subconscious are unfolded.

With the expansion of the conscious mind, the latent potentialities are fully developed. The increased contentment of the heart gives rise to compassion, and the sharpness of the mind gives rise to understanding. Such a complete individual mind accomplishes more in life, while it remains fully secure, established in the inner peace, harmony, and happiness. Such a mind is of value to the individual and the society.

These enlarged capacities improve a man's relationship with his fellow men in a natural and spontaneous way, whereas contemporary methods of improving individual relationships by counsel and advice, and social relationships by meetings and discussions, can only scratch the surface of the situation.

A gardener seeing a leaf withering away in the sun does not direct his attention directly upon it, but hastens to water the root, whereas, had he been more skillful, the root would have been watered before the leaf began to wither. Today, those who concern themselves with interrelationships of people seem unable to do much more than hurry from one withering leaf to the next, uttering vague cries of consolation and goodwill. To try to bring harmony only in this way is like running after a mirage in the hope of obtaining water. For it is obvious that as group-therapy techniques multiply, problems also multiply and tensions continue to grow. Problems of relationship and its tensions cannot be solved at the group level.

The root of every situation, on whatever scale it is, is the state of the individual mind, and it is this root that needs to be vital and healthy. Rather than attending to the effects at the level of the group, it is essential to attack the cause. This lies always in the individual mind.

A man's incapacity to cope with his environment, to dominate it, and to use it to its fullest advantage, to gain the most from it and to satisfy his needs within it — this incapacity leads to frustration and rising tension, for he becomes unable either to tolerate the situation as it is, or to change it for the better. He is then forced by the increase of tension within him to burst out into revolt and aggression against everything around him and even against himself. In this way he makes the situation continuously worse and creates confusion and unhappiness.

A man of powerful mind, in the same circumstances, interprets the situation quite differently. He behaves in such a way to make the best out of the existing circumstances for himself and, at the same time, brings about an improvement of the situation for everyone involved in it. Thus he fertilizes and enriches his whole field of influence.

All antisocial behavior, even crime and delinquency, arises from inner discontent, which finds a fertile field in the weak mind which is unable to properly come to grips with the world around it and to achieve a stable and rewarding relationship with it. No approach to these problems can hope to be truly effective unless the basic incapacity of the mind, which is their cause, is fundamentally remedied.

This can be achieved simply and without effort by the practice of Maharishi Mahesh Yogi's simple system of Transcendental Meditation, for this brings the mind to its full stature, so that it not only becomes content in itself but is also, at the same time, able to act with strength and decision in the fields of choice.

It is therefore proposed that this simple system of Transcendental Meditation should be brought to the people of each country through the department concerned with social welfare.

The following is an outline of the way in which this aim could be achieved:

Social welfare workers could be fully trained to give the technique of Transcendental Meditation to the people whom they are helping. This can be accomplished in four ways:

1. Trained meditation guides who are already conducting meditation centers of the Spiritual Regeneration Movement in the country may be utilized by the Welfare Department of the state.

2. Several of our social welfare officers could be sent to Maharishi Mahesh Yogi's Academy of Meditation in India for three months, so that they could return and train other social workers in the country.

3. Some of our social workers could go to participate in the Meditation Guides' Training Courses which Maharishi Mahesh Yogi conducts annually in different parts of Europe and America.

4. Arrangements could be made so that a large number of our social workers could be trained in our own countries. For this, arrangements could be made by contacting any of the centers of the Spiritual Regeneration Movement.

Appendix I

Health

Preservation and Betterment of Health Through Transcendental Meditation

To build more hospitals in order to remove the suffering when people have already fallen ill is certainly the responsibility of the government, but a far greater responsibility lies in finding ways and means whereby people will not fall sick. We propose to show how this new goal of good health may be achieved.

We note that preventive medicine is already an established and important part of health programs of governments. Progress in this field depends upon the application of new findings from time to time.

Here is something new which has proved its value for the preservation and betterment of health.

Individual health has both mental and physical aspects. These are very closely interdependent, and it is only for the sake of clarity that we shall consider them separately to see how health is affected by Maharishi Mahesh Yogi's system of Transcendental Meditation.

Mental Health

The mind functions through the nervous system which serves to connect the subjective nature of man with the objective world around him.

Mental health depends upon the strength of the mind. A strong mind establishes a thorough coordination with the nervous system and enables it to function normally. When the nervous system functions normally the full mind is brought to bear upon the external world. The normal functioning of the nervous system results in physical good health as well, and thereby the body is able to carry out the directives of the mind and fulfill its desires.

As long as the coordination of the mind with the nervous system is intact, mental health is maintained. When this coordination breaks down, ill health is the result. Such lack of coordination is mainly due to the weakness of the mind or lack of thought-force. A weak thought fails to stimulate the nervous system to a sufficient extent to carry out successfully the activity that is needed for its fulfillment.

For the most thorough coordination and perfect function, a profound power of thought on the part of the mind, together with a correspondingly efficient executive ability in the nervous system, is required. An improvement of the state of the mind results at once in an improved coordination between the mind and the world around it; thus the full mind is brought to bear upon the external world and the subject comes into a more perfect and rewarding apposition with the object. Happiness is clearly the result of the fulfillment of the desires of the mind, and happiness is the expression of sound mental health.

If, because of the failure to satisfy the needs and desires of the mind, discontentment begins to produce tension within it, then the way to remove these tensions will be to strengthen the mind by increasing its power to think — the force of thought. This is achieved by enlarging the conscious mind through the practice of Transcendental Meditation, as has already been explained while dealing with "The Main Principle of Transcendental Meditation for Expansion of the Conscious Mind."

When tensions build up in the mind, they are reflected through the nervous system upon the body. The anxious mind, constantly flitting back and forth amongst its problems in its discontented state, exhausts and irritates the nervous system and body. As a servant to whom his master constantly gives indecisive and confusing orders becomes tired and irritable and eventually fails to do anything, likewise, the nervous system and the body become tired and exhausted and eventually fail to function efficiently when the mind is in a state of stress due to confusion and indecision.

In this way, mental stress produces disease and even organic changes in the body. Obviously the cure of all such suffering is to create such a situation in the mind that it may become, and remain, unwavering and steady. This is achieved by expanding the conscious mind and thereby making it strong. As a result of strengthening the conscious mind, a better coordination between the mind and the nervous system is established, and smooth and efficient functioning of the body is naturally the result. Perfect mental health is maintained because of this coordination of the mind with the nervous system and with its end organ — the body.

It has been seen in hundreds of cases in many countries that worried and tense people naturally lose their tensions within a short time of starting the practice of Transcendental Meditation. Thus we find that this practice of Transcendental Meditation is a boon for mental health. It is a means for preservation of mental health; it serves as a mental tonic and at the same time is a natural and effective cure for mental illness.

Physical Health

Medical researchers have shown that a very large proportion of physical disorders arise primarily from mental tension as a result of anxieties and failures in life.

While dealing with mental health we have seen how the process of Transcendental Meditation releases tension, and this is why we find that all suffering that could be described as psychosomatic is relieved at its source by Transcendental Meditation. There are, however, purely organic diseases in which there is no evidence of a mental cause — but it is well known that a sick man, in his situation, has a mental and emotional attitude to his illness which, while not causal to the illness itself, may still be having profound effects upon its course. Certainly meditation will remove these secondary anxieties; but let us now consider what effects meditation may have upon a purely organic disease. To do this we must consider the physiological effects of Transcendental Meditation.

Physiological Effects of Transcendental Meditation

As the attention is drawn to consciously experience the subtle state of a thought during Transcendental Meditation, it is found that respiration becomes greatly reduced in amplitude; the breathing becomes soft and refined.

Physiologically it is clear that for this to take place there must be a fall in the level of carbon dioxide in the plasma. This can occur only as a result of either forced over-breathing, which washes the carbon dioxide out through the lungs, or by a fall in the production of carbon dioxide through metabolic process.

Because there is no forced over-breathing during Transcendental Meditation we can only conclude that the softening of the breath is due to the fall in the production of carbon dioxide by metabolic process.

The production of most of the energy for activity in the body involves finally the oxidation of carbon and its elimination as carbon dioxide.

Greater activity needs greater energy, which is produced by a greater amount of oxidation of carbon and its elimination as carbon dioxide. Lesser amount of activity needs lesser amount of energy, which is produced by lesser amount of oxidation of carbon and its elimination as carbon dioxide.

This shows that when a lesser amount of carbon dioxide is eliminated by way of softer breathing during Transcendental Meditation, the process of oxidation is lessened and this naturally produces a lesser amount of energy.

That is why the activity of the body and that of the nervous system is lessened during Transcendental Meditation. This explains why, during Transcendental Meditation, as the mind proceeds to experience finer states of a thought, the whole body becomes calm and quiet.

This quietening of the body naturally allows an unusual degree of rest, which itself stores energy to an unusual degree. Certainly activity of the mind and the nervous system is least in this state, and the mind quietens and becomes calm.[4] In this quiet state the mind and the nervous system are alertly poised like the arrow drawn fully back upon the bow; they are without activity, but the entire system is alert in stillness. At the same time all the mechanisms of the body are acutely balanced and steady. It is this restful alertness of the nervous system that is its most healthy state and is the basis of all energy and action.

The fall in carbon dioxide output has also another effect — that of causing a tendency to change the reaction of the blood from acidity toward

---

[4] If by means of Transcendental Meditation one does not produce this state even for a few minutes daily, then one has no chance of providing any rest to the inner machinery of the body which otherwise is kept functioning twenty-four hours of the day, for the whole of one's life as long as the breath keeps flowing.

Obviously it is to the advantage of health and longevity of life that the ever-functioning inner machinery of the body is allowed a few moments of rest and silence each day.

alkalinity. This, in its turn, has widespread effects upon the blood chemistry, all of which are beneficial to the system as a whole.

These considerations lead us to the following:

That Maharishi Mahesh Yogi's system of Transcendental Meditation is beneficial in the field of health in two ways. It is both preventive and curative:

1. It is a means of preservation of mental and physical health.
2. It is a means of providing complete rest and relaxation to body and mind which restores energy and greatly aids medical treatment toward a speedy recovery from ill health.

Following is an outline of the ways in which the preservation and betterment of health could be achieved:

1. Trained meditation guides who are already conducting meditation centers of the Spiritual Regeneration Movement may be utilized by departments of health.
2. One professor from each medical college could be trained either in Maharishi's Academy of Meditation in India or in training courses that Maharishi holds in Europe or America. This trained professor will be able to train medical students so that the future medical practitioners will be competent to impart the technique of Transcendental Meditation to their patients.
3. Officers of the health department and doctors and nurses could be trained to give the practice of Transcendental Meditation to the sick and the needy.

Appendix II

Timely Call to the Leaders of Today and Tomorrow

This is the text of an appeal made by Members of Parliament from all the States of India, in the Spring of 1963.

Dr. Harekrishna Mahatab, MP (Orissa), Former Governor of Bombay, Ex-Union Minister of Commerce & Industry, Ex-Chief Minister of Orissa; **Shri B. Ramakrishna Rao**, MP, Ex-Governor of Uttar Pradesh and Kerala, Ex-Chief Minister of Hyderabad; **Dr. M. S. Aney**, MP (Maharashtra), Ex-Governor of Bihar; **Dr. Govind Das**, MP (Madhya Pradesh); **Maharani Gayatri Devi of Jaipur**, MP (Rajasthan); **Shri Tika Ram Paliwal**, MP (Rajasthan), Ex-Chief Minister of Rajasthan; **Shri Shyam Lal Saraf**, MP (Jammu & Kashmir), Ex-Minister of Industries, Jammu & Kashmir; **Sarv Shri P. Venkata Subbiah**, MP (Andhra Pradesh); **Nihar Ranjan Laskar**, MP (Assam); **D. N. Tiwary**, MP (Bihar); **C. R. Raja**, MP (Gujarat); **Ravindra Verma**, MP (Kerala); **P. Muthiah**, MP (Madras); **T. Subramaniam**, MP (Mysore); **Sardar Gurmukh Singh Musafir**, MP (Punjab); **Raghunath Singh**, MP (Uttar Pradesh); **S. Hansda**, MP (West Bengal); **Shiv Charan Gupta**, MP (Delhi); **Partap Singh**, MP (Himachal Pradesh); **S. T. Singh**, MP (Manipur); and **Col. Satyavrata Siddhantalankar**, Vice-Chancellor of Gurukula Kangri Vishwavidyalaya.

LIVE in peace or perish is the challenge of the nuclear age. The state of increasing tension cannot continue indefinitely; it must give way to peace or annihilation.

Hundreds of educated, intelligent, energetic, and devoted persons are needed to serve the cause of world peace, by popularizing the practical formula of peace and harmony in the life of the individuals in every corner of India and abroad.

His Holiness Maharishi Mahesh Yogi, the founder of the worldwide Spiritual Regeneration Movement, expounds a simple system of Transcendental Meditation whereby any man may turn his mind within himself and tap the source of unlimited energy, happiness, peace, and creative intelligence.

Maharishi's simple system of Transcendental Meditation bridges the gulf between the inner and outer aspects of life. It regenerates the personality improving all phases of life, resulting in a harmonious development of body, mind, and soul.

Thousands of people all over the world are now enjoying "a tension-free life" through Maharishi's simple system of Transcendental Meditation.

Three times Maharishiji has gone round the world establishing Meditation Centers in India, Burma, Malay, Singapore, Hong Kong, United States of America, Canada, Germany, Sweden, Norway, Denmark, England, Scotland, Ireland, France, Italy, Greece, East Africa, South Africa, Australia, and New Zealand.

Hundreds of Meditation Guides trained by Maharishiji in India and abroad are satisfactorily conducting the Meditation Centers in all these countries.

This is an attempt to spiritually regenerate all mankind and create a lasting world peace for which Maharishiji started the Spiritual Regeneration Movement four years ago, and for which His Holiness has recently established the Academy of Meditation as the world headquarters for training Meditation Guides.

The need for more Meditation Guides is increasing day by day with the universal acceptance of Maharishi's philosophy of simple and deep meditation.

A 40-day training program of Meditation Guides will commence from 20th May 1963, at the Academy of Meditation at Shankaracharya Nagar, near Ṛishikesh.

The National Outlook

Experience has shown us that we, even in India, cannot live in peace if we have not spread peace in our surroundings. Even to maintain a balance of mind and peace within our society, it is imperative that we should rise to the challenge of the day and carry the practical message of peace and harmony to every part of the world.

The present grave situation of the national life of our country demands strength and unity, which is only possible by increasing the consciousness of our people.

Increased consciousness means greater energy, creative intelligence, better health, and also greater harmony in social relationships. Maharishi's simple technique of Transcendental Meditation is a direct way to it. It is only necessary for us all to adopt it.

We are by tradition a peace-loving nation. We know by experience that peace is not possible in weakness. Let us rise to strengthen ourselves. Let us unfold our latent faculties and begin to use our full potential. Let each of us realize that in the strength and intelligence of each one of us lies the strength of India.

Let us not forget that every one of us is responsible for our national crisis. What is the cause of such a collective calamity? It is the collective tensions of the individuals. And what causes collective tensions? Individual tensions appearing as anger, fear, hatred, jealousy, wrong thought, speech, action; and corrupt practices of all sorts.

Individual tensions accumulate in the atmosphere as collective tensions and produce collective calamities, national crises, and international conflicts.

Elimination of the existing tensions in the atmosphere is the urgent need of India. When a boil develops on any part of the body, surgery is, of course, necessary. But the treatment to purify the blood is also of vital importance. Meeting the national crisis on its level is certainly necessary, but a remedy to eliminate the existing tension in the atmosphere must be considered to be of equal importance, if not more.

It is our national duty to alleviate the atmospheric tensions as soon as possible by eliminating the tensions in the lives of every individual. This can best be accomplished by giving the people a simple technique of creating powerful influences of peace and harmony from the deepest level of their consciousness — by a few minutes of daily practice of Transcendental Meditation.

His Holiness is now traveling throughout India to make available to all the people his simple technique of Transcendental Meditation to combat the fear of war, and enable everyone to live in peace and strength.

Invitation

Those desirous of participating and helping in this nation-building project of training Meditation Guides and establishing Meditation Centers all over the country are invited to participate in the forthcoming program of training Meditation Guides at the Academy of Meditation, Shankaracharya Nagar, Rishikesh (U.P.), India.

Read Maharishiji's book, written in America: *The Science of Being and Art of Living.*

Maharishi's simple system of Transcendental Meditation has opened interesting avenues for scientific research in the physical, mental, and environmental spheres of individual life. Interested research scholars are advised to read the pamphlets entitled "Health" and "New Fields of Research" for lines of possible experiment.

All enquiries are to be addressed to: The Registrar, Academy of Meditation, Shankaracharya Nagar, P.O. Swargashram, Rishikesh, U.P.[5]

---

5 For current contacts, refer to "Contact Information for Maharishi's Global Programs," p. 435.

Afterword

Sequential Unfoldment of Maharishi's Teaching

In 1955 Maharishi Mahesh Yogi began to offer to the world the quintessence of the ancient Vedic[1] Wisdom of the Himalayas. In that year he introduced the simple, natural, and universal technique of Transcendental Meditation. This extraordinary technique, founded by Maharishi, allows anyone to directly experience and utilize the field of pure Being — the transcendental field of existence at the basis of everything in the universe.

In the succeeding decade, during ten world tours, Maharishi explained to the people of over one hundred nations that Being is a limitless ocean of life, out of the realm of time, space, and causation, while the different aspects of creation are the ripples and waves of this vast ocean of eternal Being. The Transcendental Meditation technique enables any individual to contact this field of pure Being, and to begin to utilize the unlimited treasures of this field — infinite happiness, creativity, intelligence, and organizing power — for maximum success and fulfillment in daily life.

Maharishi's Master — Shri Guru Dev

Maharishi acquired this great wisdom of pure Being at the feet of his beloved Master, Shri Guru Dev, His Divinity Brahmananda Saraswati, Jagadguru Bhagavan Shankaracharya of Jyotir Math, Himalayas — most illustrious embodiment of Vedic Wisdom in the eternal tradition of Vedic Masters. Through the fullness of the Vedic Wisdom of his great Master, Maharishi

1 The Sanskrit word "Vedic" is from Veda, meaning complete knowledge of Natural Law.

was able in a very short span to gain mastery of the Science of Being, and become not just a *Ṛishi* — a seer of the truth about our universe — but a *Maharishi* — a great *Ṛishi* — who has supreme skill in teaching that wisdom to others, and raising them to experience Being and enjoy its infinite riches.

Maharishi Founds the *Spiritual Regeneration Movement*

When Maharishi began to teach this ancient wisdom to the people of India, he became deeply inspired by the beautiful, enriching experiences of inner bliss, peace, and unboundedness gained through the Transcendental Meditation program by tens of thousands of people from every age group, walk of life, and religion. Thrilling with this inspiration and with new hope for the world family, Maharishi on January 1, 1958, inaugurated the Spiritual Regeneration Movement, in order to bring the supreme knowledge given to him by his Master to everyone, and create a spiritual regeneration of all life on Earth. This initiative to turn the trends of time on Earth toward the highest spiritual wisdom was desperately needed at that moment in world history, when the rise of fear, devastating weaponry, and other life-threatening trends and technologies endangered the very survival of the human race.

Maharishi Presents His Teaching to the World in *Science of Being and Art of Living*

Almost as soon as Maharishi began his world tours, his students urged him to commit this great teaching to paper. By 1963 he had completed this fascinating book, *Science of Being and Art of Living*, which systematically unfolds for our scientific age the wisdom of the Veda and Vedic Literature taught to Maharishi by Guru Dev.

In this volume Maharishi presents the Science of Being as the systematic investigation into the ultimate reality of the universe. Like other sciences, it begins its investigation from the gross, obvious level of life, and delves more deeply into the subtle levels of the experience of Nature. The Science of Being, however, eventually transcends these subtle regions, and reaches the transcendental field of eternal Being.

Modern Science Glimpses Being

At the time this volume was written, modern science had not yet glimpsed the existence of a single universal field at the basis of all natural phenomena, even though the discovery of this unified field of the laws of nature had been Einstein's final scientific quest some decades before. By the 1990s, however, the unified field of the laws of nature had become the greatest focus of theoretical physics, and modern science may now be said to have glimpsed the field of transcendental pure Being. It is fascinating to observe that the recent descriptions of the unified field of natural law by modern physicists, such as Dr. John Hagelin, correspond with great precision to the description of pure Being given in 1963 by Maharishi in this book, and to the classical accounts given by the Vedic *Ṛishis* throughout the ages. In *Science of Being and Art of Living*, Maharishi predicted that science, through its continuing investigations deeper and deeper into the structure of Natural Law, would eventually arrive at the field of Being, and this has now happened.

But this book is still far ahead of the objective traditions of modern scientific inquiry in one crucial sense: to modern science, the theory of the unified field of natural law is a mathematical abstraction — beautiful and profound, but irrelevant to practical life. To Maharishi and the Vedic Tradition the discovery of Being — the Unified Field of Natural Law — is the most practical and useful discovery ever made. It is relevant to practical life because it is completely easy for any human being anywhere in the world to have access to pure Being, and utilize its unlimited potential to make daily life joyful and successful. This is achieved effortlessly through the twice-daily practice of the Transcendental Meditation technique.

Maharishi Transforms the World's Understanding About Meditation

Before Maharishi brought the Transcendental Meditation technique to light, meditation was thought to be extremely difficult, involving feats of concentration few could ever accomplish. It was thought to be painfully slow to produce results, and impractical — only for the recluse lost in otherworldly pursuits, not for ordinary people in the midst of their daily responsibilities.

Maharishi reversed all these understandings in a single stroke. He found from his own experience and from the expressions of the Vedic Literature that the nature of inner life is bliss, and that this is true for everyone on Earth. Pure Being is Pure Bliss. It is everyone's birthright to discover this inner field of bliss through the Transcendental Meditation program, and enjoy it in the midst of all activity.

The *Transcendental Meditation* Program Is Based on the Natural Tendency of the Mind

This experience of Bliss Consciousness within, Maharishi discovered, is easy to accomplish, because it is the natural tendency of the mind to go toward a field of greater happiness. In the Transcendental Meditation program the conscious mind is set on the way to experiencing transcendental Being, whose nature is Bliss Consciousness. Because it is moving in the direction of bliss, the mind naturally finds increasing charm at every step of its march.

Effortlessly and spontaneously the mind flows to ever more refined and charming levels of the thinking process, until it transcends (goes beyond) even the finest aspect of thought to experience pure Being in the state of Transcendental Consciousness. This is the state of pure consciousness, self-referral consciousness, which is Bliss Consciousness. Experiencing Transcendental Consciousness several times during each twenty-minute meditation, the mind comes out enlivened with the bliss and peace and energy of Being. The treasures of Being become available in daily living for more successful and fulfilling personal, professional, and family life.

Maharishi Trains Teachers of the *Transcendental Meditation* Program

Soon after Maharishi started to teach the Transcendental Meditation program widely in the world, he realized that in order to bring this precious wisdom to everyone on Earth, he would have to "multiply himself." Therefore in 1961, he began holding special courses to train teachers of the Transcendental Meditation program. Maharishi trained thousands of teachers of this technique throughout the world. Together these teachers have taught the Transcendental Meditation program to nearly 10 million people in more than 108 countries on all six continents.

These expert teachers of the Transcendental Meditation technique were trained by Maharishi to offer personal instruction in this technique through a seven-step course, which takes about one and a half hours a day over one week, with a follow-up program for a year. Through these trained teachers, human beings of every age, religion, culture, and race can experience for themselves that to meditate is easy and natural, and does not involve concentration or effort. They can discover that the Transcendental Meditation technique is the most practical of all technologies, vital to success and fulfillment in life. They can experience for themselves that Maharishi has revolutionized the understanding and practice of meditation, and provided a new basis for the development of the life of everyone.

The Art of Living — the *Applied* Science of Being

The Science of Being, applied to our lives through the technique of Transcendental Meditation, provides us with the Art of Living — thinking, speaking, acting, and behaving while established at the level of pure Being. Experiencing pure Being twice daily through the Transcendental Meditation technique, any individual in any nation can rise to enjoy higher states of consciousness, in which the transcendental state of eternal Being is experienced along with the ever-changing experiences of relative existence. This alone, Maharishi explains in this book, is truly normal life, free of the stress and strain that usually block the full display of our infinite potential. In higher states of consciousness human life becomes filled with peace and joy, is vibrant with the infinite creative intelligence of Being, and enjoys the support of the almighty power of Nature, the infinite organizing power of Natural Law.

Locating the Teaching of Transcendental Meditation in the Bhagavad-Gītā

Having brought experience of effortless transcending to the world, Maharishi turned his attention to locating this knowledge in the Vedic Literature, initially in the Bhagavad-Gītā, the Song of Life, which expresses the quintessence of the Vedic Wisdom.

Maharishi immediately located in the teachings of Shri Kṛishṇa in the Gītā the very same Science of Being and Art of Living that he had received from his Master, Guru Dev. Especially, seeing the Gītā from the platform of Unity Consciousness, he noted three key verses in the second chapter.

First, in verse 40 of the second chapter, Lord Kṛishṇa describes the **effortless, obstacle-free practice of the supreme Yoga**:

Nehābhikramanāsho 'sti pratyavāyo na vidyate — (2.40)
In this (Yoga) no effort is lost and no obstacle exists.

Next, in verse 45, Lord Kṛishṇa directs Arjuna to **TRANSCEND** — go beyond the field of activity to experience pure Being, the source of everything:

Nistraiguṇyo bhavārjuna — (2.45)
Be without the three Guṇas (the field of action), O Arjuna.

And third, Lord Kṛishṇa in verse 48 of the second chapter gives the **key to supreme success** in the art of living in his instruction to Arjuna:

Yogasthaḥ kuru karmāṇi — (2.48)
Established in Yoga (Union), perform action.

Maharishi's translation of and commentary on the Bhagavad-Gītā, published in 1967, has revealed for the world for all time the practical wisdom of Yoga, taught by Shri Kṛishṇa in the scripture of Yoga, the Bhagavad-Gītā.

What a change for the world! For so many centuries the Gītā had been misinterpreted as expounding the difficulty of gaining enlightenment and as advocating indifference to the field of activity. This has caused a great loss to human life, and the rise of suffering in the world.

Every reader of *Science of Being and Art of Living* should also read *Maharishi Mahesh Yogi on the Bhagavad-Gītā*, which is in itself the ocean of practical Vedic Wisdom.

Maharishi's Discovery of Seven States of Consciousness

Maharishi, during his many world tours, spent thousands of hours explaining the experiences of unfolding higher consciousness to practitioners of the Transcendental Meditation technique throughout the world. Over the course of ten years, the progressive evolution of the experiences of the meditators inspired him to unfold step by step the knowledge that there are seven distinct states of human consciousness with seven corresponding and distinct kinds of physiological functioning, and distinct worlds of experience:

Waking — *Jāgrat Chetanā*
Dreaming — *Swapn Chetanā*
Sleeping — *Sushupti Chetanā*
Transcendental Consciousness — *Turīya Chetanā*
Cosmic Consciousness — *Turīyātīt Chetanā*
God Consciousness — *Bhagavat Chetanā*
Unity Consciousness — *Brāhmī Chetanā*

Transcendental Consciousness

When he began to teach the Transcendental Meditation program in 1955, Maharishi first presented the vision of three relative changing states of consciousness — waking, sleeping, and dreaming — and one absolute, non-changing field of consciousness — *Transcendental Consciousness*. Transcendental Consciousness, the fourth state of consciousness, is experienced during the Transcendental Meditation technique when the mind transcends even the finest aspect of thought, and becomes completely silent and at rest, yet fully awake inside. This is the state of pure consciousness, self-referral consciousness — the state of quiet wakefulness within, where consciousness knows itself alone, and the mind makes direct contact with Being.

Cosmic Consciousness

By 1960, Maharishi's Year of Cosmic Consciousness, the experiences of the meditators had evolved to the point where Maharishi was able to bring out the reality of the fifth state of consciousness — Cosmic Consciousness. In Cosmic Consciousness, the deep silence of Transcendental Consciousness is never lost whether one is waking, sleeping, or dreaming. Perpetually established on the platform of transcendental Being, life is lived in eternal freedom, and is filled with infinite bliss twenty-four hours a day.

God Consciousness

By 1963, when *Science of Being and Art of Living* was published, experiences of the meditators had enabled Maharishi to bring out the sixth state of human consciousness — God Consciousness. On the basis of this beautiful new level of experience dawning in the family of meditators throughout the world, Maharishi declared 1964 to be his Year of God Consciousness.

The part of this book entitled "Paths to God-Realization" clearly brings out the reality of this sublime level of human development. Maharishi explains that the individual who has risen to Cosmic Consciousness has unbounded, unlimited love overflowing in all directions for everything. When this overflowing, unlimited, unbounded universal love becomes concentrated in devotion to God, then the entire life in its tremendous diversity is nothing but fullness of love, bliss, and contentment — eternal and absolute. This is God Consciousness. While remaining established in the eternal continuum of Transcendental Consciousness, the individual in God Consciousness overflows in love and devotion to God, and in unlimited appreciation of the majesty and glory of God's creation, from its grossest levels to its levels of infinite subtlety where the light of God is eternally shining. Such individuals, Maharishi says in *Science of Being*, see, yet see the glory of God, hear, yet hear the music of Nature, speak, yet speak the words of eternal Being — their lives are the stream of cosmic Being.

Unity Consciousness

Finally, in 1967, Maharishi's Year of Unity Consciousness, he brought out a thrilling vision of the pinnacle of human development — the seventh state of consciousness, Unity Consciousness. Now Maharishi was able to explain the experiences of Transcendental Meditation in terms of Transcendental Consciousness, Cosmic Consciousness, God Consciousness, and Unity Consciousness. The whole structure of the seven states of consciousness and their seven corresponding worlds of experience was now revealed to the world.

This most exalted level of human consciousness is beautifully described in a verse of Ṛk Veda:

Dūre dṛishaṁ gṛihapatim atharyum — (Ṛk Veda, 7.1.1)
The light of God, which was experienced within one's Transcendental Consciousness, is found shining throughout the whole creation to the very farthest point.

In Unity Consciousness every particle of creation, even the farthest, most distant point of the universe, is experienced as a wave in the unbounded ocean of Transcendental Consciousness, which is one's own Self. Everything in the universe — even at the very ends of the universe — is found to be the reverberation of my own Self, of my own unbounded consciousness.

In Unity Consciousness, the whole field of existence from the gross manifest universe to the infinite subtlety of the light of God is discovered to be one limitless sea of cosmic Being. And the supreme knowledge dawns — I am That — I am that wholeness, that totality that encompasses in its range the infinite activity of the universe and infinite silence of its source in Being. Here is the experience of *Ahaṁ Brahmāsmi* — I am the totality, I am Brahm.

An individual in Unity Consciousness gains total mastery of Natural Law and lives a life of all possibilities. This is perfection of life, life lived on the level of the ultimate Unity of all life. The individual life stream then is a tidal wave of the eternal ocean of cosmic Being, a wave that holds within itself the entire ocean of cosmic life.

When many such enlightened individuals exist on Earth the world enjoys supreme fortune, and a heavenly age dawns. The supreme awakening of the enlightened who live Unity Consciousness is the hope of all humanity. Never before has this been seen so clearly as in the life of Maharishi Mahesh Yogi, whose whole sublime work is to make Unity Consciousness the normal experience of everyone.

Scientific Research on the *Transcendental Meditation* Program

From the very earliest days of his worldwide tours, Maharishi invited Western scientists to examine rigorously the effects of the Transcendental Meditation program on the physiology, psychology, and behavior of the individual, and on society as a whole. In the years after the publication of *Science of Being and Art of Living*, scientific research on the ancient Vedic technology of the Transcendental Meditation technique began in earnest, led by Dr. Keith Wallace at the University of California at Los Angeles. He discovered that the Transcendental Meditation technique spontaneously produces a unique restfully alert style of physiological functioning. Thus from the point of view of modern science, the Transcendental Meditation technique produces a fourth major state of consciousness, in which the human physiology functions in a way quite distinct from the physiology of waking, sleeping, and dreaming.

Subsequently over 675 scientific studies on the effects of the Transcendental Meditation program have been completed at more than 300 universities and research institutions in 30 countries, and articles have been published in academic journals throughout the world. These studies have also been published in the eight volumes of *Scientific Research on the Transcendental Meditation and TM-Sidhi Programme: Collected Papers*.

Research findings on the Transcendental Meditation technique have astonished the brilliant scientific minds of this age. They show that this technique creates a unique, highly ordered style of brain functioning, producing highly coherent brain waves and greater use of the latent reserves of the brain. Other scientific findings include increased intelligence and creativity, and improved academic performance; lower stress and anxiety; improved physical and mental health (reductions of 50 percent or more in health-care costs have been observed in all age groups); effective rehabilitation of prison inmates; reduced substance and alcohol abuse; improved productivity, job satisfaction, and profitability in the workplace; and increases in measures of human development and moral reasoning, often to unprecedented levels. The health benefits of the Transcendental Meditation technique not only have been independently verified at numerous universities and research institutes, but also have been clearly demonstrated in a study conducted under the auspices of the National Institute of Industrial Health of the Ministry of Labor of Japan, and by scientific studies supported by the National Institutes of Health of the United States.

The *Maharishi Effect*: Creating Coherence in World Consciousness

In 1971, Maharishi founded the first Consciousness-Based^{SM}, enlightenment-based, educational institution — Maharishi International University — which integrated rigorous academic study with the knowledge of and research in the field of consciousness. In 1974, scientists at Maharishi International University in Fairfield, Iowa, USA, discovered that even one percent of the population practicing the Transcendental Meditation program in a city improves the quality of life of the whole community as shown by reductions in crime and accident rates and improvements in other indicators of collective health. This overall increase of positivity in societal trends arises from the increasing purity in the collective consciousness of the entire population created by hundreds of individuals experiencing the pure silence and peace of Transcendental Consciousness. This phenomenon — developing the collective life of the whole society through just a small percentage of the population practicing the Transcendental Meditation technique — was named the *Maharishi Effect* by the scientists who discovered it, in honor of Maharishi who had predicted it more than a decade earlier.

The discovery of the *Maharishi Effect* by modern science established a new formula for the creation of an ideal society, free from crime and problems. With this discovery, Maharishi envisioned through the window of science the dawning of a whole new age of perfection for human life — the

Age of Enlightenment. On January 12, 1975, he inaugurated the Dawn of the Age of Enlightenment for the whole world, and subsequently inaugurated the Dawn for all six continents.

Soon afterward Maharishi saw the urgent need to establish a global organization to administer the Age of Enlightenment. Therefore, on January 12, 1976, he inaugurated the World Government of the Age of Enlightenment, a non-political, non-religious, global organization with sovereignty in the domain of consciousness, authority in the invincible power of Natural Law, and activity in purifying world consciousness, with the participation of the people of over 120 countries, and twelve hundred Capitals of the Age of Enlightenment around the world.

Maharishi's Discovery of the *Transcendental Meditation Sidhi*℠ Program and the *Yogic Flying*® Technique

In 1976 Maharishi made an historic discovery that proved crucial to the creation of peace on Earth. Researching into Patanjali's Yoga Sūtras, he brought to light the Transcendental Meditation Sidhi program, which includes the technique of Yogic Flying. This advanced technology enables those who practice the Transcendental Meditation technique not only to experience Transcendental Consciousness, but also to gain the habit of spontaneously projecting thought and action from this simplest form of awareness, pure consciousness, the total potential of Nature's intelligence. This makes thought and action most natural and therefore most spontaneously evolutionary; it brings the support of all the Laws of Nature to the individual, and thus opens the field of all possibilities for the fulfillment of every desire.

The Transcendental Meditation Sidhi program, including Yogic Flying, is Maharishi's unfoldment of the complete theoretical and practical knowledge of Yoga after thousands of years. Yoga means union, the union of the individual awareness with the field of pure Being in the state of Transcendental Consciousness. It needed a scientific age to dawn on Earth for the world to appreciate the significance of the philosophy of Yoga, and its practical application in creating integrated individuals, integrated nations, and an integrated world family.

Maximum Coherence of Brain Functioning During Yogic Flying

The most powerful of all the Transcendental Meditation Sidhi techniques is Yogic Flying, which demonstrates the ability of the individual to act from the level of Transcendental Consciousness, and thereby enliven the total potential of Natural Law in all its expressions — mind, body, behavior, and environment. During the first stage of Yogic Flying, the body — motivated only by the effortless mental impulse of the TM-Sidhi® technique — rises up in the air in a series of blissful hops. The ancient Vedic texts, such as the Patanjali Yoga Sūtras, record that in advanced stages, this technology leads to actual floating in the air, or flying.

The mind-body coordination displayed by Yogic Flying shows that consciousness and its expression, the physiology, are in perfect balance. Scientific research has found that there is maximum coherence in brain waves during Yogic Flying, indicating highly orderly and holistic functioning of the brain.

Yogic Flying Reduces Environmental Conflict and Increases Positivity and Creativity in Society

Even in its first stage — the hopping stage — the practice of Yogic Flying creates waves of bubbling bliss in the consciousness and physiology of the practitioner. This intensely blissful experience of the Yogic flyer radiates into the environment, creating coherence in the atmosphere and spreading waves of upliftment and peace to the surrounding population. This phenomenon is clearly expressed in the Yoga Sūtras:

> ***Tat-sannidhau vaira-tyāgaḥ*** — (Yoga Sūtra 2.35)
> *In the vicinity of the phenomenon of Yoga [Yogic Flying], conflicting tendencies disappear. The unifying influence neutralizes the diversifying qualities in the area.*

Maharishi explains that when Yogic flyers practice together in groups, "every hop becomes a cosmic smile for the whole creation." By the year 2020 more than 300,000 people worldwide have learned Yogic Flying, and 50 scientific studies have demonstrated that groups of Yogic flyers are extremely effective in generating the *Maharishi Effect*. In fact, scientists have found that such groups create such a strong influence of coherence in collective consciousness that the square root of one percent of the population practicing Yogic Flying together creates the *Maharishi Effect* for the whole society.

8,000 Yogic Flyers Create Coherence in the Entire World Consciousness — the *Global Maharishi Effect*

It has been found, for example, that when 8,000 Yogic flyers — approximately the square root of one percent of the world's population — gather in one place to create coherence, as they did from December 1983 to January 1984 at Maharishi International University in the USA, worldwide trends become more positive, with decreasing international violence and crime, and increases in harmonious, peaceful tendencies in world events.

The discovery of this *Global Maharishi Effect* in 1983–84 demonstrated for the first time that there existed an actual world peace technology. In succeeding years the increasing number of groups using this technology in different parts of the world led to the greatest outbreak of peace in modern history — the end of the Cold War and the dangerous rivalry of the superpowers.

If every government would create and sustain a coherence-creating group of Yogic flyers — what Maharishi called *A Group for a Government* — it is clear that the world could be rid of war forever. Soon this will happen, and permanent world peace through the *Maharishi Effect* will be recognized as one of Maharishi's enduring legacies to the world — a legacy precious to every one of us and to the entire family of nations.

Science of Being and Art of Living Brought to Fulfillment Through Maharishi's Formulation of His Vedic Science and Technology

In this volume Maharishi examines in detail how this ancient Science of Being offers a key to good health, a solution to the failures of education, an effective means of rehabilitation, and a way to naturally restore virtue in human life and bring peace to the billions of peaceless and unfulfilled people in our world. He applies the Science of Being to bring fulfillment to the quests of philosophers and psychologists, and of those religious devotees who yearn for spiritual realization.

Now Maharishi has brought complete fulfillment to this beautiful promise of the Science of Being by structuring his Vedic Science and Technology. Maharishi Vedic Science and Technology[SM] is the full unfoldment of the Science of Being and Art of Living.

Maharishi Formulates His *Vedic Science and Technology*[SM]

Maharishi has formulated his Vedic Science and Technology on the basis of the complete theoretical and practical knowledge of Veda, available in the traditional Vedic Literature, and on the basis of the personal experience of Transcendental Consciousness and higher states of consciousness of millions of people practicing his Transcendental Meditation throughout the world.

Maharishi defines his Vedic Science and Technology as the science of Veda. Since Veda means knowledge — the complete knowledge of Natural Law — Maharishi Vedic Science and Technology is the *science of the complete knowledge of Natural Law*. It also includes the technologies of Natural Law, such as the Transcendental Meditation program and Yogic Flying, which harness the infinite organizing power of Natural Law to transform human life to be Heaven on Earth.

Preservation of the Vedic Literature by the Vedic Families of India

Throughout time the sounds of the Veda and Vedic Literature have been preserved in India, passed on perfectly from generation to generation, so that the Vedic expressions and the wisdom they contain would never be lost to human life at any time. But over the centuries the many texts of the Vedic Literature became scattered and separated into different traditions and competing understandings. The sequential structure of the Veda and Vedic Literature was forgotten, and the depth of its significance and practical import for human life became obscured.

With this forgetfulness of the total Vedic Wisdom, life on Earth fell into suffering. Maharishi's genius has been in one generation to restore from the platform of Unity Consciousness the total vision of the reality of the Veda and Vedic Literature as complete knowledge of Natural Law — the knowledge whose practical benefit is the creation of Heaven on Earth.

The Veda and Vedic Literature Are the Unmanifest Sounds of Natural Law

The greatest of all misunderstandings about the Vedic Literature has been the belief that the Veda and Vedic Literature is a set of books written by the ancient Seers. In fact the Vedic Literature is not the thoughts or writings of the Vedic Seers (*Ṛishis*), but rather exists eternally in the field of Being itself, ready to be discovered by anyone who experiences Being. The impulses of the Veda and Vedic Literature are in fact the Unmanifest Sounds of the self-referral dynamism of the field of Being, heard by the self-referral state of consciousness, Being itself.

These sounds are the Laws of Nature in their fundamental state, residing perpetually in the transcendental field of Being, and conducting the whole evolution of the universe from there. Since they are the fundamental set of laws that organize the whole activity of the universe, the Ṛk Veda and other aspects of the Vedic Literature together comprise the *Constitution of the Universe*. The Veda and Vedic Literature, Maharishi has discovered, is in reality the functioning constitution of creation, the Government of Nature, which is ceaselessly governing the entire universe, and sustaining it in absolute order and harmony. This historic discovery by Maharishi of the fundamental structure of Natural Law at the basis of the universe is present in seed form in *Science of Being and Art of Living* in the part entitled "Being, the Plane of Cosmic Law."

Maharishi's Discovery of Veda Eternally Reverberating in Being

In unfolding his Vedic Science^{SM}, Maharishi has described in extraordinary detail the profound mechanics by which Being begins to reverberate within Itself in the eternal impulses of the Veda. These insights have come from Maharishi's direct experience of the self-interacting dynamics of Being, through which pure Being expresses Itself in the forms and phenomena of the universe throughout all eternity of time and space.

In his Veda-Leela^{SM} (play of the Veda), Maharishi has explained that Being, the unbounded sea of Nature's intelligence, is the field of *unbounded awareness*. It is pure wakefulness; It is fully awake within Itself. In Its transcendental self-referral state, It knows only Itself and nothing else. Knowing Itself only, It is the knower, It is the process of knowing, and It is also the known — It is all three Itself — It is the togetherness of knower, knowing, and known. In the language of the Veda, the knower is called Ṛishi, the dynamics of knowing is Devatā, the known is Chhandas, and the togetherness of these three is called Saṁhitā. In this three-in-one reality of the Saṁhitā of Ṛishi, Devatā, and Chhandas is the eternal self-referral structure of the field of pure Being.

Through the self-interactions of Ṛishi, Devatā, and Chhandas within the wholeness of Saṁhitā, the unbounded field of consciousness begins to vibrate within itself. It hums within itself in the Unmanifest Sounds of Ṛk Veda. From the Unmanifest Sounds of Ṛk Veda and also from the gaps between these sounds, all the Vedic Sounds unfold sequentially within the sea of consciousness. From Veda to Vedānga, Upānga, Upa-Veda, Brāhmaṇa, and Prātishākhya, the Vedic Sounds unfold in a precise sequence, each elaborating and commenting upon Ṛk Veda and the preceding branches of the Vedic Literature. This unique insight of Maharishi — that the Vedic Literature is its own commentary — is called Maharishi's *Apaurusheya Bhāshya* — the Self-expressed commentary of the Veda.

Veda Is Structured in Consciousness

These Unmanifest Sounds are not the sounds that can be heard by the human ear. Rather they are the sounds that Being makes when It interacts with Itself, and which are automatically heard by the *Ṛishis*, because their awareness is fully awake and open to the field of Being. This they accomplish through the established practice of the Transcendental Meditation technique and Yogic Flying. Fully awake inside, completely identified with the field of pure Being, the *Ṛishis* experience the sounds of the Veda zooming forth spontaneously in their own unbounded ocean of consciousness. Over the course of human history, they have recorded these sounds in the texts of the Vedic Literature, and also passed them on through the oral tradition of the Vedic Pandits, for the joy and benefit of the whole world. But true study of the Veda and Vedic Literature is not in the books — it is in the direct experience of the Vedic impulses reverberating in one's own self-referral consciousness.

Veda as the Structuring Dynamics of Creation

There are 40 branches of the Veda and Vedic Literature in all, and each Maharishi describes as a different creative quality of the unbounded field of Being — the unbounded ocean of consciousness. Veda is structured in consciousness, and its *structuring dynamics* are within the nature of this unbounded ocean of consciousness.

From the structuring dynamics of these 40 sets of Unmanifest Sounds of the Veda the physical form of creation unfolds. The Vedic Sounds take expression in the form of creation. In fact, the entire diversity of the universe unfolds from the Vedic Sounds, from the Unmanifest Sounds of the self-referral dynamics of Nature's intelligence.

Discovery of Veda in Human Physiology

Professor Tony Nader, MD, PhD, a brilliant scientist, has, with Maharishi's inspiration, discovered that the Veda and Vedic Literature are fully and completely expressed in human physiology. The profound insights into the

Veda and Vedic Literature revealed by Maharishi in his Vedic Science have guided this discovery that the same laws that construct the human mind and body are those that give a structure to the syllables, verses, chapters, and texts of the Vedic Literature.

Professor Nader's research has demonstrated that the human physiology (including DNA at its core) has the same structure and function as the holistic, self-sufficient, self-referral reality expressed in Ṛk Veda. The specialized components, organs, and organ systems of the human physiology, including all parts of the nervous system, match the 40 branches of the Vedic Literature one to one, both in structure and function.

In the summary of his book, *Human Physiology: Expression of Veda and the Vedic Literature*[2], Professor Nader states:

This discovery has unfolded the secrets of orderly functioning of all the organs in the body and how this orderliness can unfold its supreme quality, expressed as the absolute order in the infinite diversity of the universe. This discovery has opened the possibility for human existence to rise to the level of order that is sustaining the universe, and thereby gives the experience of Ahaṁ Brahmāsmi — *"I am Totality"* — *to everyone.*

This discovery has rendered the study of physiology to be the actualization of the supreme philosophy of life, which establishes individual consciousness and national consciousness on the level of Cosmic Life.

Study of physiology in terms of the structure of Veda is that revelation of our scientific age which raises the individual dignity of human beings to the cosmic dignity of the universe.

Fundamentally, Professor Nader's discovery means that the inner administrator of our own life is the same as the administrator of the whole universe — Veda, the total potential of Natural Law. Our own physiology is, in fact, the Vedic Literature in manifest form. Thus to anyone who approaches us we may say, "Thou art the Veda." And if we look to ourselves we may say, "I am the Veda — the Constitution of the Universe."

2 Maharishi Vedic University, Vlodrop, Holland, 2001.

The Practical Benefit of the Discovery of Veda and the Vedic Literature in Human Physiology

Through the study and practice of Maharishi Vedic Science and Technology all 40 aspects of the Vedic Literature become lively both in our intellect and on the level of direct experience. Through Vedic technologies such as Yogic Flying, every human being is able to create such graceful, integrated functioning of mind and body, that not only are all these 40 aspects of Natural Law fully awake in *consciousness* but they are fully awake in the *physiology* also.

Through the practice of Yogic Flying, the inner aspect of our lives can easily be fully awakened in the structure of the Veda, and then whatever we think will be supported by the total potential of Natural Law — by all the 40 values of Natural Law that govern the universe with infinite creativity and infinite organizing power, and without problems or mistakes. As Yogic flyers we can gain access to this enormous intelligence and power in our own self-referral consciousness — Transcendental Consciousness — and in our own physiology. The reality is that the infinite organizing power of Natural Law is at hand for all of us.

This beautiful new science of life is offered to the world in Professor Nader's book, which was first published in January 1994, soon after Maharishi declared 1994, the twentieth year of the Age of Enlightenment, to be his Year of Discovery of Veda and Vedic Literature in Human Physiology.

With this vision of the Veda and Vedic Literature, Maharishi has not only transformed the understanding of the Veda, but opened a new era for life on Earth, where the Veda and Vedic Literature are utilized to accomplish the supreme goal of the human race to live a life in Heaven on Earth generation after generation.

Enlightened Education Through *Consciousness-Based* Education

There are many precious disciplines of Maharishi Vedic Science and Technology that bring fulfillment to Maharishi's practical teachings about the Art of Living recorded by Maharishi in *Science of Being and Art of Living* over fifty years ago.

For example, Maharishi designed a new future for education through Consciousness-Based education. He pointed out that modern education develops only part of the brain because of its segmented approach, in which students focus on specific fields of Natural Law, such as physics, mathematics, management, or art, therefore only enlivening specific parts of the brain, and never the total brain.

Consequently, students' total creative potential and intelligence remain undeveloped. Such a system gives a small gain, but creates a total loss. It is "penny wise and pound foolish." This partial development of the brain is the cause of all stress and strain and failure witnessed in the world.

The only experience that awakens total brain functioning is the experience of inner silence, pure consciousness, through the practice of Transcendental Meditation. This is the key technology of Consciousness-Based education — to develop holistic functioning of the brain so that every student can enjoy higher states of consciousness, enlightenment. Through this technology, students gain benefits that have been scientifically documented, including increased creativity and intelligence, improved memory, better academic grades, reduced anxiety, and improvements in moral reasoning and in self-development.

In 1971 Maharishi founded the first educational institution to offer Consciousness-Based education to develop total brain functioning — Maharishi International University (Maharishi University of Management, 1995–2019). In 1974 the University began its own primary and secondary school, Maharishi School of the Age of Enlightenment, which has had extraordinary success both academically and in developing the highest quality of life for students. Since then Consciousness-Based education has been introduced, with extraordinary results, in more than 800 educational institutions worldwide, including Maharishi universities and schools and private and public education in 67 countries. Professors and teachers have reported a significant reduction in classroom stress, a more disciplined and focused educational environment, with fewer behavioral infractions, and an atmosphere of serenity and mutual respect pervading the classrooms.

This is Maharishi's gift for all generations to come — Consciousness-Based education through which everyone everywhere can live their full potential as enlightened human beings.

Perfect Health Through *Maharishi Vedic Approach to Health*[SM]

In the field of creating perfect mental and physical health, Maharishi emphasized the need of modern medicine to take a holistic, preventive approach, involving the body, the mind, the surroundings, and Being itself. Maharishi elaborated these profound principles twenty years later by bringing to the world his Vedic Approach to Health, the most ancient, complete, and scientific system of natural health care.

Though the Vedic tradition of medicine has continued to be lively in India up to modern times, it has become fragmented and lost its integrity as a holistic system of natural medicine bringing balance to consciousness, physiology, behavior, and environment.

Maharishi looked deeply into Vedic texts relating to health, bringing to light that all 40 areas of the Vedic knowledge are essential for complete consideration of health. These natural approaches, combined with the development of a stress-free, balanced consciousness and physiology through the Transcendental Meditation program, restore balance to the system and disallow diseases from developing in mind and body. Maharishi also restored the vital understanding of how to create collective health by bringing the collective consciousness of a society into harmony with the total potential of Natural Law, so that the violation of Natural Law, which is the cause of all sickness and suffering, is prevented. This restoration of a holistic and complete understanding of health as found in the original Vedic texts is called *Maharishi Vedic Approach to Health.*

Other Practical Disciplines of Maharishi Vedic Science and Technology

Maharishi Vedic Science and Technology is complete knowledge of the Science of Being and Art of Living — an unlimited field of riches in both knowledge of Natural Law and powerful technologies to glorify human life on Earth. It took Maharishi thirty years to unfold all the fine fabrics of Being and to have them verified through scientific research. Now all the precious disciplines of Maharishi Vedic Science℠ are being made available throughout the world.

The *Maharishi Jyotish*® program is the knowledge of past, present, and future that allows future trends to be predicted and problems prevented before they arise. *Maharishi Yagya*® performances are Vedic performances to neutralize any negative trends or enhance positive trends in individual and collective life. *Maharishi Gandharva Veda*℠ music is Vedic music, the eternal music of Nature, which creates a balancing and harmonizing influence in the individual and in the environment. *Maharishi Sthapatya Veda*® design is the Vedic Science of building, which is Nature's own system of structuring that harmonizes individual life with Cosmic Life.

Maharishi's Supreme Political Science brings out all the principles by which the government of a nation can rise to be on a par with the perfect administration of the universe by Natural Law. *Maharishi Vedic Management*℠ offers managers the opportunity to develop supreme alertness, supreme creative intelligence, and supreme support of Natural Law for maximum success in life. These are some of the precious disciplines of Maharishi Vedic Science and Technology. However, each of the 40 aspects of the Vedic Literature contributes profound and practical knowledge for daily living, based on the total knowledge of Natural Law.

Maharishi Vedic Approach to Health in Maharishi Vedic Universities, Maharishi Ayur-Veda Universities, and Colleges of Maharishi Vedic Medicine

The knowledge of Maharishi Vedic Science and Technology is the foundation of all Consciousness-Based educational institutions. In addition, programs specifically in Maharishi Vedic Approach to Health are being made available in Maharishi International University, Maharishi Vedic Universities, Maharishi Ayur-Veda Universities, and Colleges of Maharishi Vedic Medicine now being established worldwide.

These universities, in addition to offering certificate programs, will also offer Associate of Science, Bachelor of Science, Master of Science, Doctoral and Post-Doctoral degree programs in Maharishi Vedic Science and Technology, and in Maharishi Vedic Approach to Health. These degrees will lead to mastery of new Vedic professions, such as Professor of Maharishi Vedic Science, Maharishi Vedic® Prevention-Oriented Health Educator, Maharishi Jyotishī, Maharishi Gandharvan, Maharishi Sthāpati, and Vedic Manager.

Maharishi's New Definition of Government

In the final part of *Science of Being*, Maharishi calls upon governments to be the channel for the benefits of the Transcendental Meditation program to reach all the people of society. Now he is offering to the political leaders of the world *a new definition of government* — that a government is only worthy of the name government *if it can prevent problems*. Unless it can prevent problems, it is only a football of situations and circumstances. A government that cannot prevent problems, Maharishi points out, is a problem in itself.

These days governments are clearly powerless to prevent problems. Why? Because they are the innocent mirror of the collective consciousness of the people of their nations. When the people are stressed, the collective consciousness is stressed, and the whole society is filled with problems and negative, disease-producing habits and tendencies. What can governments do in the face of such a collective consciousness? History shows us that they watch powerlessly as misery upon misery is heaped upon the people whom the government is paid to protect. In fact, unless stress is systematically reduced in collective consciousness, no government will ever satisfy Maharishi's new definition of a government — that it must be able to prevent problems before they arise, and thereby create a society without suffering.

Maharishi's Group for a Government — the Basis of Preventing Problems

The need for governments to prevent problems is why the creation of Maharishi's Group for a Government — a group of Yogic flyers in every capital city — is so vital. Every government should maintain a group of 8,000 Yogic flyers, which has been shown to create a coherent influence in the whole world consciousness. The blissful performance of the Yogic flyers awakens the field of pure Being in the life of the whole society. Stress dissolves in the atmosphere and society enjoys waves of peace and happiness as if the sun had come out on a cold and cloudy day to bring waves of warmth to all.

Administration Through Natural Law — Automation in Administration

In his book, *Maharishi's Absolute Theory of Government*,[3] Maharishi explains that every government, just by creating and maintaining a group of Yogic flyers, will actualize the ideal of administration, the supreme quality of administration of government in every generation. Through the group of Yogic flyers the infinite organizing power of the supreme intelligence of the universe — known in the Vedic Literature as *Puruṣhottama* — can be fully awakened in the life of every individual, every family, and in the nation as a whole. Then the government will administer the nation as silently and efficiently as the Government of Nature; the same nourishing power of Nature that administers the universe without mistakes and problems will administer life in every nation.

This is Administration through Natural Law — automation in administration — expressed in the Ṛk Veda in the following verse:

3 Maharishi Vedic University, Vlodrop, Holland, 1994.

Yatīnāṁ Brahmā bhavati sārathiḥ — (Ṛk Veda 1.158.6)
For those who are established in the singularity of fully awake, self-referral consciousness, the total potential of pure knowledge and its infinite organizing power — the lively Constitution of the Universe, Natural Law — becomes the charioteer of all activity.

In his Absolute Theory of Government, Maharishi explains the profound significance of this expression of Ṛk Veda for all human life. When our activity is promoted from the level of self-referral consciousness or Transcendental Consciousness, which is the home of Natural Law, then our activity is upheld by the infinite organizing power of Natural Law. This is commonly known as Support of Nature, and it can be gained not only by the individual who experiences Transcendental Consciousness through the Transcendental Meditation technique, but can even be gained by national consciousness — the collective consciousness of the nation — through the collective practice of the Transcendental Meditation and Transcendental Meditation Sidhi programs. With Support of Nature rising in national life, the problems of any nation will disappear, as darkness disappears at the onset of light.

Soon every government will maintain its own group of Yogic flyers as the essential requirement of national administration, and every nation will enjoy the support of Natural Law. All troubles on Earth will fade into distant memories, and life will be lived in perfection and fulfillment by every citizen of every nation, now and for countless generations to come.

Maharishi's Master Plan to Create Heaven on Earth

In 1988 Maharishi provided a blueprint for the creation of a heavenly world for new, enlightened governments to follow — a Master Plan to Create Heaven on Earth that calls for the reconstruction of the whole world to glorify both inner and outer levels of life (see Appendix D). The inner level of life will be glorified through the development of higher states of consciousness that brings the blossoming of noble qualities, bliss, and Support of Nature from within. The outer level of life will be brought to perfection by applying the Vedic approaches to education, health, agriculture, architecture and city planning, defense, and technologies for sustainable living.

Maharishi's vision for a heavenly life on Earth includes ideal villages, towns, and cities constructed according to the scientific principles of Maharishi Sthapatya Veda design, creating such a beautiful environment that everyone feels: "I am living in Heaven." Through Maharishi Vedic Approach to Health, a disease-free world will be created, in which both individual and collective health are perfect, and sickness and suffering are prevented before they arise. Through the application of *Maharishi Vedic Organic Agriculture*[SM] — the cultivation of unused fertile land using organic agricultural methods — every nation will become self-sufficient in food production, and enjoy an abundance of natural, healthy food.

Through Consciousness-Based education based on Maharishi Vedic Science and Technology, every student will undertake study and research in consciousness and rapidly rise to live in happiness, peace, and fulfilling progress in the state of enlightenment. Such enlightened citizens will bring perfection to every profession, and enjoy the fruit of all knowledge, a life free from mistakes and suffering.

With the rise of Support of Nature in every land, every project of the government and private business to create new wealth will hit the target. Poverty will be eradicated and economic self-sufficiency will be achieved by every nation.

Through Maharishi's Master Plan to Create Heaven on Earth every citizen of every nation will enjoy all the treasures of human life — material and divine. The destructive power so dominant in world consciousness for many centuries will be replaced by the influence of the nourishing, harmonizing, integrating power of Natural Law that unrestrictedly upholds the evolution of everyone and everything on Earth. As a result, every nation will lovingly support every other nation, and all nations together will nourish every nation — everyone and every nation will enjoy Heaven on Earth.

Global Country of World Peace

In support of all the nations of the world, Maharishi established the Global Country of World Peace on October 7, 2000, to create global world peace by unifying all nations in happiness, prosperity, invincibility, and perfect health, while supporting the rich diversity of our world family. The Global Country of World Peace enjoys a parental and nourishing role in the family of nations. Its sovereignty is in the domain of consciousness and its authority is in the invincible power of Natural Law, which brings fulfillment to and upholds and nourishes every country's constitution.

The Constitution of the Global Country of World Peace is the Constitution of the Universe — the total knowledge of Natural Law — that guides the infinite diversity of the ever-expanding universe with perfect order.

On October 12, 2000, Maharishi crowned Professor Tony Nader, MD, PhD, as Maharaja Adhiraj Rajaraam, First Ruler of the Global Country of World Peace, in recognition of Professor Nader's supreme scientific discovery that human physiology is an expression of Veda and Vedic Literature: in structure and function, the physiology is an exact replica of Veda and Vedic Literature. Through this discovery, the cosmic potential of human life has become a living reality for everyone.

Maharishi summarizes the purpose of the Global Country of World Peace: "We have created a Global Country of World Peace in order to eliminate poverty and problems in the world, and to raise the level of education — create higher intelligence so that no man makes a mistake; to introduce prevention-oriented health care so that no one falls ill; and to create invincible defense (through the group practice of Yogic Flying) so that no enemy is born to the nation."[4]

Rise of Purity in World Consciousness Through Maharishi's Teaching

Already during the past decades of Maharishi's worldwide teaching the purity of world consciousness has been steadily rising; the light of pure

---

4 Maharishi, *Ideal India: The Lighthouse of Peace on Earth* (Delhi, India: Age of Enlightenment Publications, 2001).

knowledge has been steadily rising; life according to Natural Law has been steadily rising. With the blossoming of Maharishi's great wisdom in the life of humanity, the world is already witnessing the signs of a new awakening in every field in the direction of Heaven on Earth.

The many groups of Yogic flyers in different countries — such as the groups Maharishi established at Maharishi Ved Vigyān Vishwa Vidyā Peeth (Maharishi Vedic University) in India, and at Maharishi International University in Fairfield, Iowa, USA — have created a dramatic change in world consciousness, as indicated by the end of the Cold War and its many attendant wars, and by the fading away of many crudely materialistic philosophies and the rise of spiritual trends in global life.

Maharishi Purusha Program[SM] and *Mother Divine Program*[SM] [5]

The vital importance of creating coherence in world consciousness led to Maharishi's formation in 1981 of the Maharishi Purusha Program for men, and the Mother Divine Program for ladies.

These groups, established around the world, are enjoying higher states of consciousness and bubbling bliss twenty-four hours a day. They perpetually radiate an indomitable influence of harmony and positivity in world consciousness through their practice of the Transcendental Meditation and Transcendental Meditation Sidhi programs, including the Yogic Flying technique.

Maharishi's Unprecedented Achievements

Maharishi began his worldwide movement endowed only with the confidence he possessed in the knowledge of life and living bestowed on him by his Master, Shri Guru Dev. He realized that with that knowledge alone he could spiritually regenerate the whole world, and he embarked on this task with all the simplicity and unboundedness of vision possessed by only the greatest of great Maharishis of the Vedic Tradition. Because of Maharishi's tireless devotion to the welfare of humanity, every day the world

---

5 In the Vedic Tradition, the word "Purusha" refers to the infinite silent consciousness of everyone, and "Mother Divine" refers to the nourishing, evolutionary power of Natural Law.

draws closer to total spiritual regeneration of life, and to the establishment of Heaven on Earth.

All That Remains Is to Fully Implement This Knowledge

Maharishi's unique and historic discoveries in the field of Veda and Vedic Literature have established the world today on a Himalayan plateau of knowledge. With such command and authority in the field of knowledge, Maharishi made it possible for the world now to enter Heaven on Earth for all times through the full implementation of all the ancient Vedic wisdom (including the establishment of groups of Yogic flyers everywhere) by establishing Maharishi Universities of Management, Maharishi Vedic Universities, Maharishi Ayur-Veda Universities, and Colleges of Maharishi Vedic Medicine around the world.

Maharishi — A Quiet Guardian of All Nations

From the highest peak of Unity Consciousness, Maharishi experienced the whole world family as his own family. Moved by unbounded compassion for the troubles of the nations of the world, he spent every moment of his life on the creation of Heaven on Earth for everyone now and for all generations to come. This has been Maharishi in the world, a quiet guardian of all nations.

Soon the work that Maharishi began in founding the Spiritual Regeneration Movement in 1958 will reach its fulfillment. The goal of his worldwide activity and of this historic book will be achieved, and a golden era will dawn, an enlightened age, in which, as Maharishi writes in the introduction to this work, "A new humanity will be born, fuller in conception and richer in experience and accomplishments in all fields. Joy of life will belong to every man, love will dominate human society, truth and virtue will reign in the world, peace on Earth will be permanent, and all will live in fulfillment in fullness of life in God Consciousness."

— DR. BEVAN MORRIS
Prime Minister, Global Country of World Peace
September 12, 1994 (updated 2020)

APPENDIX A

Overview of the Scientific Research on the *Transcendental Meditation* and *Transcendental Meditation Sidhi* Programs Including *Yogic Flying*
(updated 2020)

SCIENTIFIC RESEARCH on the Transcendental Meditation and Transcendental Meditation Sidhi programs of Maharishi documents their profound benefits for the individual and for society.[1] Physiological changes produced during the practice of the Transcendental Meditation technique include profound relaxation and a high degree of orderliness in brain functioning. As a result of continued practice of the technique, mental potential develops, social behavior becomes more effective and rewarding, health improves, and the individual radiates a harmonious and nourishing influence for the whole society.

When applied in different areas of society, the Transcendental Meditation technique develops academic excellence and a high quality of life; increases productivity, health, and job satisfaction in business; improves behavior and reduces recidivism among prisoners; and increases positive trends in society.

Beneficial effects have been found on national and global levels when this technology is practiced by large numbers of people. As little as one percent of a population practicing the Transcendental Meditation technique, or the square root of one percent of a population practicing the Transcendental Meditation Sidhi program with Yogic Flying together in one place, produces an influence of orderliness and coherence in the environment, as reflected by improved quality of life and decreased negative trends in society and the world.

[1] Visit www.tm.org/research for additional information about scientific research studies.

Maharishi explains that this one simple technology is able to produce such an extraordinary range of benefits because it enlivens the most basic level of existence, known to ancient Vedic Science since time immemorial as the Saṁhitā, the ultimate field of unity — which by interacting within itself gives rise to the innumerable streams of Natural Law in creation. This field has recently been glimpsed by modern physics in its Unified Quantum Field Theories. From this level everything in the universe is supported and nourished. Creating an influence of coherence in world consciousness from this level can make every nation self-sufficient and perpetuate world peace.

Over 675 scientific studies on the Transcendental Meditation program of Maharishi have been conducted by researchers at more than 300 independent universities and research institutions in 30 countries.

Studies have been published in almost 200 major scientific journals, including *Science*; *Lancet*; *Scientific American*; *American Journal of Physiology*; *International Journal of Neuroscience*; *Experimental Neurology*; *Electroencephalography and Clinical Neurophysiology*; *Psychosomatic Medicine*; *Journal of the Canadian Medical Association*; *Archives of Internal Medicine*; *American Journal of Cardiology*; *American Journal of Hypertension*; *Stroke*; *American Psychologist*; *Psychological Bulletin*; *British Journal of Educational Psychology*; *Journal of Counseling Psychology*; *The Journal of Mind and Behavior*; *Academy of Management Journal*; *Journal of Conflict Resolution*; *Criminal Justice and Behavior*; *Journal of Clinical Psychiatry*; and *Social Indicators Research*.

Many studies have been presented at professional scientific conferences, and others have been part of doctoral dissertations prepared under the guidance of thesis committees at leading universities.

Much of the research has been gathered together in eight volumes (totaling 6,000 pages) of scientific research on the Transcendental Meditation and Transcendental Meditation Sidhi programs of Maharishi including Yogic Flying.[2]

These eight volumes document the benefits of the Technology of the Unified Field of Natural Law, the Technology of Transcendental Consciousness, by presenting research findings in the major areas of human concern: education, health, government, defense, rehabilitation, agriculture, and business and industry.

2 MERU (Maharishi European Research University) Press publication: *Scientific Research on the Transcendental Meditation and TM-Sidhi Programme: Collected Papers.*

In the field of education: Extensive scientific research and decades of experience in schools and universities around the world validate the benefits of the Transcendental Meditation and Transcendental Meditation Sidhi programs.

Findings include: increased intelligence and creativity; improved learning ability and memory; improved academic performance; increased graduation rate; improved behavior in school; improved perception and mind-body coordination; increased self-confidence and self-actualization; broader comprehension and greater ability to focus; higher levels of moral judgment; improvement in mental and physical health; improved social-emotional learning; integration of brain functioning; and reduction of symptoms among students diagnosed with attention deficit disorder.[3]

In the field of health: Scientific research has repeatedly proven the effectiveness of the Transcendental Meditation and Transcendental Meditation Sidhi programs for improving individual and collective health.

Findings include: decreased need for medical treatment; marked reduction of health care costs; decreased risk factors for disease, including reduction of high blood pressure, reduced atherosclerosis, decreased serum cholesterol, reduced cigarette smoking, and decreased alcohol and drug abuse; reduction of mortality, heart attacks, and strokes; protection against toxic effects of free radicals, which are associated with aging and as much as 80 percent of all diseases; effective stress reduction; improved resistance to stress; more healthy aging and increased longevity; improved mental health and well-being; improved collective health for the whole nation, reduction of crime, accidents, and other negative factors; and improvements of positive trends in all areas of society.[4]

3 For example, *Education* 139(3): 111–119, 2019; *Annals of the New York Academy of Sciences*, doi: 10.1111/nyas.13071, 2016; *Brain and Cognition* 111: 86–94, 2017; *Brain and Cognition* 125: 100–105, 2018; *Intelligence* 29: 419–440, 2001; *The Journal of Creative Behavior* 13: 169–180, 1979; *International Journal of Neuroscience* 15: 151–157, 1981; *Memory & Cognition* 10: 207–215, 1982; *Education* 107: 49–54, 1986; *British Journal of Educational Psychology* 55: 164–166, 1985; *Perceptual and Motor Skills* 39: 1031–1034, 1974; *Personality and Individual Differences* 12: 1105–1116, 1991; *British Journal of Psychology* 73: 57–68, 1982; *Journal of Social Behavior and Personality* 17: 93–121, 2005; *Health and Quality of Life Outcomes* 1: 10, 2003; *Journal of Clinical Psychology* 45: 957–974, 1989; *Journal of Instructional Psychology* 22: 308–319, 1995; *Current Issues in Education* [online], 10(2), 2008; *Education* 131: 556–564, 2011; *Education* 133: 495–501, 2013.

4 For example, *Psychosomatic Medicine* 49: 493–507, 1987; *American Journal of Health Promotion*

In the field of government: Scientific research on the Transcendental Meditation and Transcendental Meditation Sidhi programs has shown that this technology rapidly reduces negative tendencies in society, including crime, sickness, accidents, and social turbulence and conflict, and promotes positive trends such as improved economic and governmental performance.[5]

In addition, research has shown that Maharishi Vedic Science develops all skills necessary for efficient administration of government.

As every government is basically governed by the collective consciousness of the people, it is vital for every government to create and maintain a strong and indomitable influence of coherence, positivity, and harmony in national life.

Maintaining integrated national consciousness is the key to successful administration. This is attainable by maintaining a group equivalent to the square root of one percent of the population practicing the Transcendental Meditation and Transcendental Meditation Sidhi programs in the country.

This group of Yogic flyers, creating the *Maharishi Effect*[6] in the country, will spontaneously enable the government to prevent problems. A government with the ability to prevent problems will be the supreme level of government, which will promote automation in administration.

Along with this one coherence-creating group in the capital of each country — Maharishi's Group for a Government — it is advisable to introduce the Maharishi Science and Technology of Consciousness, the complete knowledge of Natural Law, on every level of education.

14: 284–291, 2000; *Current Hypertension Reports* 9: 520–528, 2007; *American Journal of Hypertension* 21: 310–316, 2008; *Stroke* 31: 568–573, 2000; *Circulation: Cardiovascular Quality and Outcomes* 5: 750–758, 2012; *Journal of Human Stress* 5: 24–27, 1979; *Alcoholism Treatment Quarterly* 11: 13–87, 1994; *Psychosomatic Medicine* 60: 38–41, 1998; *Psychosomatic Medicine* 35: 341–349, 1973; *American Psychologist* 42: 879–881, 1987; *Journal of Behavioral Medicine* 15: 327–341, 1992; *American Journal of Cardiology* 95: 1060–1064: 2005; *Social Indicators Research* 22: 399–418, 1990; *Social Indicators Research* 47: 153–201, 1999; *The Journal of Mind and Behavior* 8: 67–104, 1987; *Journal of Conflict Resolution* 32: 776–812, 1988.

5 For example, *Psychology, Crime, and Law* 2: 165–174, 1996; *Social Indicators Research* 47: 153–201, 1999; *Social Indicators Research* 22: 399–418, 1990; *The Journal of Mind and Behavior* 8: 67–104, 1987; *Psychological Reports* 76: 1171–1193, 1995; *Proceedings of the Business and Economics Statistics Section of the American Statistical Association* (Alexandria, Virginia: American Statistical Association): 799–804, 1987; *Proceedings of the Social Statistics Section of the American Statistical Association* (Alexandria, Virginia: American Statistical Association): 38–43, 1996; *Dissertation Abstracts International* 58(6): 2385A, 1997.

6 See page 369.

In the field of defense: Scientific research has repeatedly shown that the Transcendental Meditation and Transcendental Meditation Sidhi programs can reduce domestic and international conflicts and terrorism, improve international relations, and thereby raise the defense of any country to the level of invincibility.[7]

In the field of rehabilitation: Scientific research has repeatedly shown that the Transcendental Meditation and Transcendental Meditation Sidhi programs successfully treat post-traumatic stress disorder (PTSD) and also effectively rehabilitate prison inmates, reduce recidivism, and are immediately effective in reducing crime at the city, provincial, and national levels.[8]

This approach is the only scientifically verified method to consistently, immediately, and substantially reduce crime in the whole society.

In the field of agriculture: Scientific research has found that the Transcendental Meditation and Transcendental Meditation Sidhi programs increase creativity, productivity, intelligence, and energy; progressively develop higher states of consciousness; and bring more Support of Nature to the individual.

Additional findings of importance to farmers include increased physiological adaptability, improved cardiovascular health, increased effectiveness, and work satisfaction, reduced accidents and sickness, and improved quality of life in society.[9]

---

7 For example, *Military Medicine* 183(1–2): e144–e150, 2018; *The Lancet Psychiatry* 5(12): 975–986, 2018; *Journal of Conflict Resolution* 32: 776–812, 1988; *Journal of Social Behavior and Personality* 17: 285–338, 2005; *Journal of Offender Rehabilitation* 36: 283–302, 2003; *Proceedings of the Social Statistics Section of the American Statistical Association* (Alexandria, VA: American Statistical Association): 297–302, 1990.

8 For example, *The Permanente Journal* 20(4): 16–007, 2016; *The Permanente Journal* 21(1): 16–008, 2017; *Military Medicine* 176: 626–630, 2011; *Journal of Traumatic Stress* 26: 295–298, 2013; *Journal of Traumatic Stress* 27: 112–115, 2014; *Criminal Justice and Behavior* 5: 3–20, 1978; *Journal of Offender Rehabilitation* 36: 127–160, 2003; *Journal of Criminal Justice* 15: 211–230, 1987; *Journal of Offender Rehabilitation* 36: 161–180, 2003; *Journal of Offender Rehabilitation* 36: 181–203, 2003; *Psychology, Crime, and Law* 2: 165–174, 1996; *The Journal of Mind and Behavior* 8: 67–104, 1987; *The Journal of Mind and Behavior* 9: 457–486, 1988; *Social Indicators Research* 47: 153–201, 1999; *Journal of Conflict Resolution* 32: 776–812, 1988.

9 For example, *The Journal of Creative Behavior* 13: 169–180, 1979; *Academy of Management Journal* 17: 362–368, 1974; *Personality and Individual Differences* 12: 1105–1116, 1991; *Dissertation Abstracts International* 38(7): 3372B–3373B, 1978; *Psychologia* 32: 91–103, 1989; *Psychosomatic Medicine* 35: 341–349, 1973; *Archives of Internal Medicine* 166: 1218–1224, 2006; *Anxiety, Stress and Coping: An International Journal* 6: 245–262, 1993; *Japanese Journal of Industrial Health* 32:

In the field of business and industry: Scientific research has repeatedly shown that the Transcendental Meditation and Transcendental Meditation Sidhi programs produce the following benefits: increased creativity, leading to enhanced productivity, efficiency, and profitability; increased job performance and job satisfaction, and decreased unemployment and inflation; improved health of industrial workers; reduced need for medical care; reduced stress, absenteeism, and health care costs; as well as overall improved national and international economic trends.[10]

The Transcendental Meditation and Transcendental Meditation Sidhi programs of Maharishi have proved to be enriching and fulfilling to all fields of life.

All the research together scientifically establishes the reliability of the Maharishi Science and Technology of Consciousness, which is supported by the principles of all the different disciplines of modern science, validated by a large body of scientific research, upheld by the ancient Veda and Vedic Literature, and verified by the personal experience of millions of people throughout the world and, further, by the growing coherence in collective consciousness and rising positivity in world consciousness.

The results of the application of the Maharishi Science and Technology of Consciousness are so convincing that the emergence of a better quality of life in many countries is now being acknowledged to be the result of the collective practice of the Transcendental Meditation and Transcendental Meditation Sidhi programs.

656, 1990; *Japanese Journal of Public Health* 37(10 Suppl.): 729, 1990; *The Journal of Mind and Behavior* 8: 67–104, 1987.
10 For example, *The Permanente Journal* 22: 17–172, 2018; *The Journal of Creative Behavior* 13: 169–180, 1979; *Academy of Management Journal* 17: 362–368, 1974; *Anxiety, Stress and Coping: An International Journal* 6: 245–262, 1993; *Career Development International* 4: 149–154, 1999; *Dissertation Abstracts International* 57(6): 4068B, 1996; *Japanese Journal of Industrial Health* 32: 656, 1990; *Japanese Journal of Public Health* 37(10 Suppl.): 729, 1990; *Psychosomatic Medicine* 49: 493–507, 1987; *American Psychologist* 42: 879–881, 1987; *Journal of Social Behavior and Personality* 17: 235–273, 2005; *Health and Quality of Life Outcomes* 1: 10, 2003; *The American Journal of Managed Care* 3: 135–144, 1997; *American Journal of Health Promotion* 10: 208–216, 1996; *American Journal of Health Promotion* 14: 284–291, 2000; *Proceedings of the Business and Economics Statistics Section of the American Statistical Association* (Alexandria, Virginia: American Statistical Association): 799–804, 1987.

A review of all the scientific research on the Transcendental Meditation and Transcendental Meditation Sidhi programs reveals how the sequential unfoldment of pure knowledge and its infinite organizing power, brought about by the experience of pure consciousness through the Transcendental Meditation and TM-Sidhi programs, gives rise to higher states of consciousness in the individual and purifies world consciousness, as evidenced by the rising waves of achievement over the past six decades of Maharishi's teaching throughout the world.

Maharishi Effect

The *Maharishi Effect* is an influence of coherence and harmony generated in society through a sufficient number of individuals enlivening the field of pure consciousness, the Unified Field of Natural Law, through the Transcendental Meditation and Transcendental Meditation Sidhi programs. The *Maharishi Effect* is a "field effect" of consciousness, in which the beneficial influence of these programs is shared by everyone in the society.

In 1974 it was discovered in cities in the USA that when the number of people participating in the Transcendental Meditation program reached one percent of the city's population, the trend of rising crime rate was reversed, indicating increasing order and harmony in the life of the whole city.

Research scientists named this phenomenon of rising coherence in the collective consciousness of the whole society the *Maharishi Effect*, in honor of Maharishi, who predicted this effect as early as 1960, near the beginning of his worldwide Transcendental Meditation movement. Research involving several hundred other cities subsequently replicated this original finding.

The **Extended Maharishi Effect**[11]: In 1976, with the introduction of the more advanced Transcendental Meditation Sidhi program, a more powerful effect was expected. The first major test of Maharishi's prediction took place in 1978 during Maharishi's Global Ideal Society Campaign in 108 countries: crime rate was reduced and quality of life improved.

11 Over 50 independent research studies on the city, provincial, national, and international levels confirm that the *Maharishi Effect*, the *Extended Maharishi Effect*, and the *Global Maharishi Effect* improve the quality of life in society and the trends of life in the entire world.

This global research demonstrated a new formula: the square root of one percent of a population practicing the Transcendental Meditation and Transcendental Meditation Sidhi programs morning and evening together in one place is sufficient to neutralize negative tendencies and promote positive trends throughout the whole population. This much-reduced requirement — in many cases just a few hundred individuals practicing Maharishi's technology of Transcendental Meditation and the Transcendental Meditation Sidhi programs to bring life in accordance with Natural Law for a whole nation — enabled this discovery to be repeatedly verified on the city, provincial, and national levels.[12]

The *Global Maharishi Effect* was created when Maharishi promoted Yogic Flying in large groups — approximately the square root of one percent of the world's population. The basis of the *Global Maharishi Effect* is the phenomenon known to physics as a "field effect," the effect of coherence and positivity produced from the field of infinite correlation, the field of Transcendental Consciousness, the Unified Field of Natural Law, which is basic to creation and permeates all life everywhere.

Through the *Global Maharishi Effect*, the "field effect" was witnessed, strengthening positive and harmonious trends in world consciousness.

The greatest evidence of this effect was when the enmity between the two superpowers (the Soviet Union and the USA) ended in a friendly handshake in 1988.[13]

The phenomenon of the *Maharishi Effect* (like the phenomenon of the Meissner Effect[14] in physics) discovered by scientists has repeatedly verified

---

12 For example, *Journal of Consciousness Studies* 24: 53–86, 2017; *Journal of Health and Environmental Research* 3: 32–43, 2017; *SAGE Open* 6(2): 1–16, 2016; *SAGE Open* 7(1): 1–15, 2017; *Studies in Asian Social Science* 6(2): 1–45, 2019; *Psychology, Crime, and Law* 2: 165–174, 1996; *The Journal of Mind and Behavior* 9: 457–486, 1988; *Social Indicators Research* 47: 153–201, 1999; *The Journal of Mind and Behavior* 8: 67–104, 1987; *Journal of Conflict Resolution* 32: 776–812, 1988; *Social Indicators Research* 22: 399–418, 1990; *Psychological Reports* 76: 1171–1193, 1995; *Journal of Social Behavior and Personality* 17: 285–338, 2005.

13 For example, *Journal of Offender Rehabilitation* 36: 283–302, 2003; *Proceedings of the Social Statistics Section of the American Statistical Association* (Alexandria, VA: American Statistical Association): 297–302, 1990; "*U.S–Soviet relations and the Maharishi Effect: A time series analysis*," paper presented at the Annual Meeting of the American Statistical Association, Social Statistics Section, Atlanta, Georgia, August 1991.

14 A universal principle in Nature is that internally coherent systems possess the ability to repel external influences, while incoherent systems are easily penetrated by disorder from outside.

that coherence in collective consciousness and positivity and harmony in national consciousness are produced by the group practice of the Transcendental Meditation and Transcendental Meditation Sidhi programs, with Yogic Flying. This has proved to be a formula to create irreversible world peace and Heaven on Earth — all good to everyone and non-good to no one — the basis of a coherent, integrated society and a perfect government.

With this, thousands of years of suffering are soon coming to an end, and a new civilization, Vedic Civilization of enlightenment and fulfillment, is dawning.[15]

Many carefully controlled experiments on the *Maharishi Effect* have appeared in leading scientific journals such as the *Journal of Conflict Resolution*; *Psychology, Crime, and Law*; *Journal of Social Behavior and Personality*; *Social Indicators Research*; and *The Journal of Mind and Behavior*.

These studies have utilized the most advanced and rigorous research designs and statistical methodologies (time series impact assessment analysis and transfer function analysis as well as dynamic regression methods) to precisely evaluate the effect of large coherence-creating groups on standard sociological measures of the quality of life in cities, provinces, nations, and the world.

These studies have rigorously demonstrated the power of the *Maharishi Effect* to a degree of certainty that is extremely rare in the sociological sciences. The *Maharishi Effect* in itself proves the existence of the Unified Field of Natural Law and man's ability to operate from this level.

The *Maharishi Effect* is rising in the world. World consciousness is being constantly purified. Already a new awakening of freedom is being witnessed in the world. The transformation of political, economic, and social values is taking place in the whole world at a fast pace.

As the *Maharishi Effect* is purifying world consciousness, old principles that were guiding life in the age of ignorance are being replaced by new principles to guide life in the world in the dawning Age of Enlightenment.

This principle of invincibility is clearly illustrated in physics as the Meissner Effect, and in the functioning of a nation as the *Maharishi Effect*.
15 Maharishi inaugurated the Dawn of the Age of Enlightenment in 1975, on the basis of the discovery of the *Maharishi Effect*.

Meissner Effect
An Example of Invincibility in the Quantum Physics of Superconductivity

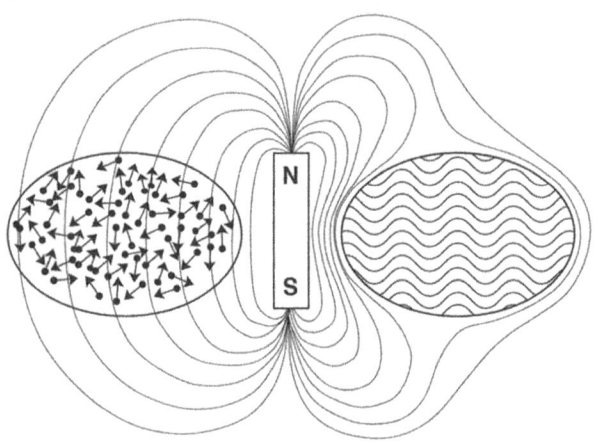

ORDINARY CONDUCTOR
In an ordinary electrical conductor, incoherent, disordered electrons allow penetration by an external magnetic field.

SUPERCONDUCTOR
In a superconductor, coherent collective functioning of the electrons spontaneously excludes an external magnetic field, and maintains its impenetrable status.

This example of invincibility is not unique in Nature; parallel phenomena of invincibility can be found in many aspects of the physical and biological sciences. In each case, it is found that the ability is always based on coherent collective functioning.

Maharishi Effect
Creating an Invincible Armor for the Nation

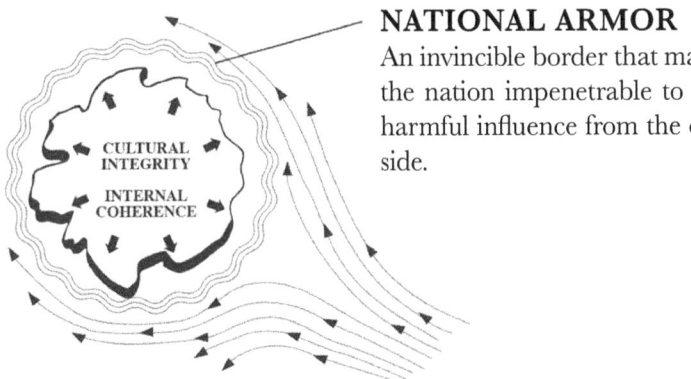

NATIONAL ARMOR
An invincible border that makes the nation impenetrable to any harmful influence from the outside.

CULTURAL INTEGRITY

INTERNAL COHERENCE

The *Maharishi Effect* refers to the growth of harmony in society resulting from the practice of Maharishi's Technology of Consciousness — the technology of Natural Law — by a small fraction of the population. When the influence of coherence generated by this technology reaches sufficient intensity, an integrated national consciousness is created. This in turn strengthens the cultural integrity of the nation by promoting life in accord with Natural Law. The result is the development of self-sufficiency and an invincible armor for the nation, which automatically repels any negative influence coming from outside.

Thus, the integrated state of national consciousness created by the *Maharishi Effect* produces a "Meissner Effect" for the nation, rendering it impenetrable to external disorder.

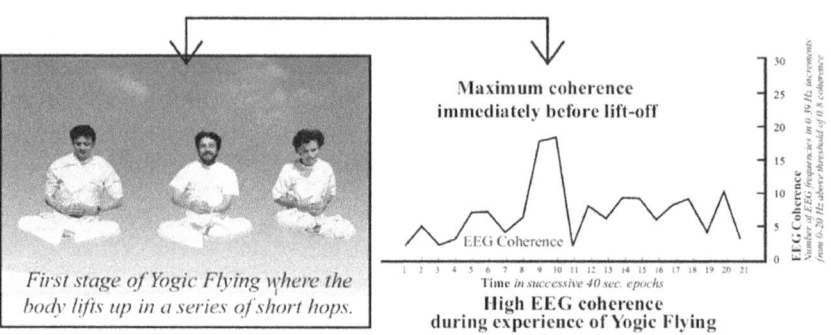

> # Optimizing Brain
> ## the *Transcendental*
> ## *Transcendental Meditation*
> Creating the *Maharishi Effect* — radiating a purifying
>
> *First stage of Yogic Flying where the body lifts up in a series of short hops.*
>
> Maximum coherence immediately before lift-off
>
> High EEG coherence during experience of Yogic Flying
>
> The Transcendental Meditation Sidhi program is a breakthrough in the development of human potential. Enlivening and activating Transcendental Consciousness, and developing the habit to spontaneously project thought and action from this simplest form of awareness, pure consciousness, total potential of intelligence,

Transcendental Meditation Sidhi Program of *Yogic Flying*

Yogic Flying is a phenomenon created by a specific thought projected from Transcendental Consciousness, the Unified Field of Natural Law, the field of all possibilities. This is the simplest state of human consciousness, self-referral consciousness, easily accessible through Transcendental Meditation and enlivened by the Transcendental Meditation Sidhi program, including Yogic Flying.

Yogic Flying demonstrates perfect mind-body coordination and is correlated with maximum EEG coherence, indicating maximum orderliness and integration of brain functioning.[16] Even in the first stage of Yogic Flying, where the body lifts up in a series of short hops, the individual experiences bubbling bliss, generating coherence, positivity, and harmony for the environment.

---

16 For example, *International Journal of Neuroscience* 38: 427–34, 1988; *International Journal of Neuroscience* 54: 1–12, 1990.

Functioning through *Meditation* and *Sidhi* Programs of Maharishi
influence to neutralize negative trends in society

> **Original finding** — During the Transcendental Meditation Sidhi Yogic Flying technique, maximum coherence is measured immediately before the body lifts up. **Replication study** — Broadband global EEG coherence among all brain areas increases during the 2.12-second period immediately before the body lifts up during the TM-Sidhi Yogic Flying technique, compared to a control condition. **References:** *Scientific Research on the Transcendental Meditation Programme: Collected Papers*, Volume 1, 1977, 705–712; *International Journal of Neuroscience*, 1990, 54: 1–12.

makes thought and action most natural, and therefore spontaneously evolutionary, and opens the field of all possibilities for the fulfillment of every desire. Here is the scientifically validated formula for enlightenment — life in fulfillment.

Yogic Flying places the individual in control of Nature's central switchboard, from where Natural Law governs the entire universe. From here, individuals grow to command all channels of Nature's infinite creativity and invincible organizing power. An order from the Prime Minister commands the total authority and resources of a nation for its implementation. Similarly, any intention projected from the Unified Field of Natural Law commands the infinite organizing power of Natural Law for its immediate fulfillment.

The practice of Yogic Flying is a practical demonstration of the ability to project thought from the Unified Field of Natural Law, and develops the ability to act spontaneously in accord with Natural Law for the fulfillment of desires. The phenomenon of Yogic Flying proves that through the Transcendental Meditation and Transcendental Meditation Sidhi programs, anyone can gain the ability to function from the simplest form of their own awareness and develop mastery over Natural Law.

Appendix B

Human Physiology

Expression of Veda and the Vedic Literature:
Modern Science and Ancient Vedic Science Discover the Fabrics of Immortality in the Human Physiology

A Textbook of Life for Everyone

**by Professor Tony Nader, MD, PhD
honored by Maharishi as Maharaja Adhiraj Rajaraam,
First Ruler of the Global Country of World Peace[1]**

THE inner intelligence of the body is at the basis of every aspect of human physiology. With the discovery of the structuring dynamics of Natural Law — the sound vibrations of the Veda and Vedic Literature — at the basis of the structures and functions of the physiology, enlivenment of the inner intelligence of the body has now become practical.

The Vedic Literature provides the structuring dynamics of Natural Law which create the structures and functions of specific Laws of Nature from the holistic field of intelligence. These specific Laws of Nature in turn create the specific structures and functions of the physiology.

It is fortunate that the structuring dynamics of Natural Law, as available in the 40 aspects of the Vedic Literature, have now been identified as the creative intelligence that structures every aspect of the physiology.

[1] See Appendix E, "A Glimpse of Maharishi's Achievements 1957–2008 Continuing," year 2000.

APPENDIX B

This discovery, in the field of physiology, of the connection between the structures of the physiology and the structures of the Vedic Literature (Vedic Sounds) has given us the opportunity to maintain a healthy physiology by maintaining wakefulness, or alertness, of the inner intelligence of every aspect of the physiology, and this is possible through the *experience* of the total field of intelligence through Transcendental Meditation and *verifying experiences* through the Vedic Literature.

Application of any aspect of the Vedic Literature will enliven the corresponding value of the physiology. *This has given rise to a practical program, popularly known as* Maharishi Vedic Vibration Technology^{SM}, *leading everyone to unfold his Cosmic Potential, supporting development of a balanced physiology.*

The following chart illustrates the correlation between the 40 aspects of the physiology and the 40 aspects of the Vedic Literature.

Celebrating the Discovery of the Veda and Vedic
Forty Qualities of Intelligence at the

Qualities of Intelligence		Terminology of Vedic Literature		Terminology of Modern Physiology
1. HOLISTIC (DYNAMIC SILENCE) quality of intelligence	fully expressed in	Ṛk Veda	which in turn expresses itself in	the Whole Physiology
2. FLOWING WAKEFULNESS—FLOWING quality of intelligence	fully expressed in	Sāma Veda	which in turn expresses itself in	the Sensory Systems—the "1000 doorways of perception"
3. OFFERING and CREATING quality of intelligence	fully expressed in	Yajur-Veda	which in turn expresses itself in	the physiology of the Processing Systems
4. REVERBERATING WHOLENESS—REVERBERATING quality in every point of HOLISTIC intelligence	fully expressed in	Atharva Veda	which in turn expresses itself in	the physiology of the Motor Systems
5. EXPRESSING quality of intelligence	fully expressed in	Shikshā	which in turn expresses itself in	the physiology of the Autonomic Ganglia
6. TRANSFORMING quality of intelligence	fully expressed in	Kalp	which in turn expresses itself in	the physiology of the Limbic System
7. EXPANDING quality of intelligence	fully expressed in	Vyākaraṇ	which in turn expresses itself in	the physiology of the Hypothalamus
8. SELF-REFERRAL quality of intelligence	fully expressed in	Nirukt	which in turn expresses itself in	the physiology of the Pituitary Gland
9. MEASURING and QUANTIFYING quality of intelligence	fully expressed in	Chhand	which in turn expresses itself in	the physiology of the Neurotransmitters, Neurohormones
10. ALL-KNOWING quality of intelligence	fully expressed in	Jyotish	which in turn expresses itself in	the physiology of the Basal Ganglia, Cerebral Cortex, Cranial Nerves, Brain Stem
11. DISTINGUISHING and DECIDING quality of intelligence	fully expressed in	Nyāya	which in turn expresses itself in	the physiology of the Thalamus
12. SPECIFYING quality of intelligence	fully expressed in	Vaisheshik	which in turn expresses itself in	the physiology of the Cerebellum
13. ENUMERATING quality of intelligence	fully expressed in	Sāṁkhya	which in turn expresses itself in	the physiology of the Cells, Tissues, Organs—Types and Categories
14. UNIFYING quality of intelligence	fully expressed in	Yoga	which in turn expresses itself in	the physiology of the Association Fibers of the Cerebral Cortex
15. ANALYZING quality of intelligence	fully expressed in	Karma Mīmāṁsā	which in turn expresses itself in	the physiology of the Central Nervous System
16. LIVELY ABSOLUTE (LIVING WHOLENESS—I-NESS, or BEING) quality of intelligence	fully expressed in	Vedānt	which in turn expresses itself in	the physiology of the Integrated Functioning of the Central Nervous System
17. INTEGRATING and HARMONIZING quality of intelligence	fully expressed in	Gandharva Veda	which in turn expresses itself in	the physiology of the Cycles and Rhythms, Pacemaker Cells
18. INVINCIBLE and PROGRESSIVE quality of intelligence	fully expressed in	Dhanur-Veda	which in turn expresses itself in	the physiology of the Immune System, Biochemistry
19. ESTABLISHING quality of intelligence	fully expressed in	Sthāpatya Veda	which in turn expresses itself in	the physiology of the Anatomy
20. NOURISHING quality of intelligence	fully expressed in	Hārīta Saṁhitā	which in turn expresses itself in	the physiology of the Venous and Biliary Systems

… APPENDIX B

Literature at the Basis of the Human Physiology
Basis of the Human Physiology

Qualities of Intelligence		Terminology of Vedic Literature		Terminology of Modern Physiology
21. DIFFERENTIATING quality of intelligence	fully expressed in	Bhel Saṁhitā	which in turn expresses itself in	the physiology of the Lymphatic System and Glial Cells
22. EQUIVALENCY quality of intelligence	fully expressed in	Kāshyap Saṁhitā	which in turn expresses itself in	the physiology of the Arterial System
23. BALANCING—HOLDING TOGETHER and SUPPORTING quality of intelligence	fully expressed in	Charak Saṁhitā	which in turn expresses itself in	the physiology of the Cell Nucleus
24. SEPARATING quality of intelligence	fully expressed in	Sushrut Saṁhitā	which in turn expresses itself in	the physiology of the Cytoplasm and Cell Organelles
25. COMMUNICATION and ELOQUENCE quality of intelligence	fully expressed in	Vāgbhatt Saṁhitā	which in turn expresses itself in	the physiology of the Cytoskeleton and Cell Membrane
26. DIAGNOSING quality of intelligence	fully expressed in	Mādhav Nidān Saṁhitā	which in turn expresses itself in	the physiology of the Mesodermal Cells
27. SYNTHESIZING quality of intelligence	fully expressed in	Shārngadhar Saṁhitā	which in turn expresses itself in	the physiology of the Endodermal Cells
28. ENLIGHTENING quality of intelligence	fully expressed in	Bhāva-Prakāsh Saṁhitā	which in turn expresses itself in	the physiology of the Ectodermal Cells
29. TRANSCENDING quality of intelligence	fully expressed in	Upanishad	which in turn expresses itself in	the physiology of the Ascending Tracts of the Central Nervous System
30. STIRRING quality of intelligence	fully expressed in	Āraṇyak	which in turn expresses itself in	the physiology of the Fasciculi Proprii
31. STRUCTURING quality of intelligence	fully expressed in	Brāhmaṇa	which in turn expresses itself in	the physiology of the Descending Tracts of the Central Nervous System
32. BLOSSOMING OF TOTALITY quality of intelligence	fully expressed in	Itihās	which in turn expresses itself in	the physiology of the Voluntary Motor and Sensory Projections
33. ANCIENT AND ETERNAL quality of intelligence	fully expressed in	Purāṇ	which in turn expresses itself in	the physiology of the Great Intermediate Net
34. MEMORY quality of intelligence	fully expressed in	Smṛiti	which in turn expresses itself in	the physiology of the Memory Systems and Reflexes
35. ALL-PERVADING WHOLENESS quality of intelligence	fully expressed in	Rk Veda Prātishākhya	which in turn expresses itself in	the physiology of the Plexiform Layer—Horizontal Communication *Cerebral Cortex Layer 1*
36. SILENCING, SHARING and SPREADING quality of intelligence	fully expressed in	Shukl-Yajur-Veda Prātishākhya	which in turn expresses itself in	the physiology of the Corticocortical Fibers *Cerebral Cortex Layer 2*
37. UNFOLDING quality of intelligence	fully expressed in	Atharva Veda Prātishākhya	which in turn expresses itself in	the physiology of the Cortico-striate, -tectal, -spinal Fibers *Cerebral Cortex Layer 5*
38. DISSOLVING quality of intelligence	fully expressed in	Atharva Veda Prātishākhya (*Chaturadhyāyi*)	which in turn expresses itself in	the physiology of the Corticothalamic and Corticoclaustral Fibers *Cerebral Cortex Layer 6*
39. OMNIPRESENT quality of intelligence	fully expressed in	Krishṇ-Yajur-Veda Prātishākhya (*Taittiriya*)	which in turn expresses itself in	the physiology of the Commisural and Corticocortical Fibers *Cerebral Cortex Layer 3*
40. UNMANIFESTING THE PARTS BUT MANIFESTING THE WHOLE quality of intelligence	fully expressed in	Sāma Veda Prātishākhya (*Pushpa Sūtram*)	which in turn expresses itself in	the physiology of the Thalamocortical Fibers *Cerebral Cortex Layer 4*

Appendix C
Introduction to the Bhagavad-Gītā
by Maharishi Mahesh Yogi[1]

THE Bhagavad-Gītā is the Light of Life, lit by God at the altar of man, to save humanity from the darkness of ignorance and suffering. It is a scripture which outlives time, and can be acknowledged as indispensable to the life of any man in any age. It is the encyclopedia of life, and this commentary provides an index to it.

There will always be confusion and chaos in the relative fields of life, and man's mind will always fall into error and indecision. The Bhagavad-Gītā is a complete guide to practical life. It will always be there to rescue man in any situation. It is like an anchor for the ship of life sailing on the turbulent waves of time.

It brings fulfillment to the life of the individual. When society accepts it, social well-being and security will result, and when the world hears it, world peace will be permanent.

The Bhagavad-Gītā presents the science of life and the art of living. It teaches how to be, how to think, and how to do. Its technique of glorifying every aspect of life through contact with inner Being is like watering the root and making the whole tree green. It surpasses any practical wisdom of life ever cherished by human society.

The Bhagavad-Gītā has a greater number of commentaries than any other known scripture. The reason for adding one more is that there does not seem to be any commentary which really brings to light the essential point of the whole teaching.

Wise commentators, in their attempt to fulfill the need of their times, have revealed the truth of the teaching as they found it. By so doing they have secured a place in the history of human thought. They stand out as torch-

---

1. Excerpts from the Introduction, by Maharishi, to *Maharishi Mahesh Yogi on the Bhagavad-Gītā: A New Translation and Commentary (Chapters 1–6)*, which brings to light the deeper significance of *Science of Being and Art of Living*. Available from Maharishi International University Press, Fairfield, Iowa, USA 52557.

bearers on the long corridor of time. They have fathomed great depths of the ocean of wisdom. Yet with all their glorious achievements they have not brought out the central point of the Bhagavad-Gītā. It is unfortunate that the very essence of this ancient wisdom should have been missed.

The Bhagavad-Gītā needs a commentary which restates in simple words the essential teaching and technique given by Lord Krishna to Arjuna on the battlefield. There are commentaries to extol the wisdom of the paths of knowledge, devotion, and action in the Bhagavad-Gītā, but none to show that it provides a master key to open the gates of all these different highways of human evolution simultaneously. No commentary has yet shown that through one simple technique proclaimed in the Bhagavad-Gītā, any man, without having to renounce his way of life, can enjoy the blessings of all these paths.

This commentary has been written to present that key to mankind and preserve it for generations to come.

The Bhagavad-Gītā is the Scripture of Yoga, the Scripture of Divine Union. Its purpose is to explain in theory and practice all that is needed to raise the consciousness of man to the highest possible level. The marvel of its language and style is that every expression brings a teaching suitable to every level of human evolution.

It will be of interest to the reader to know that this commentary is being brought out only after the technique has been verified in the lives of thousands of people of different nationalities throughout the world, under the auspices of the Spiritual Regeneration Movement founded with the sole purpose of spiritually regenerating the lives of all men in every part of the world. It presents a truth that is timeless and universal, a truth of life equally suited to all men, irrespective of differences of faith, culture, or nationality.

The overall conception of this commentary is supplementary to the unique vision and profound wisdom of the great Shankara, as set forth in his Gītā-Bhāshya. The wisdom is a gift from Guru Dev. All glory to Him! It presents the Light of Life and sets the stream of life to find its fulfillment in the ocean of eternal Being, in devotion to God, and in the bliss of God Consciousness.

May every man make use of the practical wisdom given in the 45th verse of the second chapter and thereby glorify all aspects of his life and gain eternal freedom in divine consciousness.

Appendix D
Maharishi's Master Plan
Reconstruction of

INNER

GLORIFICATION OF INNER LIFE

- Development of higher states of consciousness;
- Blossoming of noble qualities and bliss;
- Gaining Support of Nature from within—happiness, peace, and fulfilling progress through:

The **TRANSCENDENTAL MEDITATION**
and **TM-SIDHI** PROGRAMS
the practical aspects of
MAHARISHI VEDIC SCIENCE

which develops all the seven states of consciousness in the individual and develops a perfect man with the ability to employ Natural Law to work for him and achieve anything he wants.

The seven states of consciousness are:

- Waking—*Jāgrat Chetanā*
- Dreaming—*Swapn Chetanā*
- Sleeping—*Sushupti Chetanā*
- Transcendental Consciousness—*Turīya Chetanā*
- Cosmic Consciousness—*Turīyātīt Chetanā*
- God Consciousness—*Bhagavat Chetanā*
- Unity Consciousness—*Brāhmī Chetanā*—awakening of the pure nature of consciousness to its own self-referral reality—the unified reality of the diversified universe—which renders individual life to be a lively field of all possibilities—infinite organizing power of the unified field of Natural Law, spontaneously upholding individual life.

From *Maharishi's Master Plan to Create Heaven on Earth*,

TO CREATE HEAVEN ON EARTH
THE WHOLE WORLD

OUTER

GLORIFICATION OF OUTER LIFE

- **Building Ideal Villages, Towns, and Cities** based on **Maharishi Sthapatya Veda** design—the science of building in accord with Natural Law—to create a beautiful and healthy environment free of pollution, noise, and stress so that everyone feels, "I am living in Heaven."
- **Creating Global Green Revolution**—farming all the unfarmed lands in the world using the scientific principles of **Maharishi Vedic Farming** to produce naturally grown, healthy food to achieve food **self-sufficiency** in every country.
- **Achieving global eradication of poverty** and achieving economic self-sufficiency in every nation through Maharishi's programs to develop agriculture, forestry, mining, and industry in every country.
- **Realizing Global Rural Development and Urban Renewal**—providing better living conditions for an integrated life of the rich and poor throughout the world.
- **Achieving economic balance** in the world family through **Maharishi Global Trading**.
- **Achieving ideal education** through **Maharishi Vedic Science and Technology**, which offers the **fruit of all knowledge** to everyone—life free from mistakes and suffering.
- **Achieving perfect health** for everyone and every nation through prevention-oriented **Maharishi Vedic Approach to Health**.
- **Achieving coherence, harmony, and balance in Nature** for everyone and every nation through **Maharishi Gandharva Veda** music.
- **Achieving invincible defense** for every nation through **Maharishi Dhanur-Veda**, which will disallow the birth of an enemy.
- **Achieving perfect government** in every country modeled on nature's government, which silently governs through Natural Law from the unified level of all the laws of nature—the common basis of all creation, the unseen prime mover of life eternally, fully awake within itself and available to everyone on the level of one's own self-referral consciousness—transcendental consciousness.
- **Achieving the rise of a supremely nourishing power in the world**, which will unrestrictedly uphold the power of evolution in Nature, eliminating all destructive tendencies and negative trends in the world.

As a result, every nation will lovingly own every other nation, and all nations together will nourish every nation—everyone and every nation in the world will enjoy Heaven on Earth.

1989—Fifteenth Year of Maharishi's Age of Enlightenment

Appendix E

A Glimpse of Maharishi's Achievements
1957–2008 Continuing

His Holiness Maharishi Mahesh Yogi, founder of the Transcendental Meditation program and the worldwide Spiritual Regeneration Movement (1957)[1]

- Introduced research in the field of consciousness and brought to light seven states of consciousness (1957–1967);
- Inaugurated the World Plan with seven goals: (1) To develop the full potential of the individual; (2) To improve governmental achievements; (3) To realize the highest ideal of education; (4) To solve the problems of crime, drug abuse, and all behavior that brings unhappiness to the family of man; (5) To maximize the intelligent use of the environment; (6) To bring fulfillment to the economic aspirations of the individual and society; (7) To achieve the spiritual goals of mankind in this generation (1972);
- Created a new science — the Science of Creative Intelligence® — and trained 2,000 teachers of this science (1972) [and many thousands more have been trained and continue to be trained];
- Discovered the Constitution of the Universe — the lively potential of Natural Law — in Ṛk Veda, and discovered the structuring dynamics of Ṛk in the entire Vedic Literature (1975);
- Celebrated the Dawn of the Age of Enlightenment on the basis of the discovery of the *Maharishi Effect* (1975);
- Created a World Government for the Age of Enlightenment with its sovereignty in the domain of consciousness and authority in the invincible power of Natural Law (1976);

1. See footnote on p. 35.

- Introduced the Transcendental Meditation Sidhi program and the experience of bubbling bliss in Yogic Flying to create supreme mind-body coordination in the individual and coherence in world consciousness (1976);
- Formulated his Absolute Theories of Government, Education, Health, and Defense to raise every area of life to perfection (1977);
- Brought to light the commentary of Ṛk Veda, *Apaurusheya Bhāshya*, as the self-generating, self-perpetuating structure of consciousness (1980);
- Organized the centuries-old scattered Vedic Literature as the literature of a perfect science — Maharishi Vedic Science and Technology (1981);
- Brought to light the full potential of Āyur-Veda, Gandharva Veda, Dhanur-Veda, Sthāpatya Veda, and Jyotish to create a disease-free and problem-free family of nations (1985);
- Formulated the Master Plan to Create Heaven on Earth for the reconstruction of the whole world, inner and outer (1988);
- Brought to light Supreme Political Science, introduced automation in administration, and inspired the formation of a new political party, the Natural Law Party, in countries throughout the world (1992);
- Inaugurated Global *Rām Rāj* — Global Administration through Natural Law[SM]; established Maharishi Vedic Universities and Maharishi Ayur-Veda Universities throughout the world to offer mastery over Natural Law to every individual, and to perpetuate life in accordance with Natural Law — perfection in every profession — and create Natural Law-Based problem-free government in every country — governments with the ability to prevent problems; inspired the discovery of the Veda and Vedic Literature in the human physiology, which established the grand unity of all material diversity of creation, of all sciences and of all religions (1993–1995);
- Trained teachers of his universities, colleges, and schools to impart Total Knowledge to every student, to create the dawn of a new awakening in the world (1996);
- Provided Global Administration through Natural Law, offering new principles and new programs to enrich national law in all countries with the nourishing influence of Natural Law (1997);

- Established Maharishi Veda Vision^SM — the Maharishi Channel — to bring the timeless knowledge of Natural Law to every home, with a formula to bring perfection to every man on the basis of the eternal Constitution of the Universe — the Veda and Vedic Literature (1998–1999);
- Introduced his Program to Eliminate Poverty in the world through the development of unused agricultural lands, using healthy Vedic and organic farming principles and practices (2000);
- Founded the Global Country of World Peace under the rulership of Maharaja Adhiraj Rajaraam,[2] to unite all nations in a peaceful global unity (2000);
- Designed programs to create a permanent influence of world peace from one country — India — through the performance of Yoga and Yagya by thousands of Maharishi Vedic Pandits (2001);
- Designed the Raam Mudra development currency to create a balanced world economy; began to offer prevention-oriented solutions to the world through a continuum of weekly press conferences that were to continue for six years (2002);
- Launched a global initiative to build Peace Palaces in the 3,000 largest cities of the world, *"to perpetuate the knowledge that has proven itself to be complete knowledge of the nature of man"* (2003–2004);
- Inaugurated the Dawn of *Sat-Yuga* — the dawn of civilization based on pure knowledge and the infinite organizing power of Natural Law, where no one will suffer; all will enjoy the eternal glory of God — Heaven on Earth (2005);
- Began to raise whole nations to Invincibility and opened the gateway for the reconstruction of the whole world through Total Knowledge-Based programs in the areas of Education, Health, Agriculture, Science and Technology, Administration, Business and Industry, Defense, Law and Justice, Culture and Religion, Art and Music, and Architecture (city and country planning in harmony with Natural Law) (2006);
- Formulated a seven-point program to crown every nation with Invincibility — (1) Establish large groups of Maharishi Vedic Pandits and Yogic

---

[2] The Global Country of World Peace continues to guide the expansion of Maharishi's programs around the world, to bring enlightenment to every individual and invincibility to every nation.

flyers in every country; (2) Provide prevention-oriented, problem-free Administration; (3) Construct Maharishi Vedic Medical Colleges in every country to create a disease-free society; (4) Construct universities, colleges, and schools that offer total knowledge of Natural Law; (5) Produce healthy food for happy life through Maharishi Vedic Organic Agriculture; (6) Design cities and countries according to the principles of Maharishi Vedic Architecture in harmony with Natural Law; (7) Eliminate poverty in the world. Having done complete justice to the teachings of Shri Guru Dev[3] for over fifty years, which has secured the possibility of Invincibility for every nation, Maharishi inaugurated Administration through Silence, which will forever guide the destiny of the world through the Total Knowledge-Based principles of the Vedic Tradition of Masters (2007).

- On January 12, 2008, Maharishi inaugurated the Year of Invincibility — Global Raam Raj — celebrating the success of 50 years of his worldwide movement active in over 100 countries to date.

Maharishi's global plan for the spiritual regeneration of the whole human race is the greatest fortune of the world for all time. It is bringing day by day, the rising sunshine of *Sat-Yuga*. Maharishi has given the gift of enlightenment to millions of people and trained thousands to keep this bright light of Total Knowledge shining for generations to come. Maharishi's gift to the world, to all mankind, is the perpetual light of Total Knowledge fully awake in every heart and home. Maharishi's achievements will continue to unfold, and through the Grace of Guru Dev we will continue to celebrate every year and year after year and generation after generation Maharishi's achievements, as the evolving trends of time bring forth the full sunshine of Heaven on Earth — Raam Raj.

---

3 Maharishi's teacher, His Divinity Brahmananda Saraswati, Jagadguru Bhagavan Shankaracharya of Jyotir Math, Badrikashram, Himalayas, revered embodiment of Vedic Wisdom in the great Tradition of Vedic Masters who have passed down the eternal wisdom of integration of life from teacher to student since time immemorial.

Appendix F

Maharishi's Books

Enlightenment for Everyone and Every Nation

The Literature on Natural Law That Offers Freedom from Problems in Every Field of Life — the Guiding Light of Today's World and the World of Every Tomorrow for All Time

Science of Being and Art of Living —
Transcendental Meditation (452 pages)
[In Maharishi's own words] (First published in 1963)

Love and God (54 pages)
[In Maharishi's own words] (First published in 1965)

Maharishi Mahesh Yogi on the Bhagavad-Gītā
A New Translation and Commentary (Chapters 1–6) (543 pages)
[In Maharishi's own words] (First published in 1967)

Transcendental Meditation *with Questions and Answers* (158 pages)
[In Maharishi's own words] (First published in 1967)

Maharishi's Supreme Offer to the World, to Every Individual and to Every Nation
Enlightenment and Invincibility (678 pages)
[Excerpts of Maharishi's own words] (First published in 1978)

His Holiness Maharishi Mahesh Yogi
Fifty Years Around the World, Dawn of the Age of Enlightenment
Volume One, 1957–1964 (648 pages) (in press)
[Excerpts of Maharishi's own words]
(Volume One first published in 1985, as *His Holiness Maharishi Mahesh Yogi — Thirty Years Around the World, Dawn of the Age of Enlightenment*)

Maharishi's Master Plan to Create Heaven on Earth
Overview (372 pages)
[Excerpts of Maharishi's own words]
(First published in 1991)

Rām, Rāmāyaṇ, Rām Leelā, Rām Rāj (346 pages)
[In Maharishi's own words]
(First published in 1992)

Maharishi Vedic University, Introduction
Vedic Knowledge for Everyone (362 pages)
[In Maharishi's own words]
(First published in 1994)

Human Physiology — Expression of Veda and the Vedic Literature:
Modern Science and Ancient Vedic Science Discover the Fabrics of Immortality in the Human Physiology (610 pages)
by Professor Tony Nader, MD, PhD, MARR
(First published in 1994)

Maharishi's Absolute Theory of Government
Automation in Administration (565 pages)
[In Maharishi's own words]
(First published in 1995)

Maharishi Forum of Natural Law and National Law for Doctors
Perfect Health for Everyone — Disease-Free Society (480 pages)
[In Maharishi's own words]
(First published in 1995)

Maharishi University of Management
Wholeness on the Move (352 pages)
[In Maharishi's own words]
(First published in 1995)

Constitution of India Fulfilled through Maharishi's
Transcendental Meditation (370 pages)
[In Maharishi's own words]
(First published in 1996)

Maharishi's Absolute Theory of Defence
Sovereignty in Invincibility (668 pages)
[In Maharishi's own words]
(First published in 1996)

Maharishi Speaks to Educators
Mastery Over Natural Law (Volumes I–IV: 902 pages)
[Maharishi with faculty of Maharishi Vedic University]
(First published in 1996)

Inaugurating Maharishi Vedic University (258 pages)
[Excerpts of Maharishi's own words]
(First published in 1996)

Celebrating Perfection in Education
Dawn of Total Knowledge (196 pages)
[In Maharishi's own words]
(First published in 1997)

Maharishi Speaks to Students
Mastery Over Natural Law (Volumes I–IV: 978 pages)
[Maharishi with faculty of Maharishi Vedic University]
(First published in 1997)

Celebrating Perfection in Administration
Creating Invincible India (418 pages)
[In Maharishi's own words]
(First published in 1998)

Ideal India: The Lighthouse of Peace on Earth (536 pages)
[Excerpts of Maharishi's own words]
(First published in 2001)

Bhagavad-Gītā Chapters 1–6, In the Light of Maharishi's Transcendental Meditation *Scientific Research Results* (320 pages)
[Excerpts of Maharishi's own words] (First published in 2004)

Raam Raj
Global Administration through Natural Law, the Light of God (414 pages)
[Excerpts of Maharishi's own words]
(First published in 2008) (in press)

Rāmāyaṇ in Human Physiology
Discovery of the Eternal Reality of the Rāmāyaṇ in the Structure and Function of Human Physiology (425 pages)
By Professor Tony Nader, MD, PhD, MARR
(First published in 2012)

Scientific Research on the *Transcendental Meditation* and
TM-Sidhi Programme: Collected Papers (Volumes 1–8)
(over 6,000 pages) *[Forewords by Maharishi]*
(Volume 1 published in 1977; Volume 8 published in 2020)

All these publications are the waves in the ocean of knowledge. All this knowledge offers to open the gate to perfection in life. The message is that the individual is essentially Cosmic, and all that is to be known anywhere in the universe is encoded in the DNA of every cell in the human physiology.

This means that all the knowledge, all the intelligence, all the organizing power displayed in the whole creation is available to the individual within his own mind and body.

Maharishi Vedic Science and Technology of Consciousness is the natural and effortless means for every individual to unfold his Cosmic Potential and enjoy greater success and fulfillment in life.

To order these and additional books, CDs, and DVDs, please contact:

Maharishi International University Press, Fairfield, IA, USA 52557
Tel: (800) 831-6523 *From outside USA:* +1-641-472-1101
Email: miupress@miu.edu Website: miupress.shop

Maharishi AyurVeda Products, The Netherlands
Tel: +31-475-529111 Fax: +31-475-404055
Email: map@ayurveda.eu Website: ayurveda.eu

For India:
Email: vvprakashan@gmail.com Website: vvprakashan.com

Bhopal office — Maharishi Ved Vigyan Prakashan
Bhojpur Mandir Marg, Village-Chhan, Post-Misrod,
Bhopal, Madhya Pradesh 462047
Tel: +91-755-663-0100 Fax: +91-755-408-7311

New Delhi office — Flat No. 806, 8th Floor, Mercantile House,
15 Kasturba Gandhi Marg, Connaught Place, New Delhi 110001
Tel: +91-11-4302-9315

Translations of *Science of Being and Art of Living* are available in the countries of these language groups: Chinese, Dutch, Estonian, French, German, Italian, Nepalese, Norwegian, Portuguese, Russian, Spanish, Swedish, and Turkish.

Index

Absolute
  Absolute remains, 14
  Being's status as, 22
  cannot do anything, 269
  Cosmic Law disallows change in, 12
  ego, intellect, mind, senses supplemented by, 61–62, 68
  eternal bliss of, 86
  in every branch of study, 205–7, 216
  experience of, 17, 27, 37, 111, 290–91
  man projects, 49–50
  mind becomes, 111
  nothing exists without, 269
  ocean of wisdom of, 21
  senses on level of, 108–10
  source of all intelligence, 4
  transcendental nature of, 68–69
  unbounded and eternal, 8–9
  unmanifest, 268, 296
  See also Being
Absolute and relative
  Absolute assumes role of relativity, 18
  absolute bliss with relative joys, 45, 63, 245
  Absolute dances in relative, 246, 249
  Absolute is reality of all phases, 17
  Being glorifies *Karma*, 26–27
  Being is same yet different, 45–46
  Cosmic Law maintains, 10–13, 54
  cosmic *Prāṇa* assumes role of breathing, 92–96
  eternity pervades every moment, 246
  God Consciousness brings together, 245–46
  H_2O example of, 11, 14, 46
  health as coordination of, 181–82
  individual is, 80–81, 181–82
  living, 38–39
  man and surroundings are, 181–82
  ocean analogy for, 8, 13
  oneness and diversity, 13–15
  study of Absolute uplifts relative, 207
  Upanishads on, 15–16
  See also Being; relative life
academy of meditation, 301–3
accident
  collective calamity, 240–41
  to err is human, 255–56
  freedom from misfortune and, 300
  scientific findings by, 216
achievement
  capture-the-fort analogy, 84–85
  easy for everyone, 131
  of economic abundance, 210–11
  essential nature of mind for, 37
  full perception and full, 108–9
  hard work without, 152
  leaders with only partial, 76

least strain and maximum gain, 142
past *Karma* influencing, 70, 167–68
playing our part in evolution, 126
practical formula for, in speech, 136
selfish desires need great effort for, 126
ultimate, in history of physical science, 15
via concentration, 152
via strong thought force, 152n53
action
  cosmic life energy supporting, 155–57
  cycle of experience-impression-desire, 21, 94–98
  doing all good by being all good, 123–25
  far-reaching influence of, 35
  five organs of, 6, 108–11
  fixity of purpose, 162–64
  without harm, 164–65
  householders' path of, 194, 285, 294, 297
  innocent, 297–98, 297n17
  in least time, 145–46
  less effective, 141–42
  main points for art of, 144
  maximum results from, 165–68
  omnipresence of Being in, 6
  only useful, 147–48
  planning of, 172–73
  quality of doer determines quality of, 142–43
  ranges between all limits of time, space, and causation, 122
  selfish, requires great effort, 126
  taxing, boring, joyless, 169–71
  thought force behind, 61, 149–53, 152n53, 155
  See also Karma; skill in action
action-reaction, 57–58
  action's far-reaching influence, 35
  blood affinity and rebirth from, 117–19
  equal and inevitable, 71–72
  everything influences every other thing, 55–56
  of hatred, 72, 223–24, 240–41
  satellite example, 55
  stone-thrown-in-pond analogy, 34, 54, 117
  suffering resulting from, 223–24
  time duration between, 118
  as you sow so shall you reap, 72, 117, 119
  See also Karma
activity
  Absolute cannot do anything, 269
  activating deepest level of senses, 111
  balanced, 105–7
  easy and natural, to culture Being, 37–38, 100, 169
  fatigue from, 104–7, 192, 218, 291, 293–94
  God-Realization from nervous system's specific, 289–90
  mental and corresponding physical, 276, 292
  nervous system's, 192–96
  pure consciousness brought into, 128
  state neither active nor passive, 191
  stimulating any stratum for any advantage, 261
  unregulated habits of, 107
  waves reaching every strata, 55
adversity, 76–77
advice
  giving, 223
  parental, 225–29
Age of Enlightenment, xiv
air
  drawing life energy from, 156
  need good, 104, 294
  smog, 104n22
alcoholic beverages, 104, 154, 293
All this is That, 16, 266, 282
Alliata di Montereale, Giovanni Francesco, 259–60

INDEX

analogies and examples
  boil on skin, 183
  bow and arrow, 26, 68, 129, 190
  bubble of thought, 30–32, 91
  building without foundation, 4
  business
    gains and losses, 168
    investing fully, 62
    owner, 7
  butter permeates milk, 271
  calf finds mother, 119
  candlelight, 26
  capture the fort, 84–85
  castles built in air, 86
  cell and body, 54, 58
  child
    burning coal in hand of, 216, 226
    love for toys, 247
  cloth-dyeing, 38
  coconut husk, 47
  colored glasses, 178
  corpse, 251
  dirty room, 177–78
  diving, 50, 143, 260–61, 265
  dog
    at door, 153
    reciprocal love with, 73
    white teeth of rotting, 225
  family man, 163–64
  father and child
    concentrated love, 247
    father's love, 163–64, 214
    give-and-take between, 71
    social scientist like elderly father, 214
  flower arrangement, 61
  football, 63, 169
  full investment, 62
  H_2O, 11, 14, 46, 269, 281
  honeybee, 150
  husband and wife, 247
  individual sprouting from universal, 93–94
  judge's robe, 46
  Karma and posted letter, 117–27, 117n30
  king, 86, 150, 236, 284
  leaf
    recognition of more water, 39
    in wind, 4
    withering, 183
  lightbulb, 6, 295
  line drawn on stone, 98
  master and servant, 188
  millionaire
    begging in street, 50
    potential of, 78
    son of, 78, 82
  mind
    as root, 186
    thought bubble, 30–32, 91
    wandering, king not monkey, 150
    as waves in ocean, 19
  monkey, 150
  mother
    joy of, 286–87
    joyful *versus* burdensome, 170
    as Nature's almighty power, 80
    as Nature's kindness, 79
  mother and child
    Being and thought are like, 88
    child ignored, 134
    concentrated love for mother, 247
    God and devotee become one, 286–89
    mother's love saturates, 170
    mother's tolerance toward, 175–76
    path to God like mother's joy, 286–87
    rebellion against mother, 79
    reciprocity between, 71
    serving and respecting mother, 134
  ocean
    Absolute and relative as one, 8, 13
    Being *versus* watery, 8
    consciousness as, 30–32
    of divine wisdom, 246

analogies and examples (cont.)
    lover of God in, of His love, 286–87
    mind as wave of, 19
    omnipresent, of consciousness, 53
    of Oneness, 287
    pond *versus*, 263
    rising in wave, 81n14
    surface communicates with depths, 33
    time and tide wait for no man, 146
    of wisdom of Absolute, 21
    wrong action as drop in, of virtue, 72–73
oil permeates seed, 271
pond
    ocean *versus*, 263
    stone thrown in, 34, 54, 117
positive thinking "I am a king," 86, 236, 284
posted letter, 118–19
rose and thorn, 70
rubber ball, 118
saccharin, 97–98, 108
sandcastle, 76
sap
    as basis, 10, 46–47, 100
    failing to reach surface, 100–1
    tree, 61–62
satellites, 55
seed
    cycle of tree and, 19–20, 93–94
    pattern of expression within, 93–94
ship without rudder, 4
stone
    atomic energy of, 35
    thrown in pond, 34, 54, 117
submission to expert doctor, 79
Sun reflected in glass of water, 195–96
sunlight, 26
thief, 147
thought like a bubble, 30–32, 91

tree
    cycle of seed and, 19–20, 93–94
    individual sprouting from universal, 93–94
    knowledge of unseen root, xii
    leaf's recognition of water, 39
    mind as root of, 186
    perishable and imperishable nature of, 280
    sap of, 10, 46–47, 61–62, 100
    seed and, 19–20, 93–94
    water the root, 38–39, 76, 186, 241
    withering leaves, 183
water
    H_2O, 11, 14, 46, 269, 281
    diving, 50, 143, 260–61, 265
    the root, 38–39, 76, 186, 241
    stone thrown in, 34, 54, 117
    surface ripples in all directions, 34
wave
    of mind, 19
    mightier from deeper level, 33, 66–67
    individual and cosmic, 54, 77, 230
    influence on pond, 117
    ocean in a, 155
    tidal, in ocean of bliss, 246
    of love, 287
wealth
    businessman investing full, 62
    give-and-take between father and son, 71
    millionaire's, 50, 78, 82
    plentiful, 169
    power that comes with, 82
    quality of, 56–57
    stealing, 147
    that helps society, 56
    thief analogy, 147
    world as God's garden, 225
Ānanda, 4n1, 16

ancients
  Charak and Sushrut, 240
  Hatha Yoga, 291, 291n16
  psychology of, 262–63, 262n5
angels, 224, 249, 273
anger, suffering resulting from, 223–24
animals
  dog-at-door analogy, 153
  humans different from, 52–53, 55, 258
  rotting-dog-with-white-teeth anecdote, 225
  on scale of evolution, 273
  shrink from death, 52
annihilation
  of everything else in light of love of God, 288
  object's, of subject, 231–32
  prospect of world war and, 17, 180
Arjuna, 263
art of action
  ability to perform right action, 159–61
  action without harm, 164–65
  conserving mental energy, 153–54
  coordination of mind and nervous system, 154–55
  do less and accomplish more, 142
  effective execution of plan, 173–74
  favorable surroundings and circumstances, 157–58
  fixity of purpose, 162–64
  joyful, and not tedious, tiring, boring, 169–71
  with least energy, 144–45
  least strain and maximum gain, 142
  in least time, 145–46
  life energy sufficient for task, 155–57
  main points of, 144
  only useful action, 147–48
  planning, 171–73
  to produce most effective results, 148–62
  saturation in Bliss Consciousness is, 142–44
  self-confidence and, 161–62
  strong thought force, 61, 149–53, 152n53, 155
  to yield maximum results, 165–68
art of behavior
  Bliss Consciousness as basis of, 175–76
  brings satisfaction to both parties, 174–75
  See also art of action
art of Being
  art of action underlaid by, 141–44
  behavior and, 98–100
  body and, 112–13, 112n25
  breathing and, 92–96
  experiencing and, 96–98
  fulfillment through, 87–90
  good manners lie in, 179–80
  health and, 100–1
  inner fullness irrespective of surroundings, 116
  Karma-and-posted-letter analogy, 117–27, 117n30
  mind and, 101–7
  nervous system and, 113–16
  places life in harmony and intelligence, 179–80
  senses and, 108–11
  speaking and, 90–92
  thinking and, 88–90
  See also Being
art of living
  almighty power of Nature and, 77–86
  entire field of life accounted in, 143–44
  full human potential used in, 65–69
  glorifies full range of subject-object, 61, 161
  is applied science of Being, xii–xiii
  key to, 61–63
  makes full use of surroundings, 69–77
  means using full human potential, 63–65
  student of philosophy mastering, 264–67

art of speaking
  free from binding influence, 141
  harmoniously, 138–39
  with minimum energy, 134–36
  pleasingly, 139–40
  powerfully, 140
  practical formula in, 136
  rightly, 137–38, 140
  usefully, 140
  See also speaking
art of thinking
  aims of, 127–29
  art of speech emanating from, 136–37, 140
  powerful thoughts cherished by Nature, 132–33
  right thought, 130–31
  thought as means to liberate thinker, 133–34
  useful and creative thought, 131–32
  See also thinking
ascetic practices, 152
aspirant
  Being available to every, 33
  devoid of intellectual play or emotional twist, 80–81
  householder, 194, 285, 294, 297
  light of Self brightens material life, 237
  as obedient servant of Divine, 75
  reclusive, 152, 284, 294
  recognizes meditation's influence, 39
  seekers of truth, xii, 266–67
  spiritual paths for, 277–78
  union of God and, 286–89
  works out own destiny, 57
aspirations
  control is science's, 216
  of man, 146
  teaching in terms of people's, 302
atmosphere
  contamination of, 240–41
  health of, 196–99
  influence of wrong action on, 230

living Being influences, 200–5
  people's influence on, 55–56
  quietness of transcending *versus* quietness of, 199
  speech in keeping with, 138
  state of mind turns and shapes, 178
  for us to use, 178–79
  wealth which helps society and, 56
atom
  energy from, 35
  as finer layer of creation, 4–5
  immature minds and, 216
automatic nature
  of machinery produces ideal product, 172–73
  perception is mechanical and automatic, 295–96
  Transcendental Meditation's, 33
  See also mechanical path

balance
  in activity, 105–7
  Bliss Consciousness creates, 103–4, 107
  bow-and-arrow analogy, 26, 68, 129, 190
  crime results from imbalance, 217
  fixity of purpose tempered with, 164
  of Nature, 240–41
be still and know that I am God, 296
behavior
  artificiality in, 213
  Bliss Consciousness as basis of, 175–76
  fundamental of, 174–75
  of good family, 176
  indifference as weapon against negativity, 179
  innocence of, 99–100, 166–67, 179, 300
  loving heart as basis of, 73–74
  in natural flow of evolution, 99–100
  natural *versus* artificial, 171
  perseverance despite negativity, 168
  tolerance of ill-feeling toward us, 179

INDEX 399

when meeting, 174–75
See also action; right action
Being
  atmosphere influenced by humans living, 200–5
  at basis of and juncture of dream state, 114, 115
  as basis of intellect, 7, 270
  Bliss Consciousness is nature of, 4, 6
  breathing is nature of cosmic, 92–96
  conscious mind and, 37, 39, 89–90, 102–3, 115n27, 261
  beyond contemplation, 270
  Cosmic Law and, 13–15, 191
  creating is nature of, 269
  creative intelligence of, 3–4, 10–13, 19–23
  easy and natural activity to culture, 37–38, 100, 169
  ego basis is, 7, 47
  embodied in relative life, 38–39, 66–69, 112, 186, 249
  every aspirant can arrive at, 33
  beyond everything, 29, 270
  experience of, more concrete than relative experience, 17
  experience throws, out of awareness, 96–98
  experiencing, xi–xii, 17, 29–30, 37, 40–41, 96–98, 269, 290
  beyond faith, 270
  beyond feelings, 29
  freedom of eternal, 4, 40, 103–4, 126–27
  gets enlivened and vibrates in surroundings, 198–99, 198n72
  glorifies *Karma*, 26–27
  imperishability of, 15–17, 103, 124
  infusion is silent process, 39
  infusion of, 6, 39, 103–4, 108–13, 126–27
  innocence of, 18
  is Absolute and relative, 13–15, 16, 22, 53, 185, 191
  is Brahman, 15–16
  is diversity and oneness, 13–15
  is knowingness itself, 270
  is pure consciousness, 8, 12, 124
  is same yet different, 45–46
  is source of all time, space, and causation, 16
  is thought, thinker, and *Prāṇa*, 269
  is transcendental, 7–8, 17, 21–22
  Karma and, in process of creation, 19–23
  Karma brought to level of, 127
  beyond knowing, 270
  on level of body, 51–52
  lies out of realm of time, space, and causation, 8
  life is, 3–5, 8–9
  light of, 25–26
  as living presence of God, 4, 6
  located between states of consciousness, 115n27
  beyond mind, 270
  mind becomes, 37–38
  mind in constant communion with, 62
  misunderstanding about maintaining, 90
  mother-and-child analogy, 88
  omnipresence of, 6–8, 16, 270
  permanently on level of nervous system, 113–16
  Prāṇa and, 17–19, 92–93, 269
  pure consciousness radiates from center of, 6, 295–96
  retained during deep sleep, 40, 78, 102, 114, 234
  retained during dreaming, 234
  sap analogies, 10, 46–47, 100
  Self is, of everyone, 16, 278n13
  senses infused with, 108–10
  shortcut for living, 38–39, 172, 180, 236
  skill in action from level of, 25–26, 126, 142–43

400   SCIENCE OF BEING AND ART OF LIVING

speaking arises from, 90–92
at subtlest state before dream state, 115n27
thought sprouts from, and evolves into action, 94
beyond time, 4, 124
waking state retains, 234
as waking state's basis and junctures, 114, 115
water-the-root analogies, 38–39, 76, 186, 241
See also art of Being; science of Being; Transcendental Meditation
Bhagavad-Gītā
  on imperishable Being, 15–17
  Karma Yoga in, 297n17
  psychological teachings in, 262–63, 262n5
  Transcendental Meditation in, 262–63
birth-and-death cycle, 24, 97–98, 118–19
bliss
  of Absolute, 86
  of Being glorifies *Karma*, 26–27
  decreases as we proceed outward, 295–96
  field of action filled with, 171
  life is stream of, 45
Bliss Consciousness
  Ānanda, 4n1, 16
  as antidote to bondage, 142–44
  in art of behavior, 175–76
  balance created by, 103–4, 107
  Being's essential nature is, 4, 6
  circumstances not losing, 87–88, 97
  conscious mind transformed by, 25–26
  contentment from, 239
  cultivates only useful thoughts, 131–32, 140
  experience of, 53
  helps society on all levels, 98–100
  life's purpose is, 48, 49, 126
  misunderstanding about *Karma* and, 24–27

  nothing can challenge validity of, 152
  radiates from Being, 6, 295–96
  relative joys hand in hand with, 63, 245
  relative joys with Absolute, 45, 63, 245
  saccharin analogy, 97–98, 108
  Sat-Chid-Ānanda, 4n1
  senses receive full contentment in, 108–10
  as source of all yet out of relative existence, 3–4
  steady concentration from, 152, 152n53
  surroundings of full use to him in, 75
  virtue flourishes in, 262
  world peace basis is, 237–38
  See also Cosmic Consciousness
blood relations, 117–19
boat of love, rowing, 288
body
  art of Being and, 112–13, 112n25
  atmosphere cannot attain same quietness as, 199
  Being on level of, 51–52
  cell and, analogy, 54, 58
  coconut-husk analogy for, 47
  creation of, 21
  daily rest and silence for, 190n70
  defined, 190
  as end organ of nervous system, 184
  exercises to accelerate progress, 299
  fatigued, 104–7, 192, 218, 291, 293–94
  Hatha Yoga, 291, 291n16
  human boundaries extend beyond, 25, 58, 65, 77
  intimate and inseparable connection with Universe, 48, 53–58
  mind as fountainhead of, 95, 97, 185–86
  in psycho-physiological path, 278

reflects mental state, 187–89
in seven points of health, 181–82
trained to be still yet not passive, 292
See also mind/body coordination; nervous system
boil analogy, 183
bondage
  action that liberates is skill in action, 161
  Bliss Consciousness as antidote to, 142–44
  experience throws Being out of awareness, 96–98
  Karma with regard to, 124–27
  loss of direct path to liberation, 231
  misunderstanding about, 232–35
  as object identification, 96–98
  past life gives identity to present, 20
  subject overshadowed by object, 231–32
  thinking that leaves mind free from, 128–29
  thought as means of liberation from, 133–34
  thought by its very nature causes, 233
  to time, 146
  Transcendental Meditation and freedom from, 230–31
  See also identification
boredom, 169–71
bow-and-arrow analogy, 26, 68, 129, 190
Brahman, 15–16
Brahmananda Saraswati, xiii, 80, 266–67
brain
  awake in itself, 291–92
  cherishes state of pure consciousness, 293–94
  contamination, 293–94
  developed, 53, 292
  mental activity and, 276, 292
  purity, 292–93

states of consciousness and, 290–92
Transcendental Consciousness setup for, 290–91
breathing
  exercises to accelerate progress, 299
  Hatha Yoga, 291, 291n16
  improper air, 104, 104n22
  as impulse of eternal life, 249
  as nature of cosmic Being, 92–96
  restful alertness influences, 191–96
  softer, 189–95
  systematic refinement of, 196
  unnatural slowing of, 194
  See also Prāṇa
bubble-of-thought analogy 30–32, 91
Buddhist, 255–56
buildings
  attractive or repulsive houses, 56
  cities, 302–3
  without-foundation analogy, 4, 67
  to preserve spirit of message, 303–4
business
  full-investment-in analogy, 62
  gains overshadow losses, 168
  morality of how wealth is earned, 56–57
  owner-of analogy, 7
  quality of doer determines quality of action, 142–43
  timing for speaking, 138
  wealth that helps society, 56
  See also resources
butter-permeates-milk analogy, 271

calf-finds-mother analogy, 119
candlelight analogy, 26
capture-the-fort analogy, 84–85
castles, in-air-or-sand, analogies, 76, 86
cell-and-body analogy, 54, 58
Charak, 240
charity
  to alleviate past *Karma*, 168
  great acts of, 184–85, 229
  ill quality of wealth counteracted by, 57
  See also forgiveness

child-with-burning-coal analogy, 216, 226
children
    action-reaction in rearing, 223–24
    concentrated love for mother, 247
    delinquent, 227–28
    devoid of discipline, 225–28
    father's love for, 163–64, 214
    fear of God instilled in, 251, 255, 271–72
    ignored in infancy, 134
    innocence of, 55, 57, 215, 247
    knowing right from wrong, 160
    love-for-toys analogy, 247
    mother's love saturates, 170
    mother's tolerance toward, 175–76
    nourishing of, 227
    path to God like mother's joy in, 286–87
    rebellion against mother, 79
    resenting advice, 226–27
    serving and respecting mother, 134
    understanding their faith, 228
    See also mother-and-child analogies
cities, 302–3
civilization
    crime, 217
    crops flourishing, 240
    dignified and moderate expression of feelings, 228
    human potential for, xiv, 259–60
    laws derived from Nature's laws, 159
    laws for guidance, 120
    manners, 139–40, 174–76, 179–80
    rehabilitation issue, 217
    See also government; modern age
cloth-dyeing analogy, 38
coconut analogy, 47
cold war, 241
collective calamity, 240–41
colored-glasses analogy, 178
compassion, 72
concentration
    fixity of purpose, 162–64

    on gross surface values, 6–7
    practices of, 84–85, 153
    of thought force, 61, 149–53, 152n53, 155
    to yield maximum results, 165–68
confidence, 145–46, 161–62, 239
    grounded in own religion, 221
confusion, 88, 121
    about eternal freedom, 235
    master-and-servant analogy, 188
    See also misunderstanding
conscious mind
    ability to cognize universe, 266
    advantages of Being coming to level of, 102–3
    arrives systematically at source, 29, 115n27
    becomes one hundred percent Being, 37, 89
    Being comes within range of, 261
    Bliss Consciousness transforms, 103–4, 107
    cherishes thought of Being, 89–90
    conscious of thought at its origin, 132–33
    destiny improved by raising standard of, 168
    expansion of, 32, 33, 188
    fathoms deeper level of thought process, 102
    fatigue mars cognizing subtle states, 293–94
    full potential of, 63–65
    increased capacity of, 33
    infusion of Being as silent process, 39
    is vibrating consciousness, 185–86
    Karma is based on, 124
    levels of, 31
    ocean as range of, 30–32
    of ordinary man, 50, 111
    range of, 30–32
    reaches state of pure consciousness, 4

INDEX

recognizing meditation's influence, 39
strong steady mind through expansion of, 188
surface communicates with deeper levels, 33
transcendental Being located between thoughts, 115n27
transformed by Bliss Consciousness, 25–26
unfolding latent faculties of, 261
See also Bliss Consciousness; intellect; mind; psychology

consciousness
to determine right and wrong, 222–23
economic, 305
elevated by friends and parents, 258
feelings and purity of, 222
forgiveness through enlarged, 76–77
gradually fainter shifting into sleep state, 292
mass, 304–6
mind is vibrating, 185–86
ocean analogy, 30–32
omnipresent ocean of, 53
political, 304–5
projects itself to world, 295
radiates from center of pure Being, 6, 295–96
Sat-Chid-Ānanda, 4n1,16
Self never lost, 245
of time, 306
See also Bliss Consciousness; conscious mind; Cosmic Consciousness; God Consciousness; pure consciousness; states of consciousness; Transcendental Consciousness

contemplation
Being is beyond, 270
of creation's perishable nature, 279–81
extensive time for, 284–85
continental centers, 301–2

control
Hatha Yoga, 291, 291n16
mind, 84–85, 130–31, 153, 299
science aspiration to, 216
of surroundings, 69–72, 165–68, 263
switchboard of Laws of Nature, 78
of wandering mind, 149–53, 152n53
corpse analogy, 251
Cosmic Consciousness
alternation of transcending and activity cultures, 37–38
criterion of right and wrong in, 160
devotion to God in, 246–48
Father in Heaven and man on Earth united, 248
giving from level of, 75–77
integrated life fulfilled in, 246
Laws of Nature and, 75
millionaire-son's-use-of-wealth analogy, 82
as normal human status, 51–53
one word reveals inner quality, 137
overshadowed by selfishness, 126, 222, 249
projects all values of Absolute, 49–50
selfishness in, 249
See also freedom; God Consciousness; man; individual
Cosmic Law
Absolute and relative maintained by, 13
action attuned with, 147–48
Being as plane of, 10–13, 54
conformity with, 99
disallows Being to change, 12
disharmony in Nature from non-attunement with, 197–98
H_2O example of, 11
individual mind tuned with, 261–62
pure consciousness is plane of, 123
teachers established in, 301
Cosmic Life
Cosmic Law is rule of procedure of, 10
individual as basic unit of, 48, 53–54

speech to draw out purpose of, 249
  See also Being; life
creation *(noun)*
  atomic level of, 4–5, 35, 216
  cycles of, 273
  mastery of, 261
  perishable nature of, 279–81
  progressive scale of, 272–73
  purpose of, 18
  top level of, 248, 273
creation *(verb)*
  Being and *Karma* in process of, 19–23
  of body, 21
  creative thoughts, 131–32
  nature of Being is, 269
  Prāṇa in process of, 19–23
  of senses, 7, 21
  of subject-object, 17–18
  subtle mechanics of, 21
  surroundings are one's own, 69–72
  unintentional and intentional, 70
  creation-evolution-dissolution cycle, 11, 20
  God maintains, 273–74
  wheel of *Karma* and, 22, 24
creative intelligence
  Being's nature of, 3–4, 10–13, 19–23
  in man, 32, 40–41, 103, 135, 142, 241, 260
creativity
  Absolute wants to be creative, 18
  Being's relationship to creative intelligence, 3–4, 10–13, 19–23
  creative thoughts, 131–32
  different at different levels of creation, 45–46
  life is stream of, 45
  tension and, 50
  useful and creative thinking, 131–32
crime, 217
crops, 240
cruelty, 223
culture, traditional, 159, 227–28

cycle
  action-impression-desire, 21, 94–98
  birth and death, 24, 97–98, 118–19
  creation, 273
  creation-evolution-dissolution, 11, 20, 22, 24, 273–74
  creation-maintenance-dissolution, 273
  day and night, 20
  existence and nonexistence, 22
  seed and tree, 19–20, 93–94
day-and-night cycle, 20
daydreaming, 131
death
  animals and man shrink from, 52
  as ceasing of experience, 234
  cycle of birth and, 24, 97–98, 118–19
deep-sleep state
  Being as basis of and juncture of, 114, 115
  Being located at juncture of, 115
  Being retained during, 40, 78, 102, 114, 234
  devoid of experience, 106
  oneness of life remains during, 283
  passivity in, 192, 290
  transcendental experience is unique from, 290–91
  wakefulness between states of consciousness, 292–93
democracy
  educators' excuses in name of, 228
  holds people's faith and goodwill, 306
  political consciousness dominates, 304–5
depression, 55, 56, 196, 257, 262
  sorrow, 223–24
desire
  crime as shortcut to fulfill, 217
  cycle of impression and, 21, 94–98
  future, 94, 97–98, 121–22, 131, 179
  health and fulfillment of, 186–88
  Prāṇa and, forms mind, 95
  pure consciousness between fulfill-

ment and next, 293
  selfish, 126, 222, 249
  unfulfilled, 94–98
devotion
  fulfillment in surrender and, 80
  full value of, 246–48
  sustains emotional path to God, 285
  Transcendental Meditation as path of, 248–49
  union of devotee and God, 286–89
dictator, 76
dirty-room analogy, 177–78
discrimination, intellectual, 279–82
  See also intellect
divided mind
  music in workplace, 170–71
  weakens personality, 233
  while speaking, 92–93
the Divine
  aspirant as obedient servant of, 75
  faith yet still searching for, 253
  free from error, 255
  gaining status of, 245–49
  individual is center of, intelligence, 262
  man as tool in hands of, 75, 78–79, 83
  ocean of, wisdom, 246
  See also God
diving analogy, 50, 143, 260–61, 265
do less and accomplish more
  clear and precise speech consumes less energy, 135
  conserving mental energy, 153–54
  dividing the mind minimizes efficiency, 170–71
  proper planning enables, 173
  Transcendental Meditation enhances, 125–26, 195, 201–2
  See also art of action
doctor analogies
  boil treatment, 183
  submission to expert, 79
dog-at-door analogy, 153
dogma, 270

doubting
  beyond, 160, 264, 265
  is state of mind, 178
  in reciprocity of action and reaction, 72
  Transcendental Meditation influencing, 77, 242, 265
dream state
  Being as basis of, 114
  Being located at juncture of, 115
  Being retained during, 234
  oneness of life remains during, 283
  subtler regions of senses activated in, 115
  transcendental Being at subtlest before, 115n27
  transcendental experience is unique from, 290–91
drinking, alcoholic beverages, 104, 154, 293–94
duality
  reality of, is Unity, 19
  thought brings mind into, 233
dullness, 48, 238, 293–94
dyeing-cloth analogy, 38

easiness
  action in least time, 145–46
  action using least energy, 144–45
  in activity, 37–38, 100, 169
  increasing-charm principle, 32–33
  least effort principle, 26
  least strain and maximum gain, 142
  of locating truth in scriptures, 220
  of materializing thought, 103
  of path, xii, 65, 69, 78, 131, 145, 158, 164, 209, 266–67, 299
  of routine to make life pure, 300
  of solid foundation for generations, 83
  speaking with least energy consumption, 134–36
  taking life easy, 300
  in Transcendental Meditation practice, 36, 85, 86, 115n27
  useful thinking easily gained, 140

eating, 293–94
  improper food, 104–5
  prayer before, 105
  spoiled food, 154
  unregulated habits of, 107
economic consciousness, 305
economics, extended meaning of, 210–11
education
  from within, 209
  Absolute in every branch of, 205–7, 216
  art of living mastered through, 264–67
  to best use one's life, 206–10
  democracy as excuse in, 228
  dissection *versus* fathoming depths, 208
  duty to advise right action, 226
  for future generations, 216, 300–7
  higher values open to students, 207–9
  humanities, 211–13
  intellect unsatisfied by, 207–9
  for merely earning living, 207
  policies that weaken, 227–28
  political science, 212–13
  psychology, 214–15
  sociology, 213–14
  subtle strata/fields open to students, 207–9
  Transcendental Meditation in, 35n14, 306
  UNESCO, 242
effort
  bow-and-arrow analogy, 26
  mind control, 84–85, 153, 299
  present, is materialization of past, 70
  selfish action requires great, 126
  speaking with least, 134–36
  in Transcendental Meditation, 80–81
  See also concentration; control; straining
ego
  Absolute supplementing, 61–62, 68
  Being as basis of, 7, 47
  God's perfection of, 273–74
  theories of, 15
Einstein, Albert, 14
elders
  advice from, 225–29
  to determine right and wrong, 222–23
  social scientist like elderly father, 214
  See also parents
emotional path
  of happiness, 286–89
  main factor of, 285
  path of love is, 247, 285–87
  for those with already developed heart, 278
emotions. *See* feelings
energy
  action with least expenditure of, 144–45
  conserving mental, 153–54
  from food and drink, 155–57
  law of conservation of, 117
  loss of, 136, 168
  not overspent, 107
  relative life draws life energy from Being, 186
  speaking with minimum, 134–36
  speech consumes, 135
  stone's-atomic-level analogy, 35
  unlimited, 103, 107
enlightenment
  action that liberates is skill in action, 161
  Age of Enlightenment, xiv
  innocent action as path to, 297–98, 297n17
  loss of direct path to, 231
  misconception about, 235–36
  thought as means of liberation, 133–34
  Vedic expressions of, 16
  See also Cosmic Consciousness; integrated life; specific path: emo-

tional, intellectual, mechanical, physiological, or psycho-physiological
environment. *See* atmosphere; surroundings
error, to err is human, 255–56
eternal life
  Absolute as unlimited unbounded, 8–9
  bliss of Absolute is, 86
  breath as impulse of, 249
  eternity pervades every moment, 246
  happiness which knows no misery, 170
  See also God Consciousness; life
evolution
  all that is fearful is against, 200
  behavior in natural flow of, 99–100
  creation-evolution-dissolution cycle, 11, 20, 22, 24, 273–74
  exercises to accelerate, 299
  Laws of Nature always for, 80
  Laws of Nature provide for evolved souls, 172
  life maintains and evolves simultaneously, 10–11
  man has choice, 52–53, 234
  mind flows in accord with, 262
  Nature's kindness in bringing, 79
  Nature's one-way flow of, 80
  only to bring fulfillment, 79
  past is less evolved state, 258
  past life gives identity to present, 20
  perfection on highest level of creation, 273
  personal God as fulfillment of, 272–73
  playing our part in purpose of, 126
  as purpose of behavior, 174–75
  rate of, depends upon species, 48–49
  scientific study of evolving nervous system, 112n25
  stages of, 33
  thought sprouts from Being and evolves into action, 94
  when pleased within yourself, 200
existence
  without Absolute, 269
  angels enjoy his, 249
  cycle of nonexistence and, 22
  defined, 3
  life is flow of, 45
  mind becomes, 37
  pure consciousness is state of, 37
  refuting God's, 275
  sap is, of entire tree, 10, 46–47, 100
  See also Absolute and relative; Being
expansion
  of conscious mind, 32, 33, 188
  happiness, 18
experience
  of Absolute, 17, 27, 37, 111, 290–91
  action-experience-impression cycle, 21, 94–98
  advantages of experiencing Being, 40–41
  Being as state of no, 37
  of Being is most concrete, 17
  of Bliss Consciousness, 53
  death as ceasing of, 234
  deep-sleep state devoid of, 106
  to fulfill mind's quest, 264–67
  gross and subtle range of, 27–29
  nature of Being is expansion, 269
  of pure Being, 290
  Science of Being goes beyond, xi–xii
  senses formed to provide, 7
  throws Being out of sight, 96–98
  of transcendental Being, 29–30
  See also subtle strata/fields

faith
  approaching action with, 167
  Being is beyond, 270
  children's understanding of their, 228
  moves mountains, 253
  of people in their government, 306
  for sake of faith alone, 253
  should be productive, 253

should provide fully developed nervous system, 252
yet still searching for divine, 253
family
    blood relations, 117–19
    children of good, 176
    family-man analogy, 163–64
    quality of wealth from, 56–57
    reciprocal relationship with, 71
    traceability-of-*Karma* analogy, 118
    wife's-love analogy, 247
    See also children
famine, 240
father
    -and-child analogy, 214
    concentrated love for, 247
    Father in Heaven and man on Earth united, 248
    give-and-take between son and, 71
    love from, 163–64, 214
    millionaire's-son analogy, 78, 82
fatigue
    dullness, 48, 238, 293–94
    mars cognizing subtle states, 293–94
    master-and-servant analogy, 188
    nervous system's, 104–7, 192, 218, 291, 293–94
    as physical state of nervous system, 291
    revitalization *versus*, 218
    sleep rises from, 192
fear
    all that is fearful is against evolution, 200
    of annihilation, 17, 180
    atmospheric tension causing, 201
    lack of confidence creates, 239
    in name of God, 251, 255, 271–72
    no one need fear own Self, 272
    peace through elimination of, 41
    Transcendental Meditation relieves, 16, 180, 242
feelings
    anger, 223–24, 227–28
    aspirant devoid of emotional twist, 80–81
    Being lies beyond, 29
    crime stems from unbalanced, 217
    depression, 55, 56, 196, 257, 262
    dignified and moderate expression of, 228
    experiments on plants, 55
    ill, toward us, 179
    infringing on other's, 225–26
    intolerance results in ill-, 175
    joyfulness, xiv, 152–53, 171, 176–80
    as main factor of emotional path, 285
    non-harsh expression of, 138–39
    purity of consciousness and, 222
    sinful *versus* harmonious influence, 200
    surroundings reacting to, 73–74
    uncultured, 6–7
    See also bliss; happiness
fire cannot burn It, 16
fixity of purpose, 162–64
floods, 240
flower-arrangement analogy, 61
food
    dog-at-door analogy, 153
    dullness from, 293–94
    improper, 104–5
    taste *versus* description of, 40
    unregulated habits of diet, 107
football analogies, 63, 354
    joyful *versus* tedious tasks, 169
forgiveness
    awakening spirit of, 213
    through enlarged consciousness, 76–77
    let wrong be drop in ocean of virtue, 72–73
    in speaking, 228–29
formless, appears in form, 249
free will, 53
freedom
    Absolute as unbounded, 8–9
    action infused with Being brings, 126–27
    action that liberates is skill in action, 161

art of thinking maintains eternal,
  128–29
Being is eternal, 4
complete, for children, 225–28
free will, 53
from *Karma*, 124–27
life lived in, 229–37
life's purpose is eternal, 49
living Being is eternal, 40
mind infused with Being brings,
  103–4
misunderstanding about, 232–35
saturation in Bliss Consciousness is,
  142–43
from suffering and misfortune, 300
See also bondage; Cosmic Consciousness
friends
  child instruction duty of, 226
  consciousness elevated by, 258
  dissension among, 240
  fruit of doer's actions returning to,
    119
  seeing good in, 258
fulfillment
  art of Being brings, 87–90
  of art of breathing, 96
  in day-to-day life, xi, xiv
  in devotion and surrender, 80
  in gaining status of divine life,
    245–49
  lasting *versus* short-lived, 239
  of mind's quest, 264–67
  nature of senses is to want more,
    109
  Nature's kindness in bringing, 79
  personal aspect of God as, 272–73
  of philosophy, 264–67
  positive thinking *versus* real, 86
  powerful and right thinking brings,
    127–31
  of psychology, 256–64
  purpose of life is, 48
  of recreation, 218–19
  of religion, 250–56
  of speech, 136, 138–40
  unfulfilled desires, 94–98
full potential
  of conscious mind, 63–65
  ocean-rising-in-wave analogy, 81n13
  requires life with solid basis, 66–69
  of resources, 50, 52, 63–69, 81, 81n14
  suffering from not unfolding, 50

Ganges, 301
gardener analogies
  knowledge of unseen root, xii
  surroundings are own creation, 70
  water the root, 38–39, 76, 186, 241
  world-as-God's-garden analogy, 225
  See also tree analogies
giving
  advice, 223
  maximum, in Cosmic Consciousness,
    75–77
  past life gives identity to present, 20
  principle of, 174–75
  receiving and, 73–74
  we receive what we give, 71–72
glass-of-water, Sun's reflection analogy,
  195–96
glasses, colored, analogy, 178
God
  annihilation of everything else in light
    of love of, 288
  be still and know that I am, 296
  Being as living presence of, 4, 6
  as cherished word, 267, 275
  created some good in everything, 225
  devotee and, become one, 286–89
  devotion sustains emotional path to,
    285
  ego of, 273–74
  Father in Heaven, 248
  fear of, 251, 255, 271–72
  found through love, 288
  individual is light of, 270
  Lord of Universe, 7–8, 105, 249, 263,
    272

love of, as greatest virtue, 286
multiplicity in unbounded existence of, 287–88
nervous system of, 273
as She and He, 272, 274
word of, 248–49
world-as-God's-garden analogy, 225
See also Being; impersonal God; personal God
God Consciousness
   Absolute and relative brought together in, 245–46
   as art of living, 61
   Cosmic Consciousness as prerequisite, 246–48
   Father in Heaven and man on Earth united, 248
   as goal, 237
   impersonal God realized in transcendent, 275–78
   Karma glorified by, 26–27
   life is unity in, 45
   lover of God drowns in ocean of His love, 286–87
   psychology's purpose of, 257
   religion's purpose is, 250–56
   waves in ocean of Oneness, 286–87
   See also Cosmic Consciousness
government
   democratic, 228, 304–5, 306
   God's, 274
   guidance from laws of, 120
   health care resolved by, 183, 306
   laws of land derived from Laws of Nature, 159
   leaders with only partial achievement, 76
   monarchs and dictators, 76
   Nature's, 53, 79–80, 122–23, 159, 273–74, 301
   political science, 212–13
   Transcendental Meditation via agencies of, 300, 306
   See also Cosmic Law; Laws of Nature

greeting, 174–75
Guru Dev, xiii, 80, 266

H_2O examples and analogies
   Absolute and relative, 11, 14, 46
   Cosmic Law, 11
   impersonal God, 269
   permanency of elements, 281
   See also water
habits, 107
hands
   children's fate in their own, 227
   hold to cosmic intentions, 249
   holding destiny of education, 210
   man as tool in Divine, 75, 78–79, 83
   as one of five organs of action, 108
happiness
   emotional path is path of, 285–89
   eternal, knows no misery, 170
   expansion of, 18
   intensity at different levels of creation, 45–46
   key to, lies in subtler levels, 288
   lasting *versus* short-lived contentment, 239
   life's purpose is, 48–51
   peace is based in, 237–38
   of scientists, 216
   See also bliss
harmful action
   action-reaction principle, 223–24
   trying to compute, 164–65
   wrong action, 175–76, 222–24, 227–28, 230, 293–94
harmony
   art of Being places life in, 179–80
   harmonious speech, 138–39
   integrated life creates, 100–101, 201–2
   Nature set free from strain and dis-, 197–99
   pure consciousness is realm of, 76
   of universe, 302
   vibrations of, 138–39, 198, 201, 240
   when pleased with yourself, 200

Hatha Yoga, 291, 291n16
hatred
    brings dissatisfaction to both parties, 174–75
    lack of confidence creates fear and, 239
    narrow vision causes misunderstanding and, 176–77
    reciprocity of, 72, 223–24, 240–41
    See also tolerance
He or She, of personal God, 272, 274
health
    art of Being brings, 100–101, 201–2
    atmospheric, 196–99
    authority, 182, 205
    cannot be considered in segments, 200–5
    as coordination of Absolute and relative, 181–82
    daily rest and silence for, 190n70
    fulfillment of desires and, 186–88
    knowledge of whole range of life for, 181–84
    mental, 180–88, 190n70, 191–96, 200–205
    physical, 188–89
    preventive measures, 183–86, 190–96, 190n70
    Transcendental Meditation given for, 306
    world, 240
heart
    controller of universe dwells in, 7–8, 272
    hardened, in modern age, 175
    listener's, 139
    loving, as basis of, 73–74
    as ocean of virtue, 72–73
    to receive you must give, 71–72
    restless, worried, troubled, 239–40
    uncultured, 6–7
    See also emotional path; feelings; love
hermit, time-consuming practices of, 294
Himalayas, 301
holiday resort, 303
honeybee analogy, 150

hot war, 241
householder
    husband-and-wife's-love analogy, 247
    intellectual path not suited to, 285
    time-consuming practices unfit for, 294
    Yogic physical culture and, 194
houses, attractive or repulsive, 56
human(s)
    ability to experience subtle strata/fields, 53
    Absolute projecting from, 49–50
    angels enjoy his existence, 249
    animals different from, 52–53, 55, 258
    boundaries extend beyond body, 25, 58, 65, 77
    can speak for Lord of Universe, 249
    civilization potential of, xiv, 259–60
    conscious mind of ordinary, 50, 111
    cosmic life's thought materialized in, 249
    creative intelligence in, 32, 40–41, 103, 135, 142, 241, 260
    family-man analogy, 163–64
    has choice for evolution, 52–53, 234
    invitation to every, on Earth, 49–50
    is master of own destiny, 57–58, 168
humanities, study of, 211–12
humanity
    Age of Enlightenment, xiv
    child-with-burning-coal analogy, 216, 226
    connection between universe and, 58
    Cosmic Life influenced by, 239–40
    Cosmic Life served by, 48, 53–54
    dignity and splendor at basis of, 7
    emancipation plan for, 301
    to err is human, 255–56
    invitation to, 49–50
    laws derived from Nature's laws, 159
    man can speak for Lord of Universe, 249

rehabilitation issue, 217
rescue from annihilation, 17, 180
shrinks from death, 52
See also modern age; individual
husband-and-wife's-love analogy, 247
hydrogen and oxygen. *See* H_2O example

I am That, 16, 266, 282
identification
    Bliss Consciousness influencing, 142–44
    Bliss Consciousness not lost under any circumstances, 87–88, 97
    coming out of what one is not, 270, 278n13
    in experience-impression-desire cycle, 21, 94–98
    forgotten in blinding light of love, 288
    misunderstanding about, 232–35
    object-, overshadowing perception, 96–98
    past life gives identity to present, 20
    Self is Being of everyone, 16, 278n13
    Self-consciousness not lost, 245
    subject overshadowed by object, 226, 231–32
    thought by its very nature causes, 233
    See also bondage
idleness, 48
ill-humored remarks, 175–78
imperishability
    Being's, infused into mind, 103
    Being's nature is opposed to *Karma*, 124
    mind's lasting contentment, 202
the imperishable
    fire cannot burn It, 16
    as God's nature, 272
    the perishable and, 279–83
    Upanishads on, 15–16
impersonal God, 267
    creator, maintainer, and sustainer of world, 268–69
    dwells in heart of everyone, 7–8, 272
    H_2O example, 269
    as knowingness itself, 270
    path to, 271–72
    pure consciousness is both subject and object, 269
    realization of, will be in transcendent, 271, 275–78
    See also personal God
impression
    action-experience-impression cycle, 21, 94–98
    as finest remains of *Karma*, 21
    line-drawn-on-stone analogy, 98
    See also identification; senses
indecision, 188, 189, 263
India
    ancient medical profession of, 240
    Bhagavad-Gītā, 15–17, 262–63, 262n5, 297, 297n17
    inauguration of Spiritual Regeneration Movement in, 35n14
    Mahābhārata, 263
    Vedic Ṛishis, xi
    Yogis of, 80
indifference, as weapon, 179
individual
    cosmic intelligence expressed in, 249
    divine intelligence centered in, 262
    full coordination with Laws of Nature, 141–44
    grounded in truths of one's own religion, 221
    innocence at basis of, life, 7
    intimate and inseparable connection with universe, 48, 53–58
    is Absolute and relative, 80–81, 181–82
    is light of God, 270
    life stream of, 123
    mechanical path suits any, 278
    mind attuned with Cosmic Law, 261–62

personality, 34, 39, 56, 249
Prāṇa and breath of, 92–96
responsible for surroundings, 177–80
righteousness, 57
seed-and-tree analogy for, 93–94
ship-without-rudder analogy, 4
sprouting from universal, 93–94
touches horizon of eternity, 77
See also human; man
infusion, of Being, 39, 103–4, 108–13, 126–27
as softness, 6
injustice, affecting us, 179
innocence
  at basis of individual, 7
  of Being, 18
  child's, 55, 57, 215, 247
  enlightenment through action in, 297–98, 297n17
  minds that miss, 6–7
  of natural easy behavior, 99–100, 166–67, 179, 300
  in speaking, 138
  of those without this wisdom, 226
  in Transcendental Meditation practice, 80–81, 297
integrated life
  Bhagavad-Gītā on, 262, 262n5
  citizens leading, 210
  of conscious and subconscious mind, 214
  fulfilled in Cosmic Consciousness, 246
  as fulfillment of philosophy, 264
  harmony and health through, 100–1, 201–2
  practical thesis of, xi
  as purpose of every religion, 250–56
  social scientist's need for, 213
  unnatural influences neutralized by, 200–1
  as wave drawing from its base, 66
  See also Cosmic Life; life
intellect
  Absolute supplementing, 61–62, 68

Being as basis of, 7
Being is beyond, 270
communion with God is not through, 273–75
computing action without harm, 164–65
computing all Laws of Nature, 79–81
education fails to satisfy, 207–9
right and wrong action computed by, 219–21
right thoughts computed by, 130–31
See also right action
intellectual path
  for already cultured intellects, 278
  discrimination between real and unreal, 279–82
  main factor of, 285
  mind-body coordination marred by, 285
  practical life on, 283–84
  Rāja Yoga belongs to, 285, 285n14
  as self-hypnotism, 282–83
  three steps on, 282
intelligence
  Absolute source of all, 4
  annihilation of, in light of love of God, 288
  art of Being places life in state of, 179–80
  Cosmic, expressed in individual mind, 249
  different at different levels of creation, 45–46
  increases as love grows, 287–88
  individual is center of divine, 262
  life is stream of, 45
  light of love is, 288
  pure consciousness is absolute, 193
  See also creative intelligence
intolerance, 175
invitation
  to custodians of all religions, 256
  every man on Earth, 49–50
  to health authorities, 182, 205

seekers of power, 85
ulterior motive, 70
irritability, 188
from atmospheric tension, 201

Jagadguru Bhagavan Shankaracharya, xiii, 80, 266–67
jealousy, in reciprocity of action and reaction, 72
joyfulness
in Age of Enlightenment, xiv
love spread through, 176
natural, 171
sacrifice of, 152–53
surroundings reflecting, 177–80
See also Bliss Consciousness
judge's-robe analogy, 46

Karma
in action-experience-impression cycle, 21, 94–98
art of Being and, 117–27
Being and, 23–27
Being and, in process of creation, 19–23
blood relations and, 117–19
bondage and, 124–27
brought to level of Being through Transcendental Meditation, 127
calf-finds-mother analogy, 119
defined, 23–24
finest remains of, 21
freedom from, 124–27
gains attribute of *Prāṇa*, 95
in God Consciousness, 26–27
imperishability *versus*, 124
Karma Yoga, 297, 297n17
law of conservation of energy and, 117
materialization of past, 70
mind and, 19–20
mind out of reach of, 24–26
misunderstandings about, 24–27, 117n30
philosophy of, 120, 125
posted-letter analogy, 118–19

Prāṇa and, 19–23
present is materialization of past, 70
beyond scope of human mind, 122–23
success reflects, 167–68
surroundings are one's, 70–71, 168
take it as it comes, 70
traceability of, 118
unfulfilled, 94–95
unity diversified by, 124
vast, unlimited, and complex field of, 221
weakness from past, 168
wheel of, 22, 24
as you sow so shall you reap, 72, 117, 119
See also action; action-reaction
Karma Yoga, 297, 297n17
kindness
contrary opinion expressed with, 139
in reciprocity of action and reaction, 72
sustains emotional path to God, 285
king analogies
positive thinking that "I am a king," 86, 236, 284
wandering mind is like king not monkey, 150
knowing
Absolute cannot know anything, 269
all, is He, 273
be still and know that I am God, 296
Being is beyond, 270
as intellectual path, 285
philosophy of *Karma*, 120
suffering due to not, 50
knowingness, 270
knowledge
of Being as essential constituent of creation, 5
to dive within oneself, 50, 63
of full scope of life, 206
incomplete, 203, 206–8
loss of, 231

INDEX 415

lost over time, 235
mysticism *versus*, 82
not just theoretical, 205
of the subject, 209
that excites thirst but cannot satisfy, 208
See also intellectual path; wisdom
Kṛishṇa, 263

law
conservation of energy, 117
for guidance in right and wrong, 120
of land, 159
See also Cosmic Law
Laws of Nature
all-powerful and all-loving, 79
always evolutionary, 80
animal activities governed by, 53
Being as basis of, 10
cannot be deceived, 72
conformity with, 99
Cosmic Consciousness and, 75
Cosmic Law expresses through, 10–13, 54
father-as-millionaire analogy, 78, 82
full coordination with, 141–44
intellect cannot compute, 79–81
laws of land derived from, 159
provide for evolved souls, 172
rigid in their character, 123
speech congenial to, 91
Transcendental Meditation imparted on plane of, 301
unveiling mystery of, 264–67
leaf-in-wind analogy, 4
least-effort principle, 26
life
Cosmic Life energy, 155–57, 186
individual and cosmic, 48, 53–58
is Being, 3–5, 8–9
is stream of bliss, 45
as light of God, 45, 270
maintains itself and evolves simultaneously, 10–11

normal, 51–53
oneness of, 266, 283
purpose of, 48–51, 126, 249
three spheres of, 40–41
See also Cosmic Life; eternal life; integrated life; material life; relative life
light
Age of Enlightenment, xiv
of Being, 25–26
candlelight analogy, 26
lightbulb analogy, 6, 295
more intense at source, 33
of Self brightens material life, 237
of Self to fathom subtle strata, 209
sunlight analogy, 26
See also enlightenment
Light of God
increases as love grows, 287–88
individual is, 270
life is, 45, 270
light of love is, 288
truth is, 229
light of love, 288
lightbulb analogy, 6, 295
line-drawn-on-stone analogy, 98
longevity, 190n70
look before you leap, 171
Lord of Universe
in Bhagavad-Gītā, 263
kindly dwells in heart of everyone, 7–8, 272
man can speak for, 249
omniscient, omnipotent, omnipresent, 7–8
prayer before eating, 105
See also God; universe
loss
of binding influence of *Karma*, 26
businessman analogy of, 168
of direct path to enlightenment, 231
of energy, 136, 168
is victory on path of love, 247
memories of past overshadowing

present, 258
　of spirit of religion, 254
love
　all-loving hand of Nature, 79
　concentrated universal, 246–48
　correction of child from state of,
　　227–28
　despite ill-feeling toward us, 179
　father's love for children, 163–64,
　　214
　God found in world through, 288
　of God is greatest virtue, 286
　mother's, saturates children, 170
　real and significant, 288–89
　in reciprocity of action and reaction,
　　72–73
　river of, gains ocean of, 287
　universal *versus* personal, 247
　vehicle on emotional path is, 247,
　　285–87

Mahābhārata, 263
Maharishi Effect, 198n72
Maharishi Mahesh Yogi, 35n14
man
　aspirations of, 146
　creative intelligence in, 32, 40–41,
　　103, 135, 142, 241, 260
　Father in Heaven and, on Earth
　　united, 248
　invitation to every, on Earth, 49–50
　is master of own destiny, 57–58, 168
　speech as medium between sur-
　　roundings and, 137–38
　vibrations reach Moon, Sun, and
　　stars, 117–18
　See also human; individual
manners
　good, 139–40, 176
　greeting, 174–75
　lie in art of Being, 179–80
Mantra, 34–35, 290–91
mass consciousness, 304–6
master of own destiny, 57–58, 168
master-and-servant analogy, 188

material life
　dissatisfaction with, 239
　light of Self brightens, 237
　misunderstanding about, 24–25
　potential glories of, 52, 64
　See also life; surface value
matter
　contamination by wrong action,
　　293–94
　Prāṇa forms, 95
　science of mind and of, 15
　See also science
mechanical path
　for anyone no matter how weak, 278
　of gaining restful alertness, 296–97
　Karma Yoga as, 297–98, 297n17
　lies in process of perception, 295–98
medical profession
　ancient India's, 240
　goodwill toward, 184
　limitations of modern, 204
　preventive measures, 183–86,
　　190–96, 190n70
　research on mental as basis of physi-
　　cal, 182, 188–89
　Transcendental Meditation advanta-
　　geous for, 190–91
　Transcendental Meditation for, 306
meditation. *See* Transcendental Medi-
　tation
meditation academies, 301–3
mental energy, conservation of, 153–54
mental health
　cannot be properly considered in
　　segments, 200–5
　coordination of mind and nervous
　　system for, 186–89
　health authorities, 182, 205
　perfect, 180–81
　preventive measures, 183–86,
　　190–96, 190n70
　requires knowledge of whole range
　　of life, 183–84
　restful alertness for, 191–96

Transcendental Meditation advantageous for, 190n70
of world, 240
See also health
mental perception (with closed eyes), 108–11
metabolic process, Transcendental Meditation influencing, 189–96
metaphysics, 20, 304, 305
   absurdity of Self-realization "path," 278n13
   misunderstandings about freedom, 232–35
   religion *versus*, 221
   Self-realization emphasized by, 237
Milky Way, 146
millionaire analogies
   forgotten his wealth and status, 50
   making full use of almighty Nature, 78
   son of millionaire, 82
mind
   Absolute supplementing, 61–62, 68
   becomes Absolute, 111
   becomes pure Being, 37–38
   Being is beyond, 270
   can stimulate any stratum of creation for any advantage, 261
   carried from lifetime to lifetime, 20
   clear thinking, 129
   in constant communion with Being, 62
   crime as result of weak, 217
   divided, 92–93, 170–71, 233
   doubting, 178
   dualistic ability of, 163
   of God, 249, 274
   indecisive, 188, 189, 263
   inward march of, 297
   is vibrating consciousness, 185–86
   Karma and, 19–20
   left awake by itself, 3–4, 39, 245, 290
   mental energy conservation, 153–54
   narrow, 108, 176–77, 275, 279
   nervous system interdependence with, 187–89
   nothing remains hidden, 102, 266
   only useful thoughts, 131–32, 140
   pettiness of, 56–57, 82, 239, 279
   point of refinement of, 215
   Prāṇa, *Karma* and, 19–23, 95
   quest of, 264–67
   restless, 150–53
   scientific discoveries by immature, 216
   as second manifestation, 20
   silencing, 238–39
   surface waves communicate with deeper levels, 33
   surroundings reflecting, 177–80
   that misses innocent field of life, 6–7
   tuned with Cosmic Law, 261–62
   tuning individual with Cosmic, 261–62
   undeveloped, refutes God's existence, 275
   See also concentration; conscious mind
mind control, 84–85, 130–31, 153, 299
mind/body coordination
   Absolute supplementing, 68–69
   art of action and nervous system, 154–55
   full coordination with Laws of Nature, 141–44
   health is coordination of Absolute and relative, 181–82
   infusion of Being, 113
   intellectual path disturbs, 285
   mental health and, 186–89
   in unity, 193
ministers, 253
misunderstanding
   artificial joyfulness as, 171
   ascetic practices as, 152
   Being maintained on thinking level as, 90
   confusion about eternal freedom, 235

confusion between mind and body, 188
about enlightenment's practicality, 235–36
to err is human as, 255–56
about eternal freedom, 232–35
general confusion, 88, 121
about incompatibility of *Karma* and Being, 24–27
of intellectual path, 285
mood-making as, 285
mystical nature of Being as, 17
narrow vision leads to, 176–77
negation of thoughts as, 238–39
power of thinking rather than being, 86
about pursuing pure consciousness, 238
of spiritual values, 24–25
suffering as religious tenet is, 254
Mithyā, 280
modern age
 children not told what to do, 225–28
 fast tempo and tension of, 50, 145–46, 157, 171, 239–40
 heart and mind development in, 175
 householder's life in, 194, 285, 294, 297
 irritability, 188, 201
 lack of time to meditate, 39
 natural sciences in, 215–16
 philosophy in, 264–67, 304
 playing music in workplace, 170–71
 religion's ineffectiveness in, 251–56
 suffering as religious tenet, 254
 unregulated habits of diet and activity, 107
 See also misunderstanding; psychology
monarchy, 76
money. *See* wealth
monkey-*versus*-king-on-throne analogy, 150
mood-making, 81, 285

Moon
 far influence of action on, 117–18
 in man's aspirations, 146
morality, is in accord with evolution, 200
mother
 children serving and respecting, 134
 concentrated love for, 247
 looks kindly upon mistakes, 175–76
 love saturates children, 170
 path to God like mother's joy, 286–87
 rebellion against, 79
mother-and-child analogies
 Being and thought are like, 88
 God and devotee become one, 286–89
 joyful *versus* burdensome treatment, 170
 Nature's almighty power, 80
 Nature's kindness, 79
 path to God like mother's joy, 286–87
 reciprocal relationship of, 71
 thought ignored at its origin, 134
music, in workplace, 170–71
mysticism, xii, 17, 81, 82

narrow vision
 causes misunderstandings, 176–77
 pettiness of, 56–57, 82, 239, 279
 refutes God's existence, 275
 senses influenced by tension cause, 108
natural behavior, 99–100
 artificial joyfulness, 171
 millionaire son's use of wealth, 82
 necessity of, 37
 religion should lead in natural manner, 252
 un-, 99, 194, 213
 white-cloth-in-yellow-dye analogy, 38
natural sciences, 215–16
natural tendency
 dividing mind between two attrac-

tions, 170–71
mind attracted to subtle strata,
  151–52
for only right action, 160–61
should not be disturbed, 302
in Transcendental Meditation practice, 32–33
See also happiness
Nature
all-powerful and all-loving hand of,
  79
almighty power of Mother Nature,
  77–86
Being gets enlivened and vibrates in,
  198–99, 198n72
calculating time and place for
  strength of, 79
cannot be deceived, 72
government of, 53, 79–81, 122–23,
  159, 273–74, 301
provides for evolved souls, 172
set free from strain and disharmony,
  197–99
source of, 4, 10
unveiling mystery of, 264–67
when balance is disturbed, 240–41
See also Laws of Nature; subtle
  strata/fields; surroundings
negativity
indifference as weapon against, 179
negation of thoughts, 238–39
perseverance despite, 168
nervous system
Being permanently on level of,
  113–16
body as end-organ of, 113, 184
fatigue as physical state of, 291
of God, 273
God realization from specific functioning of, 289–90
impression of experience on, 21,
  94–98
master-and-servant analogy, 188
mind interdependence with, 186–89

purpose of, 48–51
rate of evolution depends on species,
  48–49
religion adherence should develop, 252
scientific study of evolving, 112n25
in state neither active nor passive,
  192–96
in steps of creation, 21
subjective and objective connected
  through, 185
tired from activity, 104–7, 192, 218,
  291, 293–94
See also body
night-and-day cycle, 20
nonexistence and existence cycle, 22
normal life, 51–53
nothing remains hidden, 102, 266
nuclear physics, 5, 14

object-identification. *See* identification
obstacles, perseverance despite, 168
ocean
Absolute-and-relative analogy, 8, 13
Being *versus* watery, 8
of divine wisdom, 246
lover of God in, of His love, 286–87
mind as wave of, 19
omnipresent ocean of consciousness,
  53
of Oneness, 287
pond *versus*, analogy, 263
as range of consciousness, 30–32
rising-in-wave analogy, 81n14
surface communicates with deeper
  levels, 33
time and tide wait for no man, 146
of wisdom of Absolute, 21
of your virtue, 72–73
oil-permeates-seed analogy, 271
omnipotence, 3–4, 7–8, 23, 41, 64,
  77–86, 236
See also power
omnipresence
of Being, 6–8, 16, 270
individual as expression of, 249

of pure consciousness, 53
omniscience
   expressed in limitations, 249
   God's, 274
   Lord of Universe's, 8
oneness
   Being is diversity and, 13–15
   of Being radiates outward, 6, 295–96
   confusion about, 266, 282–84
   of God and lover of God, 286–87
   of life, 266, 283
   maintained in waking, deep-sleep, and dreaming, 283
   as ultimate reality, 16
   Upanishads declaring, 266
   See also unity
organs of action, 108–11
omnipresence of Being in, 6
oxygen and hydrogen. *See* H_2O example

parents
   advice from, 225–29
   consciousness elevated by, 258
   family wealth damaging heirs, 56–57
   See also elders; father; mother
passivity
   as misguided practice, 238–39
   religious life incompatible with, 253
past life. *See* rebirth
path
   absurdity of, 278n13
   as coming out of what one is not, 270–71, 278n13
   discrimination of real and unreal on intellectual path, 279–82
   easiness of, 65, 131, 145, 158, 164, 209, 266–67, 299
   five paths to realization, 277–78
   to God like mother's joy in child, 286–87
   of goodness, 252–53
   householder, 194, 285, 294, 297
   to impersonal God, 271–72
   innocent action as, 297–98, 297n17
   intellectual path as self-hypnotism, 282–83
   loss of direct, 231
   of love, 247, 285–87
   mechanical path lies in process of perception, 295–98
   need for, 270
   practical life on intellectual, 283–84
   Rāja Yoga belongs to intellectual path, 285, 285n14
   recluse, 152, 284, 294
   Transcendental Meditation as, 248–49
   See also emotional path, intellectual path, mechanical path, physiological path, psycho-physiological path
peace
   art of Being places life in, 179–80
   at different levels of creation, 45–46
   by eliminating fear, 41
   happiness as basis of, 237–38
   opposite of, 239–40
   practicality via Transcendental Meditation, 242
   pure consciousness as realm of, 76
   scientists in harmony and, 216
   world, xiv, 237–40, 242
perception
   Absolute supplementing all senses, 61–62, 68
   activating deepest level of senses, 111
   Being infused on level of, 108–10
   God's senses, 273–74
   is automatic and mechanical, 295–96
   limits of, 27–29
   mental (with closed eyes), 108–11
   nature of senses is to want more, 109
   object-identification overshadowing, 96–98
   reason for forming of senses, 7
   seeing good in others, 223, 224, 258
   starts from unmanifest, 296
   steps of creation of senses, 21

white-teeth analogy, 225
perfection
  at highest level of creation, 273
  mental health, 180–81
  personal God's, 273–74
  in purity of brain, 292–93
personal God
  communion with, 274–75
  merges into impersonal aspect, 273
  as perfection in all features, 274
  prayer before eating, 105
  realization of, will be on level of perception, 275–78
  senses of, 273–74
  in whose person evolution finds fulfillment, 272
  See also God; impersonal God
personality
  attractive or repulsive, 56
  dividing mind weakens, 233
  each has own quality, 34
  inexpressible expressed in, 249
  rejuvenation of, 39, 218–19
  See also individual
pettiness, 56–57, 82, 239, 279
philosophy, 264–67, 304
physician. *See* doctor analogies
physics
  as material science of relative field, 86
  discovering finer layers, 4–5, 14–15
  everything is vibration, 73
  immature minds experiment with nuclear forces, 216
  law of conservation of energy, 117
  nuclear, rapid development of, 14
  recent discoveries in, 4–5
  science of mind and, 15
  scientific age, 157
  theory of relativity, 14
  ultimate achievement in history of, 15
  unified field theory, 14
  waves of activity reaching all strata, 55

physiological path
  body's state of suspension, 292
  brain awake and alert in itself, 291–92
  God realization from, 289–90
  Hatha Yoga, 291, 291n16
  perfectly pure brain, 292–93
  study of evolving nervous system, 112n25
physiology, 54, 58
  See also nervous system
planning, 171–72
  execution and review of, 173–74
plant experiments, 55
point of refinement, 215
political consciousness, 305
political science, 212–13
politics, 140
pond analogies
  ocean *versus* pond, 263
  stone thrown in pond, 34, 54, 117
  waves on pond, 54
positive thinking, 85–86
posted-letter analogy, 118–19
power
  all-powerful hand of Nature, 79
  annihilation of, in light of love of God, 288
  Being as source of, 4
  in daily life, 8–9
  intensity at different levels of creation, 45–46
  -lessness is waste of life, 67
  millionaire analogies, 50, 78, 82
  from nothing hidden, 102, 266
  in subtle strata/fields, 35
  of thought, 125–26
  at top level of creation, 248, 273
  will of God, 273–74
  See also omnipotence
Prāṇa, 9n4, 17
  Being and, 17–19, 92–93, 269
  breathing and, 92–96
  as essential, 112

exercises to accelerate evolution, 299
Karma and, 19–23, 95
as subtle aspect, 47, 51
where, takes birth, 16
See also breathing
preventive medicine
  familiarity with subtle strata/fields as, 183–86
  restful alertness as, 190–96, 190n70
priest, 253
psychic powers, 83–85
  See also misunderstanding
psychoanalysis, 257–58
psychology
  father-and-child analogy, 214
  individual is Absolute and relative, 181–82
  past is lesser developed state, 257–58
  purpose and goal of, 257
  results of child, 227–28
  study of, 214–15
  summary of, 256–57
  surface value of, 76
  on tension as necessary, 50
  Transcendental Meditation opens gates of ancient, 262–63, 262n5
psycho-physiological path, 298–99
  suits those who train mind and body, 278
psychosomatic disease, 182
punishment
  fear of, as motivation, 251
  Nature's, is for evolution and good, 79
pure consciousness
  absolute intelligence is, 193
  amounts to gaining absolute purity of life, 158, 159–60
  appears as both subject and object, 269
  art of thinking brings, into activity, 128
  Being is, 8, 12, 124
  brain cherishes state of, 293–94

brain setup for, 290–91
breath neither active nor passive, 195
carries into activity, 128
at end of subtlest waking state, 115n27
between fulfillment and next desire, 293
is absolute intelligence, 193
is both subject and object, 269
is purity and bliss, 197
is state of pure existence, 37
joyful action from, 170
Karma and, transforms to mind, 124
knows no change, 12
medical professionals should know, 184
mind is left awake by itself, 3–4, 39, 245, 290
misunderstanding about, 238
Nature's mysteries revealed, 266
omnipresent ocean of, 53
perception starts from, 296
plane of Cosmic Law is, 123
as realm of harmony, 76
beyond relative existence, 15
Self-awareness is, 32
source of all, 3–4, 262, 265
source of all creation, 265
source of all intelligence and creativity, 262
source of all thinking, 3–4
state of pure existence, 37
stimulating any stratum for any advantage, 261
beyond subconscious, 215
surroundings improved by, 200–1
transcendental nature of, 21, 29
as value of human over animal, 53
purity
  basis of plan should be, 301
  brain, 292–93
  daily routine to make life pure, 158, 300

to determine right from wrong,
  222–23
life is stream of, 45
Self-realization as coming out of
  what one is not, 270, 278n13
success from, 141–42
surroundings reflect inner, 72–73
of teachers and system of teaching,
  302, 304, 306–7
white-teeth analogy, 225
yields maximum results, 166–67
purpose
  Bliss Consciousness is life's, 126
  of creation, 18
  of economic resources, 210–11
  of every religion, 250–56
  evolution as, of behavior, 174–75
  fixity of, 162–64
  happiness is life's, 48–51
  of nervous system, 48–51
  playing our part in, of evolution, 126
  psychology's, and goal, 257
  of recreation, 218
  same, for individual and Cosmic
    Life, 48
  speech draws out, of Cosmic Life, 249

rain, 240
Rāja Yoga, 285, 285n14
reality
  Absolute is, of all relative phases, 17
  Absolute is, of all subtle strata, 17
  oneness as ultimate, 16
  positive thinking *versus* living, 86
  Transcendental Meditation makes
    love, 288–89
  unity is, of duality, 19
  world as neither real nor unreal,
    279–81
  See also Absolute and relative
realization. See Self-Realization
rebirth
  birth-and-death cycle, 24, 97–98,
    118–19

one's own desire causes, 300
posted-letter analogy, 118–19
unfulfilled desires cause, 94–98
weapons cannot slay, 16
recluse
  ascetic practices, 152
  intellectual path suited to, 284
  time-consuming practices of, 294
recreation
  purpose of, 218
  Transcendental Meditation fulfilling,
    219
rehabilitation, hard nature changed,
  217
rejuvenation, 39, 218–19
relative life
  Absolute dances in, 246, 249
  art of Being places, in harmony and
    intelligence, 179–80
  Being as essential constituent of,
    3–5, 8–9
  Being at basis of, 112
  Being embodied in, 249
  Being lived in, 38–39
  Being supplementing, 66–69
  Bliss Consciousness hand in hand
    with, 45, 63, 245
  draws life energy from Being, 186
  experience of Being more concrete
    than, 17
  is highly concentrated and complex,
    57
  taken naturally and easily, 37
  theory of relativity, 14
  three aspects of, 181–82
  See also Absolute and relative; life
religion
  binds back to source (religare), 250
  coordinates individual with Cosmic,
    250
  custodians of strange, 271
  faith should be productive, 253
  fear-instilling, 251, 255, 271–72
  follow one's own, 120–21

fulfillment of, 250–56
God Consciousness as goal, 250, 255–56
ineffectiveness of modern, 251–56
is practical and has to be lived, 221
purpose of, 250–56
reduced to ritual and dogma, 304
scriptural authority, 220–21
Self-Realization emphasized by, 237
should lead in natural manner, 252
should provide God-Realization, 250–51
suffering as premise of, 254
truths of one's own, 221
religious rituals, 251
resources
of evolved souls, 172
full potential of, 50, 52, 63–69, 81, 81n14
look at, before you leap, 171
purpose of economic, 210–11
of UNESCO, 241
See also wealth
restful alertness, 190, 190n70, 296–97
as antidote to daily wear and tear, 201–2
body and breathing exercises along with, 299
as preventive medicine, 190–96, 190n70
as psycho-physiological path's main feature, 298–99
restless mind, 150–53
revival, xiv, 254
riddle, of *Karma* and mind, 19–20
right action
advice about, 225–29
criterion for, 120–22
definition, 220
fear of punishment as motivation, 251
guides to, 159–60
religion puts us on path of, 252

religious teaching and rituals insufficient for, 255–56
scriptural authority on, 220–21
spontaneously, 58, 130–31, 139, 252
universality of every influence, 219
See also wrong action
righteousness
through ability to perform right action, 159
in earned livelihood, 105
individual's influence of, 57
Karma of Absolute, 124
world health dependent upon, 240
See also right action
Ṛishis (Vedic seers), xi
ritual, Being is beyond, 270
river
Ganges, 301
of love, 287
rose-and-thorn analogy, 70
routine, daily
to make life pure, 158, 300
precepts of one's religion in, 221
Transcendental Meditation and taking life easy, 303
rubber-ball analogy, 118

saccharin analogy, 97–98, 108
sap analogies
Being as basis of everything, 10, 46–47, 100
failing to reach surface value, 100–1
imperishable and perishable nature of tree, 280
specific seed and pattern of expression, 93–94
of tree, 61–62
See also tree analogies
Sat-Chid-Ānanda, 4n1
satellites example, 55
science
aspires to control phenomena, 216
discoveries by immature minds, 216
etymology of, xii

explores actuality of forms and
  phenomena, xi
explores Laws of Nature, 203
natural, explores organization of
  objective creation, 215–216
political, 212–13
scientific age, 157
social scientist like elderly father, 214
sociologists should have complete
  view, 214
starts from known, xi
study of evolving nervous system,
  112n25
ultimate achievement of, 15
Science of Being
  Being brought to scientific scrutiny,
    xiii
  practical, results found when experi-
    ment made, 27
  starts from known and goes beyond,
    xi–xii
  theoretical and applied, xii
  topmost science in science of life, 86
  transcends science of mind, 15
scriptures
  guidance for right action in, 220–21
  Self-realization emphasized by, 237
  Transcendental Meditation found in
    all, 254
seed
  -thought, 94
  weakness in, as most important, 187
seed-and-tree analogy, 19–20, 93–94
seed-and-tree cycle, 19–20, 93–94
seeing good, 223–24
  white-teeth example, 225
  world-as-God's-garden analogy, 225
seekers of truth, 266–67
self
  brain awake within it-, 291–92
  intellectual path as self-hypnotism,
    282–83
  knowledge to dive within one-, 50, 63
self-confidence, 145–46, 161–62, 239

selfish desire, 126, 222, 249
  See also identification; subject-object
Self
  -awareness is pure consciousness, 32
  -consciousness not lost, 245
  is essential Being of everyone, 16,
    278n13
  light of, brightens material life, 237
  light of, to fathom subtle strata, 209
  mind left awake by it-, 3–4, 39, 245,
    290
  no one need fear own, 272
  See also Self-Realization
selfishness
  in Cosmic Consciousness, 249
  man overshadowed by, 126, 222,
    249
  requires great effort, 126
Self-Realization
  all religions on, 237
  as coming out of what one is not,
    270, 278n13
  five paths to, 277–78
  of impersonal God will be in
    transcendent, 275–78
  of personal God is on level of per-
    ception, 275–78
  physiological path to, 289–90
  religion should provide, 250–51
  Vedic expressions of, 16
senses
  Absolute supplementing, 61–62, 68
  activating deepest level of, 111
  Being as basis of, 7
  Being infused on level of, 108–10
  experience throws Being out of
    awareness, 96–98
  nature of, is to enjoy more, 109
  personal God's, 273–74
  reason for, 7
  in steps of creation, 21
  subtler regions of, in dream state, 115
  See also impression
She or He, of personal God, 272, 274

ship-without-rudder analogy, 4
shortcut, for living Being, 38–39, 172, 180, 236
Shri Guru Dev, xiii, 80, 266–67
sight, 108–11
silence
    be still and know that I am God, 296
    becomes vibrant, 249
    hearing, 249
    infusion of Being is silent process, 39
silencing the mind, 238–39
skill in action
    acting from level of Being is, 126, 142–43
    action that liberates is, 161
    bow-and-arrow analogy, 26, 68, 129, 190
    light of Being brings, 25–26
    opposite of, 141–42
    true knower of, 161
    See also do less and accomplish more
sleep state
    consciousness gradually fainter, 292
    unregulated habits of, 107
social behavior. *See* behavior
sociology
    scientist should have complete view, 214
    should awaken spirit of forgiveness, 213
softness
    of breath, 189–95
    infusion of Being as, 6
    rehabilitation changes hard, cruel nature, 217
sorrow, 223–24
speaking
    advice, 223, 225–29
    arises from Being, 90–92
    art of, 134–40
    clear and precise, 135
    dividing mind while, 92–93
    harmonious, 138–39
    ill-humored remarks, 175–78
    love and forgiveness in, 228–29
    as medium between man and surroundings, 137–38
    minimum energy consumption in, 134–36
    past *Karma* influencing, 168
    pleasingly, 139–40
    powerfully, 140
    practical formula for, 136
    rebuking others, 224
    responsibility for others', 178–79
    retardation of, 92
    saying no, 138
    speaker remains free while, 141
    tongue as organ of action, 108
    usefully, 140
    Vedic expressions, 16
    words of God, 249
    See also word
spirit invocation, 83–84
spiritual paths, for aspirant, 277–78
    See also path
Spiritual Regeneration Movement, xiii, 14, 35n14
spiritual values
    full value of devotion, 246–48
    gulf between, and material values, 24, 233, 235
    harmonize with outer life, xi, 41, 209, 237
    man projects all values of Absolute, 49–50
    misunderstanding about, 24–25
    open to students, 207–9
spontaneously right action, 57–58
    religion should elevate to, 252
    in thought and speech, 130–31, 139
    See also right action
stability
    Absolute remains Absolute, 14
    belongs to unchanging status, 67
    evolution and simultaneous, 10–11
    of traditional culture, 228

states of consciousness
  brain and, 290–92
  evolved souls, 172
  purity of consciousness impacting feelings, 222
  three, 102, 114–16
  transcendental Being located between, 115n27
  wakefulness between, 292–93
  See also consciousness; specific state of consciousness
stone analogies
  atomic level of stone, 35
  line drawn on stone, 98
  stone thrown in pond, 34, 54, 117
straining
  in activity, 37–38
  artificiality in relationships, 213
  dyeing-cloth analogy, 38
  least strain and maximum gain, 142
  mind control, 84–85, 130–31, 153, 299
  nature set free from disharmony and, 197–99
  to slow breath, 194
  trying to silence mind, 238–39
  See also effort; tension; unnatural behavior
subject-object
  art of living glorifies full range of, 61, 161
  creation of, 17–18
  experiencer and object of experience, 29
  impersonal God is both, 269
  knowledge of subject, 209
  in mechanics of Transcendental Meditation, 109–10
  omnipresence of Being in, 6
  pure consciousness is both, 269
  subject overshadowed by object, 226, 231–32
  See also self

subtle strata/fields
  Absolute as reality of all, 17
  attention brought to, rows boat of love, 288
  Being becomes alive and vibrates in, 198–99, 198n72
  familiarity with, 260–61
  fatigue mars cognizing, 293–94
  impersonal path to God by entering, 271–72
  key to happiness lies in subtler levels, 288
  light of inner Self to fathom, 209
  man's ability to directly experience, 53
  mind can stimulate, for any advantage, 261
  mind satisfied by, 151–52
  Nature's mysteries revealed, 266
  open to students, 207–9
  perception during meditation, 108–11
  power in, 35
  preventive medicine to consider, 183–86
  stimulating any stratum for any advantage, 261
  in study of humanities, 212–13
  Transcendental Meditation and, 109–10
  See also experience
suffering
  Being hidden from view, 7–8
  equity of action and reaction, 223–24
  eternal happiness knows no, 170
  freedom from, 300
  life lived in, 48
  as Nature's help to promote evolution, 79
  one sure cure for, xi
  as our own creation, 71
  past is less evolved state, 258
  past *Karma* bringing, 168
  as religious tenet, 254
  steady mind *versus*, 188

surroundings reflecting, 177–78
unfolding full potential *versus*, 50
Sun
    cloth-dyeing analogy, 38
    in example of two ways of experiencing, 276–77
    -reflected-in-glass-of-water analogy, 195–96
    -shine balanced with rain, 240
    vibrations reach Moon, stars, and 117–18
sunlight analogy, 26
surface value
    acting from level of Being *versus*, 126, 142–43
    attempts at harmony on, 158, 174, 241–42, 253–55
    boil analogy, 183
    concentration on gross, 6–7
    current education's, 207
    depths *versus*, 13, 30–33, 39n17
    of eternity, 45
    full potential *versus*, 65–66, 77, 81, 81n14
    functioning at will from depths *versus*, 260–61
    gross, 6
    integrated unchanging value underlying, 281
    key to happiness in subtler levels, 288
    modern psychology's, 76
    sap failing to reach, 100–1
    stone-thrown-in-pond analogy, 34, 54, 117
    waves of love lived on, 287
    See also material life
surrender
    almighty Nature harnessed by, 80–84
    in devotion and fulfillment, 80
    never on level of thinking or mood, 79–81
    on basis of Cosmic Consciousness, 247

    to spirits, limitations of, 83–84
    sustains emotional path to God, 285
    as vehicle on emotional path, 285
    to will of God, 81–82
    See also emotional path
surroundings
    Absolute and relative constitute, 181–82
    All this is That, 16, 266, 282
    are meant to assist, 71
    are one's own creation, 69–72
    art of living makes full use of, 69–77
    Being as basis of, 7
    Being gets enlivened and vibrates in, 198–99, 198n72
    consciousness elevated by, 258
    control of, 69–72, 165–68, 263
    divided mind due to, 170–71
    education for best use of, 206–10
    everything draws maximum from every other, 75
    favorable to action, 157–58, 166
    individual responsible for, 177–80
    inner fullness irrespective of, 116
    Maharishi Effect, 198n72
    past *Karma* and adverse, 70–71, 168
    plant experiments, 55
    pure consciousness improving, 200–1
    remote, 73–74
    speaking as medium between man and, 137–38
    speech in accord with, 136, 138
    subjection to one's, 263
    two types of, 73–74
    unintentional and intentional, 70
    See also Laws of Nature
Sushrut, 240
suspension
    body trained to be still, 292
    breath, 193–94
    mind is left awake by itself, 3–4, 39, 245, 290
    nervous system, 106–7, 112–16, 112n25, 190

take it as it comes, 70
teachers, of Transcendental Meditation
   from all countries, 35, 302
   established in Cosmic Law, 301
   necessity of personal guidance from, 36
   premises from which to work, 302–3
teachers, school, 228
tension
   atmospheric, causing fear, 201
   body reflects built up, 188–89
   collective, 239–40
   creativity and, 50
   from joyless tasks, 169–70
   of modern age, 50, 145–46, 157, 171, 239–40
   narrow vision brings misunderstanding and, 176–77
   past *Karma* causing, 168
   psychology on, 50
   senses influenced by, 108
   surroundings reflecting, 177–78
   war from, 17, 180, 201, 239–40
   See also straining
That alone is, 16
theory of relativity, 14
thief analogy, 147
thinking
   daydreaming, 131
   powerful and right, 127–28, 132–33
   source of, 3–4
   speaking and, are same flow, 92
   systematic refinement of, 196
   that leaves mind free from bondage, 128–29
   See also art of thinking
thorn-and-rose analogy, 70
Thou art That, 16, 266, 282
thought
   Being becomes thought, thinker, and *Prāṇa*, 269
   Being is between all thoughts, 293
   Being is beyond, 29, 270
   brings mind into duality, 233
   conscious mind established in Being, 88–90
   conscious mind fathoms deeper level of, 102
   Cosmic Life's, materialized in man's, 249
   creative, 131–32
   ignored at its origin, 134
   is abstract not concrete, 235
   at its origin, 132–33
   materializing, 103
   as means of liberation, 133–34
   only useful, 131–32, 140
   powerful, 125–26
   seed-, 94
   speech as projection of, 137–38
   spontaneously right, 58, 130–31, 139, 252
   sprouts from Being and evolves into action, 94
   as subtle form of sound, 30
   surroundings react to, 73–74
thought bubble, 30–32, 91
thought force, 61, 149–53, 152n53, 155
thought waves, 74
   transcendental Being located between, 115n27
   useless, 131
   wakefulness between thoughts, 292–93
time
   Absolute dances in relative, 246
   action in least, 145–46
   Being is beyond, 4
   changing phases of mass consciousness, 304–6
   -consuming practices, 294
   direct path to enlightenment lost over, 231
   education for future generations, 216, 300–7
   eternity pervades every moment, 246
   for extensive contemplation, 284–85
   forgetting the past, 258
   future desires and actions, 94, 97–98,

121–22, 131, 179
knowledge lost over, 235
lack of, to meditate, 39
lasting *versus* short-lived contentment, 239
Lord of Universe is omnipresent in, 8
loss of spirit in religion over, 254
memories of past overshadowing present, 258
mind carried from lifetime to lifetime, 20
as most valuable factor, 173
omnipresence of Being, 6–8, 16, 270
past is less evolved, 258
past *Karma*, 167–68
past life gives identity to present, 20
present is materialization of past, 70
as resource, 172
for speaking, 136, 138
and tide wait for no man, 146
See also eternal life; modern age
time, space, and causation
action ranges between all limits of, 122
Being is source of all, 3, 16
Being lies out of realm of, 8
individual life touches horizon of eternity, 77
intellectual discrimination about, 279
keep everything bound, 25
omnipresent means unbounded by, 275
pettiness of mind bound by, 56–57, 82, 239, 279
See also relative life
to err is human, 255–56
tolerance
of ill-feeling toward us, 179
of ill-humored remarks, 175–78
in-, 175
mother's, for child's mistakes, 175–76
See also hatred

traditional culture, 227–28
laws of land derive from Laws of Nature, 159
transcendent
Absolute remains transcendental, 68–69
experience of, 29–30
impersonal God realized in, 275–78
as nature of Being, 7–8, 17, 21–22
Transcendental Consciousness
brain setup for experiencing, 290–91
brings subtle levels to conscious mind, 260, 266
as bubble of thought's source, 32
easily arrived at, 82
impersonal God realization is in, 271, 276
is Bliss Consciousness, 262
is unique from waking state, 290–91
located between states of consciousness, 115n27
mind becomes Absolute, 111
nervous system supporting, 291
physiological approach to experiencing, 294
psycho-physiological approach to, 298–99
unlike waking, dreaming, or sleep states, 115
Transcendental Meditation
academies of, 301–3
action in least time through, 146
action planning gained by, 171–73
action with maximum results through, 166
action without harm through, 165
almighty power of Nature harnessed via, 77–86
art of Being and breathing fulfilled through, 96
art of living through, 69
Being cultivated in mind through, 132–33
Being on level of body through, 113

Being on level of senses through, 108–10
belongs to every religion, 256
body's machinery rested through, 190n70
Cosmic Consciousness gained via, 75
cultivates Being in nature of mind, 132
as daily routine, 303
do less and accomplish more during, 125–26, 195, 201–2
effective execution of plan through, 173–74
energy through, 156
everlasting freedom through, 237
every aspirant can arrive at Being, 33
to experience Transcendent, 29–30
familiarizes mind with Being, 89
favorable surroundings through, 158
fixity of purpose through, 164
freedom from bondage through, 230–31
individual life stream influenced by, 123
joyful action through, 170
Karma brought to level of Being through, 127
main principle of, 30–32
to make use of surroundings, 77
makes love real and significant, 288–89
mind becomes existence during, 37
mind established in everlasting freedom through, 234–35
natural, innocent, easy behavior with, 99–100, 166–67, 179, 300
Nature works for him, 82–86
necessity of personal guidance, 36
opens gates of ancient psychology, 262–63, 262n5
as path of devotion, 248–49
personal guidance in, 36
proper thought for, 34–35
purity of system of teaching, 302
recreation served by, 219
regular habits and, 107
relief from fear through, 16, 180, 242
religion fulfilled by, 256
as restful alertness, 191–96
as revitalizing activity, 218
right action based in, 160
self-confidence based in, 162
as shortcut for living Being, 38–39, 172, 180, 236
simple and automatic, 33
speech fulfilled by, 136, 138–40
state of Cosmic Consciousness gained via, 75
strong thought force through, 61, 149–53, 152n53, 155
taught in terms of people's aspirations, 302
taught on basis of mass consciousness, 305–6
teachers of, 35
world peace practicality with, 242
tree analogies
imperishable and perishable, 280
individual sprouting from universal, 93–94
leaf in wind, 4
leaf's recognition of more water, 39
mind as root, 186
sap is entire tree, 46–47
sap of tree, 61–62
seed and tree, 19–20, 93–94
water the root, 38–39, 76, 186, 241
withering leaf, 183
See also sap analogies
truth
in Age of Enlightenment, xiv
in giving, you receive, 174–75
is eternal, 4, 124
is in accord with evolution, 200
light of God is, 229
in one's own religion, 221
present in all scriptures, 120–21

seekers of, xii, 21–22, 266–67
-speaking, 138–39, 223
See also wisdom

UN. *See* United Nations
UNESCO, 242
unified field theory, 14, 15
union
 of devotee and God, 286–89
 prayer before eating, 105
 Upanishads declaring, 266
 See also Cosmic Consciousness
United Nations (UN), 241–42
United Nations Educational, Scientific, and Cultural Organization (UNESCO), 242
unity
 of Beingness, 18
 coordination of mind and body in, 193
 is eternal, 4, 124
 of material existence, 15
 on path of devotion, 286–89
 reality of duality is, 19
 See also Absolute and relative; oneness
universe
 ability to cognize, 266
 cell-and-body analogy, 54, 58
 change gives status to, 10
 harmony of, 302
 individual's intimate and inseparable connection, 48, 53–58
 influence of proper thought on, 34–35
 is nothing but Being, 16
 man's vibrations reach Moon, Sun, and stars, 117–18
 Milky Way, 146
 physics discovering layers of, 5
 theory of relativity, 14
 See also action-reaction; Lord of Universe
unnatural behavior
 artificiality in relationships, 213
 mind strained by, 99
 neutralized by integrated life, 200–1

straining to slow breath, 194
See also natural behavior; straining
unrighteousness, 240
See also righteousness; wrong action
Upanishads
 Ānanda in, 16
 Brahman in, 15–16
 God dwells in heart, 272
 on imperishability, 15–16
 oneness declared by, 266

Vedas
 Being is Brahman, 15–16
 practical wisdom of integrated life, xi
 Vedic *Ṛishis*, xi
 See also Bhagavad-Gītā
vegetable species, 273
vibrations
 attractive or repulsive, 56
 Being enlivened in surroundings, 198–99, 198n72
 harmonious, 138–39, 198, 201, 240
 of improper thought, 34
 mind is vibrating consciousness, 185–86
 mind radiating, of Being, 197
 reach Moon, Sun, and stars, 117–18
 silence becomes vibrant, 249
 of sound *versus* meaning, 34–35
 See also action-reaction; harmony
victory, on path of love, 247
virtue
 in Age of Enlightenment, xiv
 flourishes in Bliss Consciousness, 262
 insufficiency of religious teaching, 255–56
 is in accord with evolution, 200
 let wrong be drop in ocean of, 72–73
 love of God as greatest, 286

waking state
 Being as basis of, 114
 Being located at juncture of, 115
 Being retained during, 234
 oneness of life remains during, 283

personal God realized in, 276
pure consciousness at end of subtlest, 115n27
transcendental experience is unique from, 290–91
wandering mind, 149–53, 152n53
war
  child-with-burning-coal analogy, 216
  collective tension causing, 17, 180, 201, 239–40
  when balance of Nature disturbed, 240–41
water
  -born beings, 273
  cannot wet It, 16
  H_2O as unchanging elements of, 11, 14, 46, 269, 281
  leaf's recognition of increased, 39
  ocean of Being *versus* ocean of, 8
  pond analogies, 34, 54, 117, 263
  rain, 240
  ripples-in-all-directions analogy, 34
  snow, liquid, ice, values of, 281
  Sun-reflected-in-glass-of-, analogy, 195–96
  temperature and density levels of, 45
  water-the-root analogies, 38–39, 76, 186, 241
  See also ocean
water-the-root analogies, 38–39, 76, 186, 241
waves
  -in-all-directions analogy, 34
  mind as, of ocean, 19
  in ocean of Oneness, 287
  pond analogies, 34, 54, 117, 263
  surface, communicate with deeper levels, 33
  See also ocean
weakness
  lack of Being's life energy causes, 186
  mental, 177, 217
  past *Karma* bringing, 168
  rebuking, seen in others, 224

seed's, as most important, 187
simplicity of transforming, 263
wealth
  businessman investing his, 62
  give-and-take between father and son, 71
  millionaire-begging-in-street analogy, 50
  millionaire-father analogies, 78, 82
  natural power that comes with, 82
  plentiful, analogy, 169
  quality of, 56–57
  thief analogy, 147
  See also resources
weapons cannot slay, 16
wheel of *Karma*, 22, 24
white-cloth-in-yellow-dye analogy, 38
white teeth, example, 225
will of God, 273–74
  surrender to, 81–82
wind, cannot dry It, 16
wisdom
  child-with-burning-coal analogy, 216, 226
  child-rearing toward, 226–27
  of different religions, 221
  of elderly father, 214
  fathoming the unfathomable, 21–22, 207
  about individual and universe, 48, 53–58
  ocean of divine, 246
  practical, xi
  preserving, in buildings, 303–4
  seeing good in everything, 223–25
  study of Absolute brings, 207
  See also integrated life; truth
word
  "art," 88
  "body," 190
  can never be withdrawn, 137
  to convey nature of Being, 17
  etymology of "science," xii
  "existence," 3

far-reaching influence of, 34–35, 54–55, 117–18
"full potential," 63–65
of God, 248–49
"God" as most cherished, 267, 275
of greeting, 174–75
hundreds of unsuitable, futile against one of value, 138
to melt listener's heart, 139
reveals inner quality, 137
sound vibrations *versus* meaning of, 34–35
Vedic, 16
See also speaking

world
consciousness projects itself to, 295
creator, maintainer, and sustainer of, 268–69
as-God's-garden analogy, 225
health of, 240
is found in God, 288
as neither real nor unreal, 279–81
omnipresence of Being in, 6–8, 16, 270
pure consciousness is realm of harmony, 76
war, 17, 180

world-as-God's-garden analogy, 225

world center, for spiritual leaders, 303

world peace
Age of Enlightenment, xiv
bliss is basis of, 237–38
collective tension *versus*, 17, 180, 201, 239–40
UNESCO's surface approach to, 242

wrong action
antagonistic behavior, 147–48
binding influence of, 230
brain matter contaminated by, 293–94
mother looks kindly upon child's, 175–76
not in accord with evolution, 200
selfishness leading to, 126, 222, 249
slapping in anger, 223–24
thief analogy, 147
See also right action

Yoga
Hatha Yoga, 291, 291n16
Karma Yoga, 297, 297n17
Rāja Yoga, 285, 285n14
Yogic physical culture, 194

Contact Information for Maharishi's Global Programs

The Transcendental Meditation program is taught in over ninety countries around the world. For information on Maharishi's programs and contact details for Transcendental Meditation introductory talks and courses in your country, please visit **www.tm.org/choose-your-country**, or go to the **tm.org** home page and click on *Choose Country*.

Transcendental Meditation Program for Women

Global Mother Divine Organization
www.gmdousa.org

Global Women's Organization for Transcendental Meditation
www.tmwomenglobal.org

AUSTRALIA
www.meditationforwomen.org.au

AUSTRIA www.tmgwoaustria.org

CANADA www.tm-women.org

CHILE www.meditaciontrascendentalmujer.cl

POLAND www.tm.net.pl

UGANDA www.awago.org

UNITED STATES OF AMERICA
www.tm-women.org
www.tmwomenprofessionals.org
www.tmforwomensheartheath.org

Architecture and City Planning

Maharishi Sthapatya Veda
Architecture in Accord with Natural Law

International Institute of Maharishi Sthapatya Veda
www.maharishivastu.org

Institute of Vedic City Planning
www.vediccityplanning.com

AUSTRALIA
www.maharishivastu.org.au

CANADA www.vastu.ca

FRANCE www.vastu.fr

Publications

Maharishi International University Press, USA www.miupress.shop

HEALTH

Maharishi AyurVeda® Health Products

AUSTRALIA Maharishi AyurVeda Products www.maproducts.com.au

EUROPE Maharishi AyurVeda Products Europe B.V. (MAP) www.ayurveda.eu

INDIA www.maharishiayurvedaindia.com

NETHERLANDS Maharishi Technology Corporation B.V. www.ayurveda-produkte.de

NEW ZEALAND Maharishi AyurVeda Products www.getbalance.co.nz

SWITZERLAND www.veda.ch *and* www.ayurveda-products.ch

UNITED KINGDOM www.maharishi.co.uk

UNITED STATES OF AMERICA, Maharishi AyurVeda Products International, USA www.mapi.com

Maharishi AyurVeda Health Programs

Maharishi College of Perfect Health www.globalcountry.org/wp/current-projects-2/maharishi-college-of-perfect-health

Maharishi College of Perfect Health, USA www.miu.edu/bs-in-preintegrative-medicine

Institute of Natural Medicine and Prevention www.miu.edu/inmp

Maharishi AyurVeda Health Centers

Maharishi AyurVeda Health Spa: The Raj, Fairfield, Iowa, USA www.theraj.com

Maharishi AyurVeda Health Centre, Skelmersdale, Lancashire, UK www.maharishi.co.uk/health-spa

Maharishi AyurVeda Health Centre, Bad Ems, Germany www.ayurveda-germany.com

Maharishi AyurVeda Health Centre, Seelisberg, Switzerland www.ayurveda-seelisberg.ch

EDUCATION

International Foundation of Consciousness-Based Education www.consciousnessbasededucation.org

Maharishi International University, Fairfield, Iowa, USA www.miu.edu

Maharishi School, Fairfield, Iowa, USA www.maharishischooliowa.org

Maharishi University of Enlightenment, USA www.maharishiuniversityofenlightenment.com

Maharishi School, UK www.maharishischool.com

Maharishi School, Australia www.maharishischool.vic.edu.au

Maharishi Invincibility Institute, South Africa www.cbesa.org

OTHER PROGRAMS

Global Country of World Peace
www.globalcountry.org

Maharishi Vedic Organic Agriculture Institute www.vedicorganic.org

Maharishi Gandharva Veda,
The Eternal Music of Nature
www.gandharva.nl/page6.htm

Maharishi Purusha Program
www.purusha.org

Mother Divine Program
www.motherdivine.org

Maharishi Vedic Pandits
www.vedicpandits.org

Maharishi Veda App
www.maharishivedaapp.com

David Lynch Foundation
www.davidlynchfoundation.org

Trademark Information

For further information, contact: MVULtd@Maharishi.net

The following are protected trademarks and are used in the United States under license or with permission from their respective owners: Transcendental Meditation®, TM®, TM-Sidhi®, Maharishi Sthapatya Veda®, Maharishi University of Management®, Science of Creative Intelligence®, Maharishi AyurVeda®, Maharishi®, Maharishi Vedic®, Maharishi Jyotish®, Maharishi Yagya®, Yogic Flying®, Maharishi School, Transcendental Meditation Sidhi, Consciousness-Based, Vedic Science, Maharishi Vedic Science, Maharishi Vedic Science and Technology, Vedic Science and Technology, Maharishi Vedic Approach to Health, Maharishi Gandharva Veda, Maharishi Vedic Management, Maharishi International University, College of Maharishi Vedic Medicine, Global Administration through Natural Law, Maharishi Purusha Program, Mother Divine Program, Maharishi Vedic Vibration Technology, Maharishi Vedic Organic Agriculture, Maharishi Veda Vision, Maharishi Channel, Global Country of World Peace, Spiritual Regeneration Movement, Raam Raj, Peace Palace, Raam Mudra, Veda-Leela.

Transcendental Meditation, TM, Maharishi, Maharishi Sthapatya Veda, Maharishi AyurVeda, Maharishi Yagya, Maharishi Jyotish, Maharishi Vedic, Raam Raj, and other terms used in this publication are subject to trademark protection in many other countries around the world.

CPSIA information can be obtained
at www.ICGtesting.com
Printed in the USA
BVHW092304250822
645539BV00004B/7